鳥 山 明

Our dog had puppies! She gave birth to three in all, but unfortunately one puppy died at birth, so now we have two puppies. When our cat gave birth, she didn't do so well on her own, and we had to assist with the labor and do things like cut the kittens' umbilical cords. We got ready several days in advance to help our dog with her labor, but she managed to do it all on her own. We really don't want to give the puppies away, so we are going to keep the both of them...

—Akira Toriyama, 1991

Widely known all over the world for his playful, innovative storytelling and humorous, distinctive art style, **Dragon Ball** creator Akira Toriyama is also known in his native Japan for the wildly popular **Dr. Slump**, his previous manga series about the adventures of a mad scientist and his android "daughter." His hit series **Dragon Ball** ran from 1984 to 1995 in Shueisha's weekly **Shonen Jump** magazine. He is also known for his design work on video games such as **Dragon Warrior**, **Chrono Trigger** and **Tobal No. 1**. His recent manga works include **Cowa!**, **Kajika**, **SandLand**, and **Neko Majin**. He lives with his family in Tokyo, Japan.

**DRAGON BALL Z VOL. 10**

This graphic novel contains the monthly comic series
DRAGON BALL Z PART FIVE #4 through #7, plus the
first one-fifth of PART FIVE #8 in their entirety.

STORY AND ART BY
AKIRA TORIYAMA

ENGLISH ADAPTATION BY
GERARD JONES

Translation/Lillian Olsen
Touch-Up Art & Lettering/Wayne Truman
Cover Design/Hidemi Sahara
Graphics and Layout/Sean Lee
Edited by/Jason Thompson

V.P, of Sales and Marketing/Rick Bauer
Senior Editor/Trish Ledoux
Managing Editor/Annette Roman
Editor-in-Chief/Hyoe Narita
Publisher/Seiji Horibuchi

Printed in Canada

Published by Viz Communications, Inc.
P.O. Box 77010 • San Francisco, CA 94107

10 9 8 7 6 5 4 3 2 1
First printing, October 2002

*Vizit* us at our World Wide Web site at
**www.vizkids.com!**

VIZ GRAPHIC NOVEL

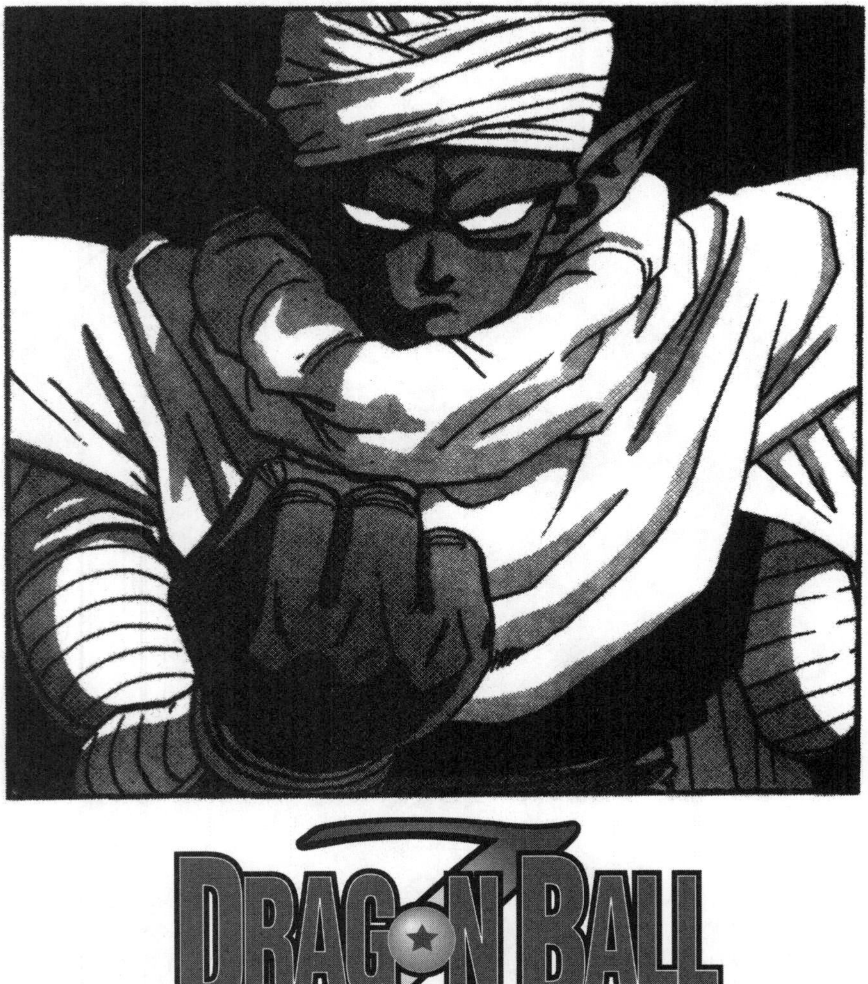

# DRAGON BALL Z

## Vol. 10

DB: 26 of 42

STORY AND ART BY
**AKIRA TORIYAMA**

# THE MAIN CHARACTERS

**Bulma**

Goku's oldest friend, Bulma is a scientific genius. She met Goku while on a quest for the seven magical Dragon Balls which, when gathered together, can grant any wish.

**Son Goku**

The greatest martial artist on Earth, he owes his strength to the training of Kame-Sen'nin and Kaiô-sama, and the fact that he's an alien Saiyan. To get even stronger, he has trained under 100 times Earth's gravity.

**Kaiô-sama**

The "Lord of Worlds," he is Kami-sama's superior in the heavenly bureaucracy. He lives in the Other World, where he occasionally trains dead heroes.

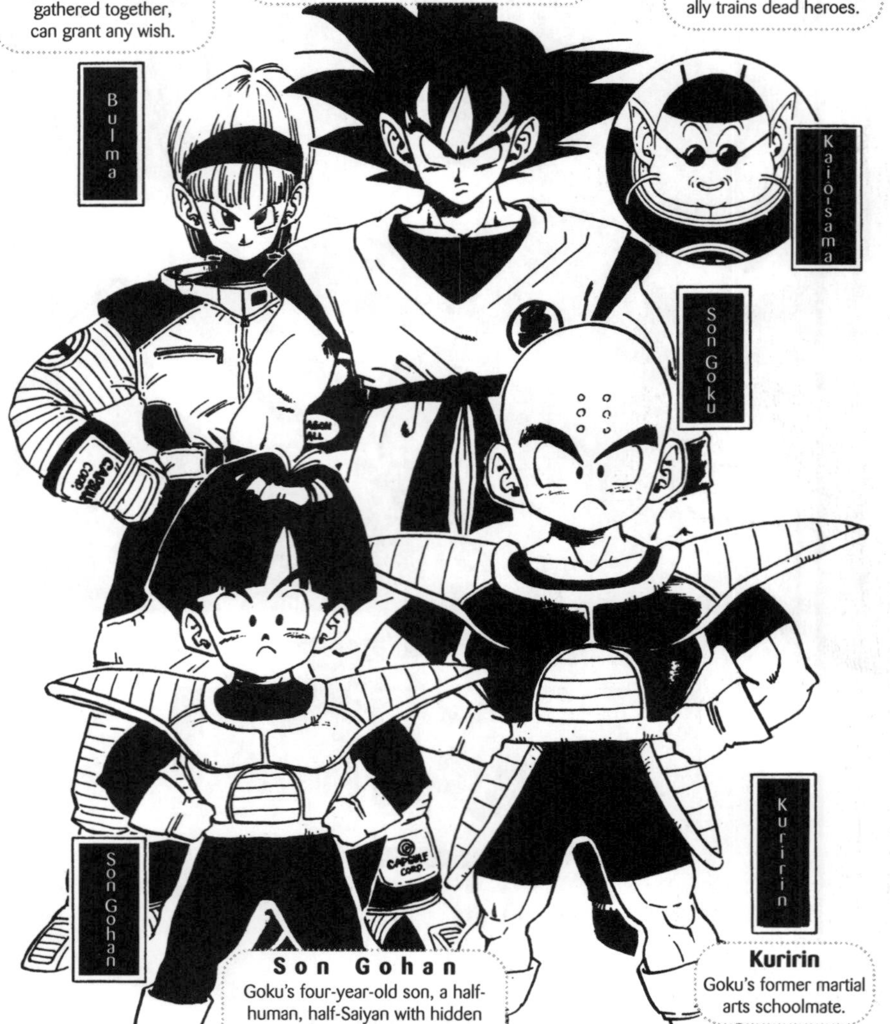
Bulma
Kaiô-sama
Son Goku
Kuririn
Son Gohan

**Son Gohan**

Goku's four-year-old son, a half-human, half-Saiyan with hidden reserves of strength. He was trained by Goku's former enemy Piccolo.

**Kuririn**

Goku's former martial arts schoolmate.

Piccolo

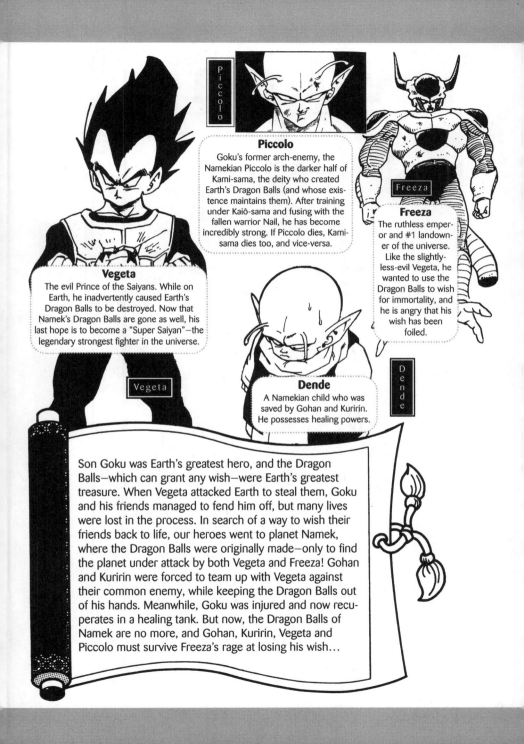

**Piccolo**

Goku's former arch-enemy, the Namekian Piccolo is the darker half of Kami-sama, the deity who created Earth's Dragon Balls (and whose existence maintains them). After training under Kaiô-sama and fusing with the fallen warrior Nail, he has become incredibly strong. If Piccolo dies, Kami-sama dies too, and vice-versa.

Freeza

**Freeza**

The ruthless emperor and #1 landowner of the universe. Like the slightly-less-evil Vegeta, he wanted to use the Dragon Balls to wish for immortality, and he is angry that his wish has been foiled.

Vegeta

**Vegeta**

The evil Prince of the Saiyans. While on Earth, he inadvertently caused Earth's Dragon Balls to be destroyed. Now that Namek's Dragon Balls are gone as well, his last hope is to become a "Super Saiyan"—the legendary strongest fighter in the universe.

Dende

**Dende**

A Namekian child who was saved by Gohan and Kuririn. He possesses healing powers.

Son Goku was Earth's greatest hero, and the Dragon Balls—which can grant any wish—were Earth's greatest treasure. When Vegeta attacked Earth to steal them, Goku and his friends managed to fend him off, but many lives were lost in the process. In search of a way to wish their friends back to life, our heroes went to planet Namek, where the Dragon Balls were originally made—only to find the planet under attack by both Vegeta and Freeza! Gohan and Kuririn were forced to team up with Vegeta against their common enemy, while keeping the Dragon Balls out of his hands. Meanwhile, Goku was injured and now recuperates in a healing tank. But now, the Dragon Balls of Namek are no more, and Gohan, Kuririn, Vegeta and Piccolo must survive Freeza's rage at losing his wish…

# DRAGON BALL Z 10

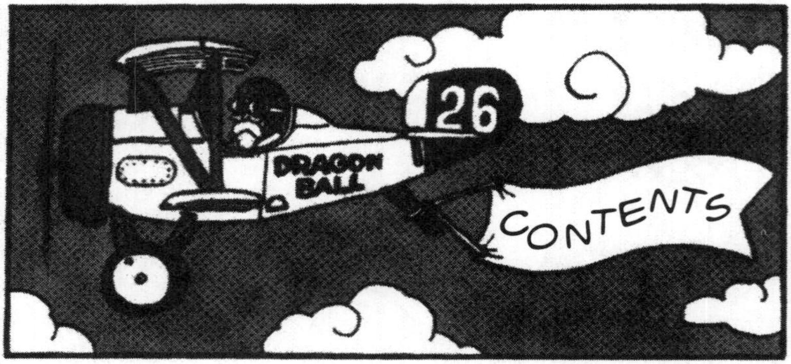
26
DRAGON BALL
CONTENTS

# DRAGON BALL

## DBZ:107 • Freeza vs. Piccolo, Part 2

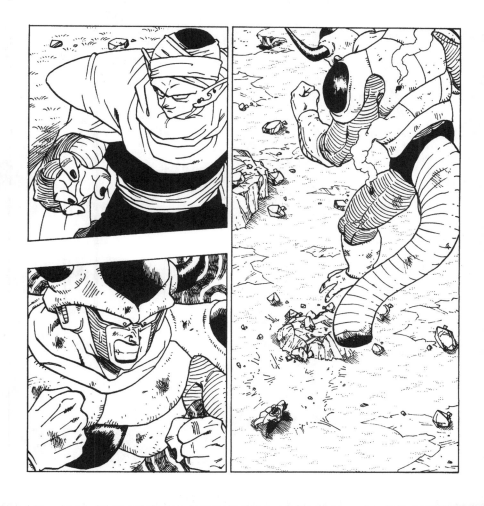

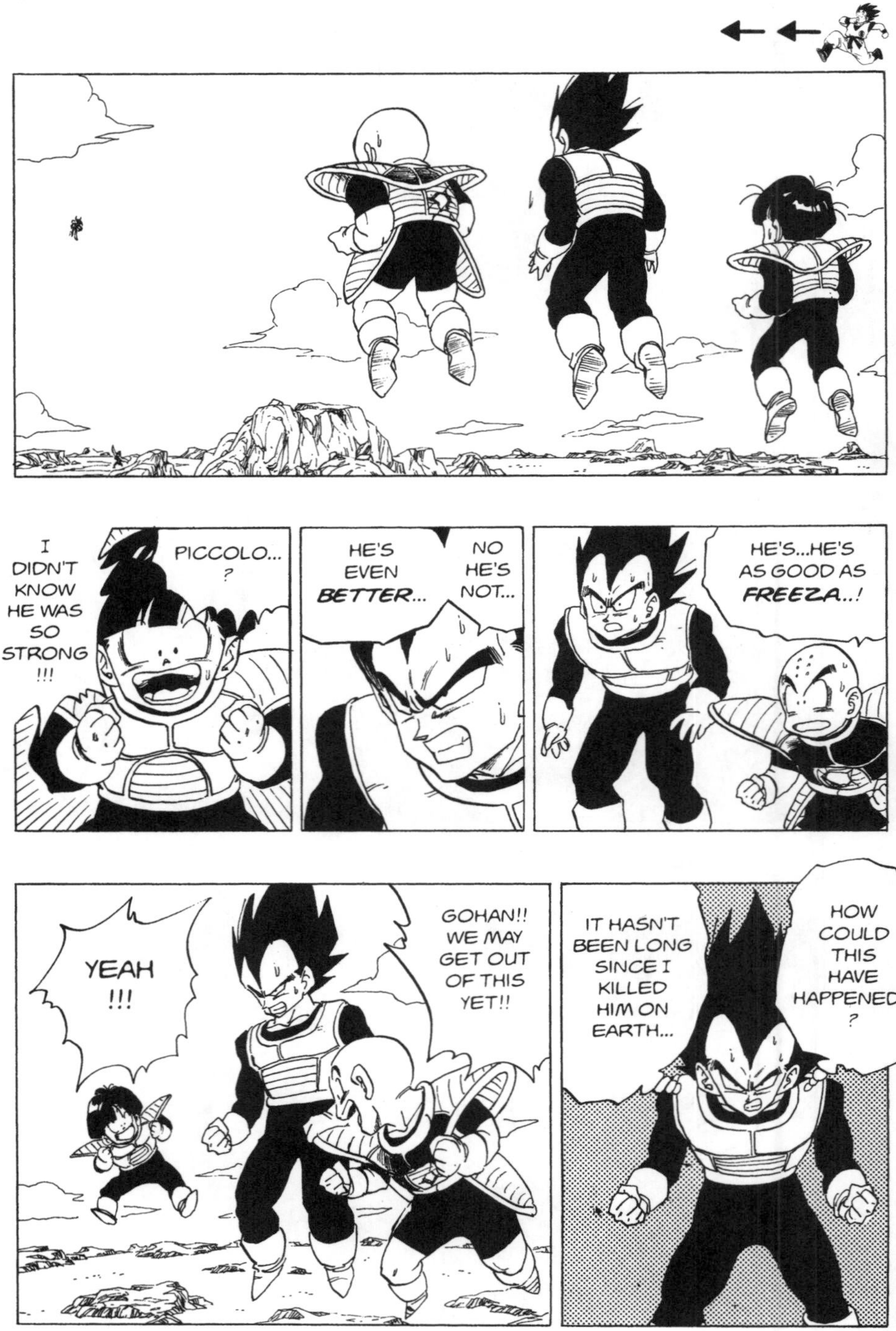
HE'S...HE'S AS GOOD AS FREEZA...!
NO HE'S NOT...
HE'S EVEN BETTER...
PICCOLO...?
I DIDN'T KNOW HE WAS SO STRONG!!!
HOW COULD THIS HAVE HAPPENED...?
IT HASN'T BEEN LONG SINCE I KILLED HIM ON EARTH...
GOHAN!! WE MAY GET OUT OF THIS YET!!
YEAH!!!

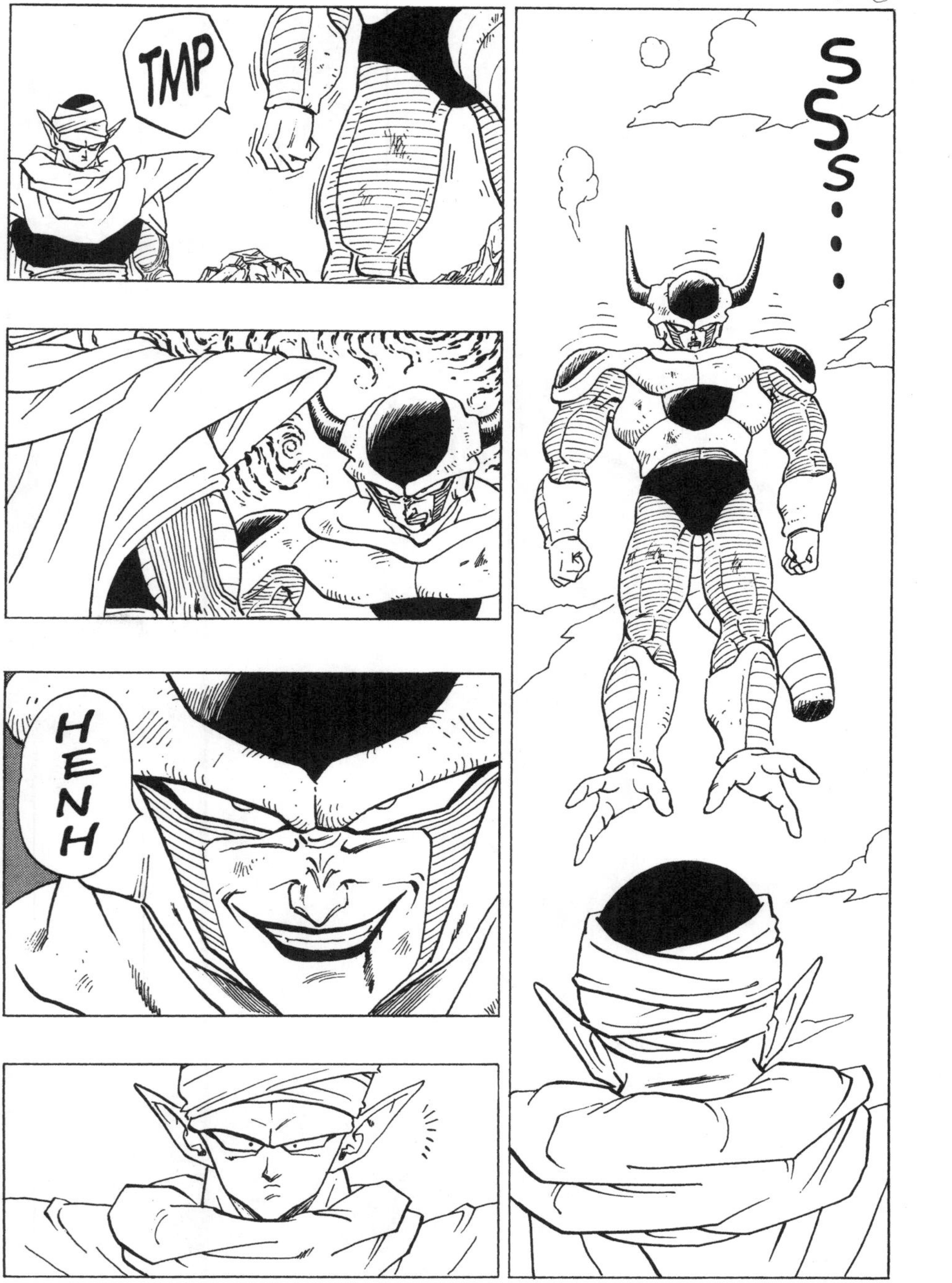
SSS...
TMP
HENH

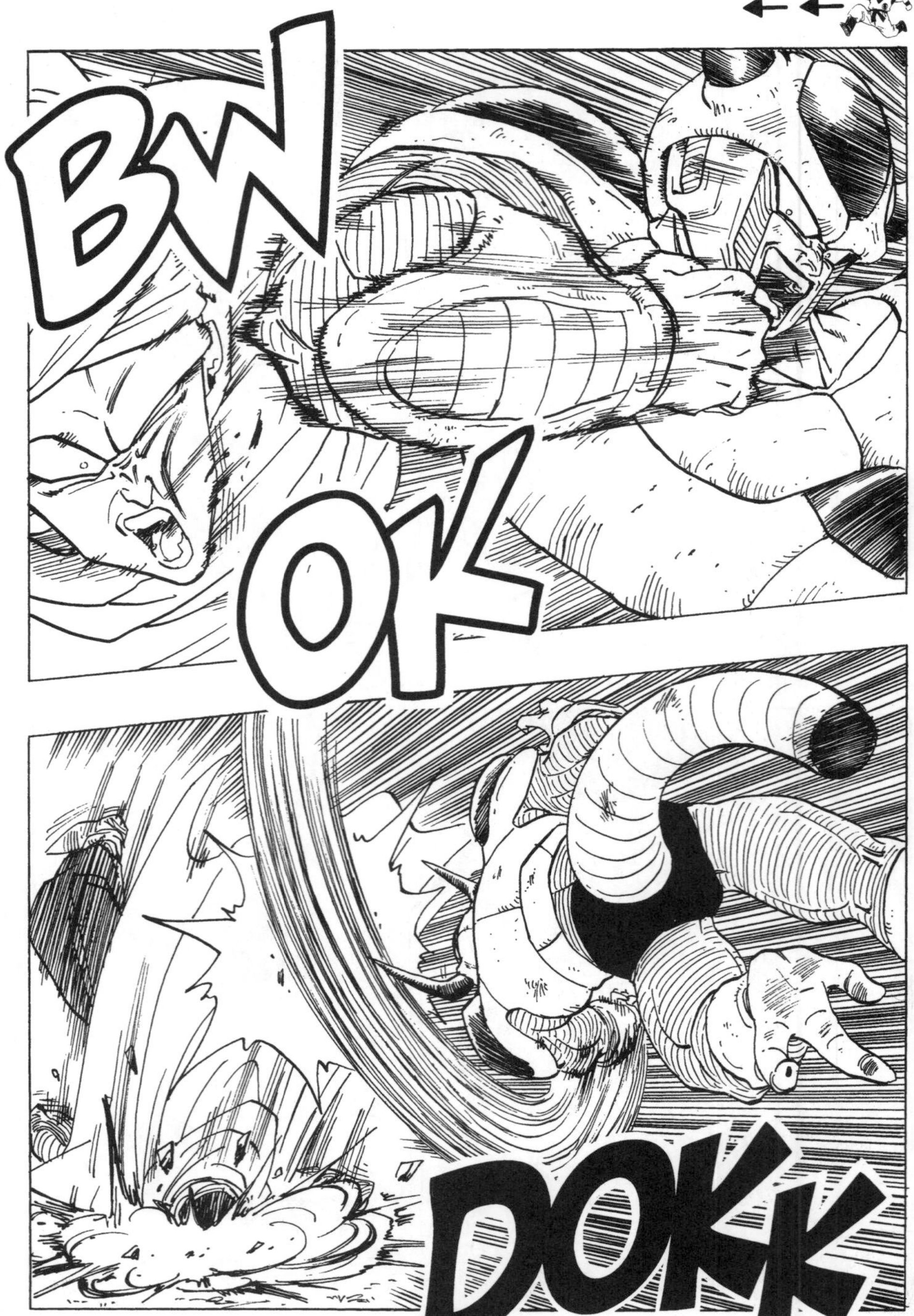
BW
OK
DOKK

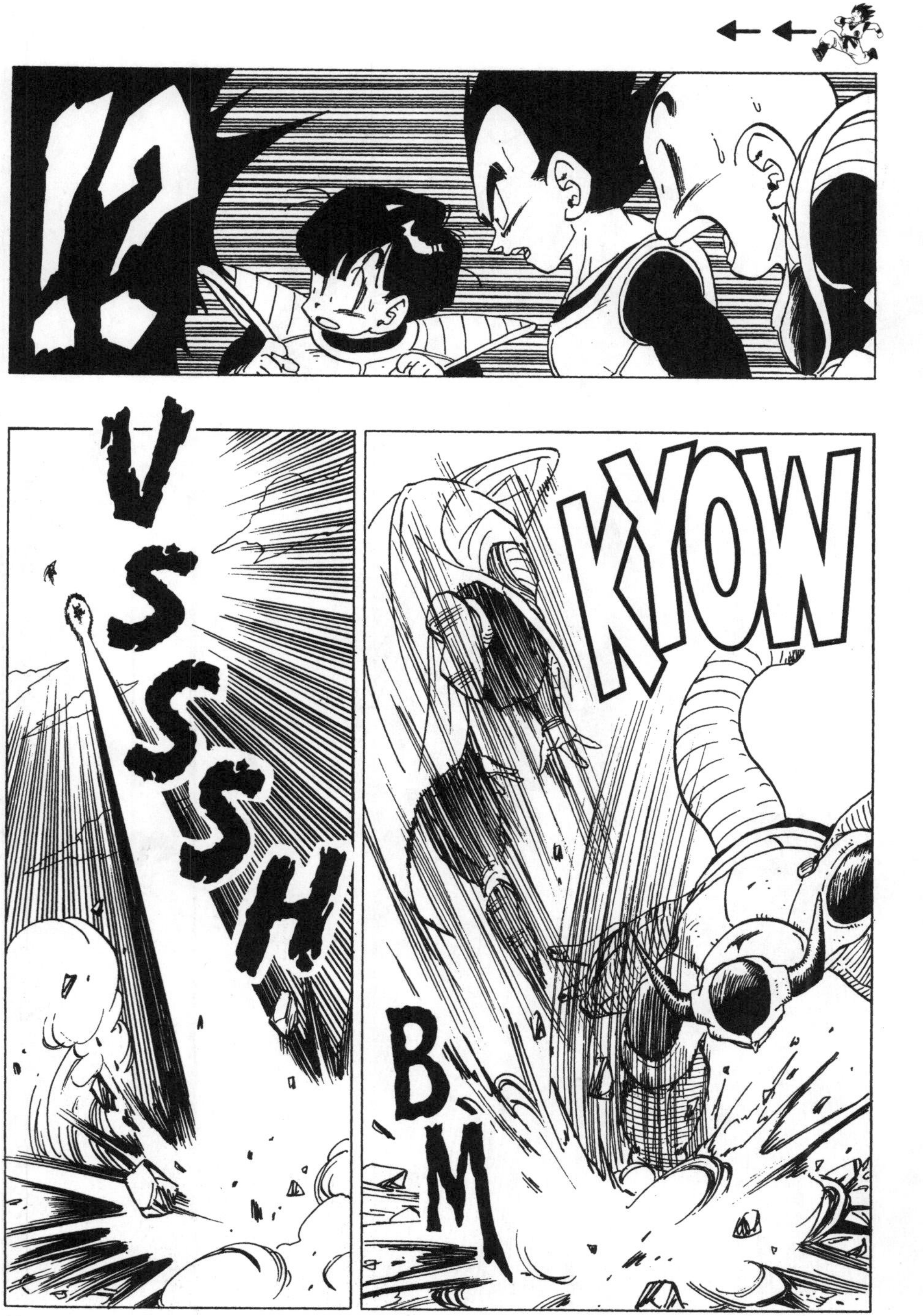
!?
KYOW
BM
VSSSH

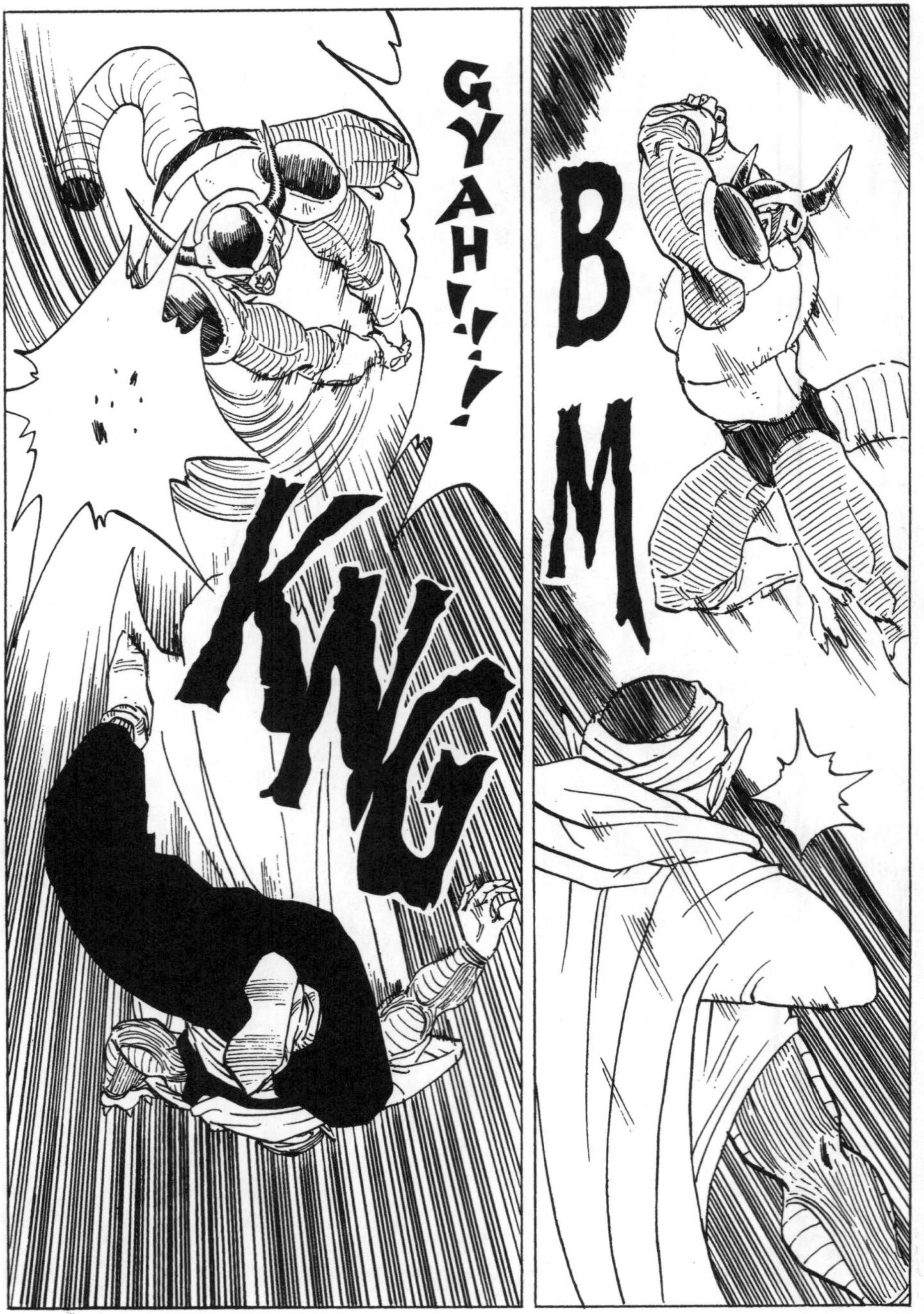
BM
GYAH!!!!
KWG

RRRMMMM

D.KOOOM

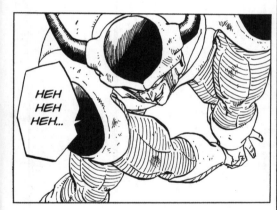

HEH
HEH
HEH...

OH GOD...
HE WAS...
JUST FAKING
IT...

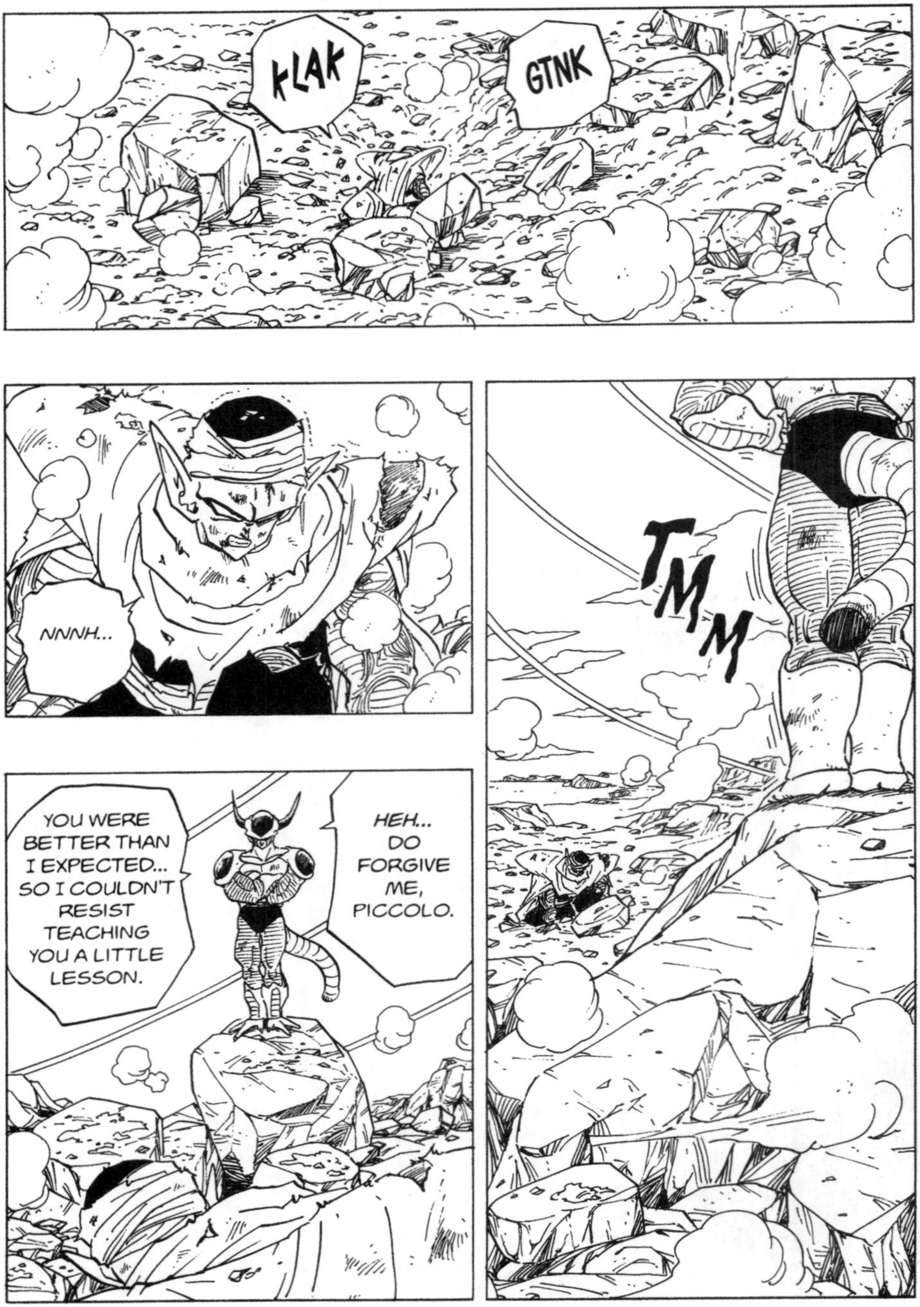
GTNK
KLAK
TMM
NNNH...
HEH... DO FORGIVE ME, PICCOLO.
YOU WERE BETTER THAN I EXPECTED... SO I COULDN'T RESIST TEACHING YOU A LITTLE LESSON.

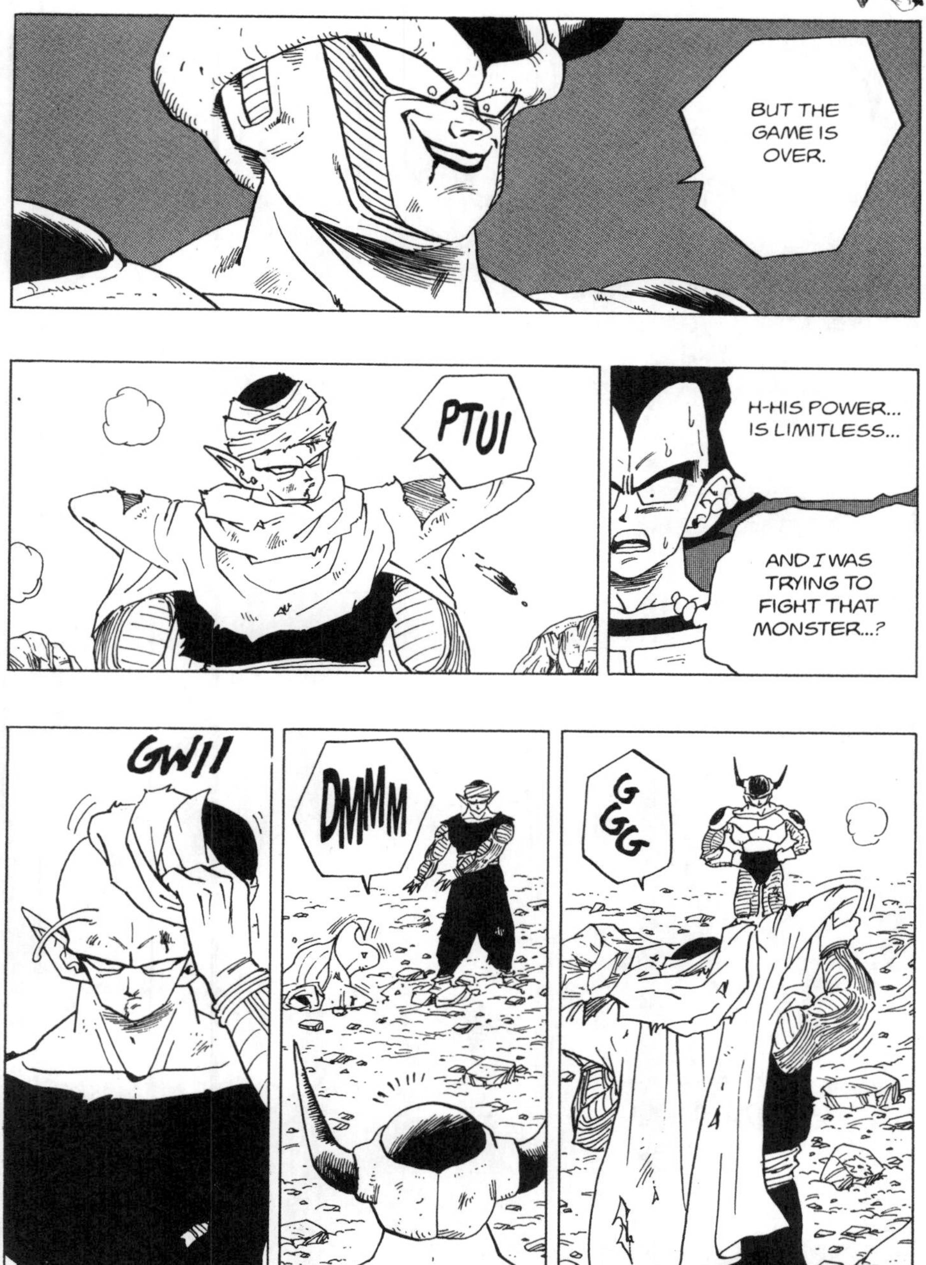
BUT THE GAME IS OVER.
H-HIS POWER... IS LIMITLESS...
AND I WAS TRYING TO FIGHT THAT MONSTER...?
PTUI
G GG
DMMM
GWII

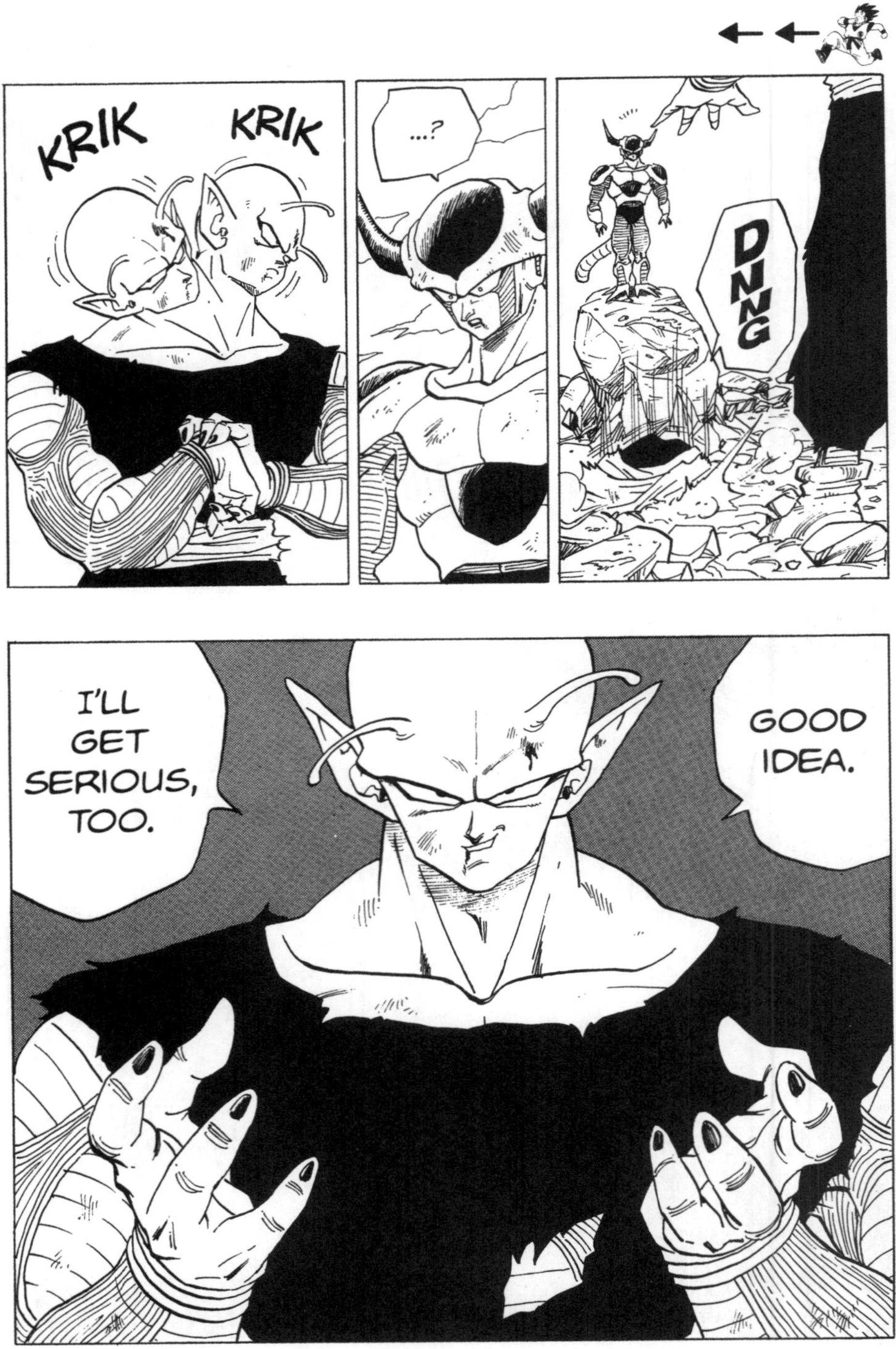
DNNG
...?
KRIK
KRIK
GOOD IDEA.
I'LL GET SERIOUS, TOO.

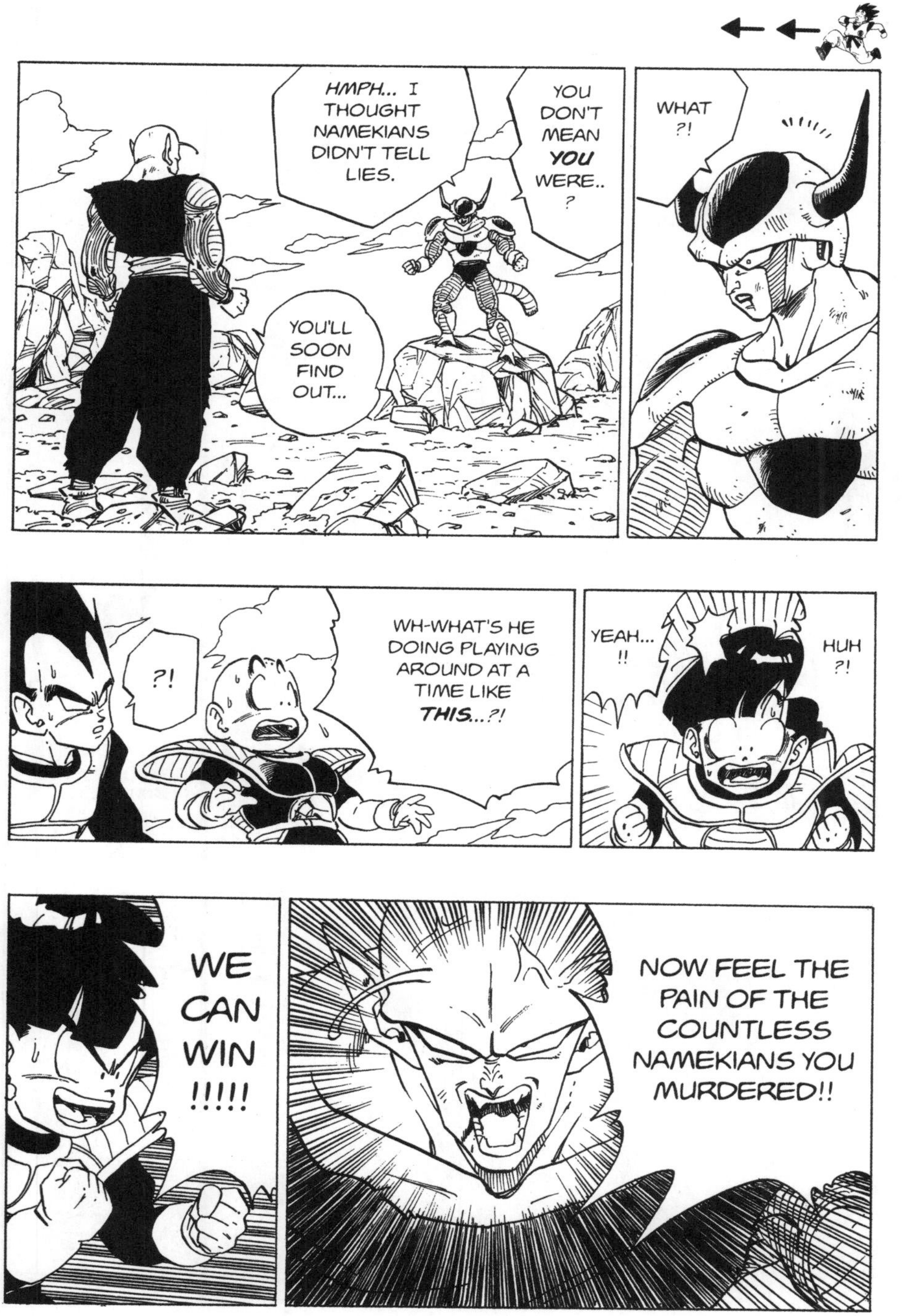
WHAT ?!
YOU DON'T MEAN ***YOU*** WERE.. ?
*HMPH...* I THOUGHT NAMEKIANS DIDN'T TELL LIES.
YOU'LL SOON FIND OUT...
HUH ?!
YEAH... !!
WH-WHAT'S HE DOING PLAYING AROUND AT A TIME LIKE ***THIS***...?!
?!
NOW FEEL THE PAIN OF THE COUNTLESS NAMEKIANS YOU MURDERED!!
WE CAN WIN !!!!!

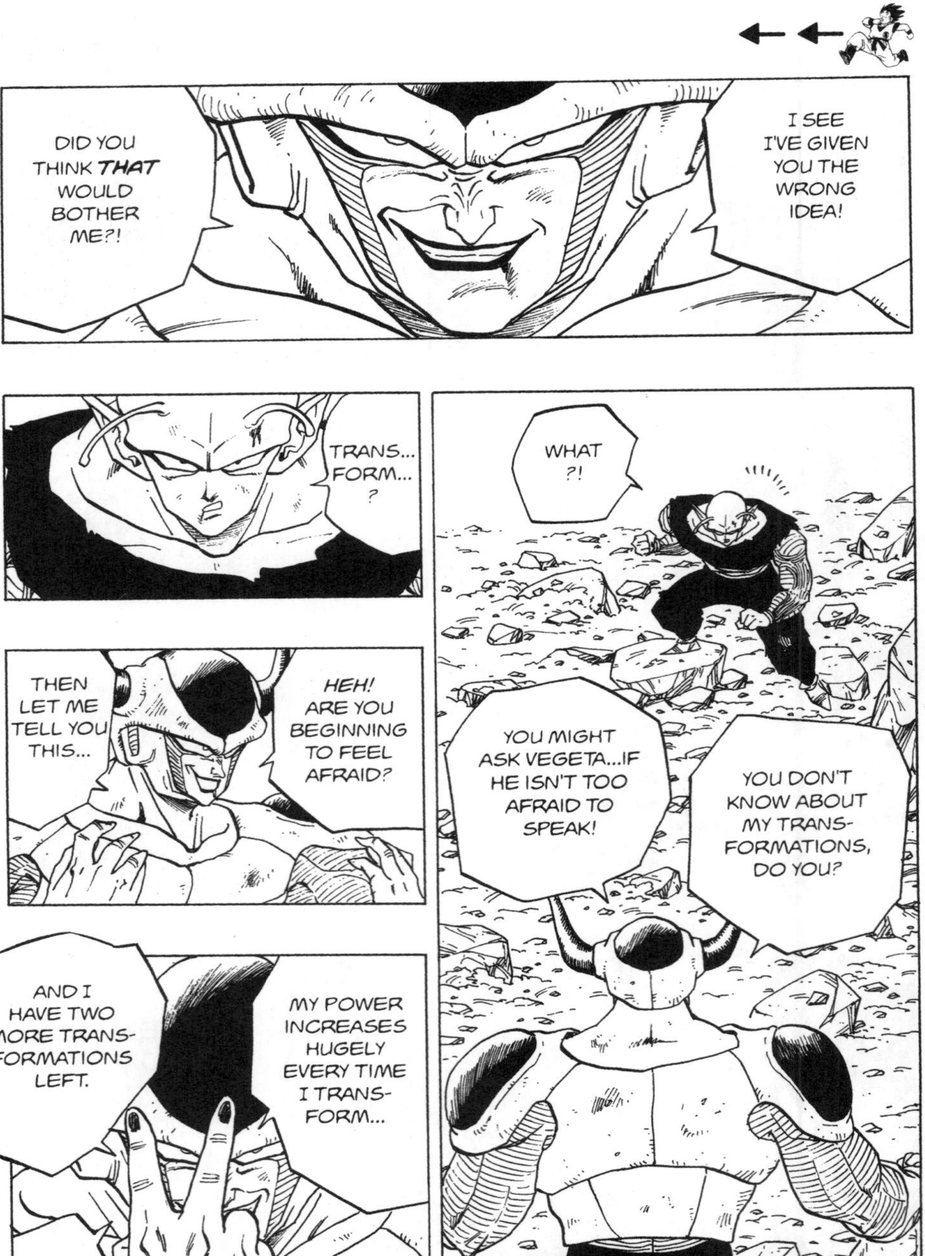

I SEE I'VE GIVEN YOU THE WRONG IDEA!
DID YOU THINK ***THAT*** WOULD BOTHER ME?!
WHAT ?!
YOU DON'T KNOW ABOUT MY TRANS-FORMATIONS, DO YOU?
YOU MIGHT ASK VEGETA...IF HE ISN'T TOO AFRAID TO SPEAK!
TRANS... FORM... ?
*HEH!* ARE YOU BEGINNING TO FEEL AFRAID?
THEN LET ME TELL YOU THIS...
MY POWER INCREASES HUGELY EVERY TIME I TRANS-FORM...
AND I HAVE TWO MORE TRANS-FORMATIONS LEFT.
NOW DO YOU UNDER-STAND ?

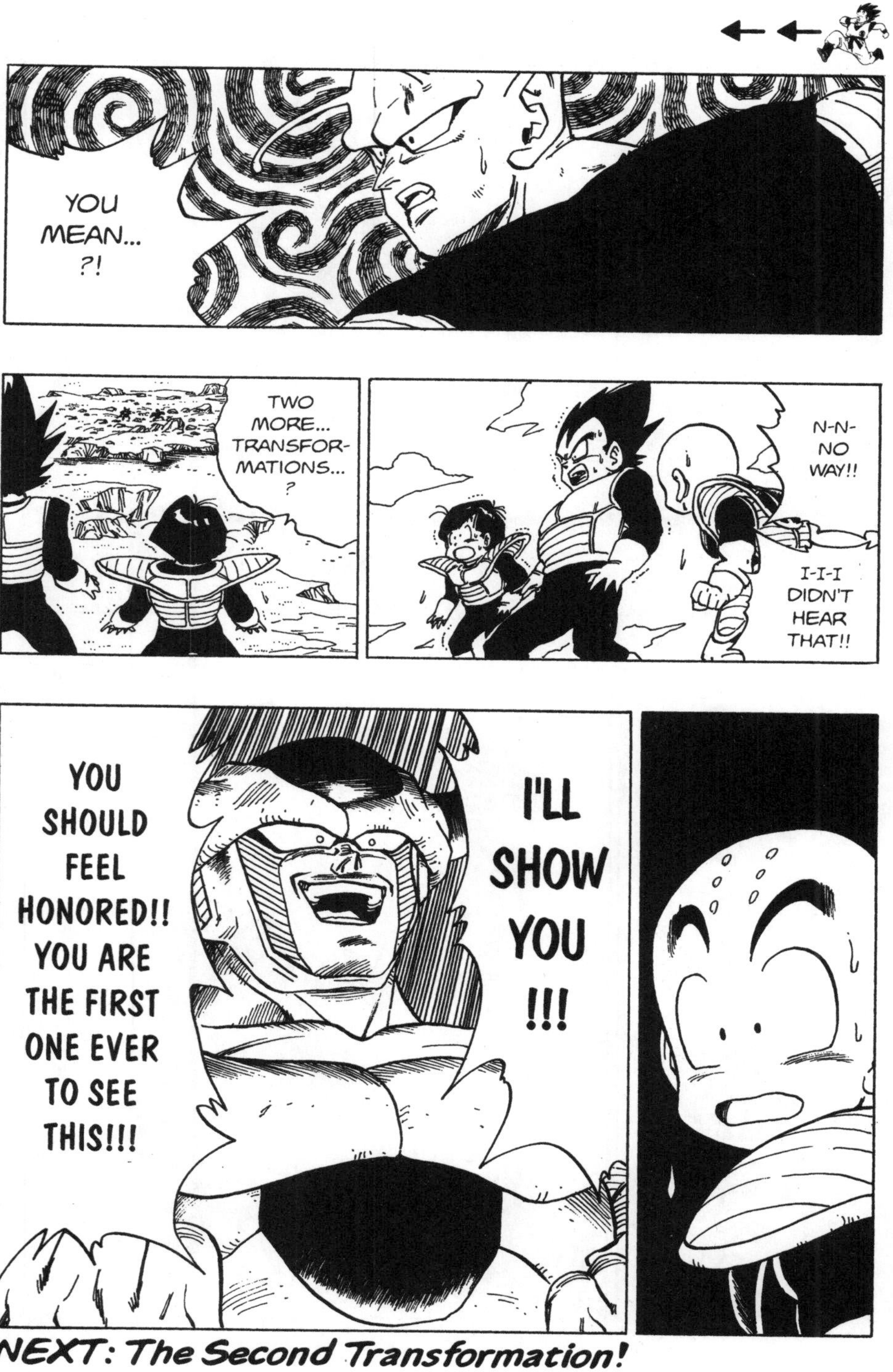
YOU MEAN... ?!
N-N-NO WAY!!
I-I-I DIDN'T HEAR THAT!!
TWO MORE... TRANSFORMATIONS... ?
I'LL SHOW YOU!!!
YOU SHOULD FEEL HONORED!! YOU ARE THE FIRST ONE EVER TO SEE THIS!!!

**NEXT**: The Second Transformation!

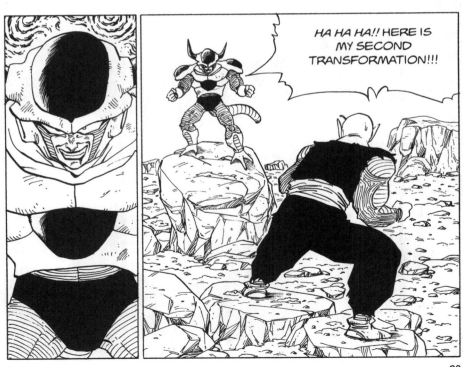

HA HA HA!! HERE IS MY SECOND TRANSFORMATION!!!

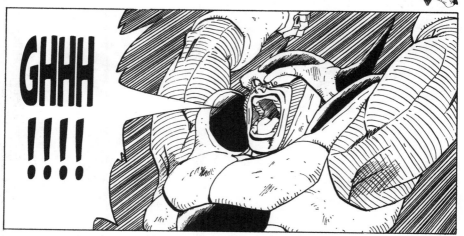

GHHH!!!!

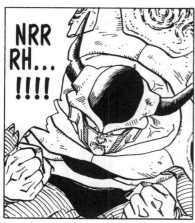

NRR RH...!!!!

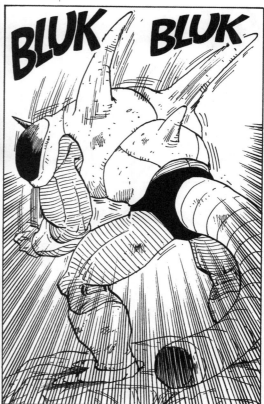

BLUK BLUK

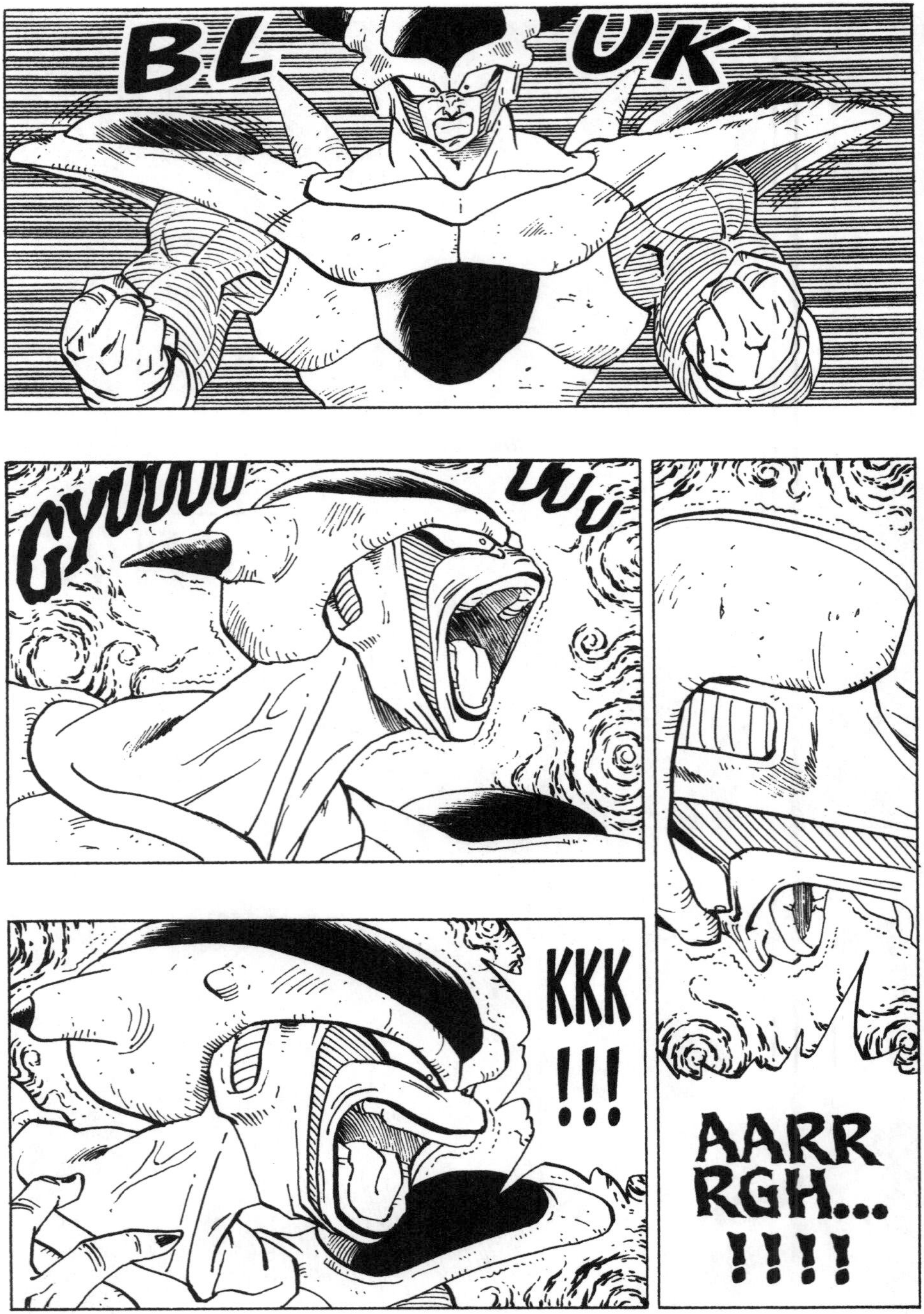
BL UK
AARR RGH... !!!!
GYUUUU UUU
KKK !!!

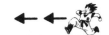

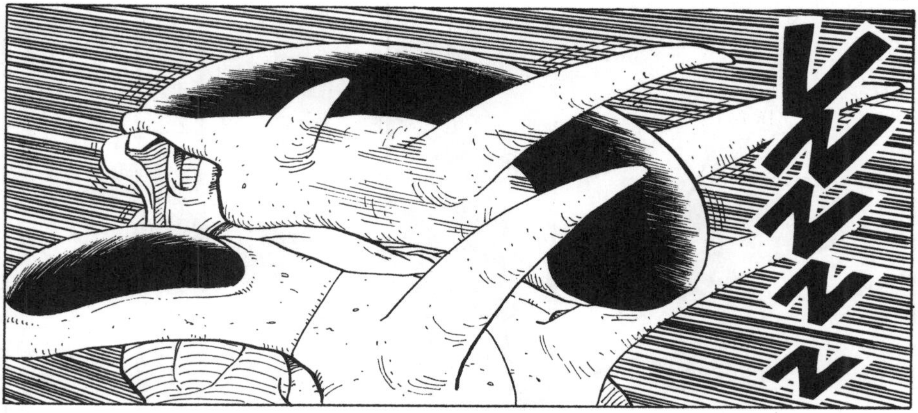
VNNNNN
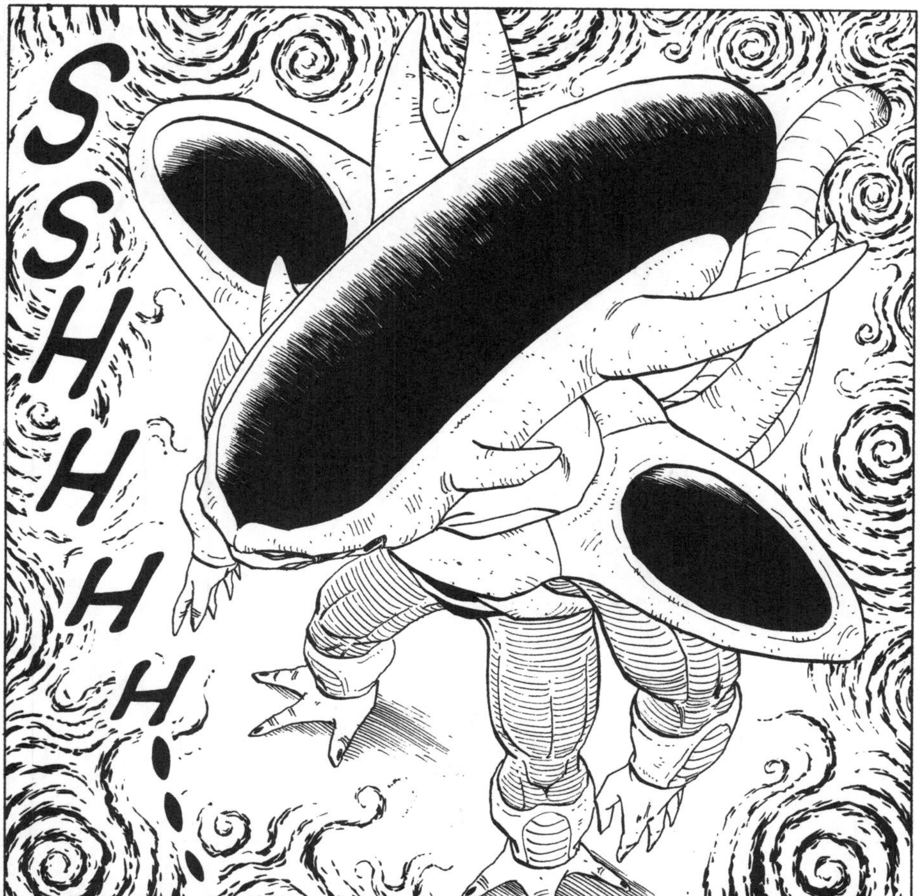
SSHHHHH...

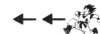

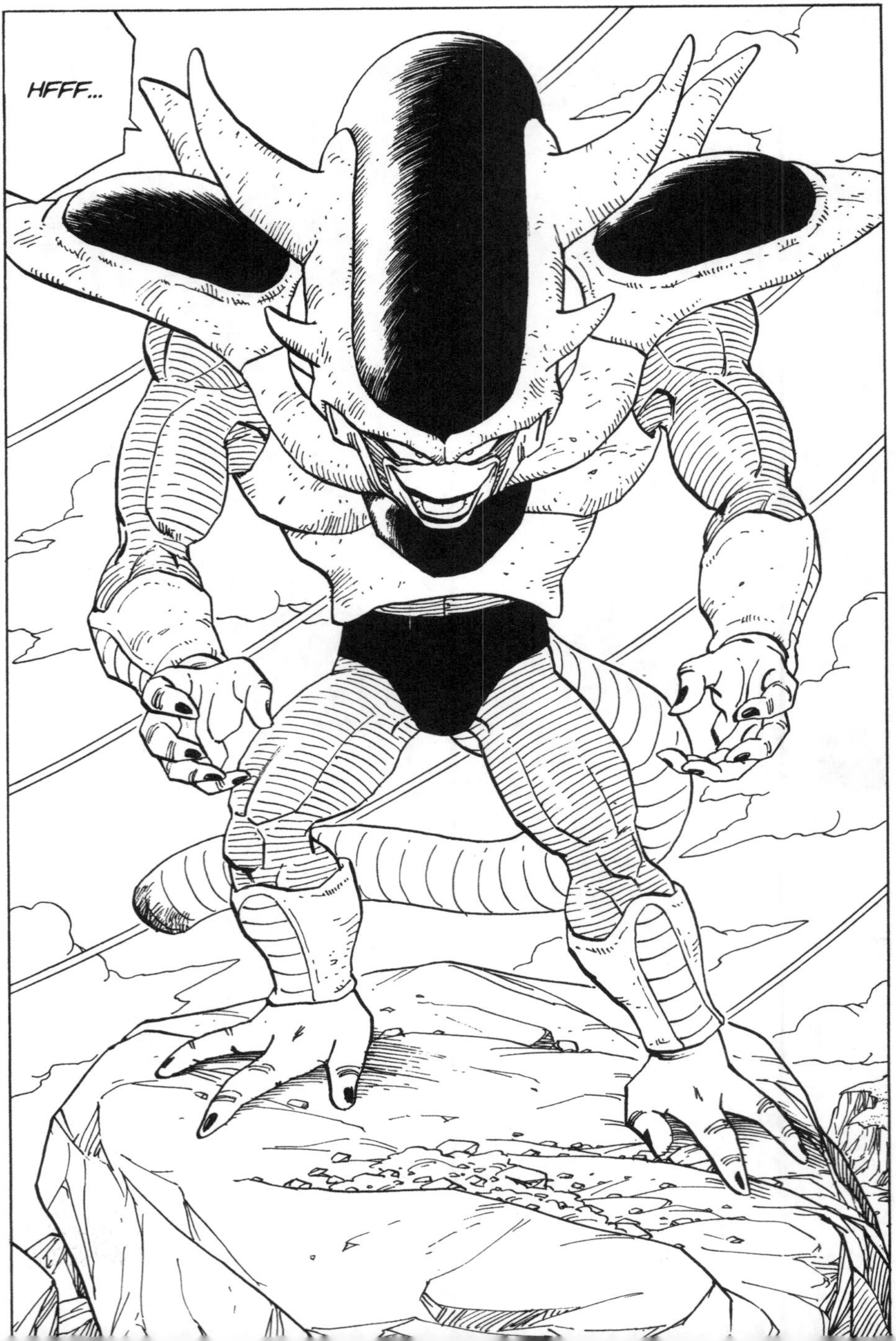
HFFF...

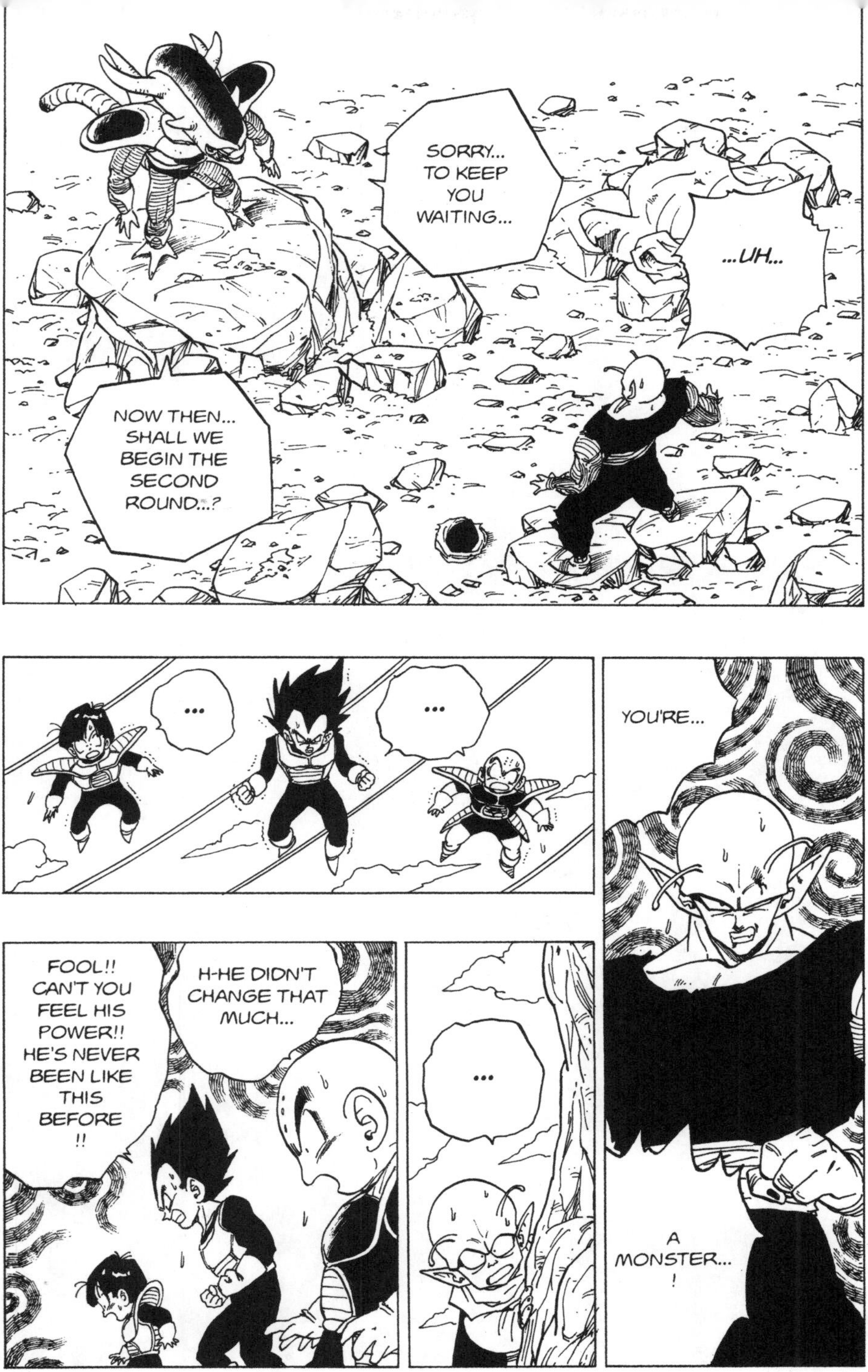
SORRY... TO KEEP YOU WAITING...
...UH...
NOW THEN... SHALL WE BEGIN THE SECOND ROUND...?
YOU'RE...
A MONSTER... !
...
...
...
H-HE DIDN'T CHANGE THAT MUCH...
FOOL!! CAN'T YOU FEEL HIS POWER!! HE'S NEVER BEEN LIKE THIS BEFORE !!

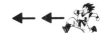

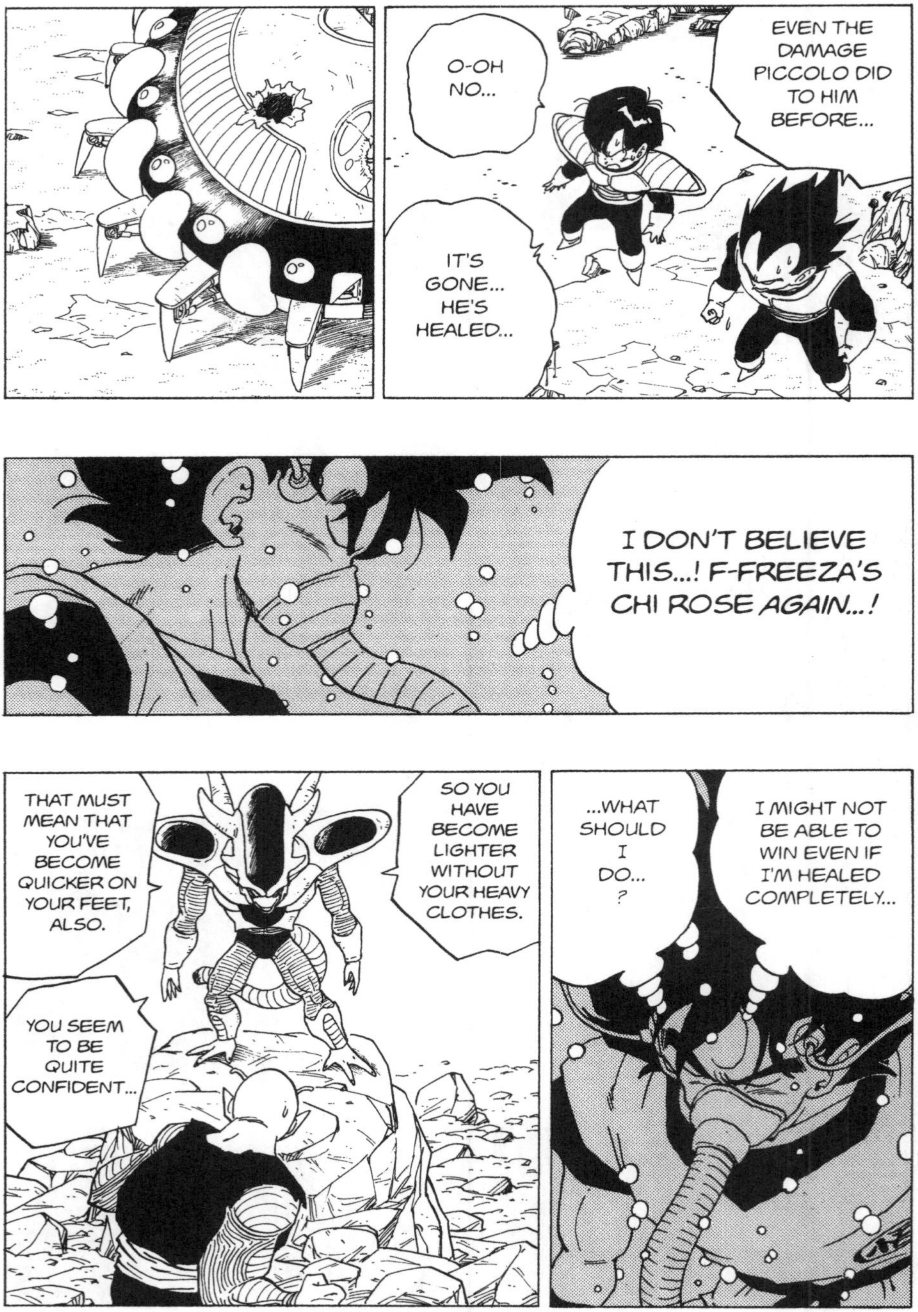
EVEN THE DAMAGE PICCOLO DID TO HIM BEFORE...
O-OH NO...
IT'S GONE... HE'S HEALED...
I DON'T BELIEVE THIS...! F-FREEZA'S CHI ROSE *AGAIN*...!
I MIGHT NOT BE ABLE TO WIN EVEN IF I'M HEALED COMPLETELY...
...WHAT SHOULD I DO...?
SO YOU HAVE BECOME LIGHTER WITHOUT YOUR HEAVY CLOTHES.
THAT MUST MEAN THAT YOU'VE BECOME QUICKER ON YOUR FEET, ALSO.
YOU SEEM TO BE QUITE CONFIDENT...

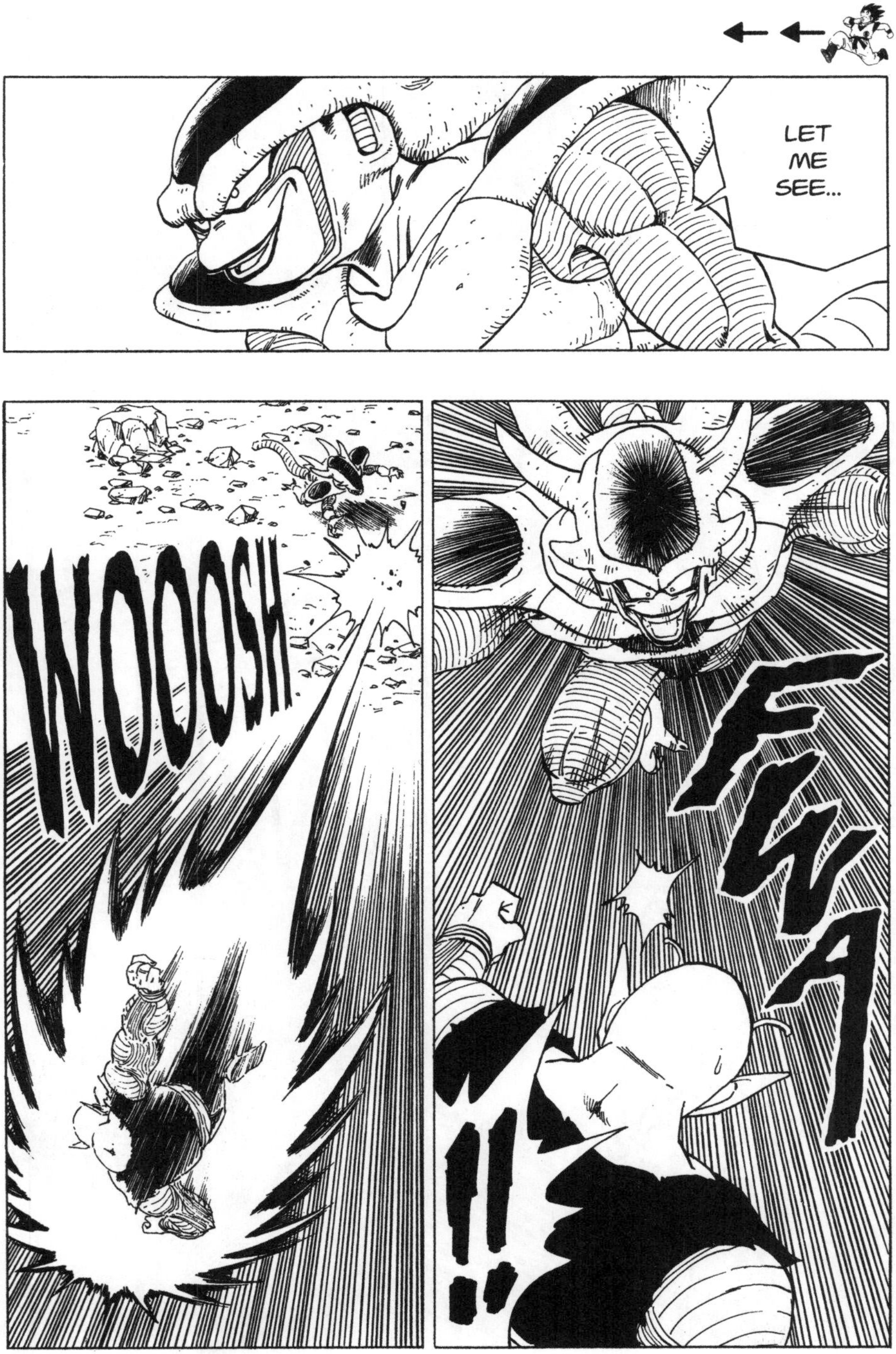
LET ME SEE...
FWA
!!
WOOOSH

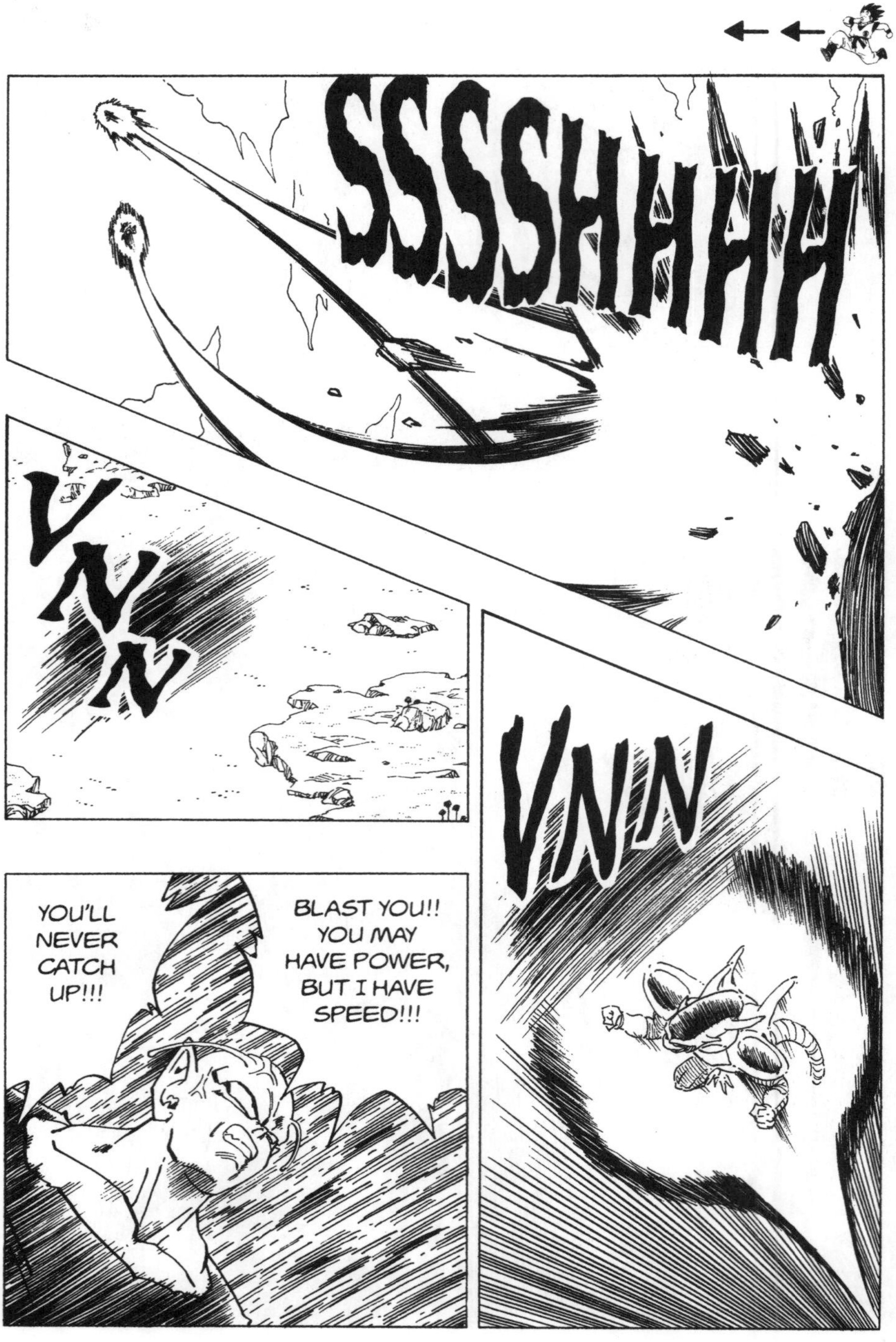
SSSSHHHH
VNN
VNN
BLAST YOU!! YOU MAY HAVE POWER, BUT I HAVE SPEED!!!
YOU'LL NEVER CATCH UP!!!

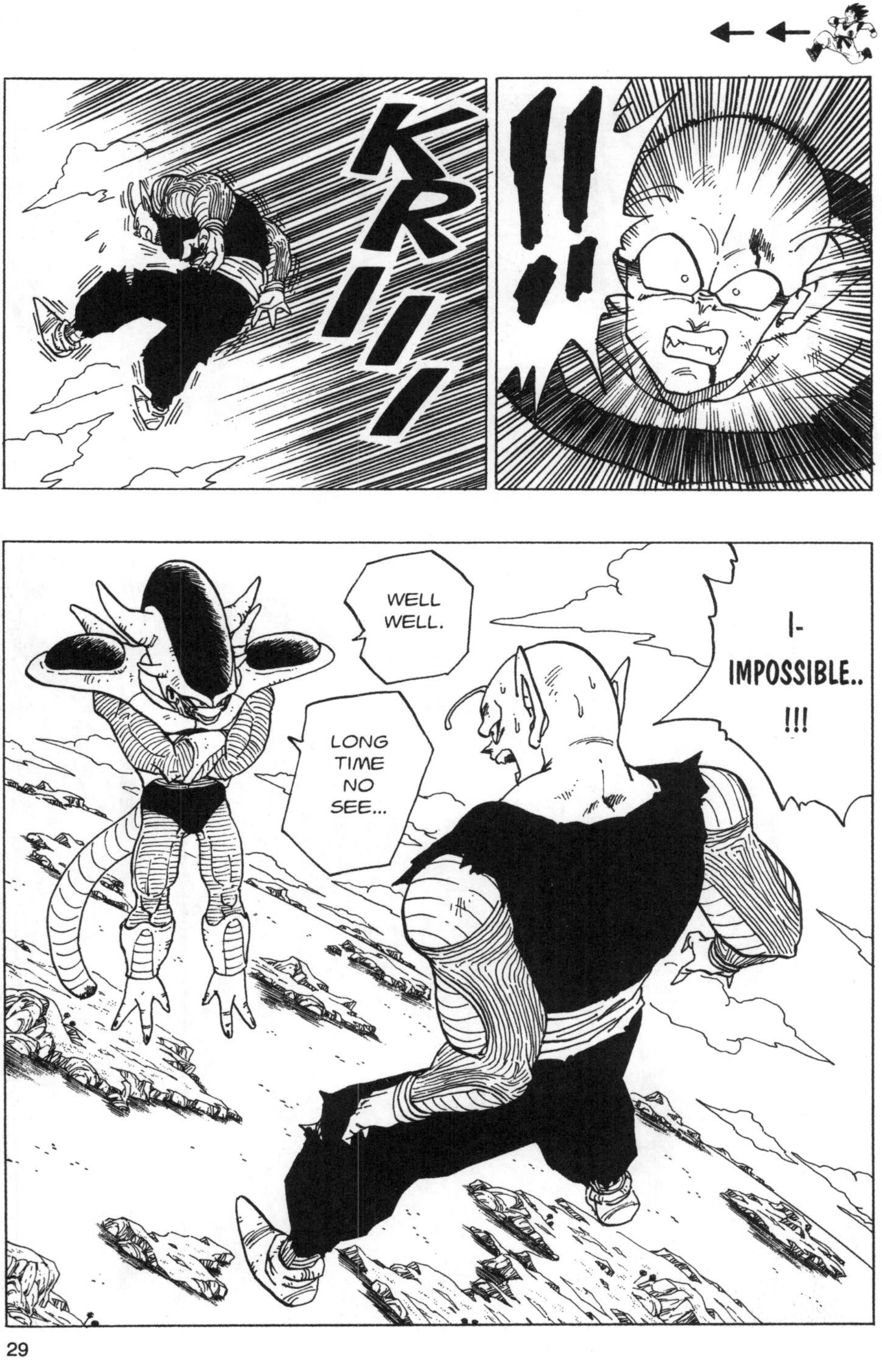
!!
KRIII
I- IMPOSSIBLE.. !!!
WELL WELL.
LONG TIME NO SEE...

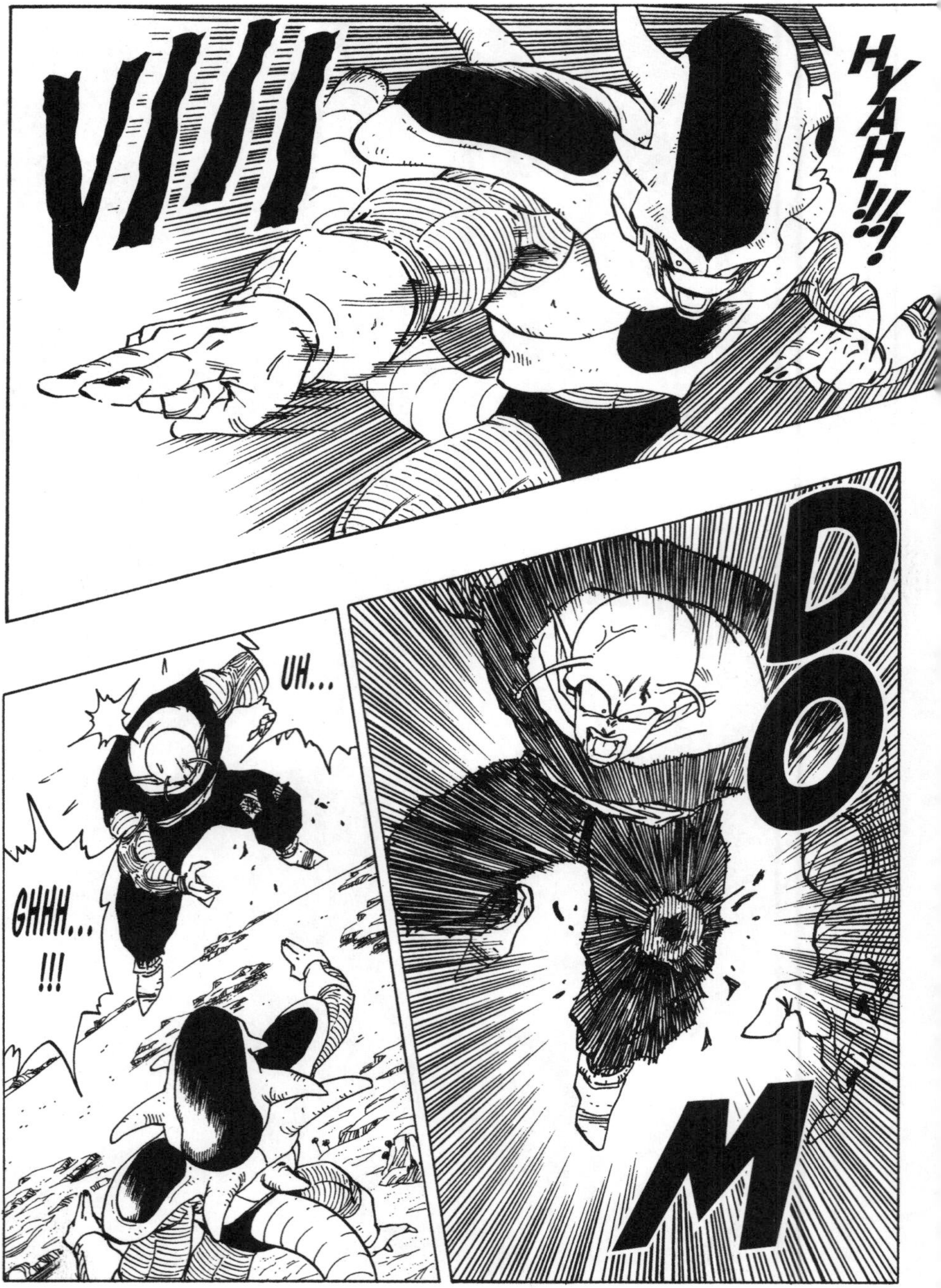
VIIII
HYAH!!!
DOM
UH...
GHHH... !!!

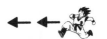

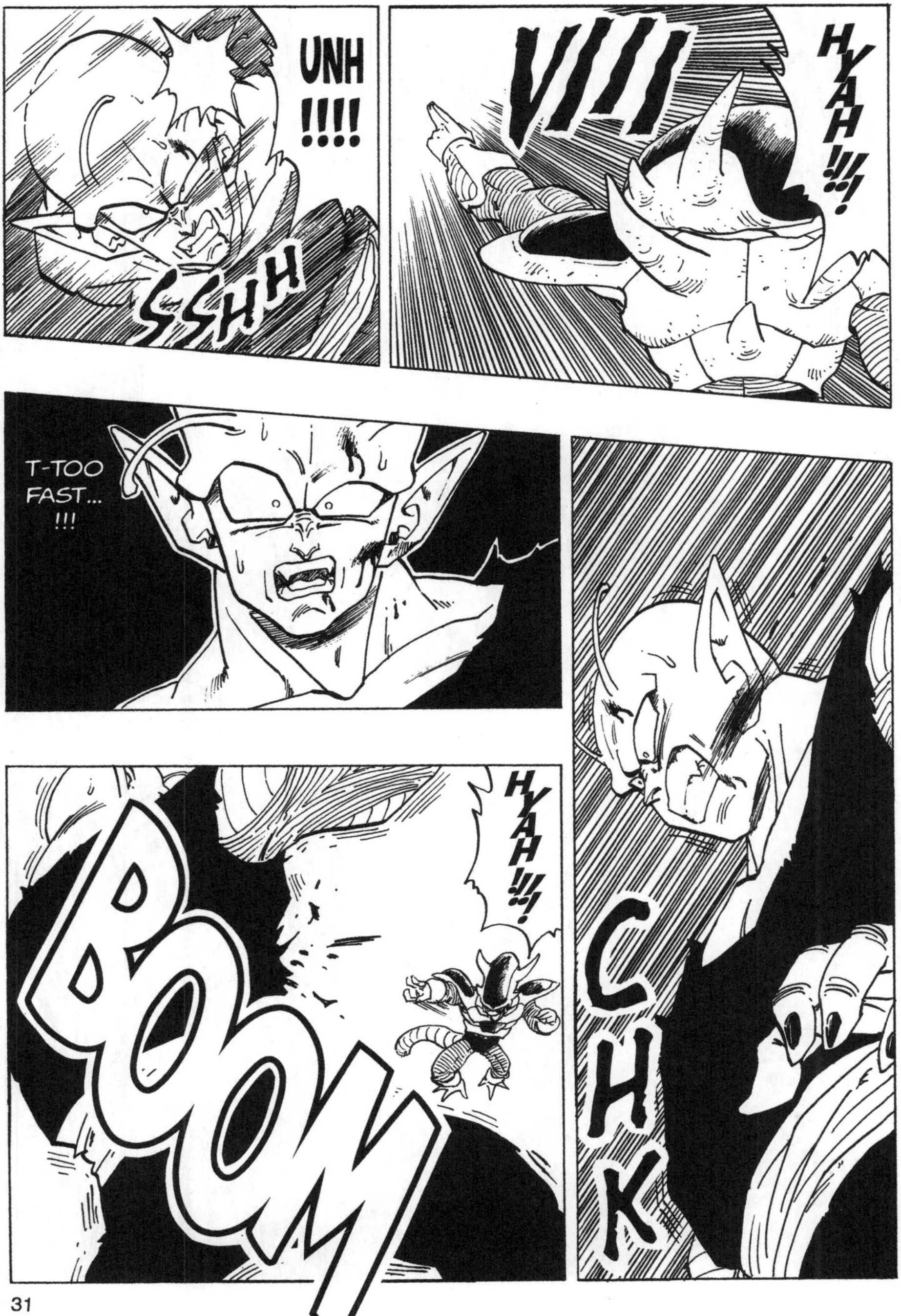
VIII
HYAH!!!
UNH!!!!
SSHH
CHK
T-TOO FAST... !!!
HYAH!!!
BOOM

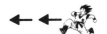

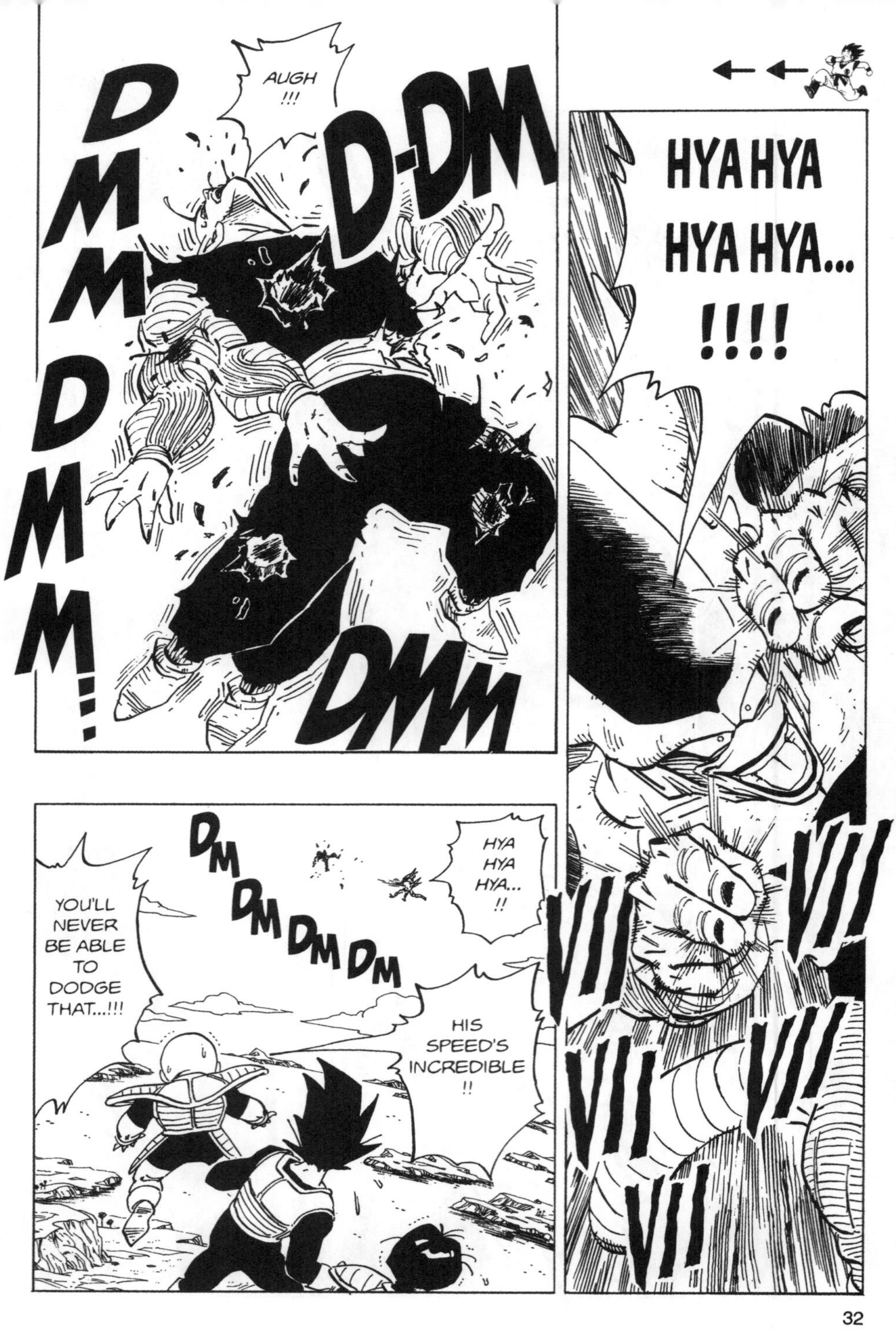
HYA HYA
HYA HYA...
!!!!
VII-VII!
VII VII
VII VII!
VII
DMMMDMMMM!!
AUGH !!!
D-DM
DMM
HYA HYA HYA... !!
DM DM DM DM
YOU'LL NEVER BE ABLE TO DODGE THAT...!!!
HIS SPEED'S INCREDIBLE !!

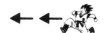

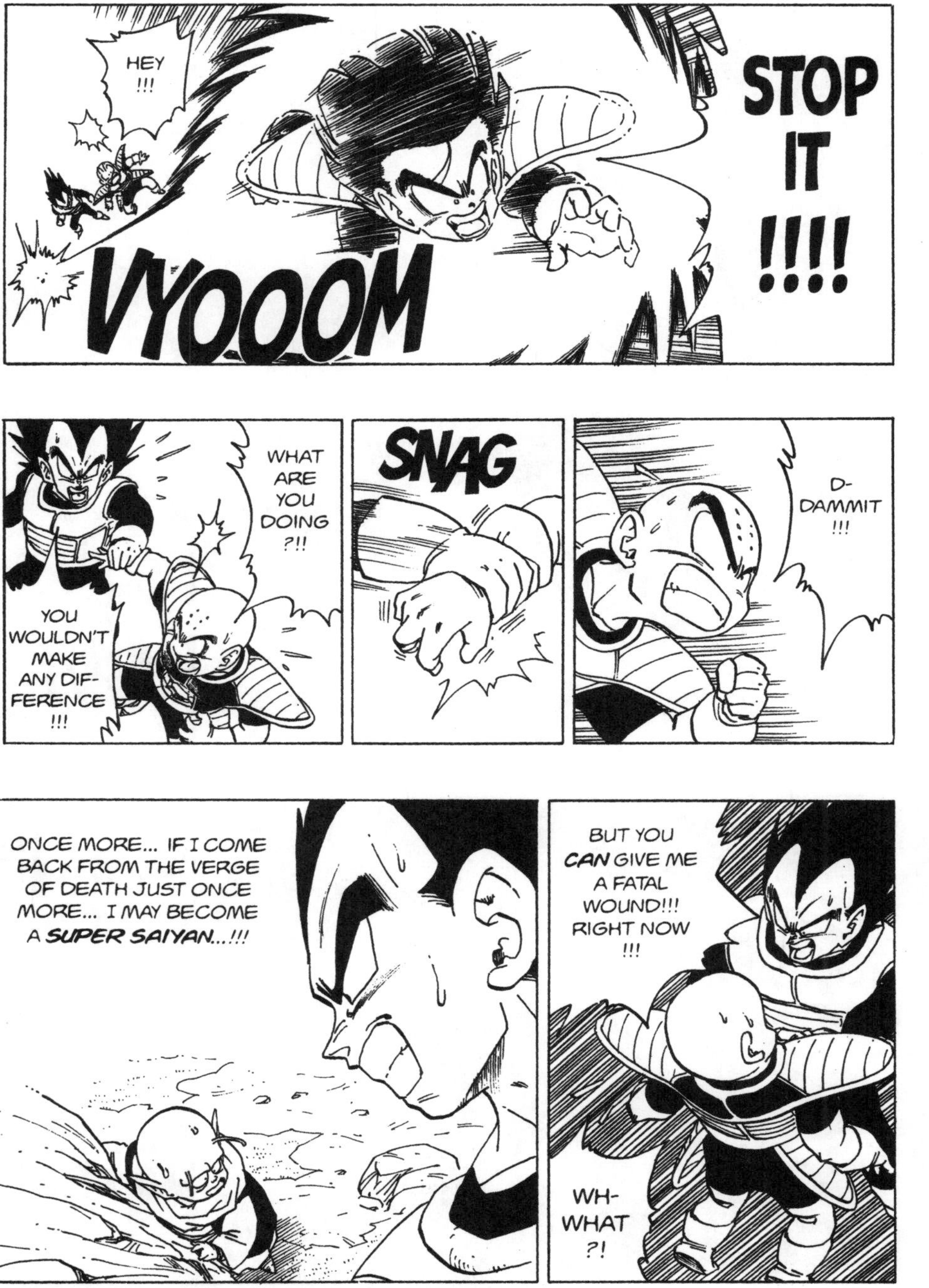
STOP IT !!!!
HEY !!!
VYOOOM
D-DAMMIT !!!
SNAG
WHAT ARE YOU DOING ?!!
YOU WOULDN'T MAKE ANY DIFFERENCE !!!
BUT YOU CAN GIVE ME A FATAL WOUND!!! RIGHT NOW !!!
WH-WHAT ?!
ONCE MORE... IF I COME BACK FROM THE VERGE OF DEATH JUST ONCE MORE... I MAY BECOME A SUPER SAIYAN...!!!

**NEXT: The Last Transformation!**

## DBZ:109 • Vegeta's Ploy

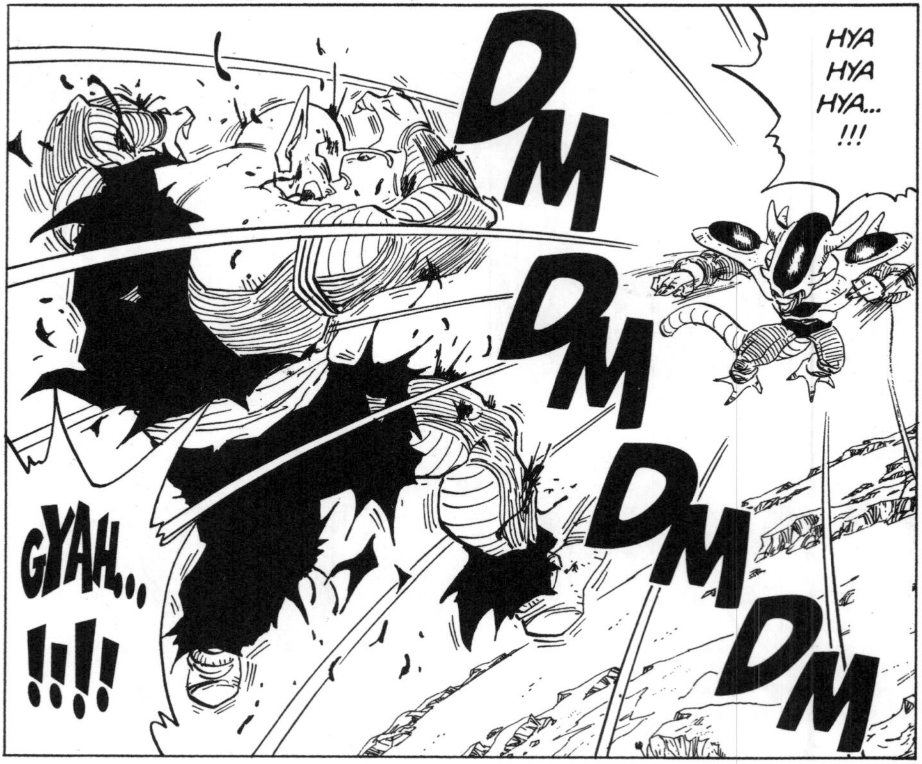
HYA
HYA
HYA...
!!!
DM DM DM DM DM DM
GYAH...
!!!!

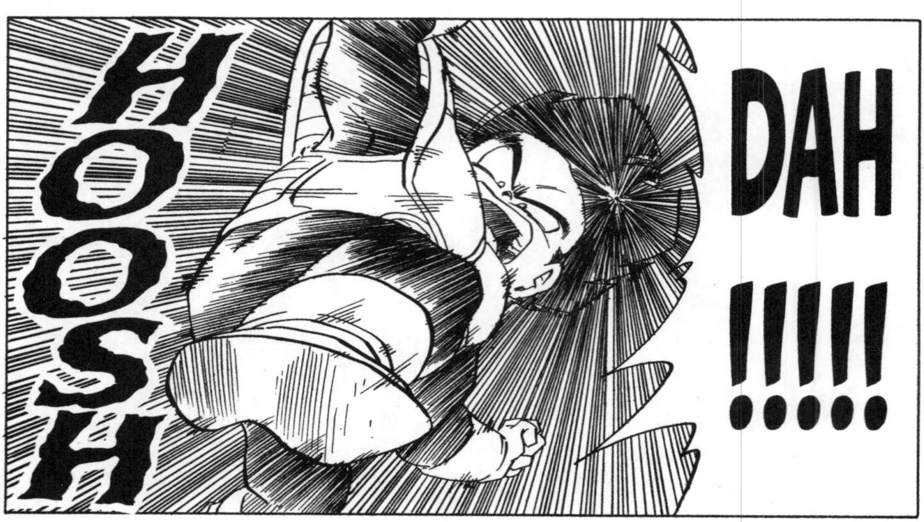
DAH
!!!!!!
HOOSH

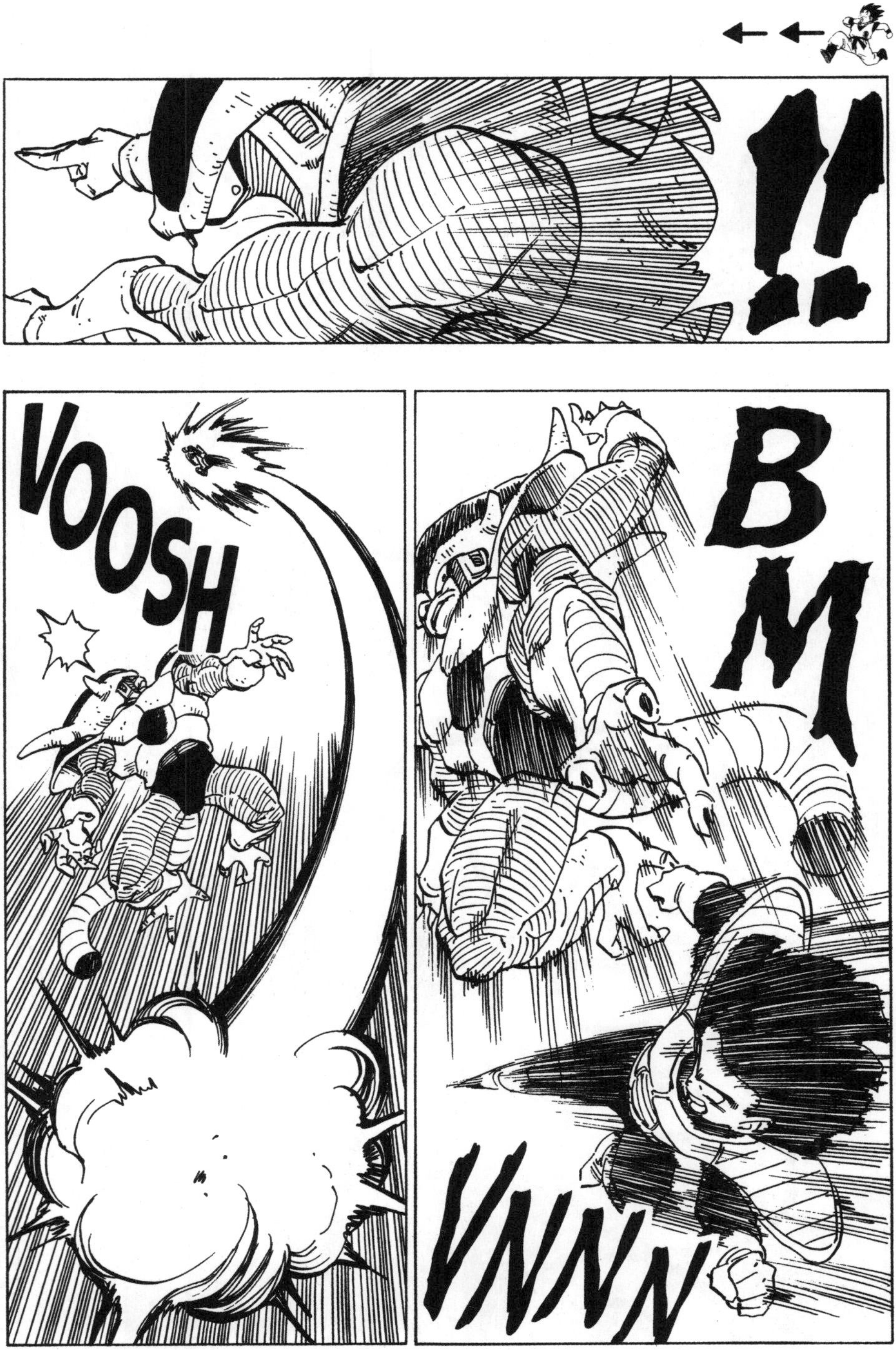

!!
BM
VNNN
VOOSH

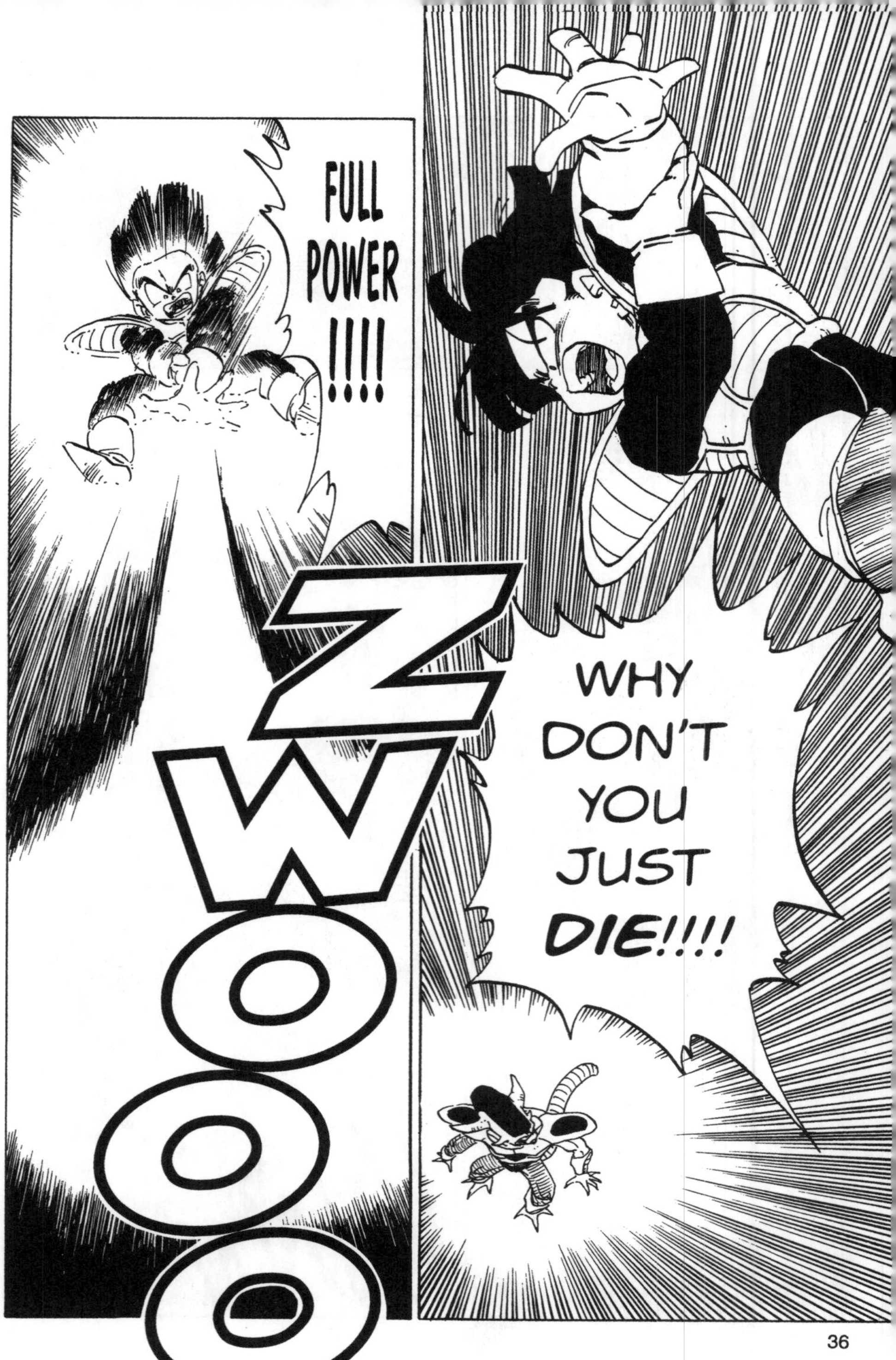
WHY DON'T YOU JUST DIE!!!!
FULL POWER!!!!
ZWOOOO

UNH
!!!!

FFFFF

DOOM

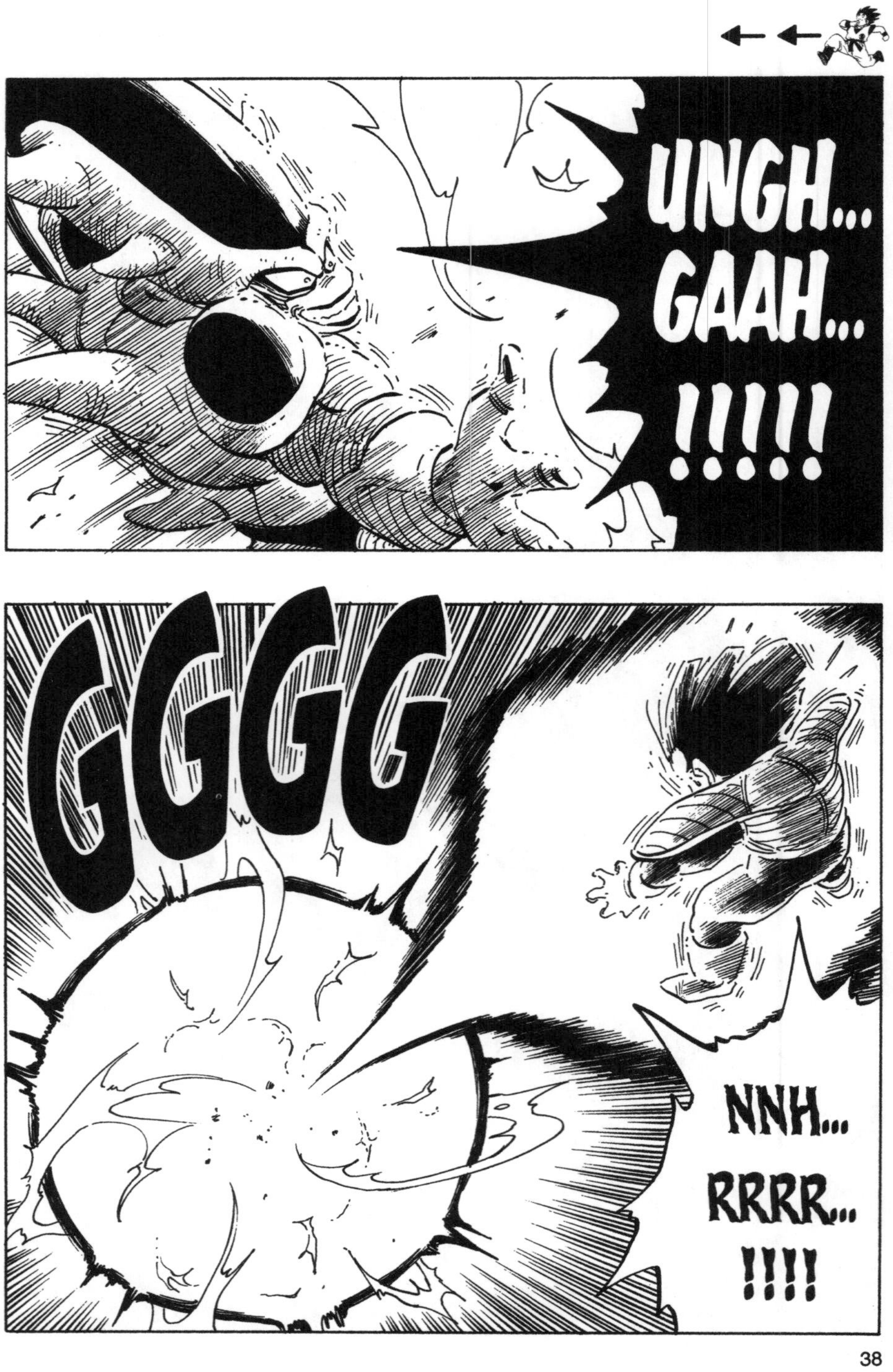

UNGH... GAAH... !!!!!
GGGG
NNH... RRRR... !!!!

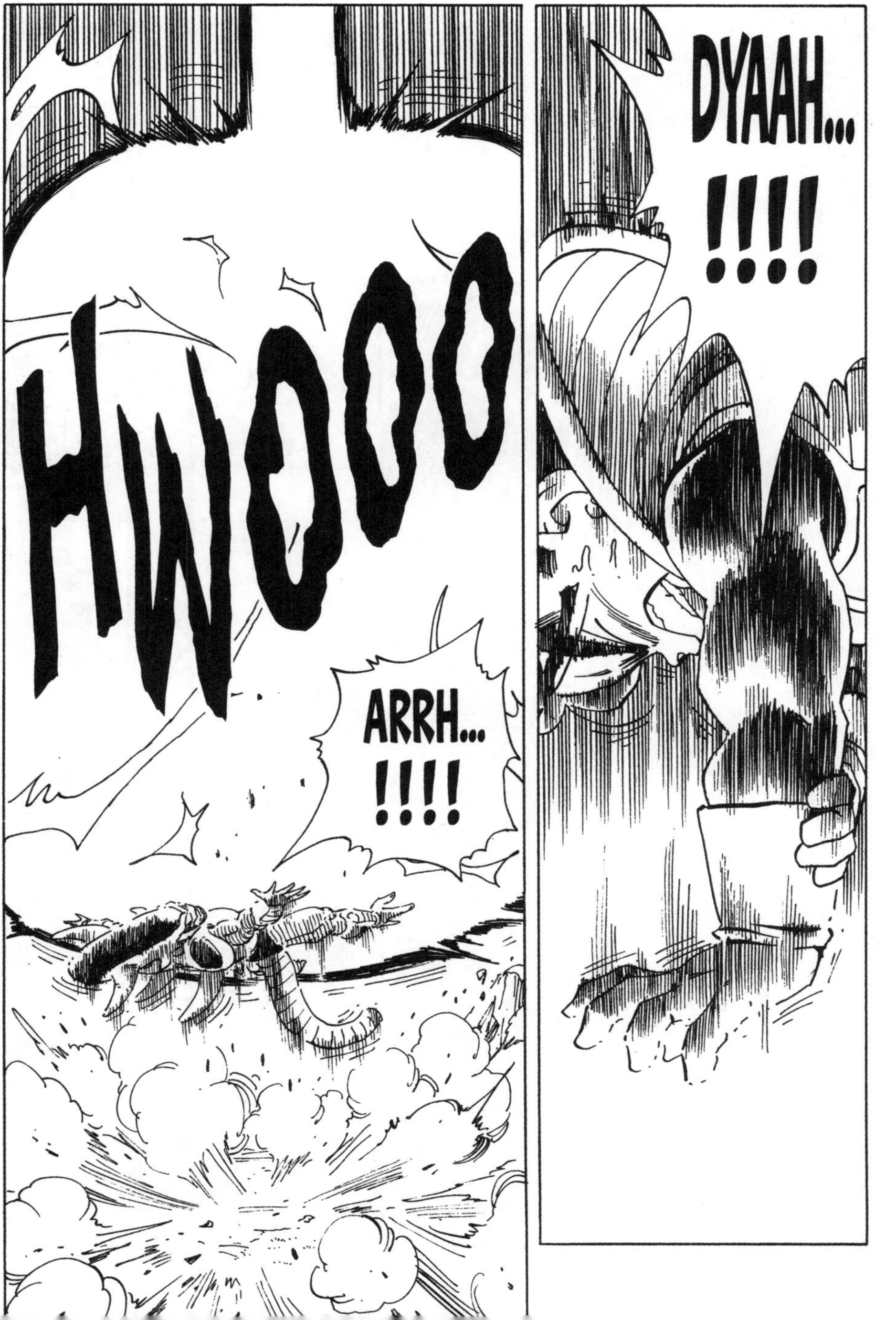
DYAAH...
!!!!
HWOOO
ARRH...
!!!!

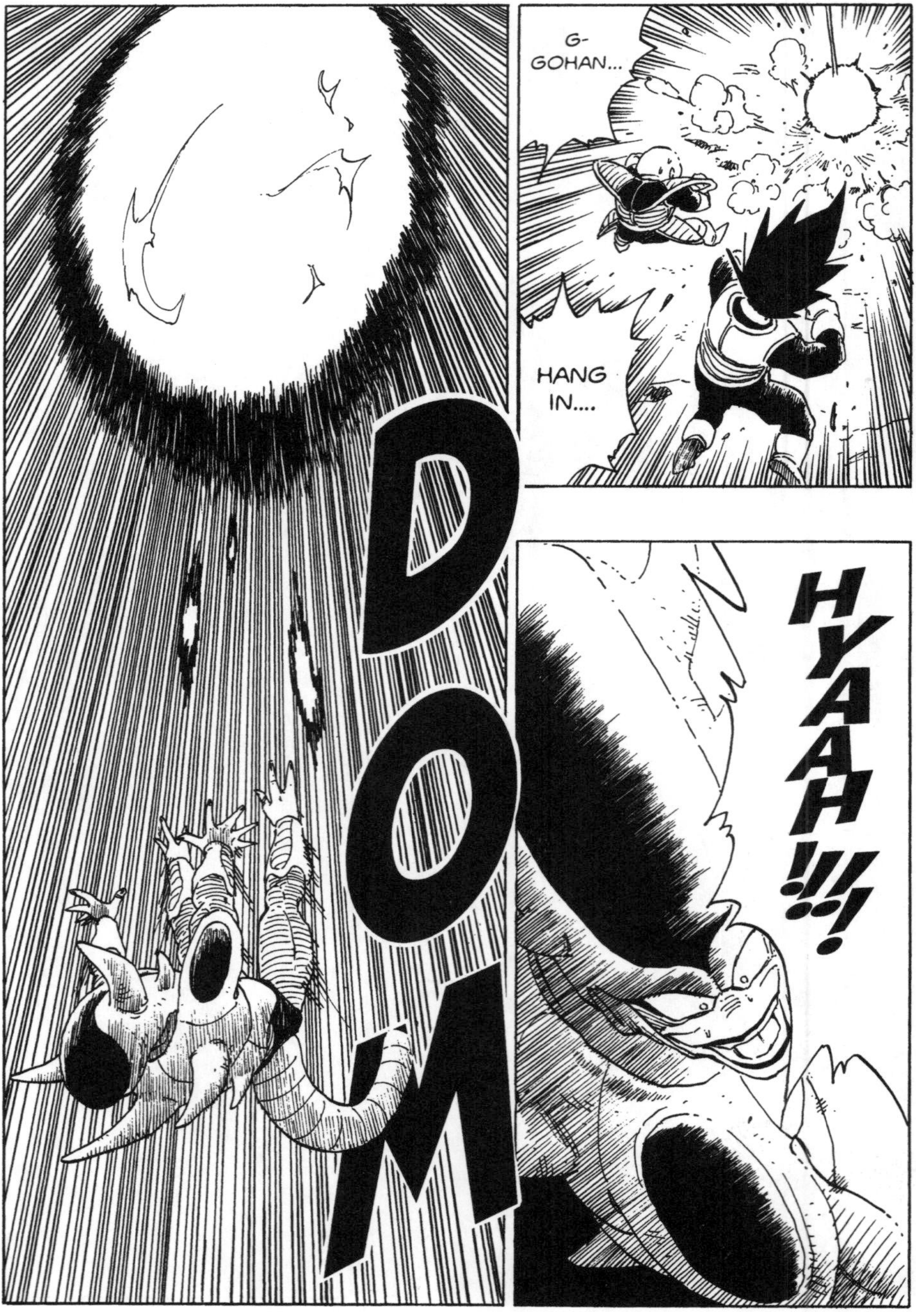
G-
GOHAN...
HANG
IN....
HYAAH!!!!
DOM

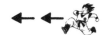

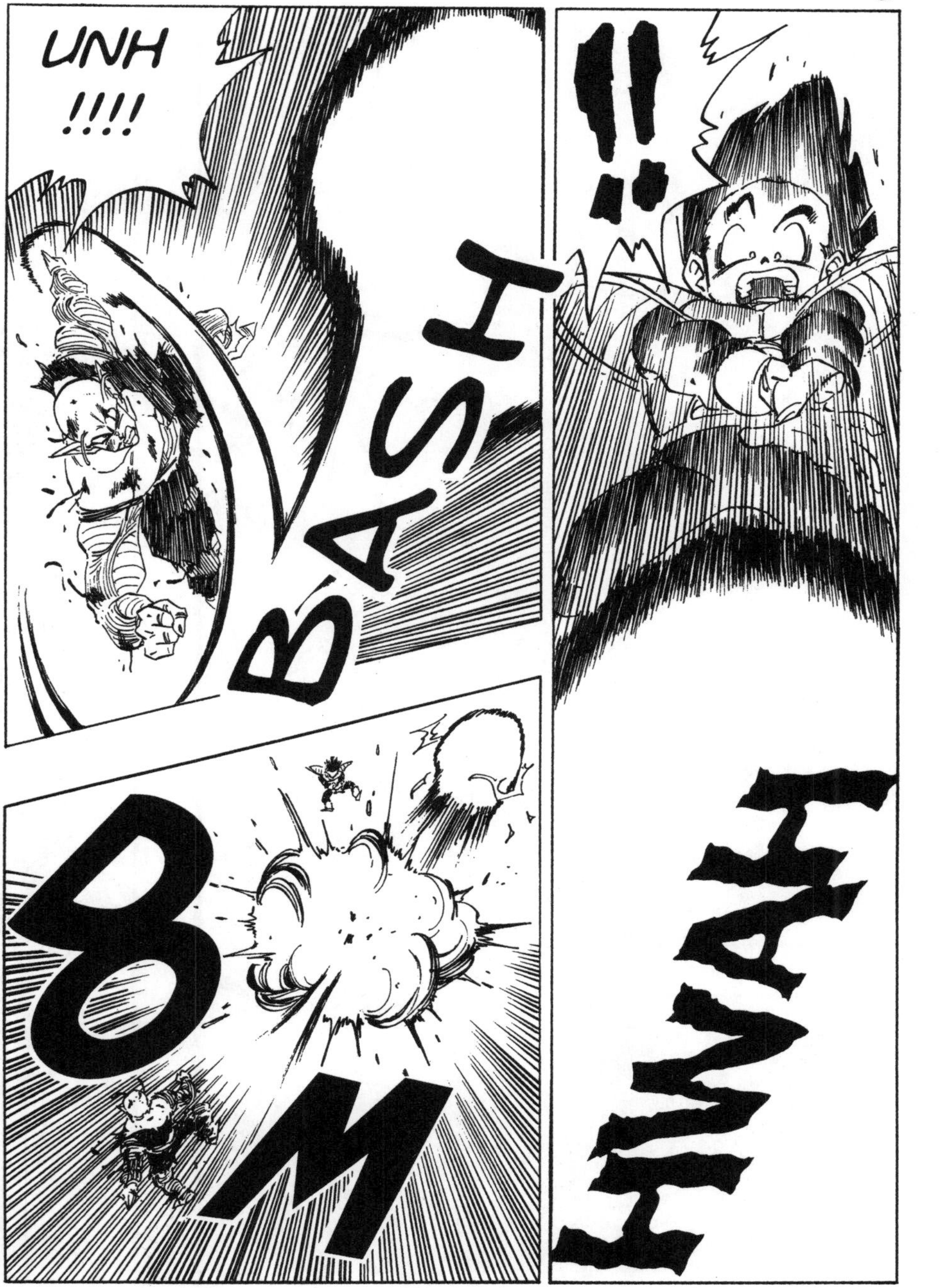
!!
HWAH
UNH !!!!
BASH
BOOM

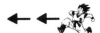

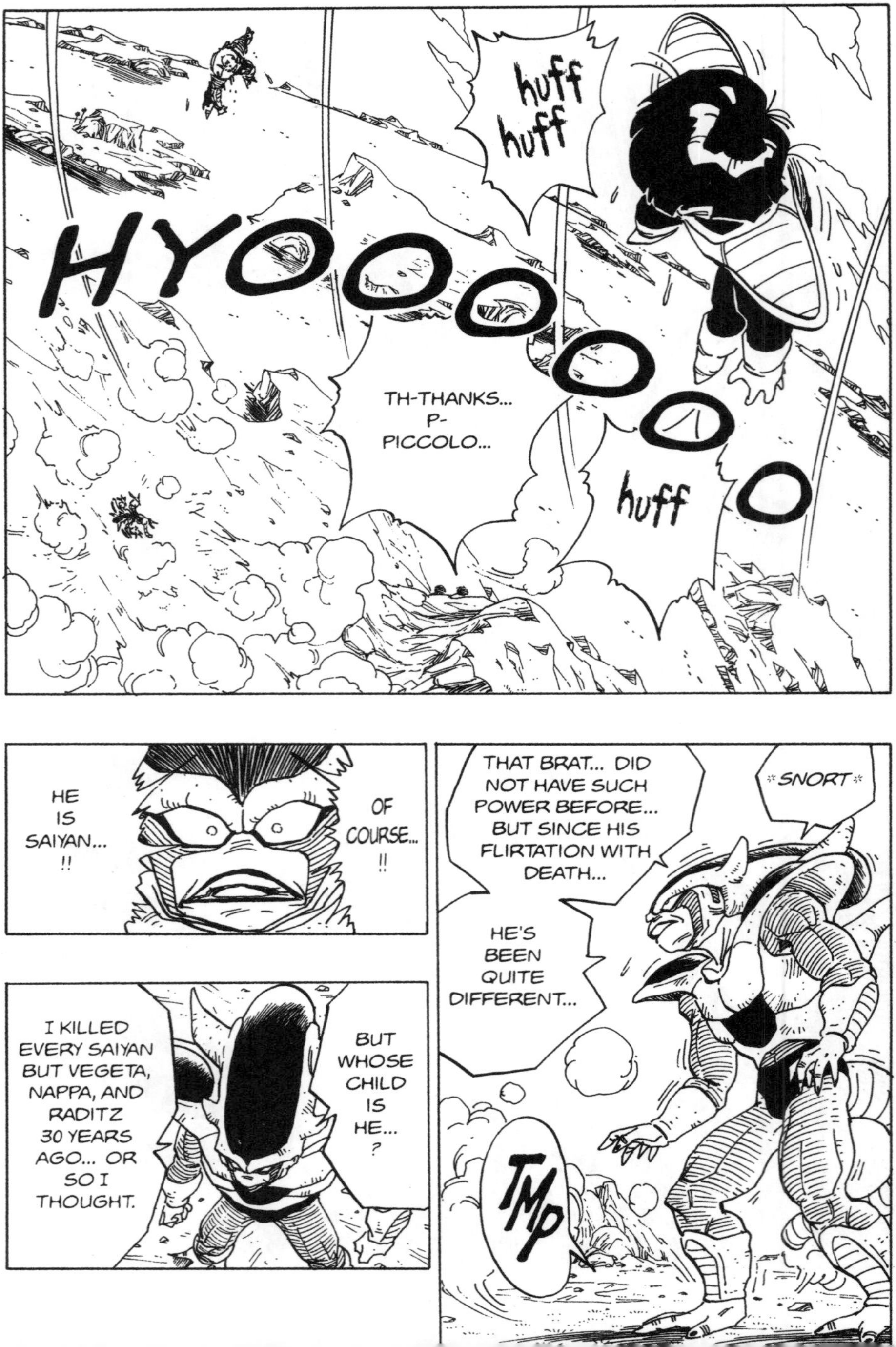
huff huff
HYOOOOOOOOO
TH-THANKS... P-PICCOLO...
huff
*SNORT*
THAT BRAT... DID NOT HAVE SUCH POWER BEFORE... BUT SINCE HIS FLIRTATION WITH DEATH...
HE'S BEEN QUITE DIFFERENT...
TMP
OF COURSE... !!
HE IS SAIYAN... !!
BUT WHOSE CHILD IS HE... ?
I KILLED EVERY SAIYAN BUT VEGETA, NAPPA, AND RADITZ 30 YEARS AGO... OR SO I THOUGHT.

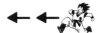

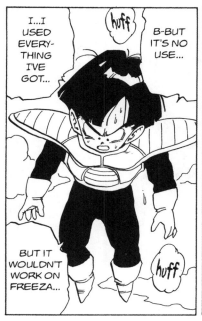

H-HE BOUNCED THAT ONE BACK...
...BUT YOU'VE GROWN STRONG, GOHAN...
IT... IT MAKES ME HAPPY...
B-BUT IT'S NO USE...
huff
I...I USED EVERYTHING I'VE GOT...
BUT IT WOULDN'T WORK ON FREEZA...
huff
HE DOES NOT LOOK LIKE VEGETA OR NAPPA...
RADITZ'S CHILD...? PERHAPS... THERE *IS* A RESEMBLANCE...
I MUST NOT ALLOW ANY SAIYAN TO LIVE ANYMORE...
I MUST EXTERMINATE ALL SAIYAN BLOOD...
I DON'T BELIEVE IN THE RIDICULOUS SUPER SAIYAN LEGEND...BUT STILL, IT DOESN'T HURT TO BE CAREFUL...
THAT BRAT AND VEGETA ARE ALREADY GROWING MORE POWERFUL...

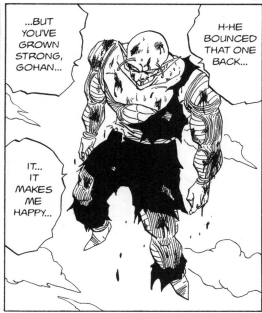

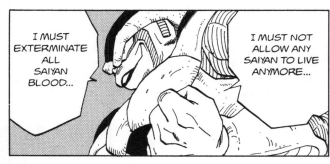

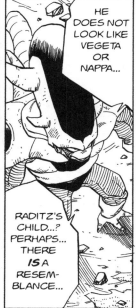

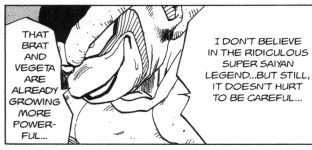

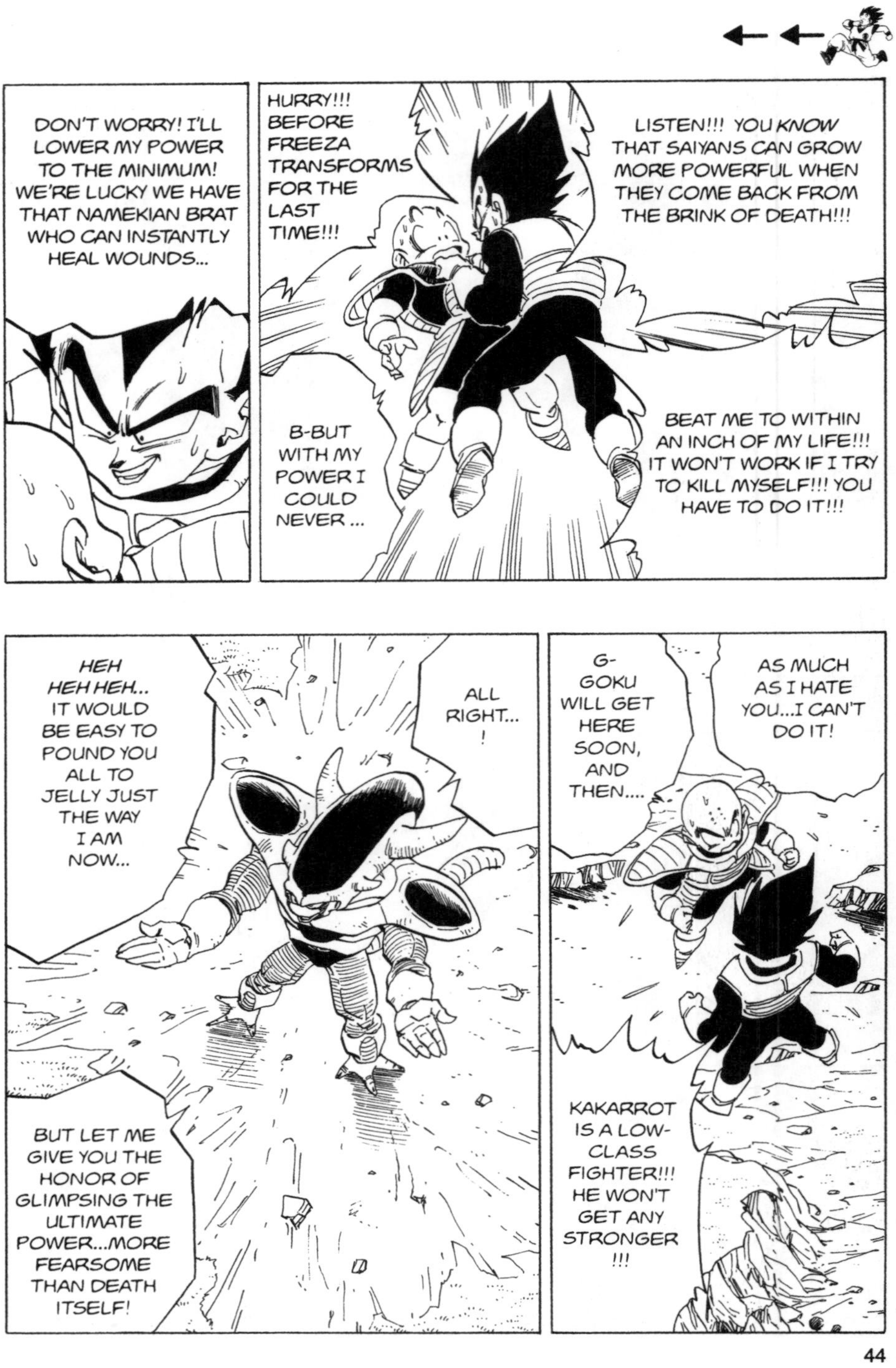
LISTEN!!! YOU *KNOW* THAT SAIYANS CAN GROW MORE POWERFUL WHEN THEY COME BACK FROM THE BRINK OF DEATH!!!
HURRY!!! BEFORE FREEZA TRANSFORMS FOR THE LAST TIME!!!
BEAT ME TO WITHIN AN INCH OF MY LIFE!!! IT WON'T WORK IF I TRY TO KILL MYSELF!!! YOU HAVE TO DO IT!!!
B-BUT WITH MY POWER I COULD NEVER ...
DON'T WORRY! I'LL LOWER MY POWER TO THE MINIMUM! WE'RE LUCKY WE HAVE THAT NAMEKIAN BRAT WHO CAN INSTANTLY HEAL WOUNDS...
AS MUCH AS I HATE YOU...I CAN'T DO IT!
G-GOKU WILL GET HERE SOON, AND THEN....
KAKARROT IS A LOW-CLASS FIGHTER!!! HE WON'T GET ANY STRONGER !!!
ALL RIGHT... !
*HEH HEH HEH...* IT WOULD BE EASY TO POUND YOU ALL TO JELLY JUST THE WAY I AM NOW...
BUT LET ME GIVE YOU THE HONOR OF GLIMPSING THE ULTIMATE POWER...MORE FEARSOME THAN DEATH ITSELF!

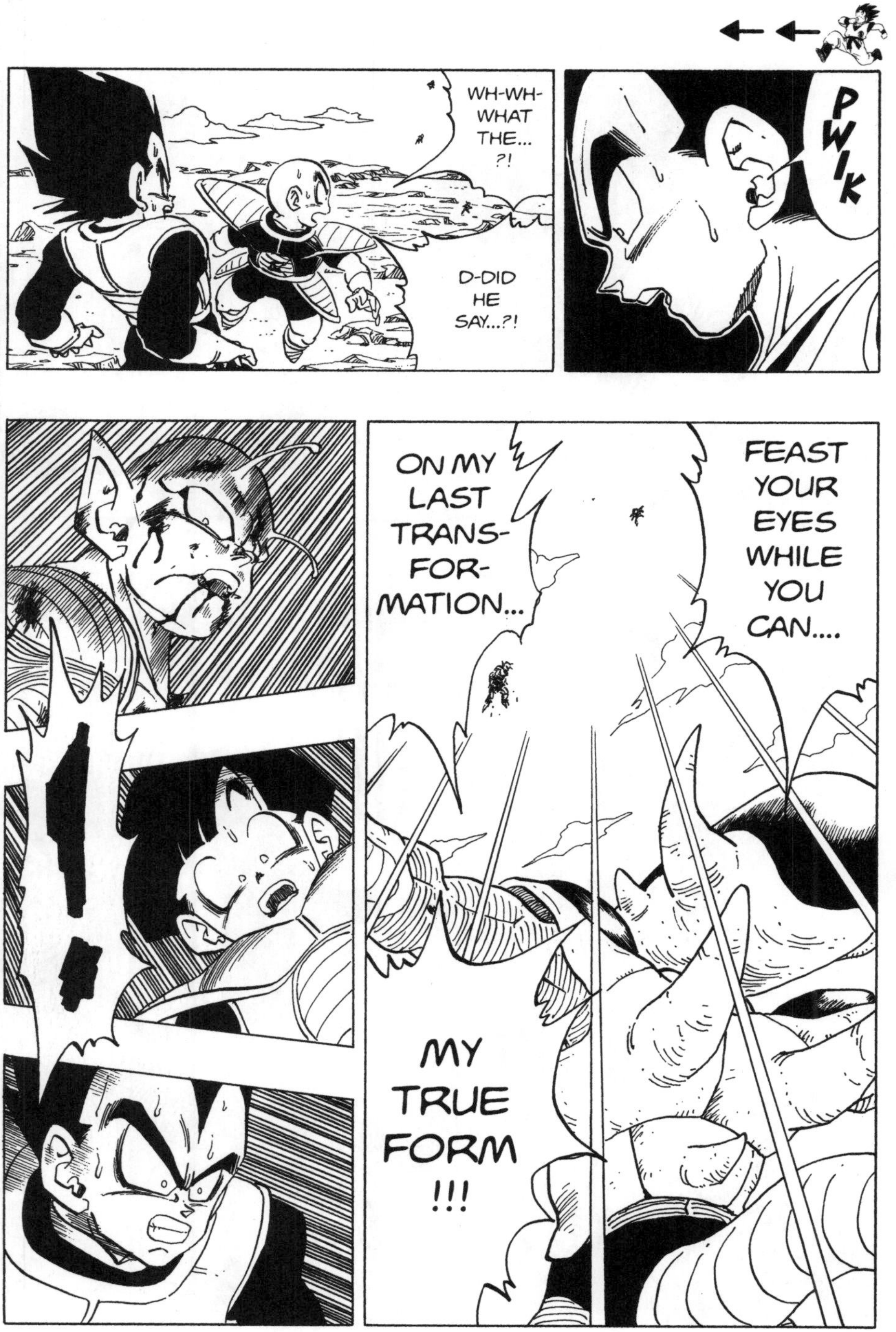
PWIK
WH-WH-WHAT THE...?!
D-DID HE SAY...?!
FEAST YOUR EYES WHILE YOU CAN....
ON MY LAST TRANS-FOR-MATION...
MY TRUE FORM!!!

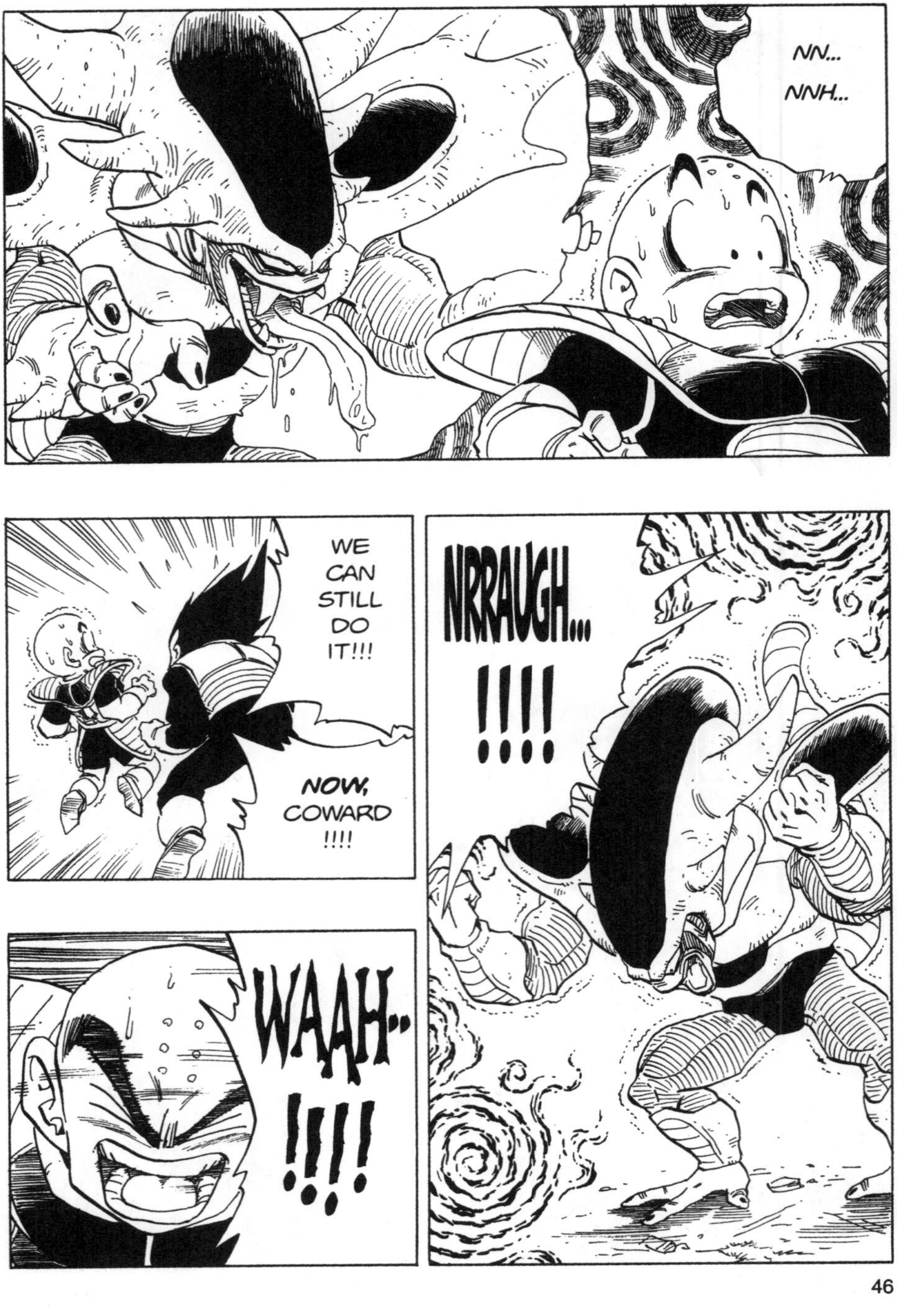
NN... NNH...
NRRAUGH... !!!!
WE CAN STILL DO IT!!!
NOW, COWARD !!!!
WAAH.. !!!!

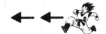

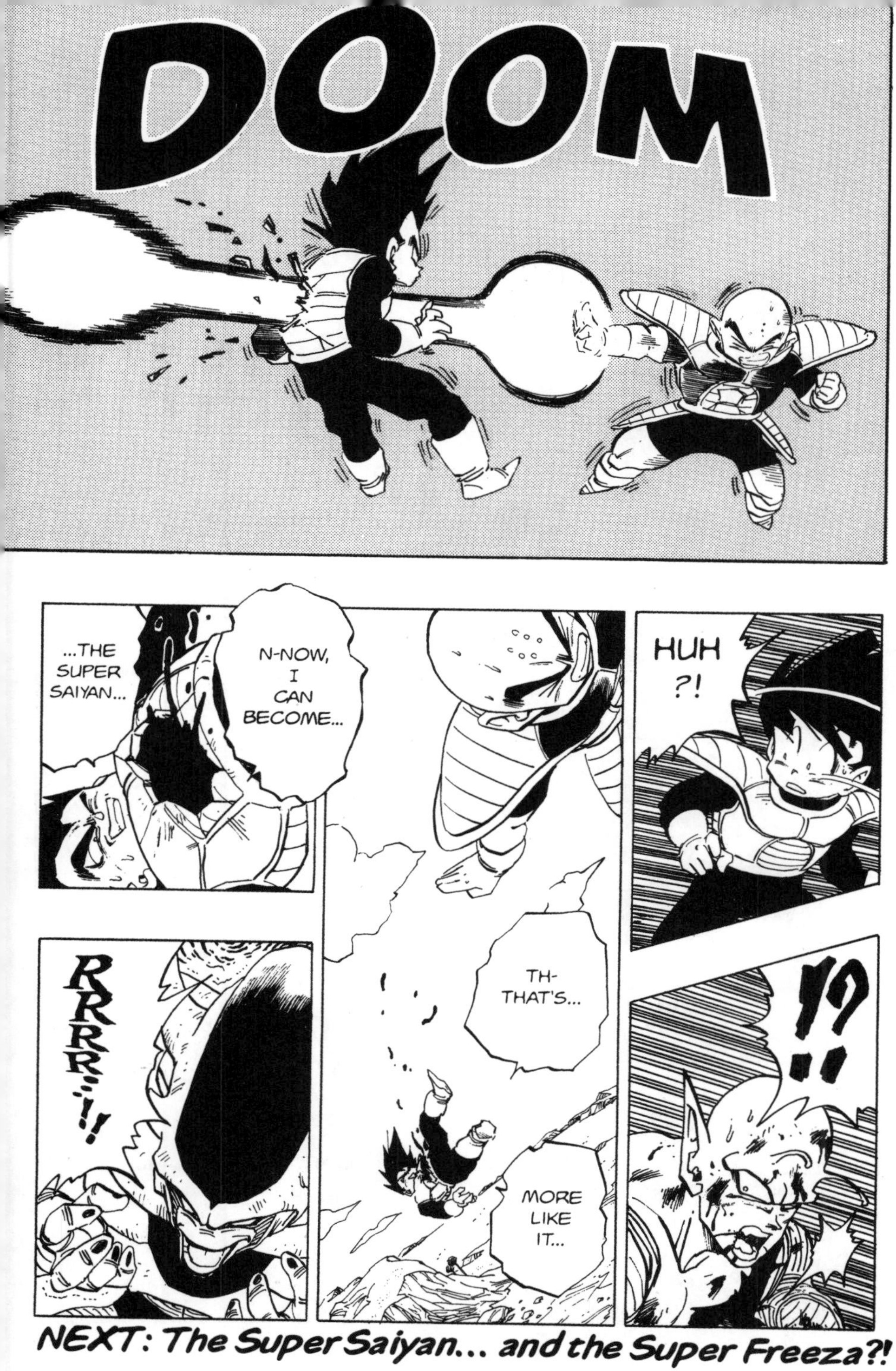
DOOM
HUH ?!
!?
!!
N-NOW, I CAN BECOME...
TH- THAT'S...
MORE LIKE IT...
...THE SUPER SAIYAN...
RRRR...!!

**NEXT: The Super Saiyan... and the Super Freeza?!**

# DBZ:110 • The Final Transformation

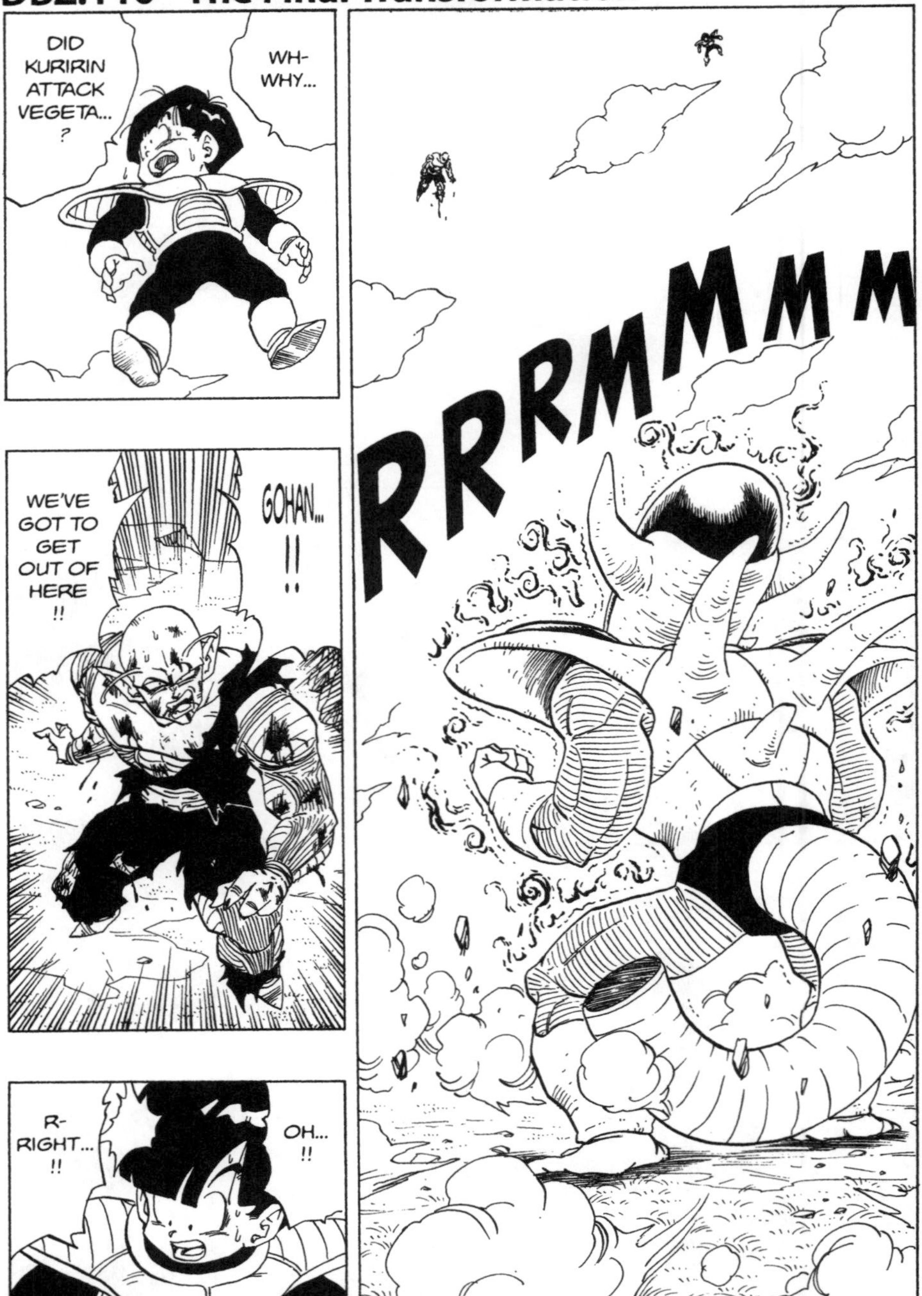

RRRMMMMM
WH-WHY...
DID KURIRIN ATTACK VEGETA...?
GOHAN... !!
WE'VE GOT TO GET OUT OF HERE !!
OH... !!
R-RIGHT... !!

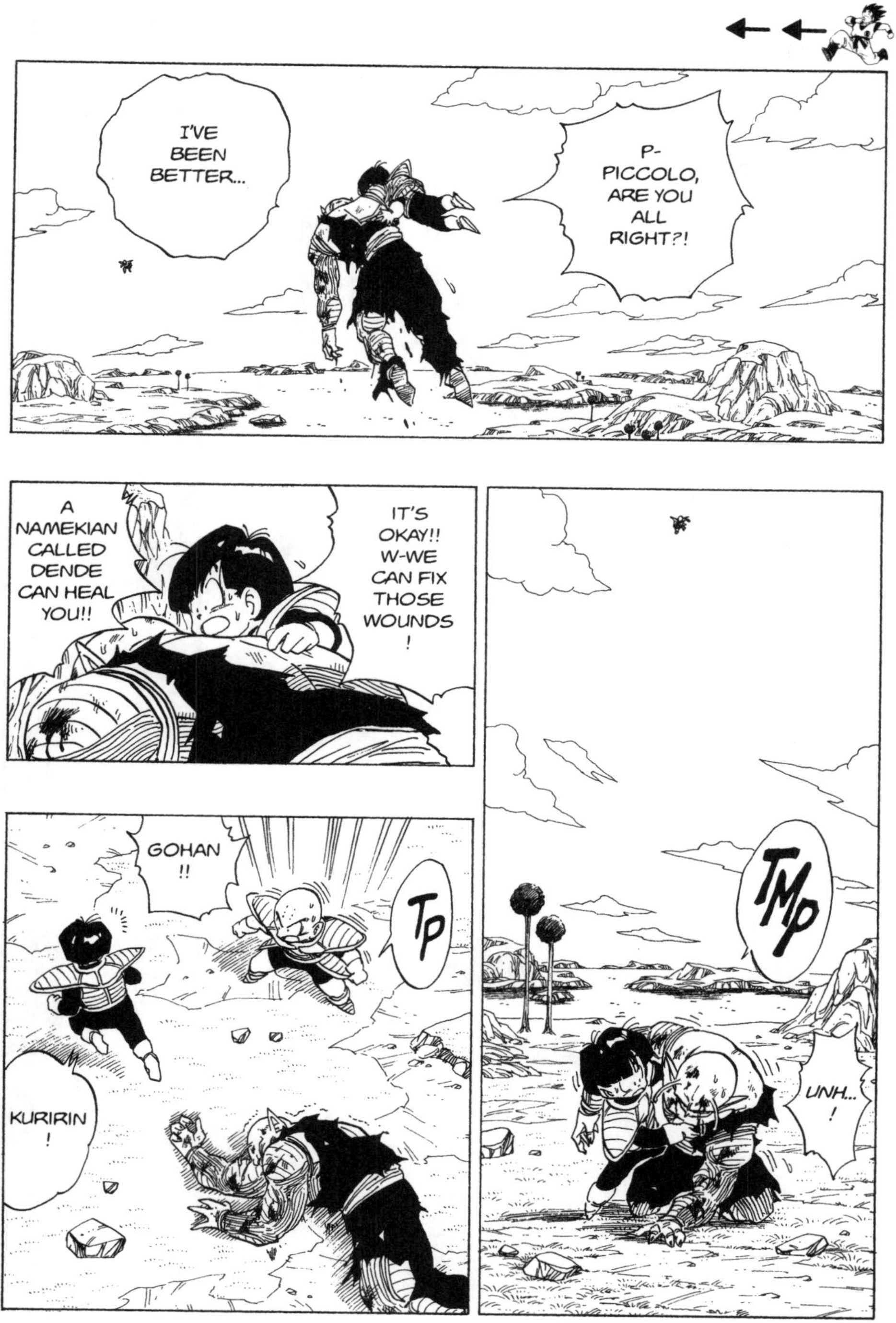
P-PICCOLO, ARE YOU ALL RIGHT?!
I'VE BEEN BETTER...
TMP
UNH...!
IT'S OKAY!! W-WE CAN FIX THOSE WOUNDS!
A NAMEKIAN CALLED DENDE CAN HEAL YOU!!
TP
GOHAN!!
KURIRIN!

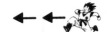

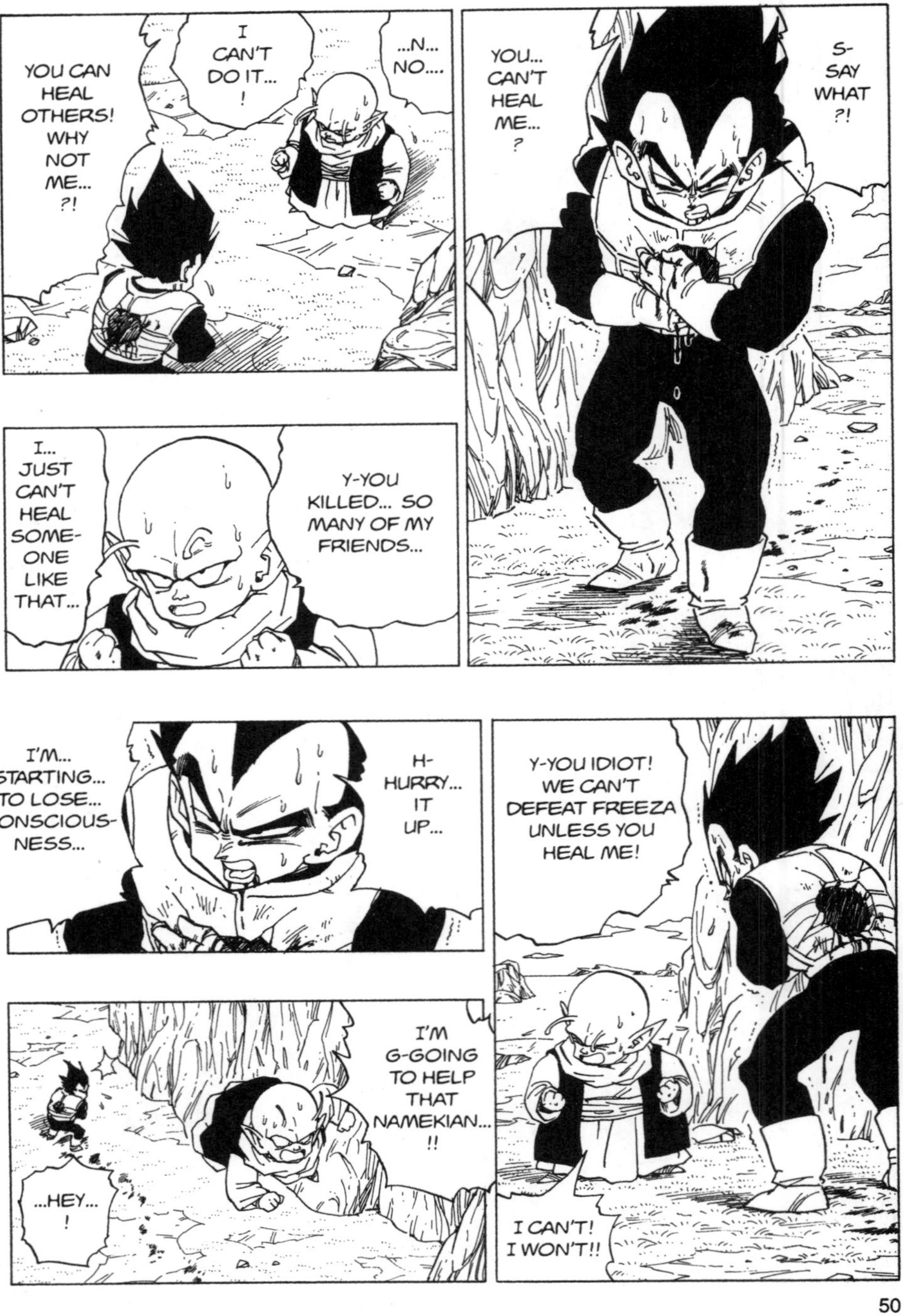
S-SAY WHAT ?!
YOU... CAN'T HEAL ME... ?
...N... NO....
I CAN'T DO IT... !
YOU CAN HEAL OTHERS! WHY NOT ME... ?!
Y-YOU KILLED... SO MANY OF MY FRIENDS...
I... JUST CAN'T HEAL SOME-ONE LIKE THAT...
Y-YOU IDIOT! WE CAN'T DEFEAT FREEZA UNLESS YOU HEAL ME!
I CAN'T! I WON'T!!
H-HURRY... IT UP...
I'M... STARTING... TO LOSE... CONSCIOUS-NESS...
I'M G-GOING TO HELP THAT NAMEKIAN... !!
...HEY... !

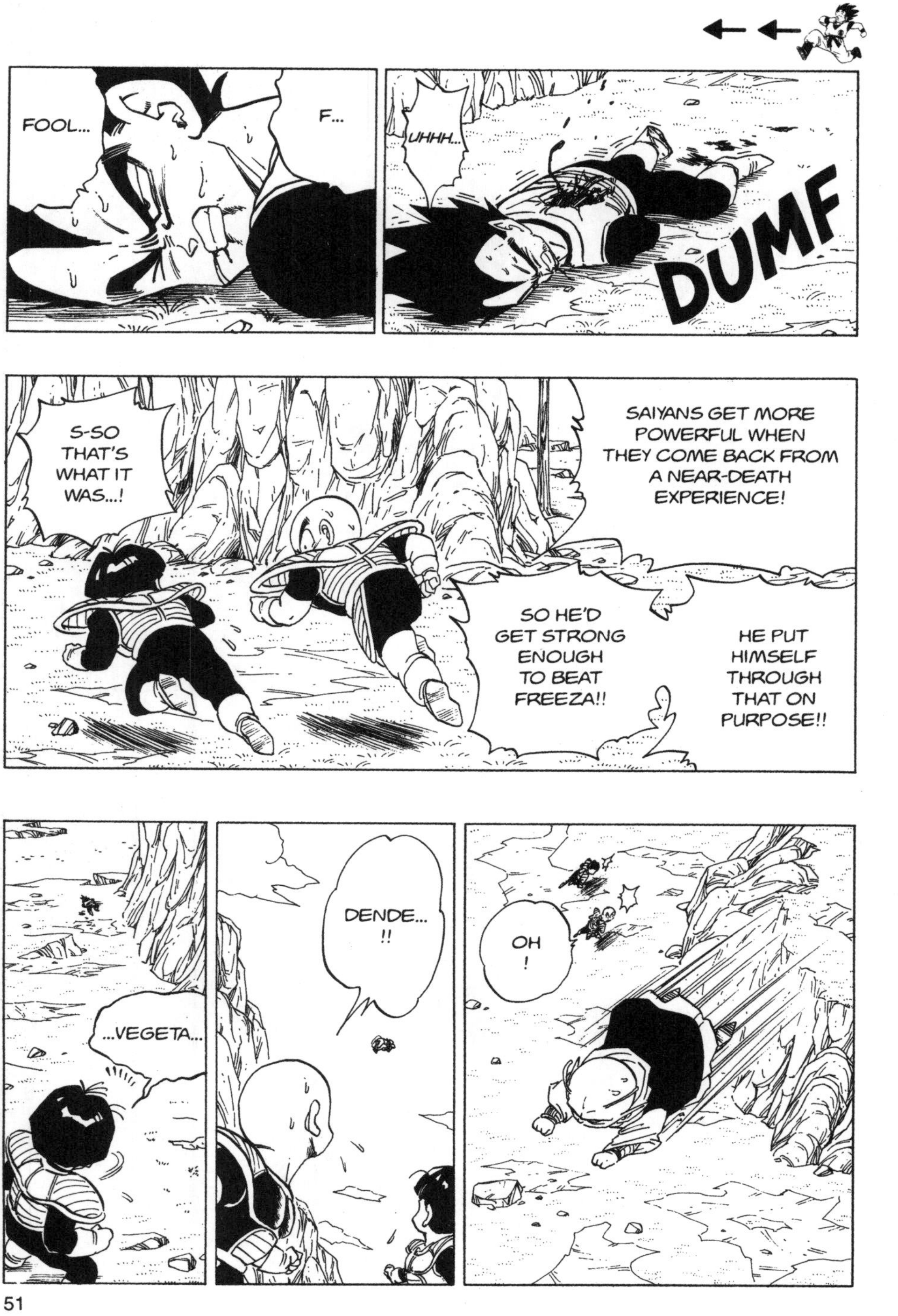
UHHH...
DUMF
F...
FOOL...
S-SO THAT'S WHAT IT WAS...!
SAIYANS GET MORE POWERFUL WHEN THEY COME BACK FROM A NEAR-DEATH EXPERIENCE!
HE PUT HIMSELF THROUGH THAT ON PURPOSE!!
SO HE'D GET STRONG ENOUGH TO BEAT FREEZA!!
OH !
DENDE... !!
...VEGETA...

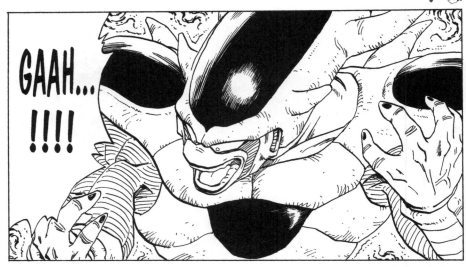

GAAH... !!!!

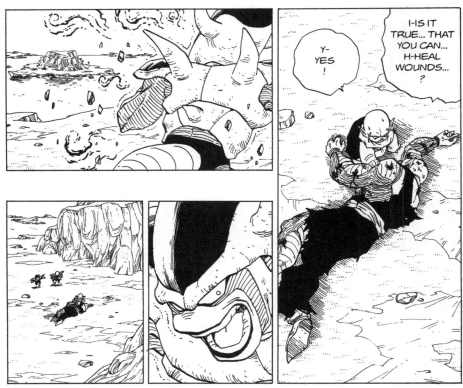

Y-YES!

I-IS IT TRUE... THAT YOU CAN... H-HEAL WOUNDS...?

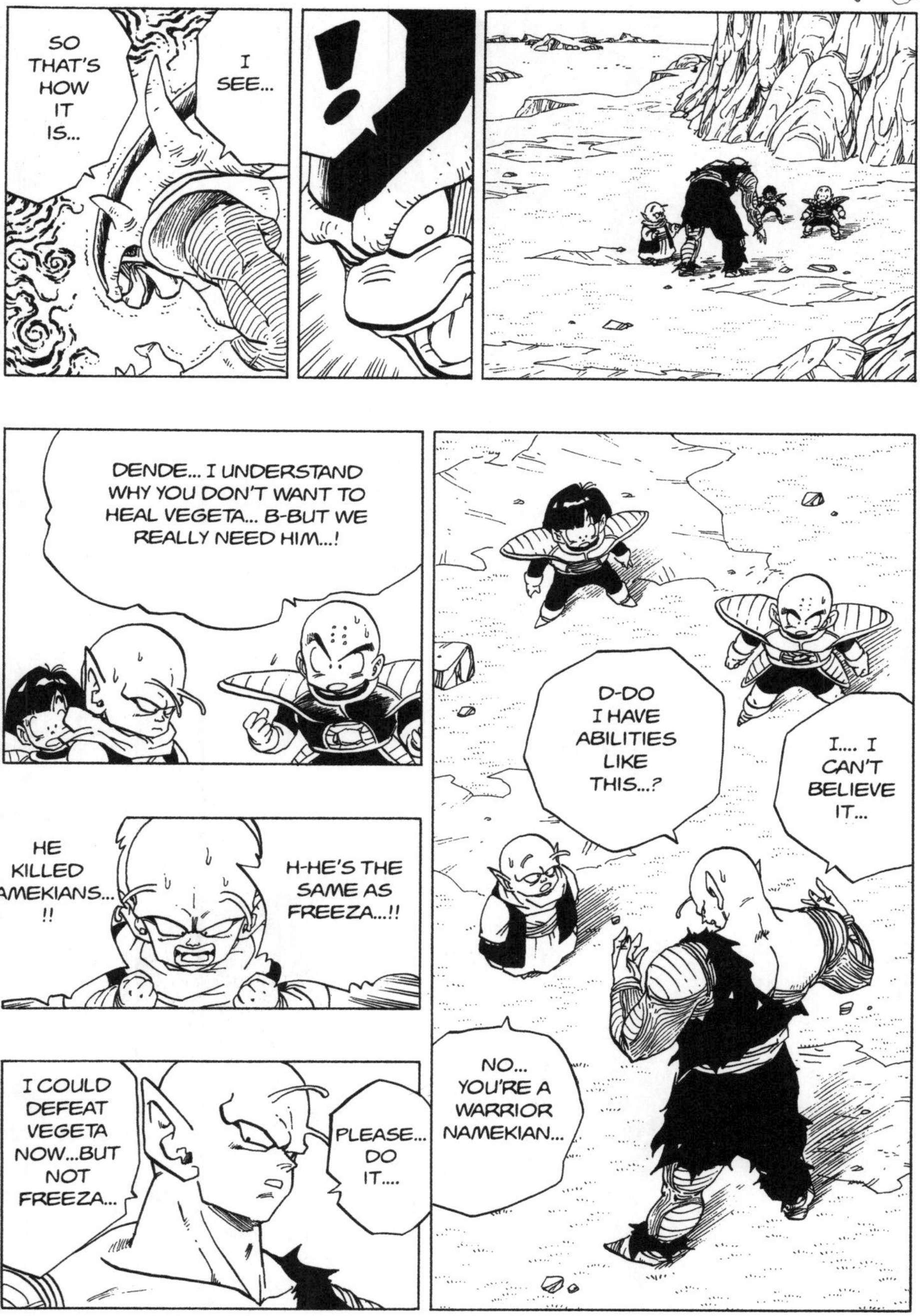

!
I SEE...
SO THAT'S HOW IT IS...
I.... I CAN'T BELIEVE IT...
D-DO I HAVE ABILITIES LIKE THIS...?
NO... YOU'RE A WARRIOR NAMEKIAN...
DENDE... I UNDERSTAND WHY YOU DON'T WANT TO HEAL VEGETA... B-BUT WE REALLY NEED HIM...!
H-HE'S THE SAME AS FREEZA...!!
HE KILLED NAMEKIANS...!!
PLEASE... DO IT....
I COULD DEFEAT VEGETA NOW...BUT NOT FREEZA...

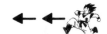

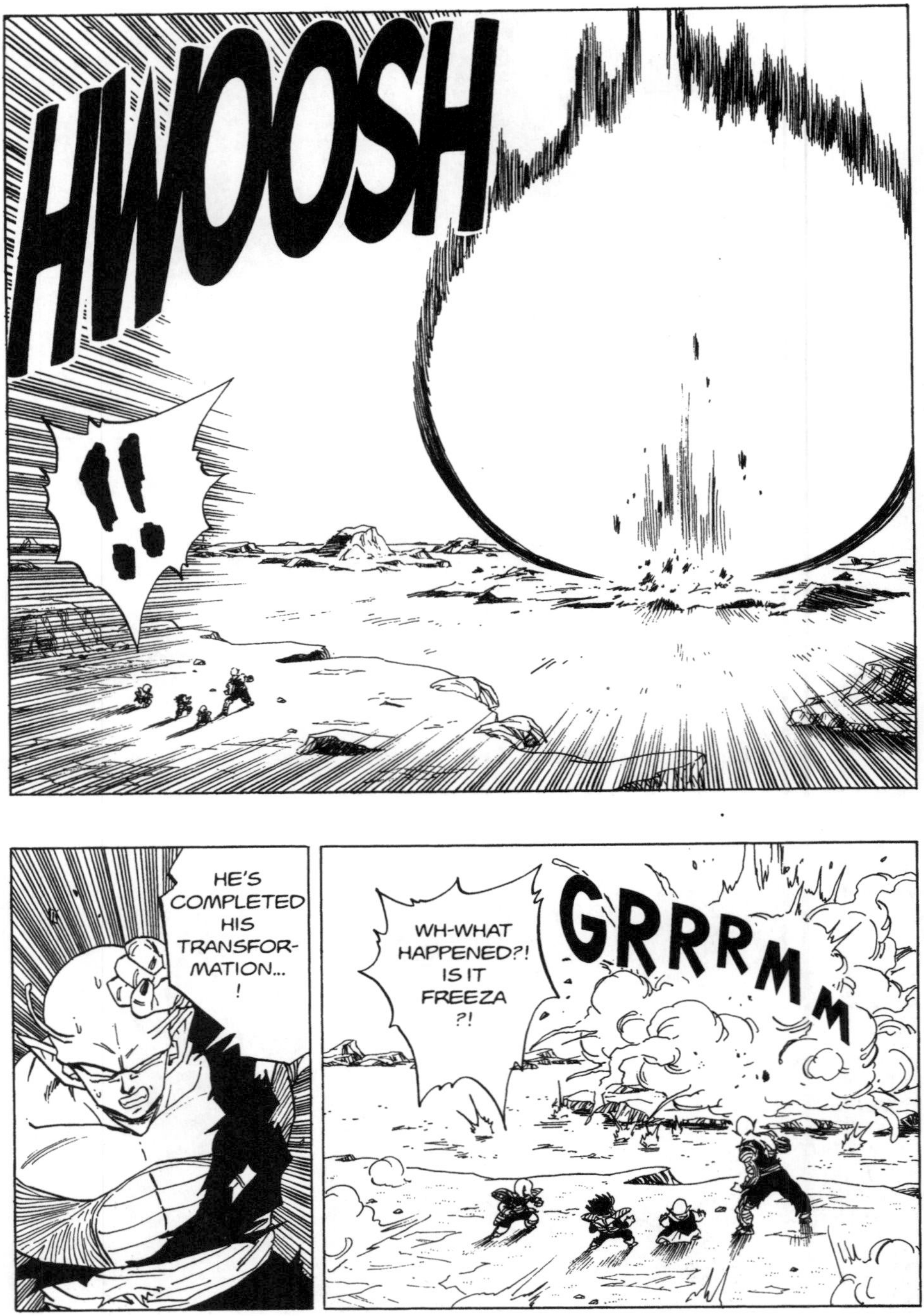
HWOOSH
!!
WH-WHAT HAPPENED?! IS IT FREEZA ?!
GRRRMM
HE'S COMPLETED HIS TRANSFOR-MATION... !

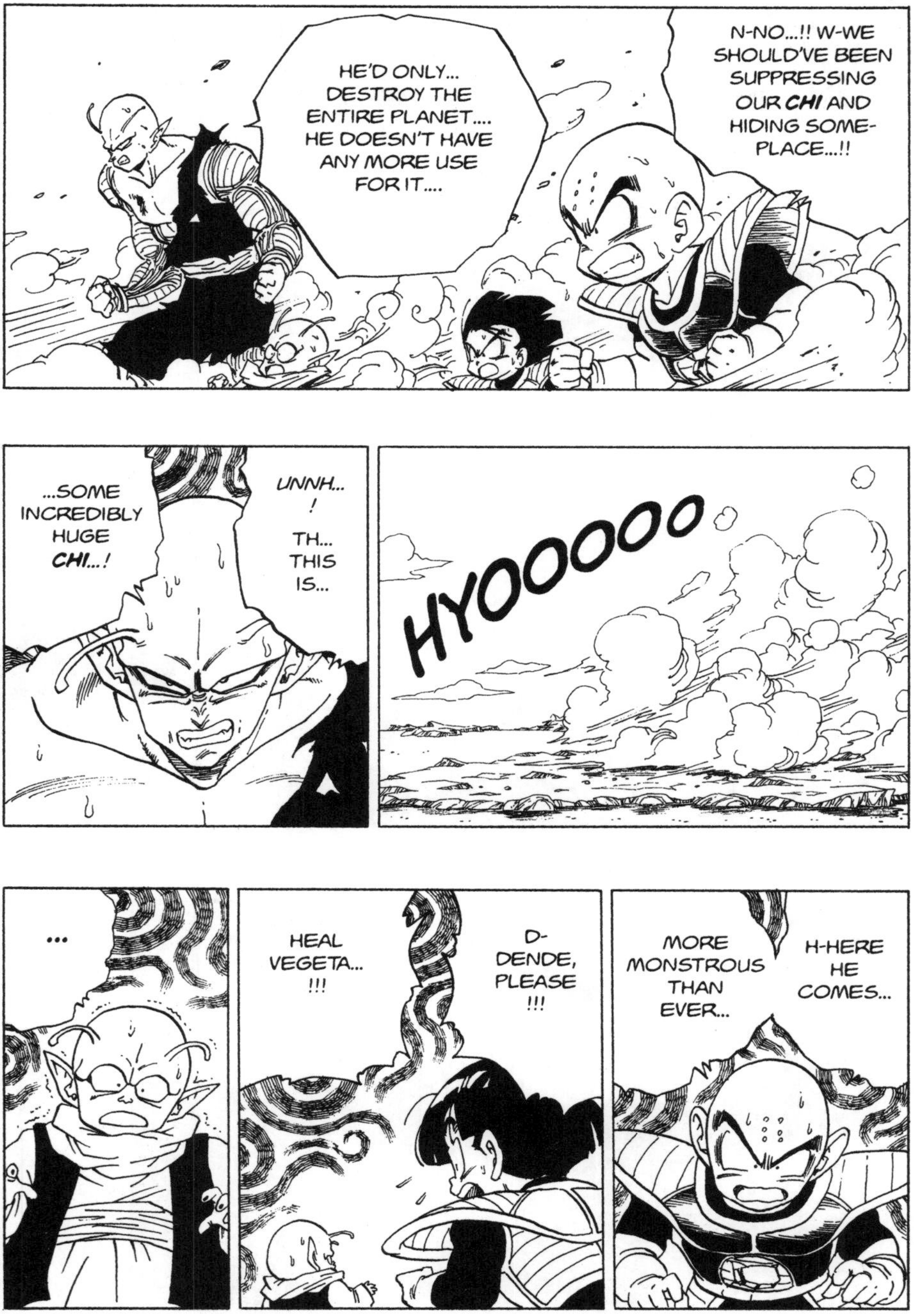
N-NO...!! W-WE SHOULD'VE BEEN SUPPRESSING OUR CHI AND HIDING SOME-PLACE...!!
HE'D ONLY... DESTROY THE ENTIRE PLANET.... HE DOESN'T HAVE ANY MORE USE FOR IT....
HYOOOOOO
UNNH...! TH... THIS IS...
...SOME INCREDIBLY HUGE CHI...!
H-HERE HE COMES...
MORE MONSTROUS THAN EVER...
D-DENDE, PLEASE!!!
HEAL VEGETA...!!!
...

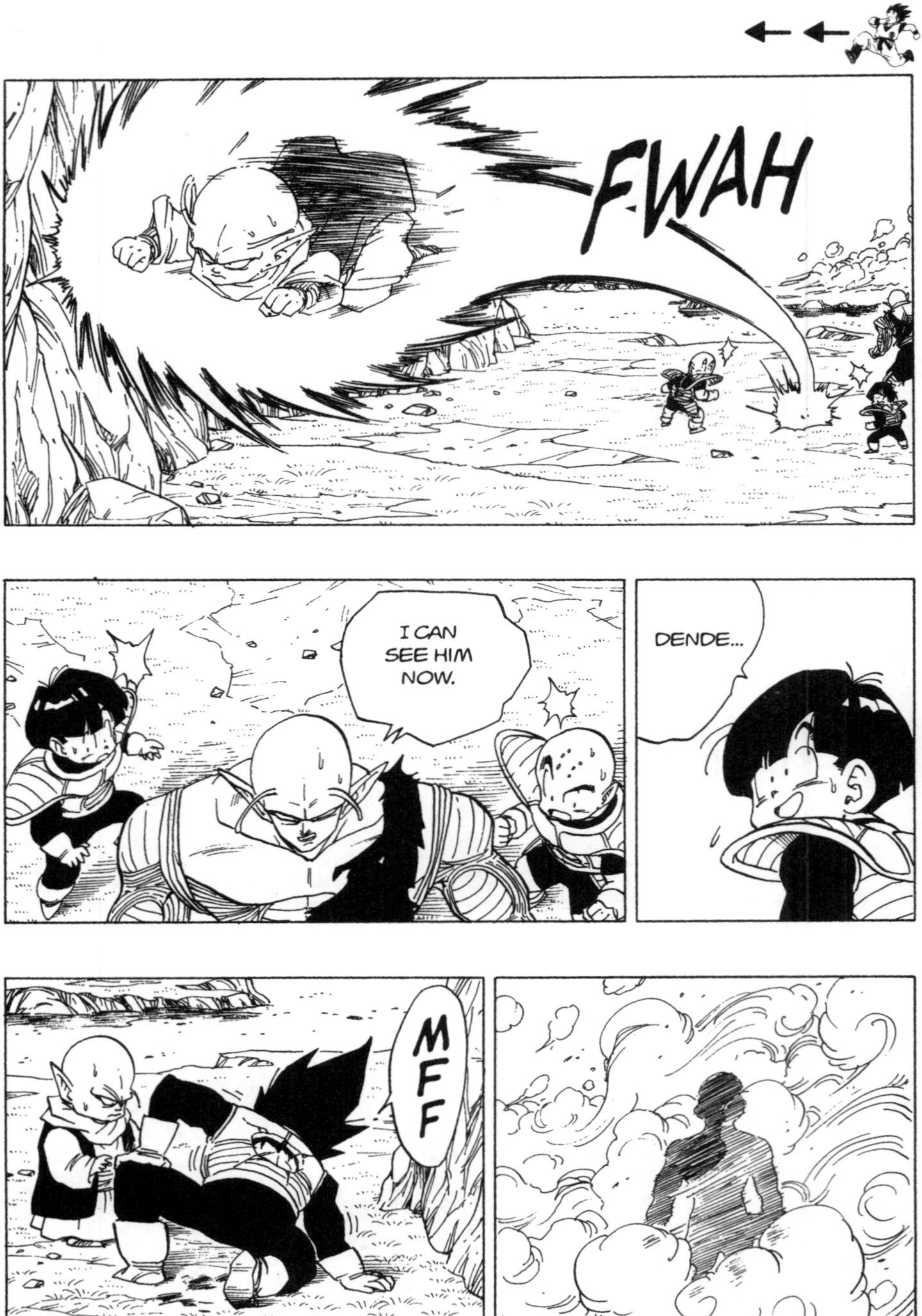
FWAH
DENDE...
I CAN SEE HIM NOW.
MFF

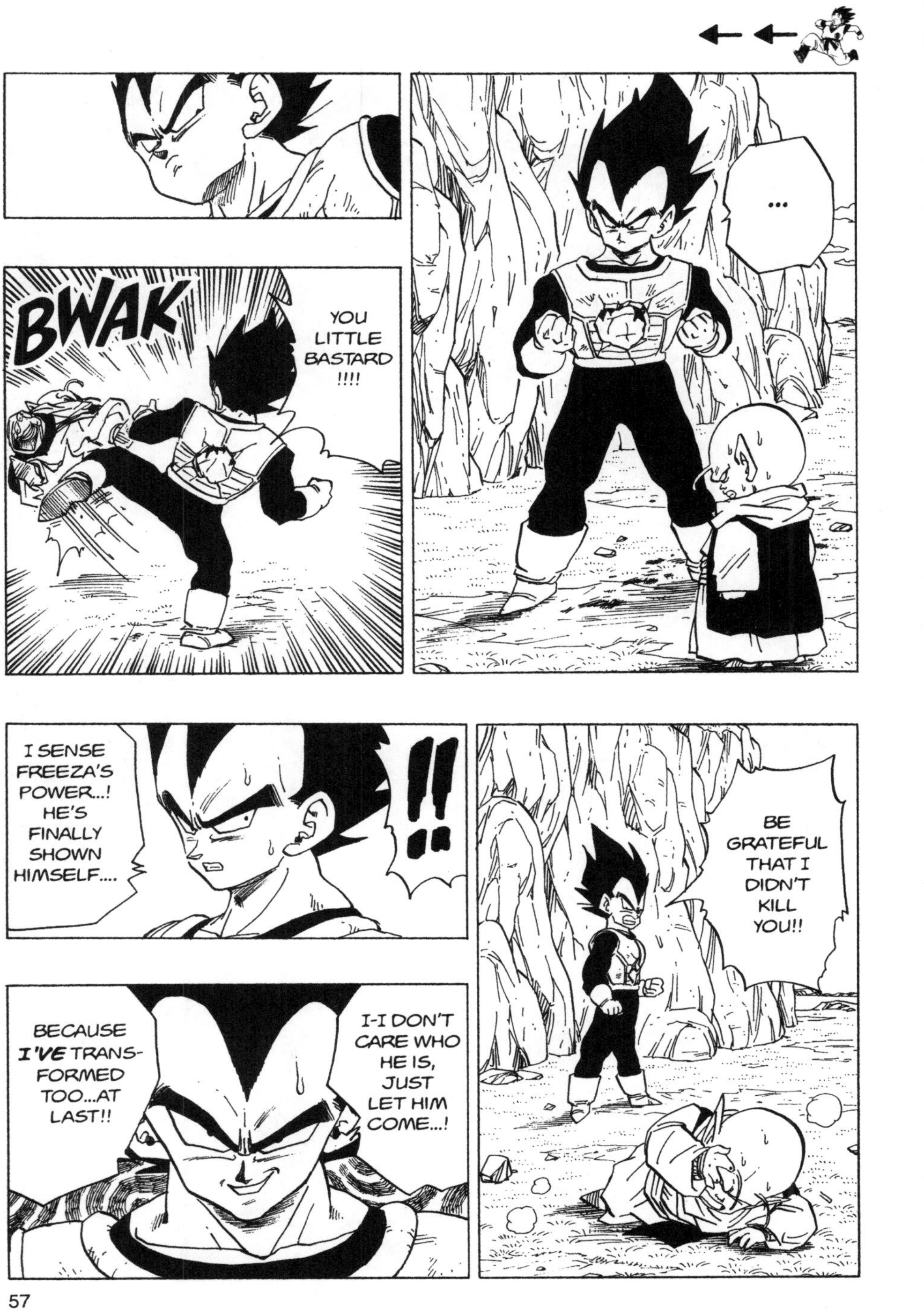
...
BWAK
YOU LITTLE BASTARD !!!!
BE GRATEFUL THAT I DIDN'T KILL YOU!!
I SENSE FREEZA'S POWER...! HE'S FINALLY SHOWN HIMSELF....
!!
I-I DON'T CARE WHO HE IS, JUST LET HIM COME...!
BECAUSE I'VE TRANS-FORMED TOO...AT LAST!!

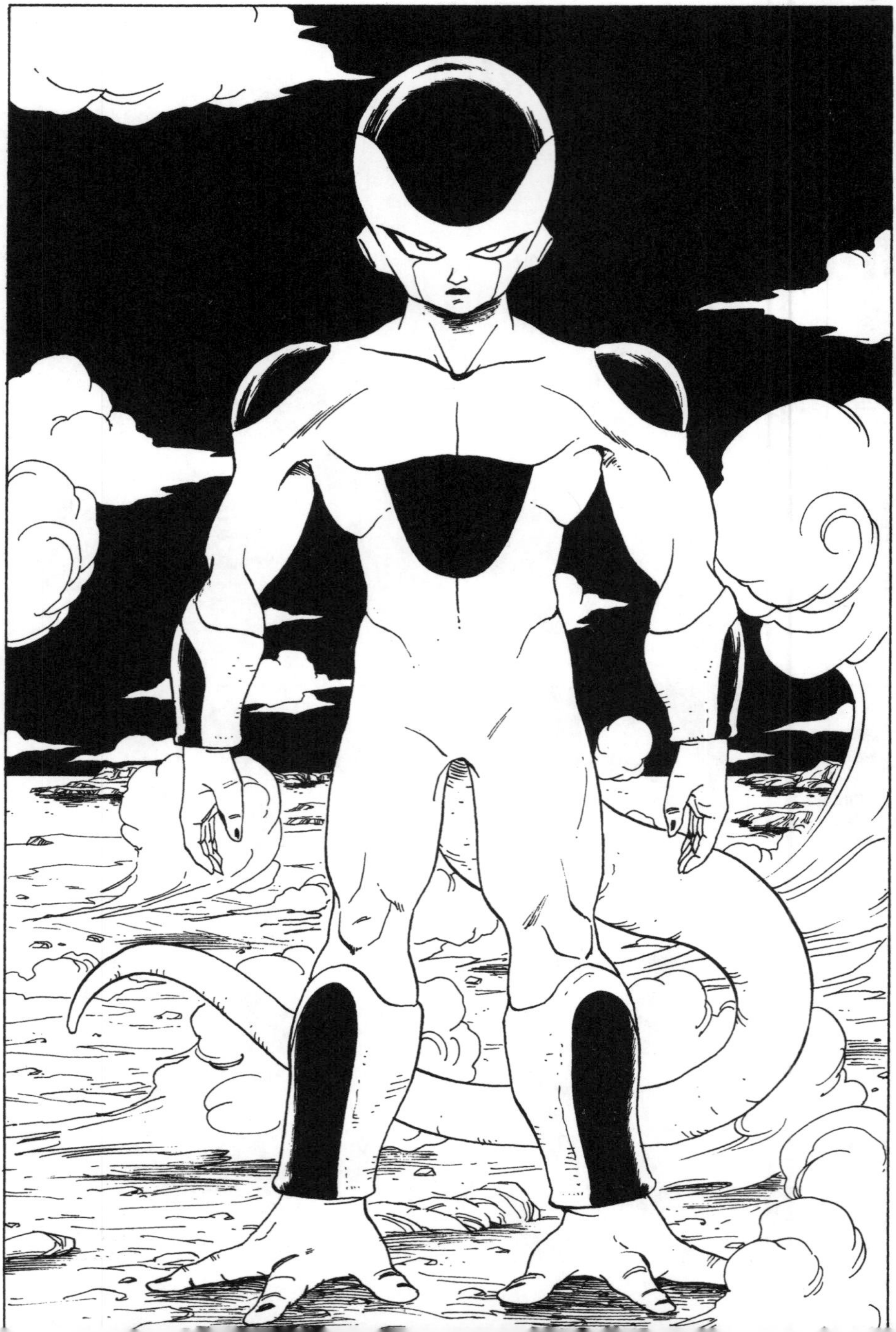

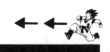

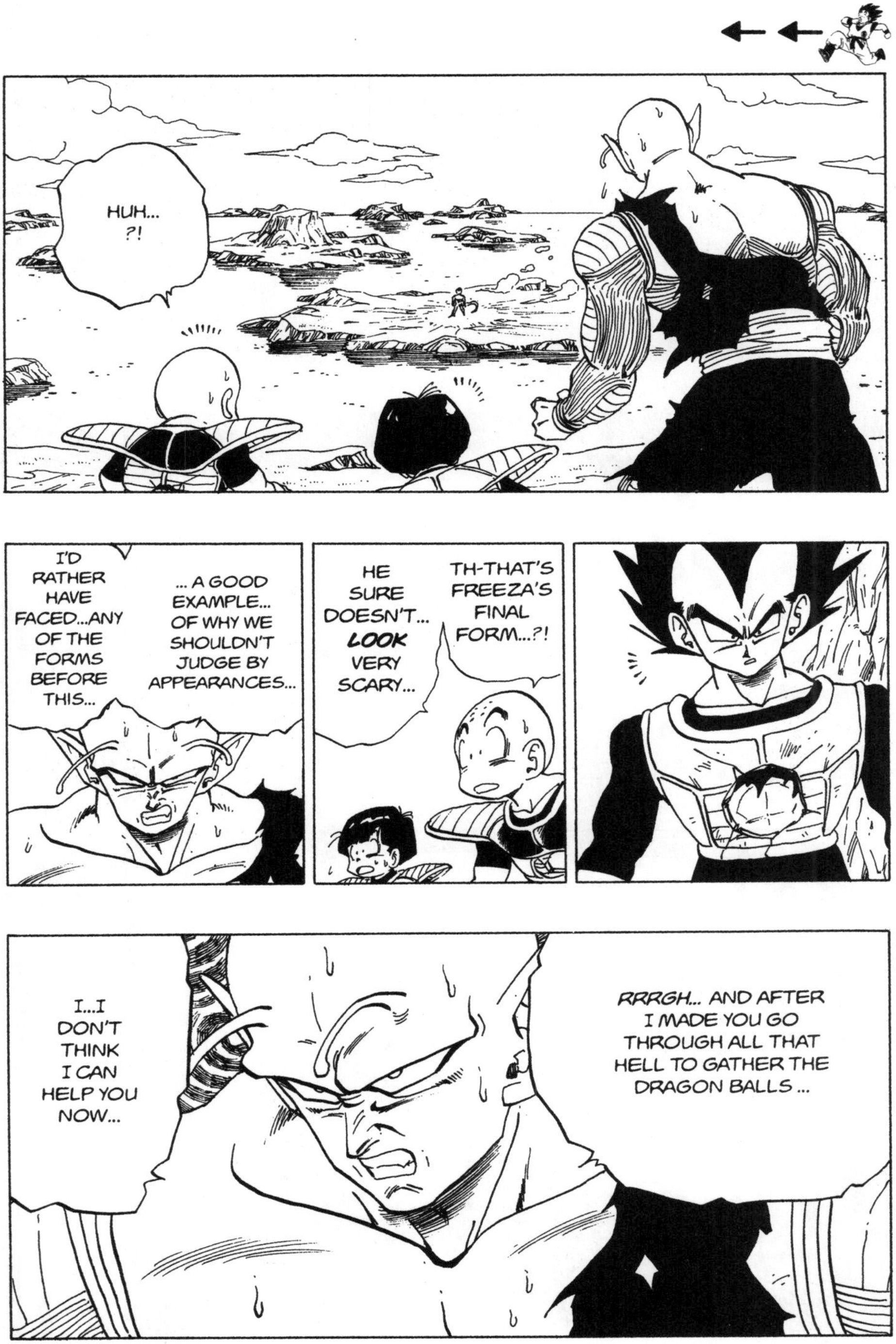
HUH... ?!
TH-THAT'S FREEZA'S FINAL FORM...?!
HE SURE DOESN'T... *LOOK* VERY SCARY...
... A GOOD EXAMPLE... OF WHY WE SHOULDN'T JUDGE BY APPEARANCES...
I'D RATHER HAVE FACED...ANY OF THE FORMS BEFORE THIS...
*RRRGH...* AND AFTER I MADE YOU GO THROUGH ALL THAT HELL TO GATHER THE DRAGON BALLS ...
I...I DON'T THINK I CAN HELP YOU NOW...

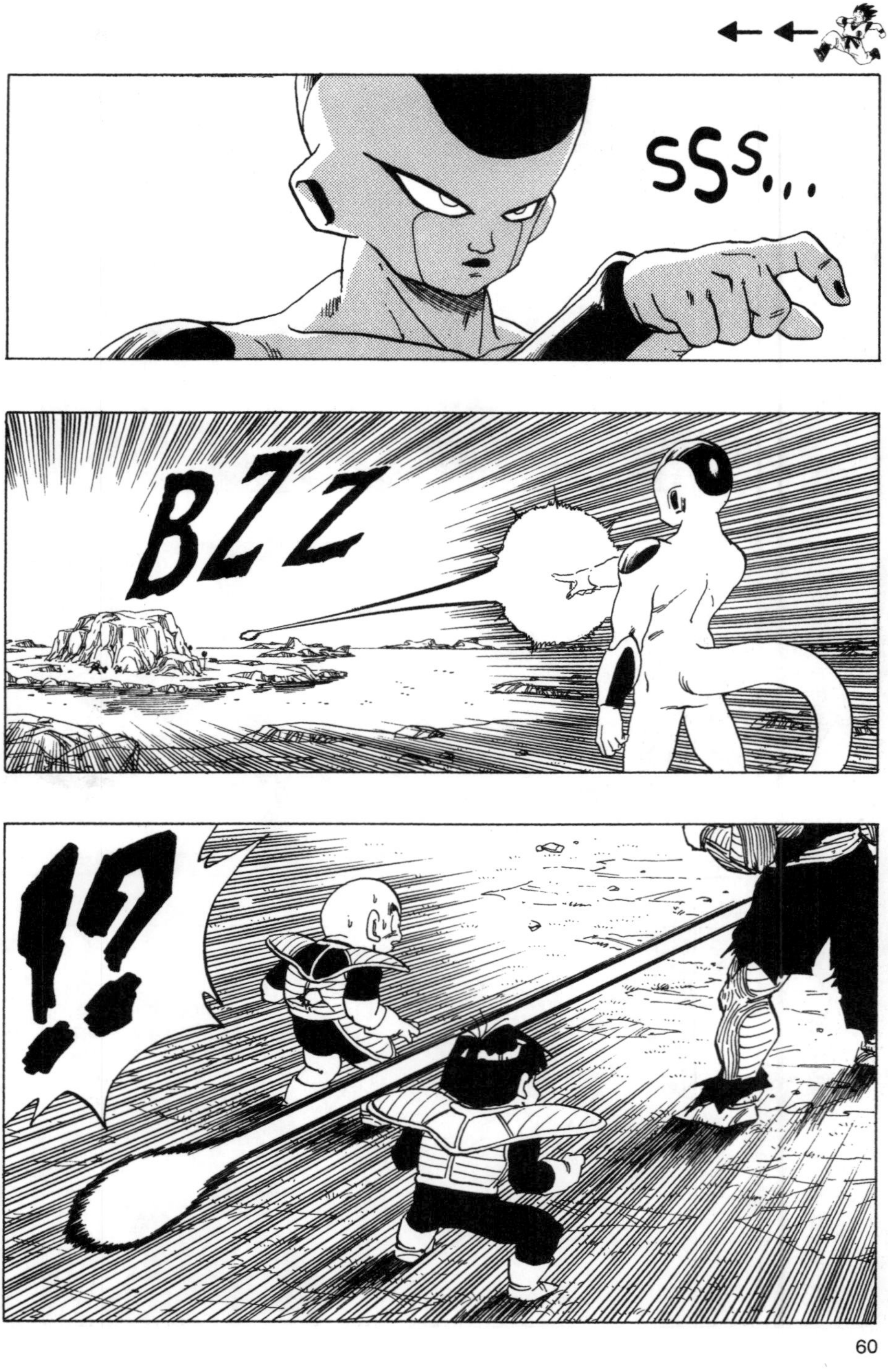
SSS...
BZZ
!?

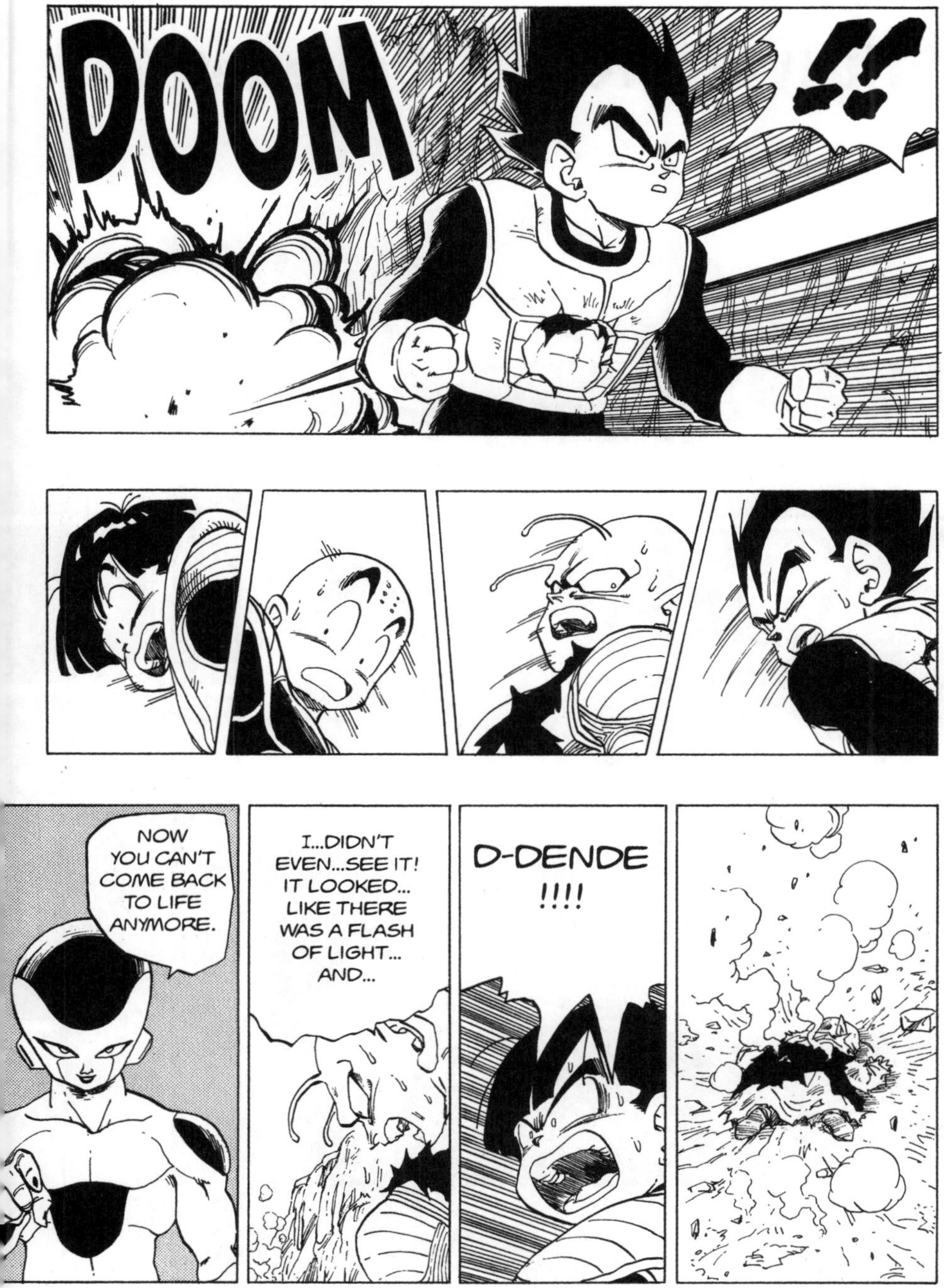
DOOM
!!
D-DENDE
!!!!
I...DIDN'T EVEN...SEE IT! IT LOOKED... LIKE THERE WAS A FLASH OF LIGHT... AND...
NOW YOU CAN'T COME BACK TO LIFE ANYMORE.

# DBZ:111 •
# Will It Be Freeza? Or Vegeta?

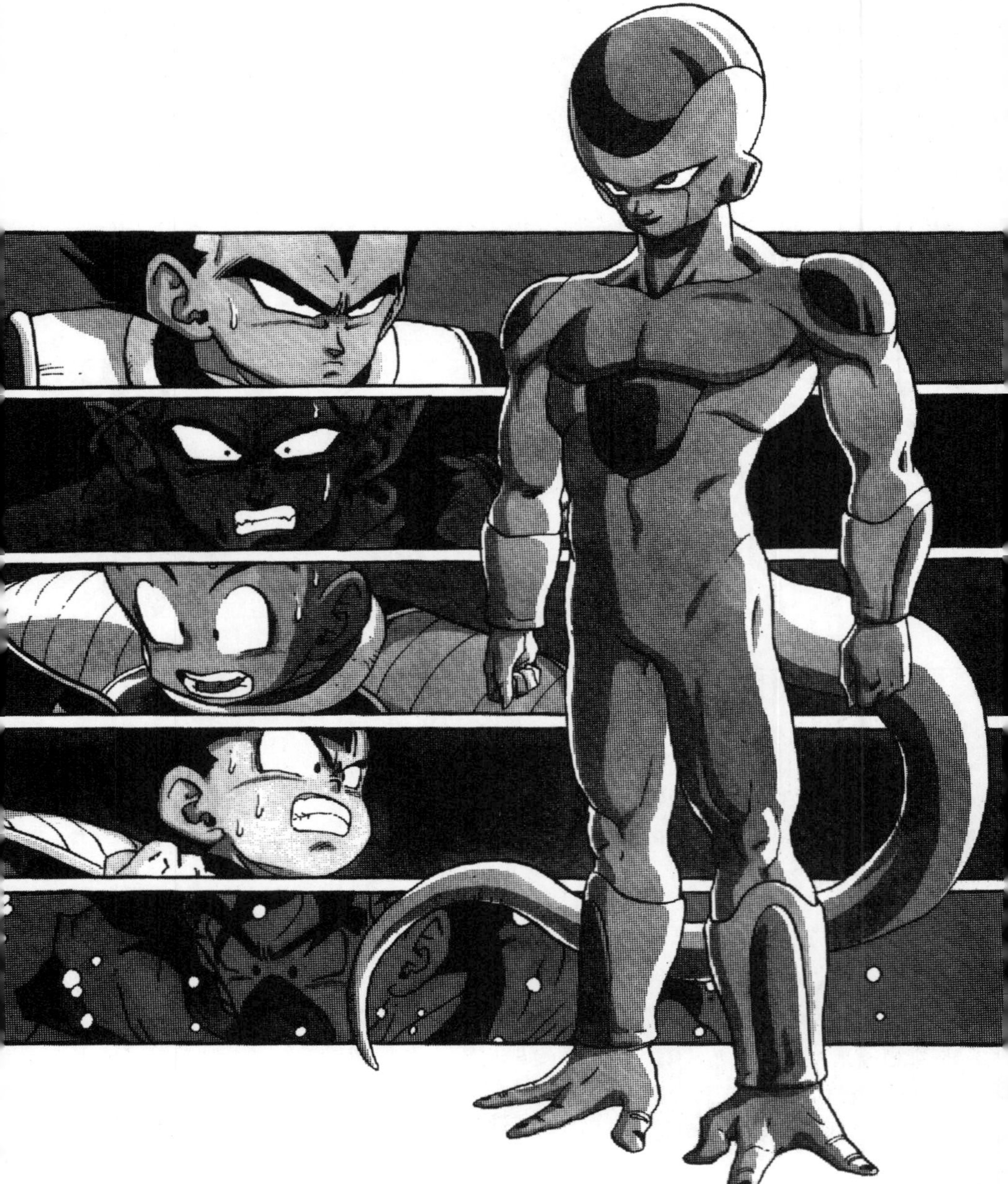

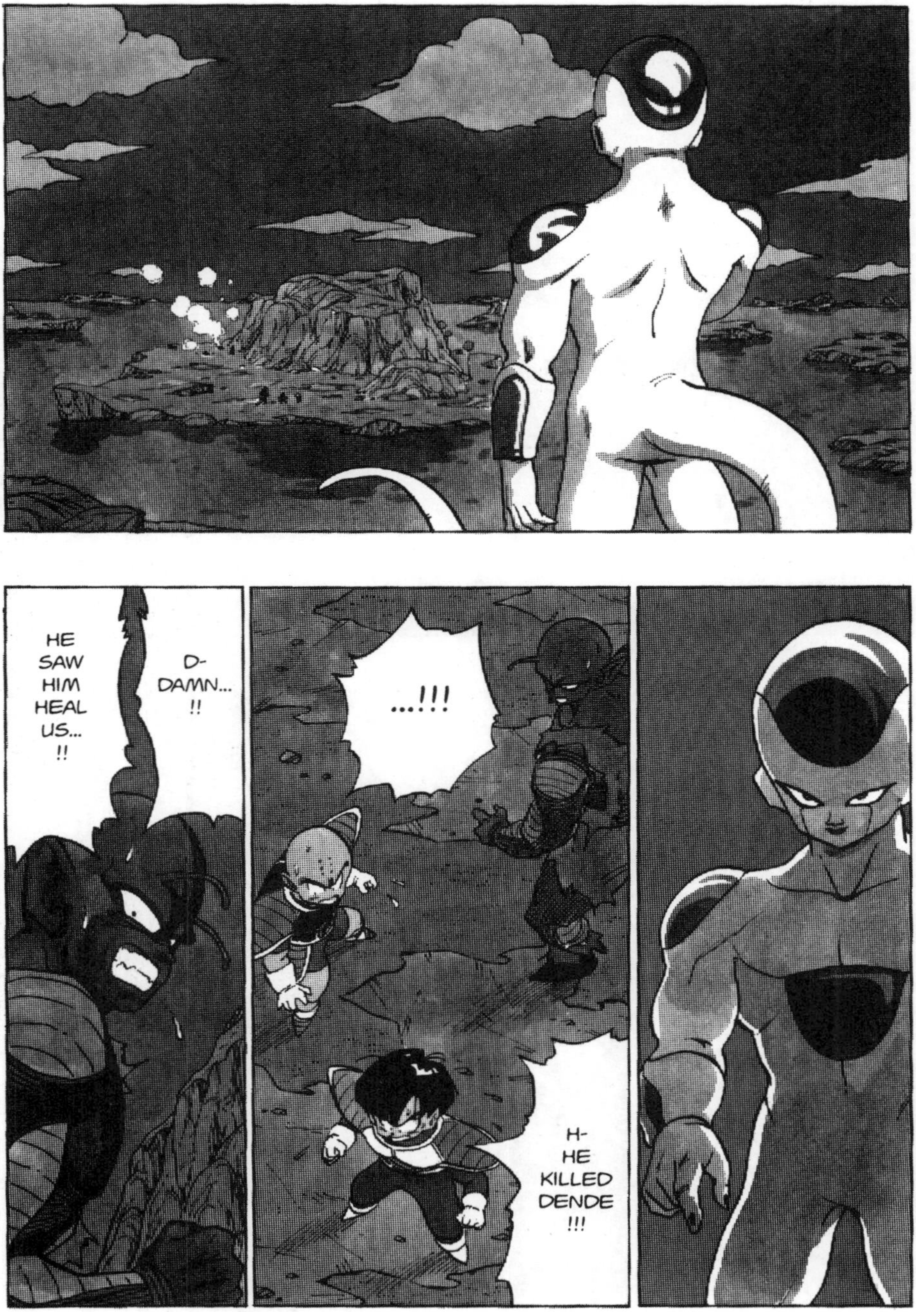
...!!!
H- HE KILLED DENDE !!!
D- DAMN... !!
HE SAW HIM HEAL US... !!

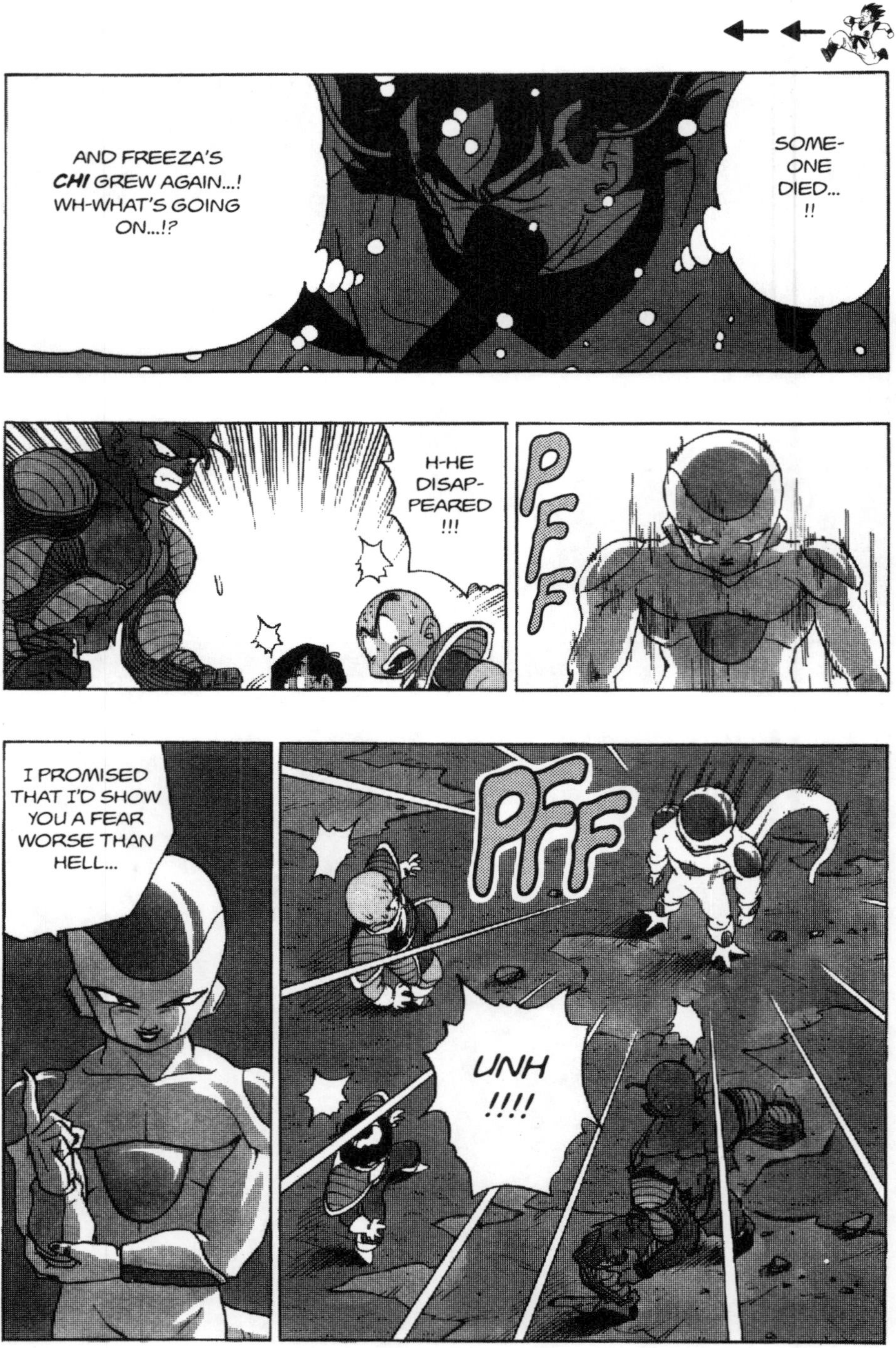
SOME-ONE DIED... !!
AND FREEZA'S **CHI** GREW AGAIN...! WH-WHAT'S GOING ON...!?
PFFF
H-HE DISAP-PEARED !!!
PFF
UNH !!!!
I PROMISED THAT I'D SHOW YOU A FEAR WORSE THAN HELL...

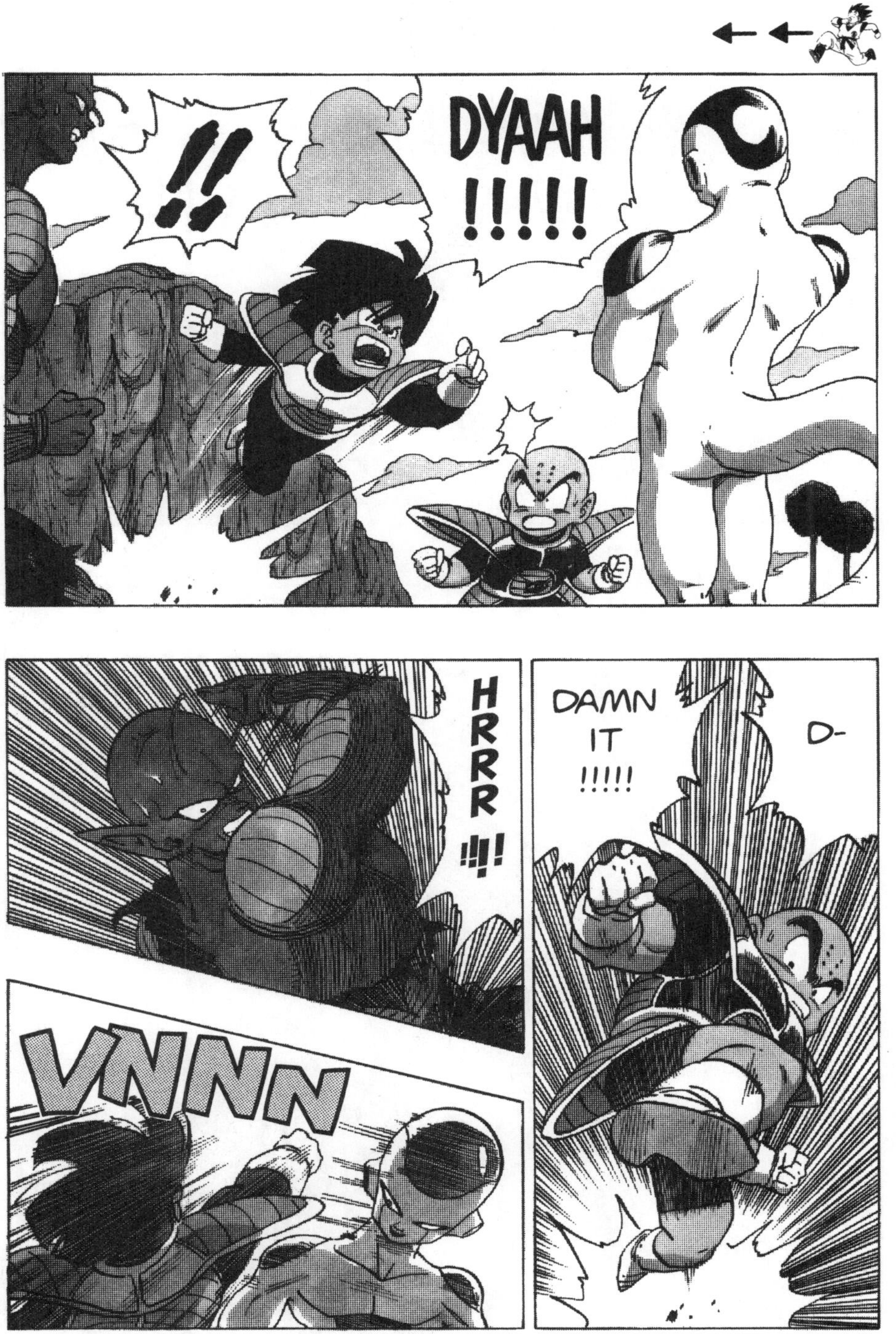
DYAAH !!!!!
!!
D-
DAMN IT !!!!!
HRRR !!!!
VNNN

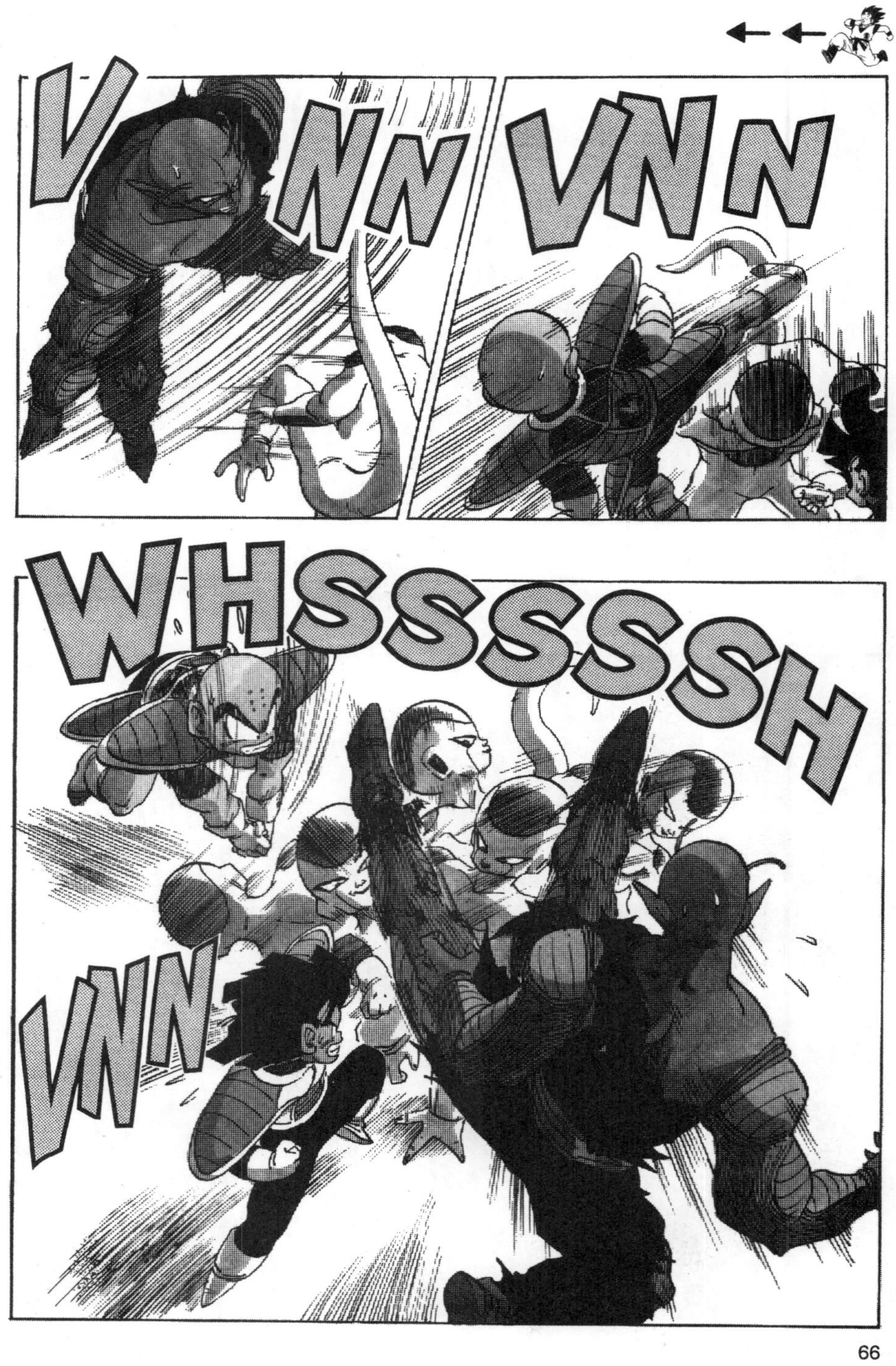
VNN
VNN
WHSSSSSH
VNN

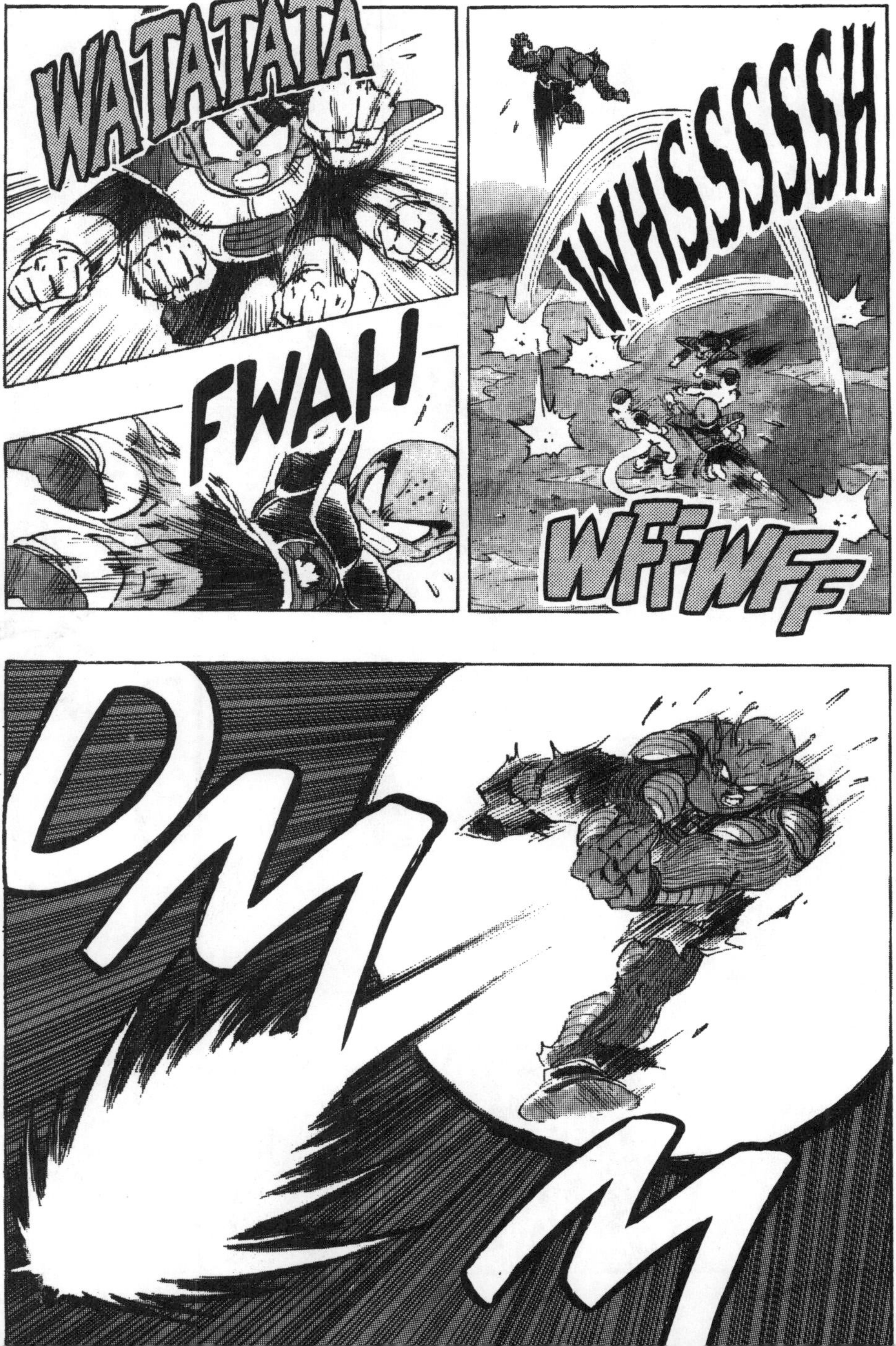
WHSSSSSH
WFFWFF
WATATATA
FWAH
DMMM

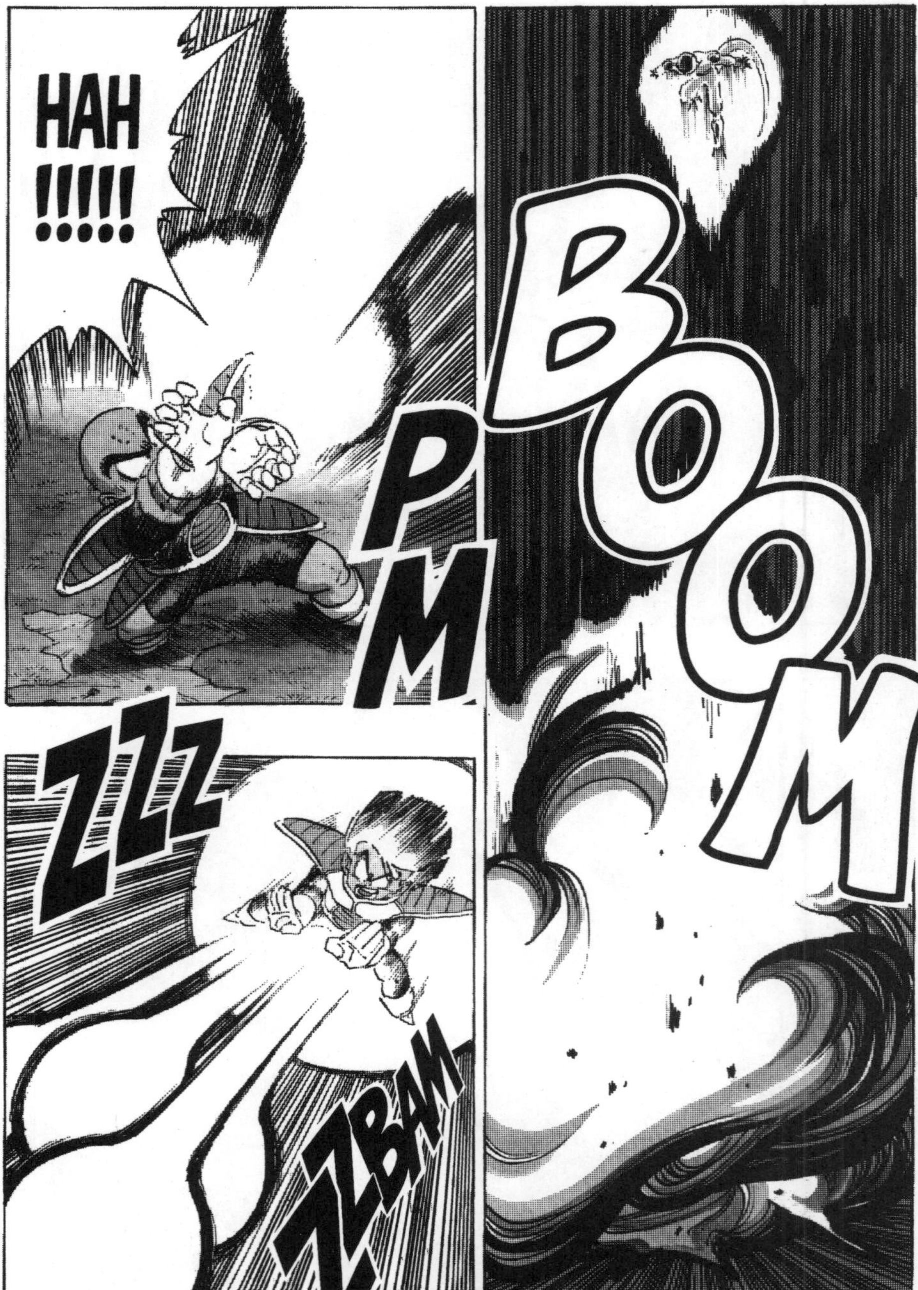
BOOOM
HAH!!!!!
PM
ZZZ
ZZBAM

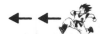

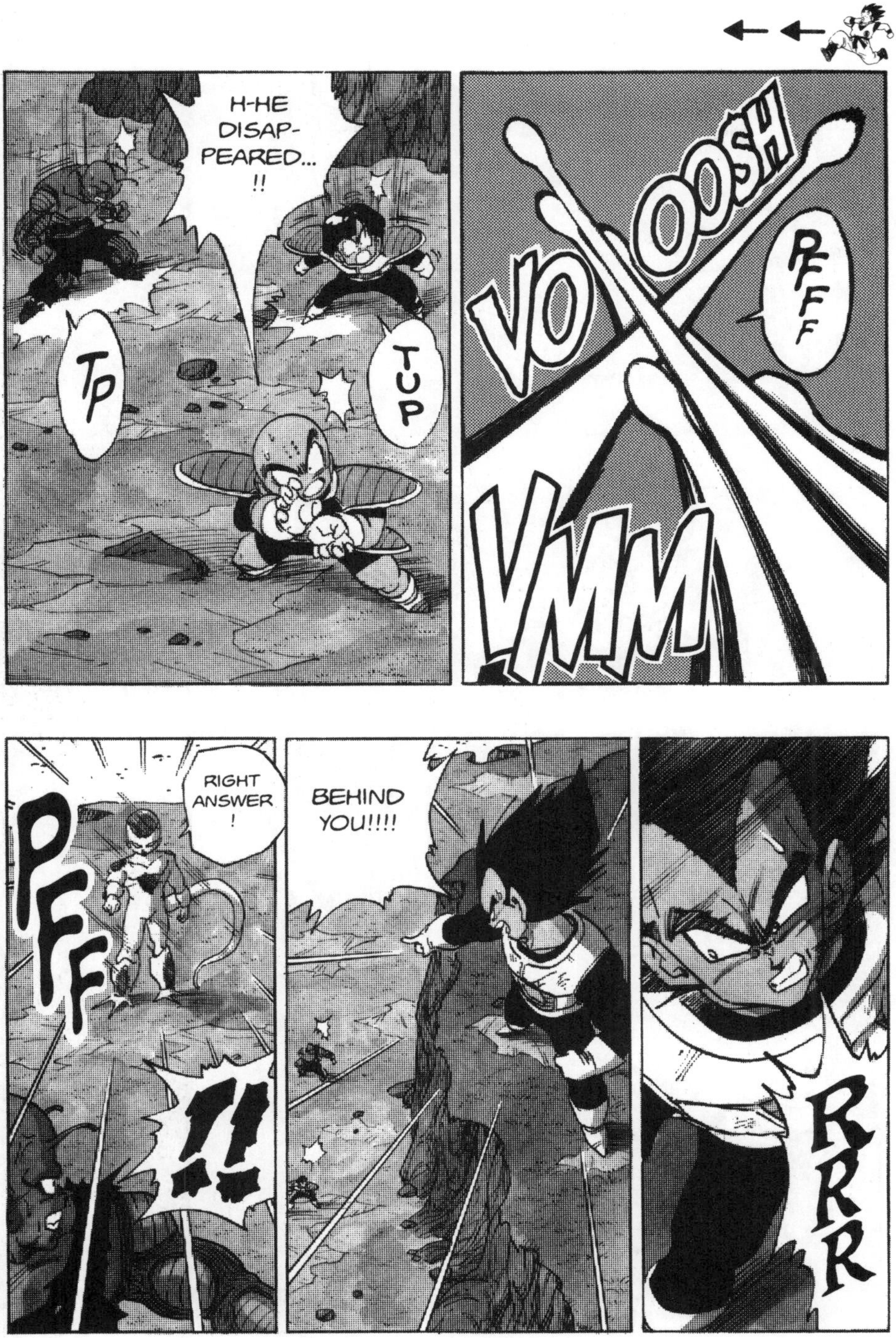
PFFF
VOOOSH
VMM
H-HE DISAPPEARED... !!
TUP
TP
RRR
BEHIND YOU!!!!
RIGHT ANSWER !
PFF
!!

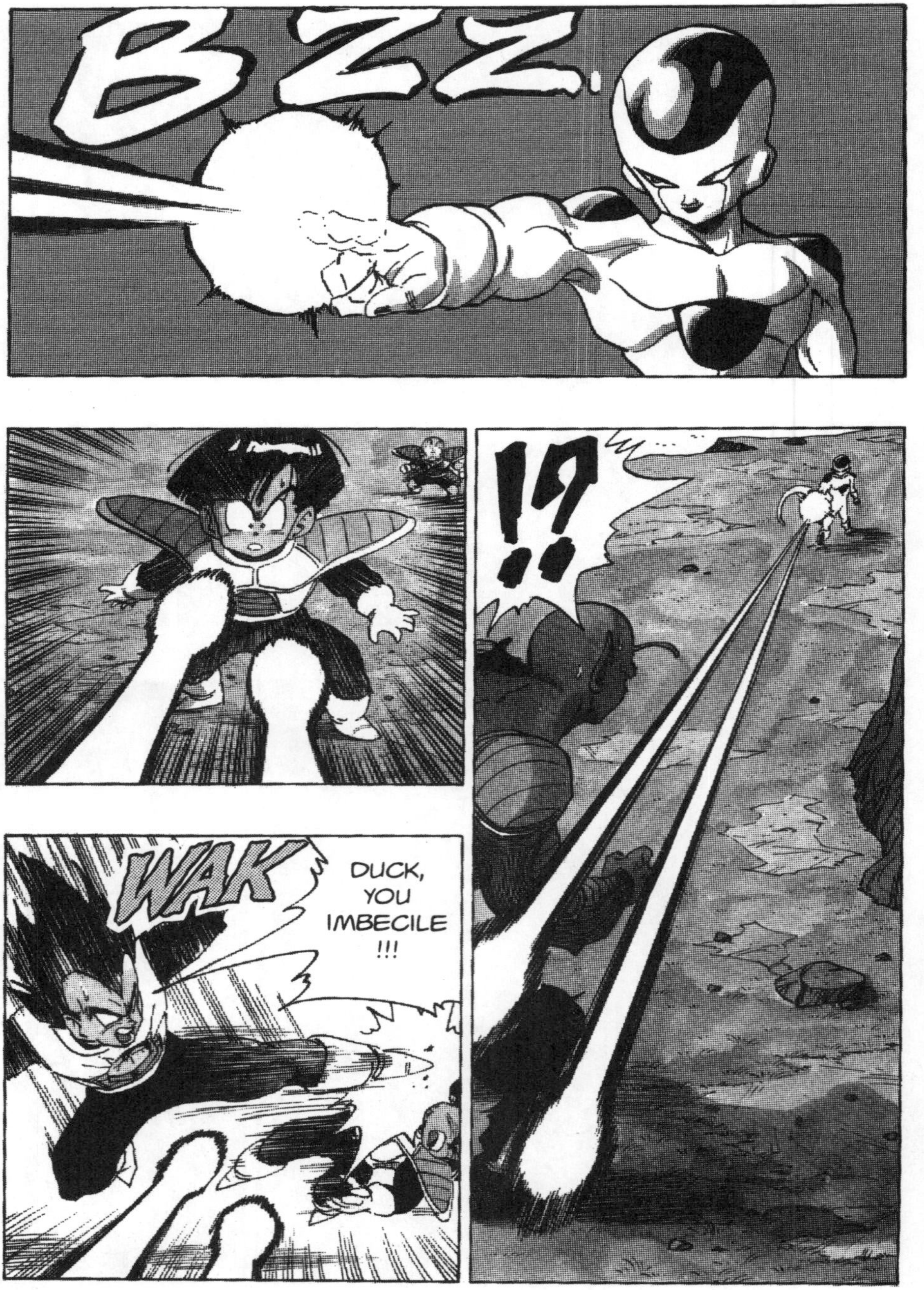
BZZ.
!?
WAK
DUCK, YOU IMBECILE !!!

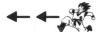

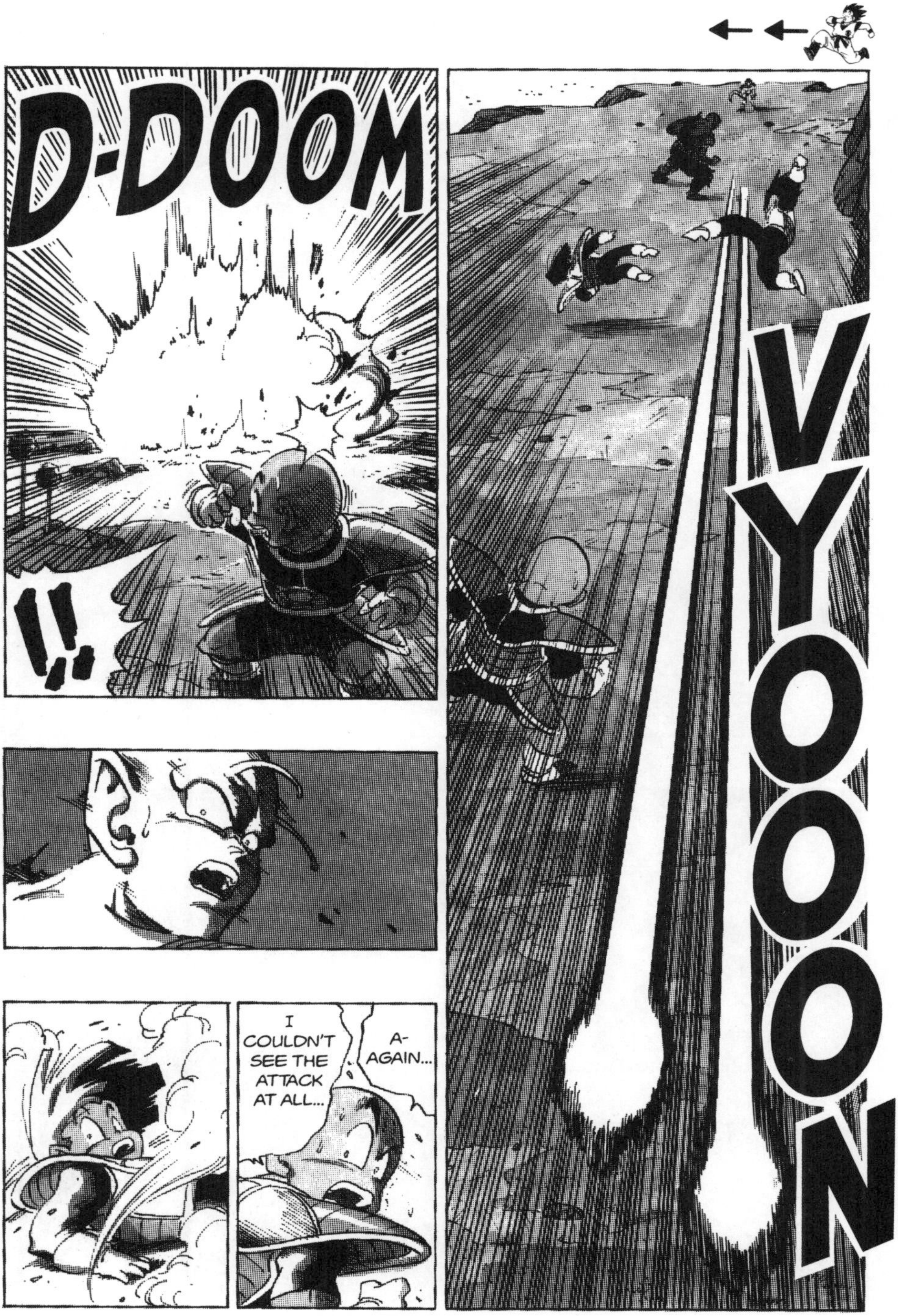
VYOOON
D-DOOM
!!
A-AGAIN...
I COULDN'T SEE THE ATTACK AT ALL...

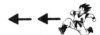

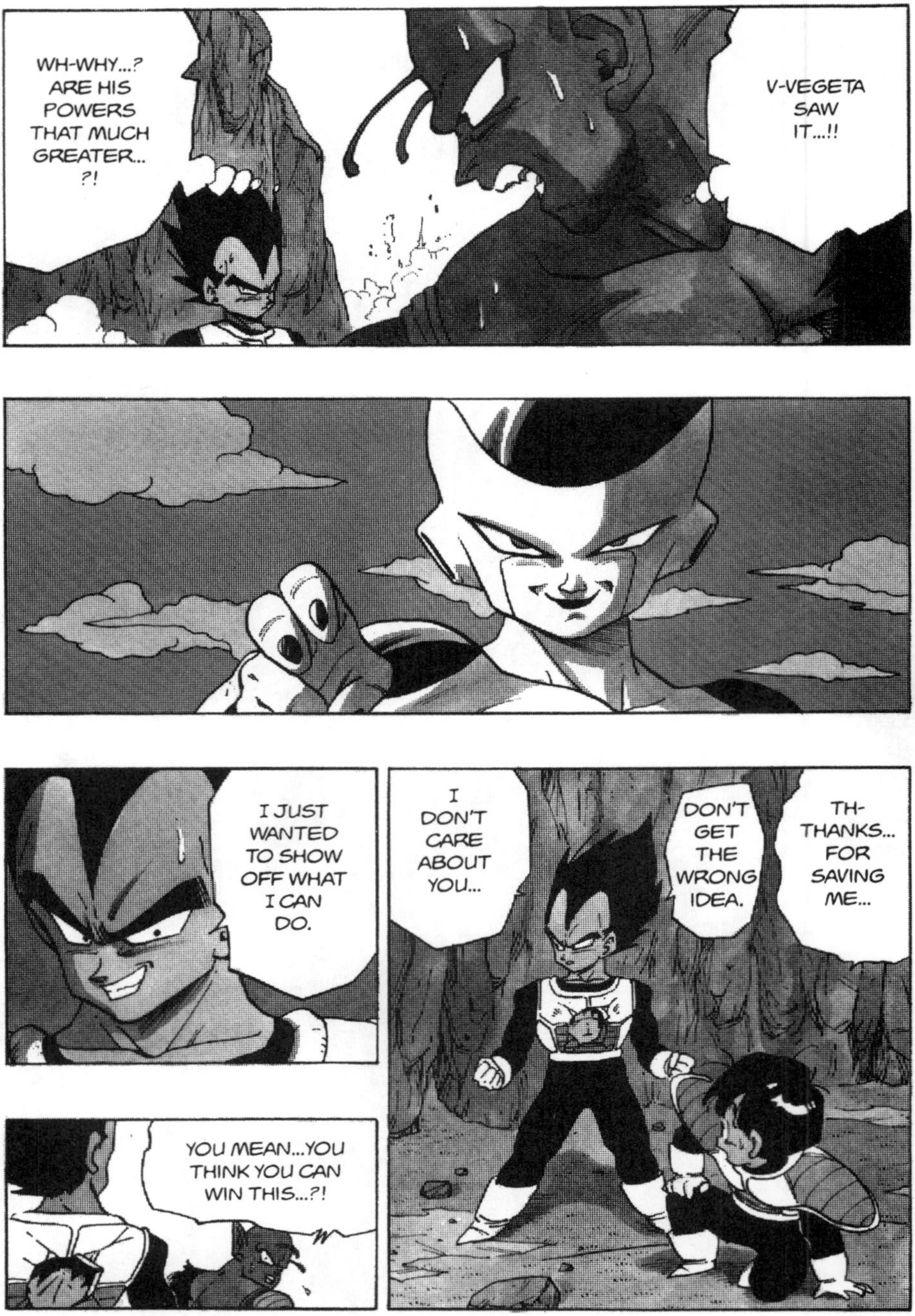
V-VEGETA SAW IT...!!
WH-WHY...? ARE HIS POWERS THAT MUCH GREATER...?!
TH- THANKS... FOR SAVING ME...
DON'T GET THE WRONG IDEA.
I DON'T CARE ABOUT YOU...
I JUST WANTED TO SHOW OFF WHAT I CAN DO.
YOU MEAN...YOU THINK YOU CAN WIN THIS...?!

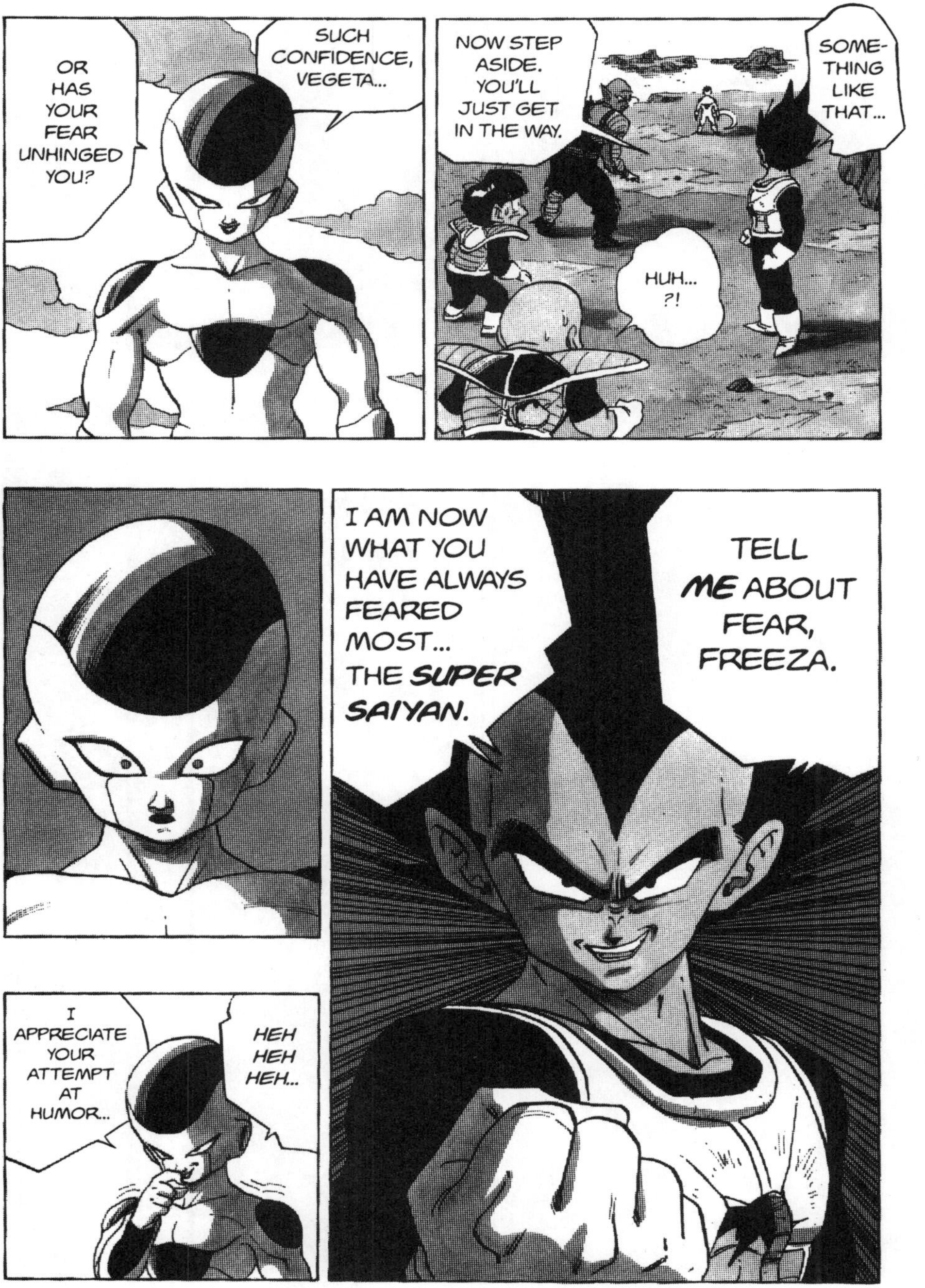
SOMETHING LIKE THAT...
NOW STEP ASIDE. YOU'LL JUST GET IN THE WAY.
HUH... ?!
SUCH CONFIDENCE, VEGETA...
OR HAS YOUR FEAR UNHINGED YOU?
TELL ME ABOUT FEAR, FREEZA.
I AM NOW WHAT YOU HAVE ALWAYS FEARED MOST... THE SUPER SAIYAN.
HEH HEH HEH...
I APPRECIATE YOUR ATTEMPT AT HUMOR...

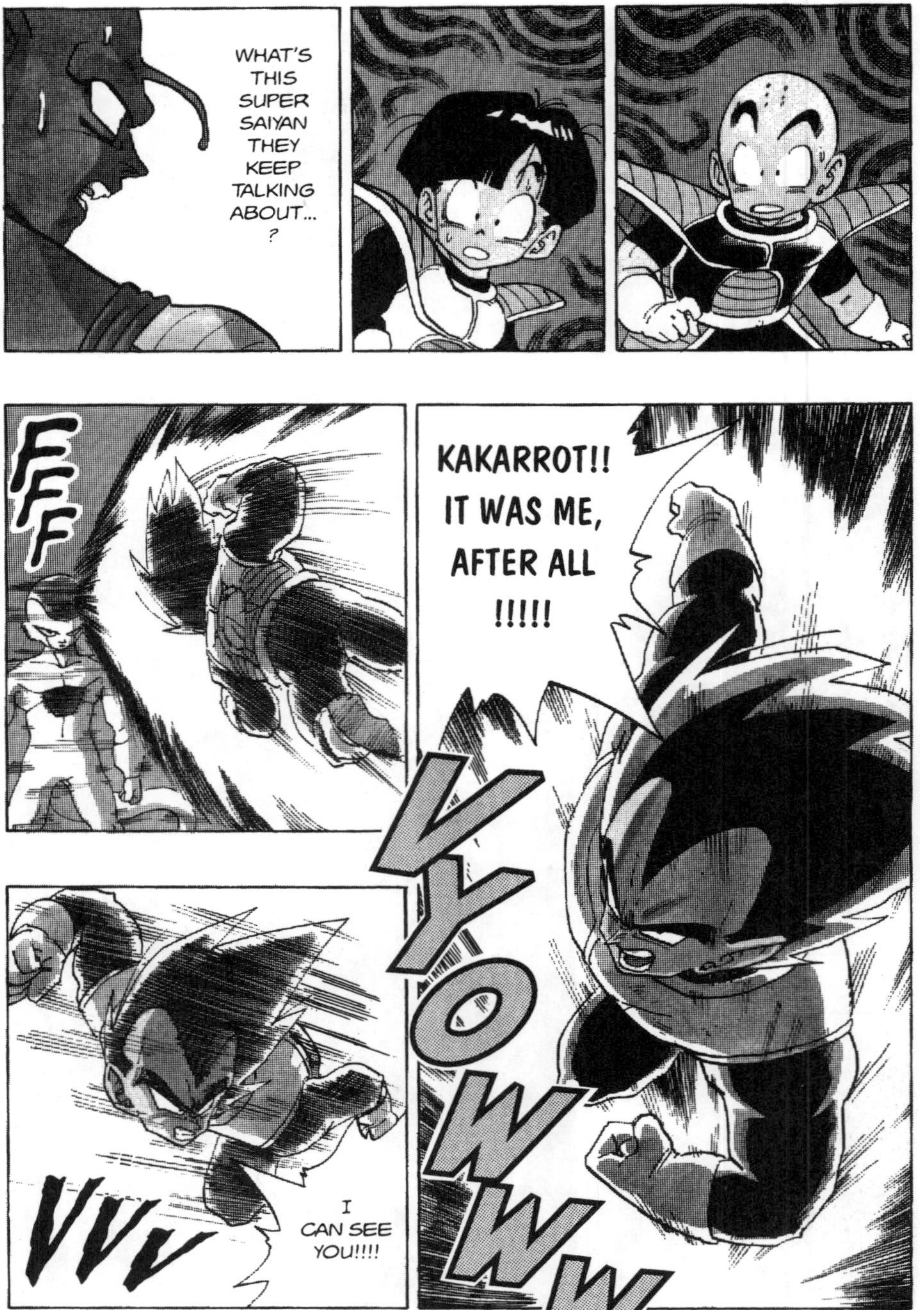
WHAT'S THIS SUPER SAIYAN THEY KEEP TALKING ABOUT...?
KAKARROT!! IT WAS ME, AFTER ALL!!!!!
VYOWWWW
FFF
VVV
I CAN SEE YOU!!!!

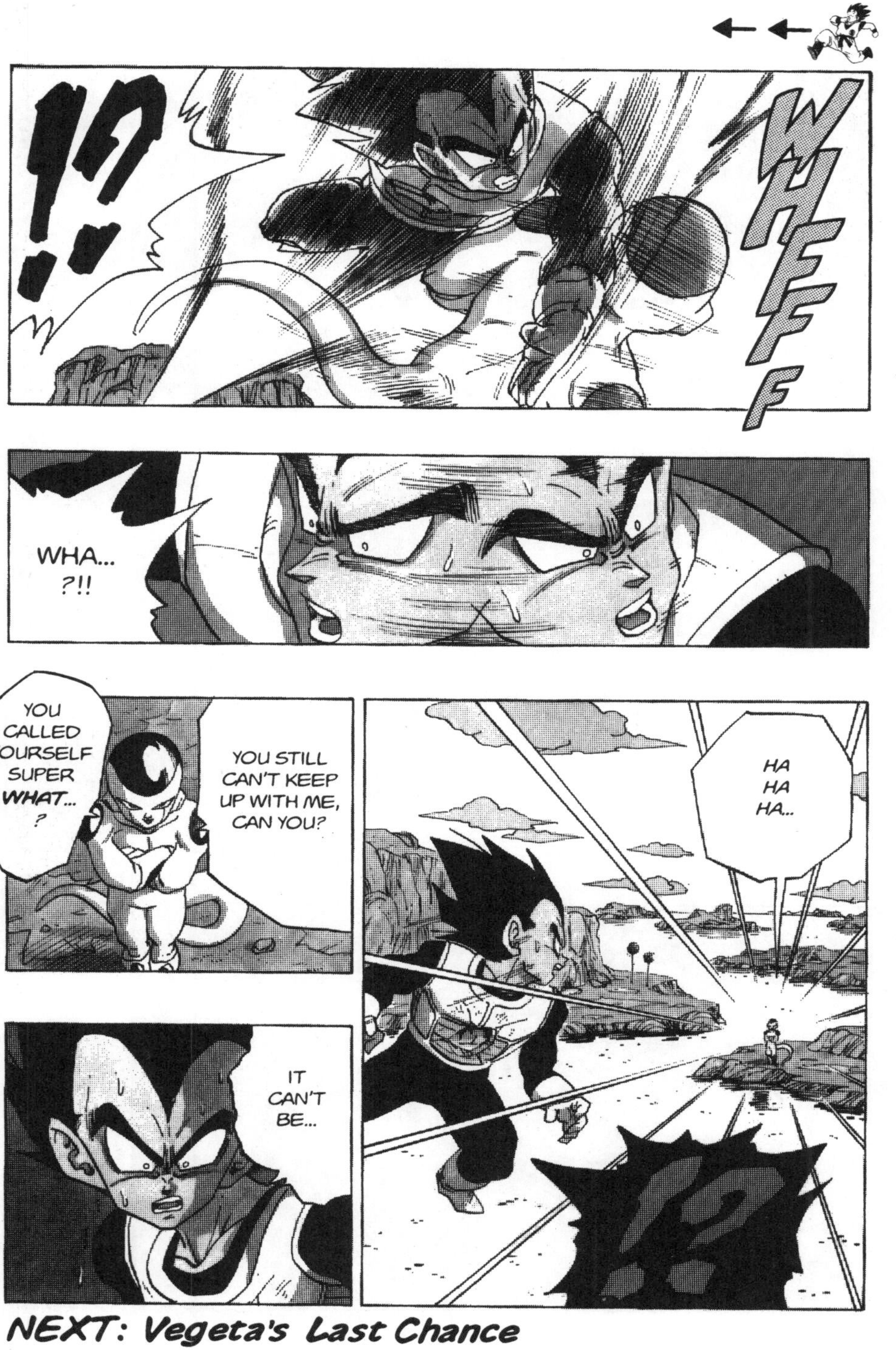
WHFFFF
!?
WHA... ?!!
HA HA HA...
!?
YOU STILL CAN'T KEEP UP WITH ME, CAN YOU?
YOU CALLED YOURSELF SUPER WHAT...?
IT CAN'T BE...

**NEXT: Vegeta's Last Chance**

# DBZ:112 • Son Goku... Resurrected!!

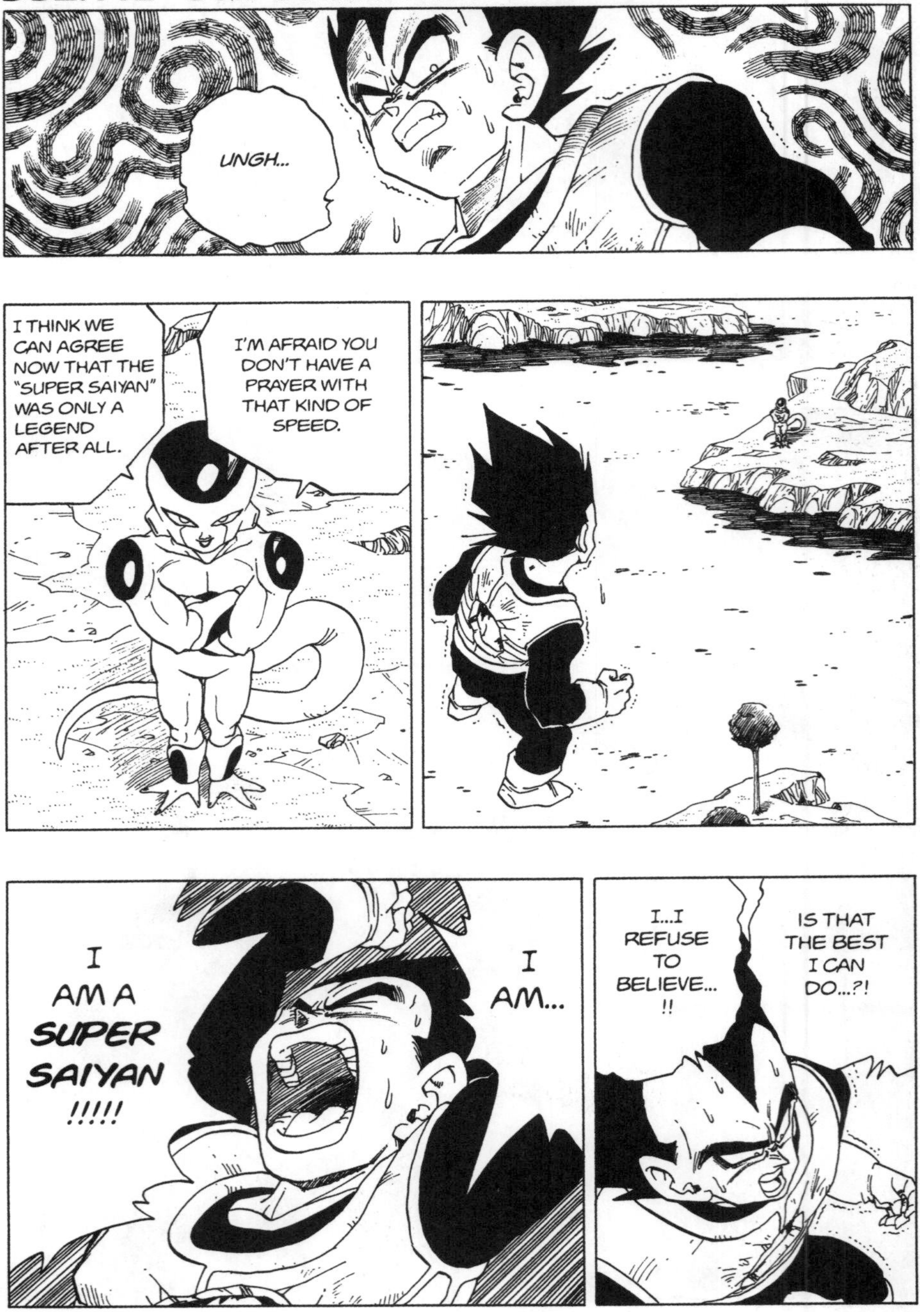
UNGH...
I'M AFRAID YOU DON'T HAVE A PRAYER WITH THAT KIND OF SPEED.
I THINK WE CAN AGREE NOW THAT THE "SUPER SAIYAN" WAS ONLY A LEGEND AFTER ALL.
IS THAT THE BEST I CAN DO...?!
I...I REFUSE TO BELIEVE... !!
I AM...
I AM A SUPER SAIYAN !!!!!

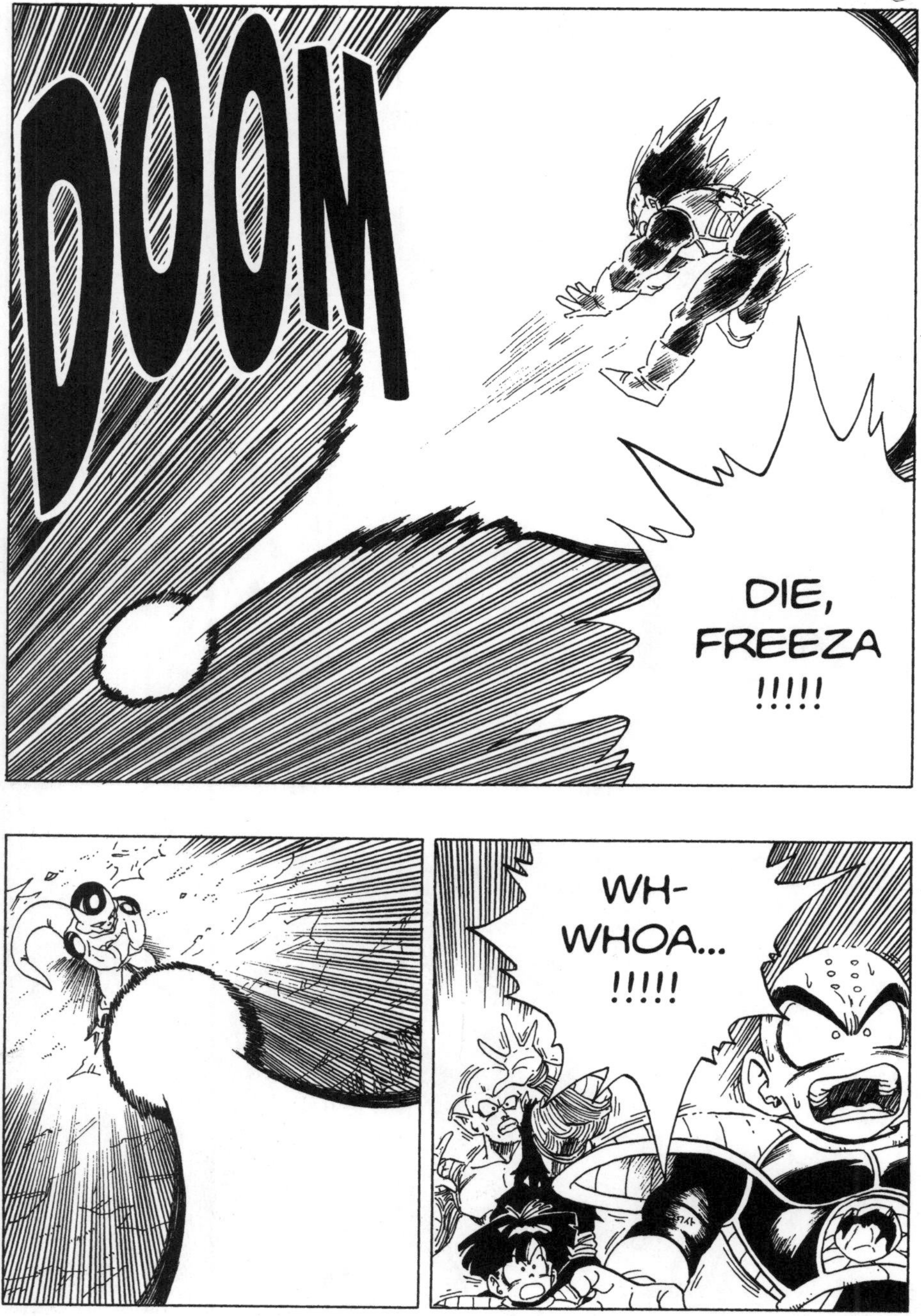
DOOM
DIE, FREEZA !!!!!
WH- WHOA... !!!!!

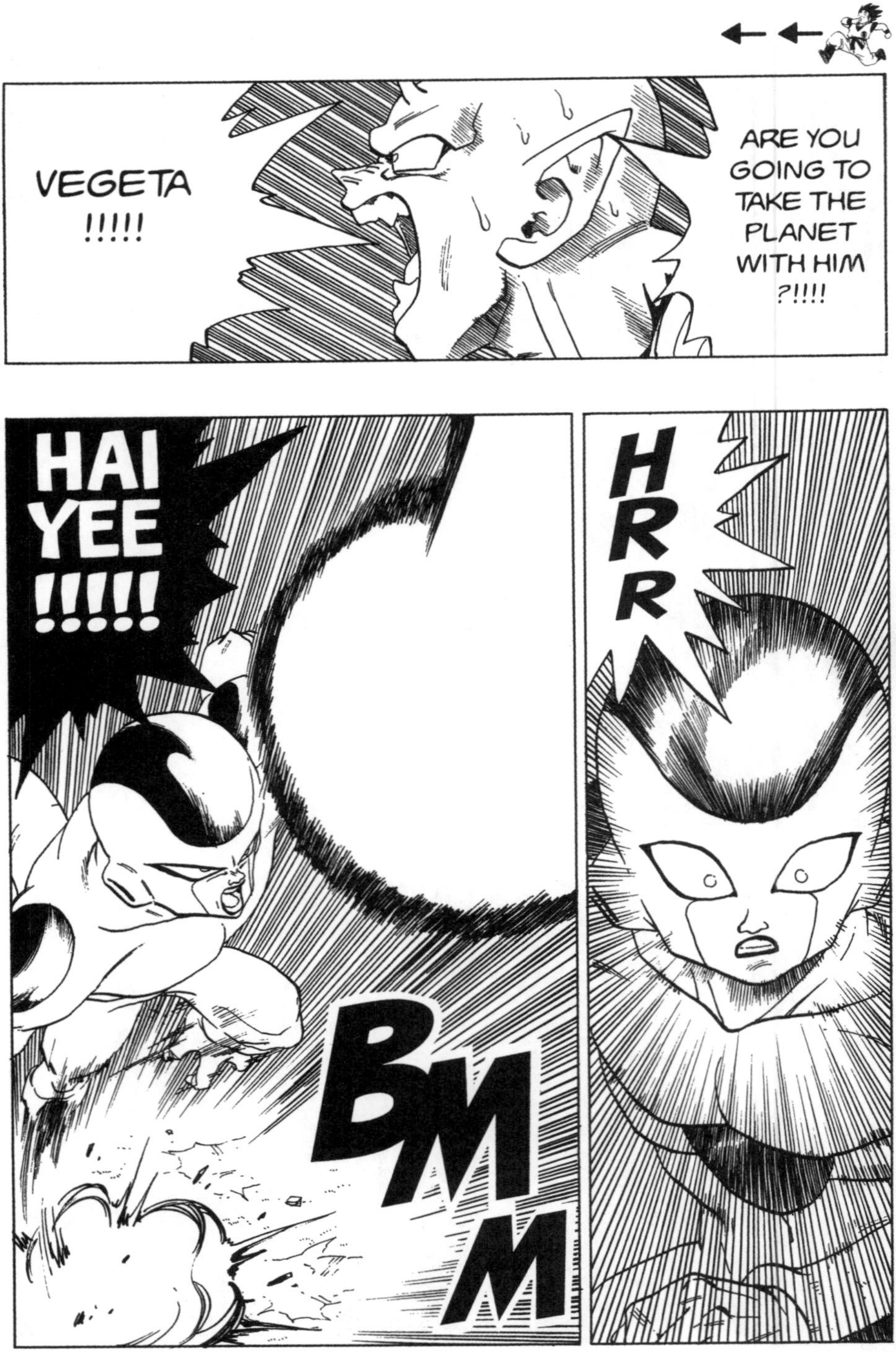
ARE YOU GOING TO TAKE THE PLANET WITH HIM ?!!!!
VEGETA !!!!!
HRR
HAI YEE !!!!!
BMM

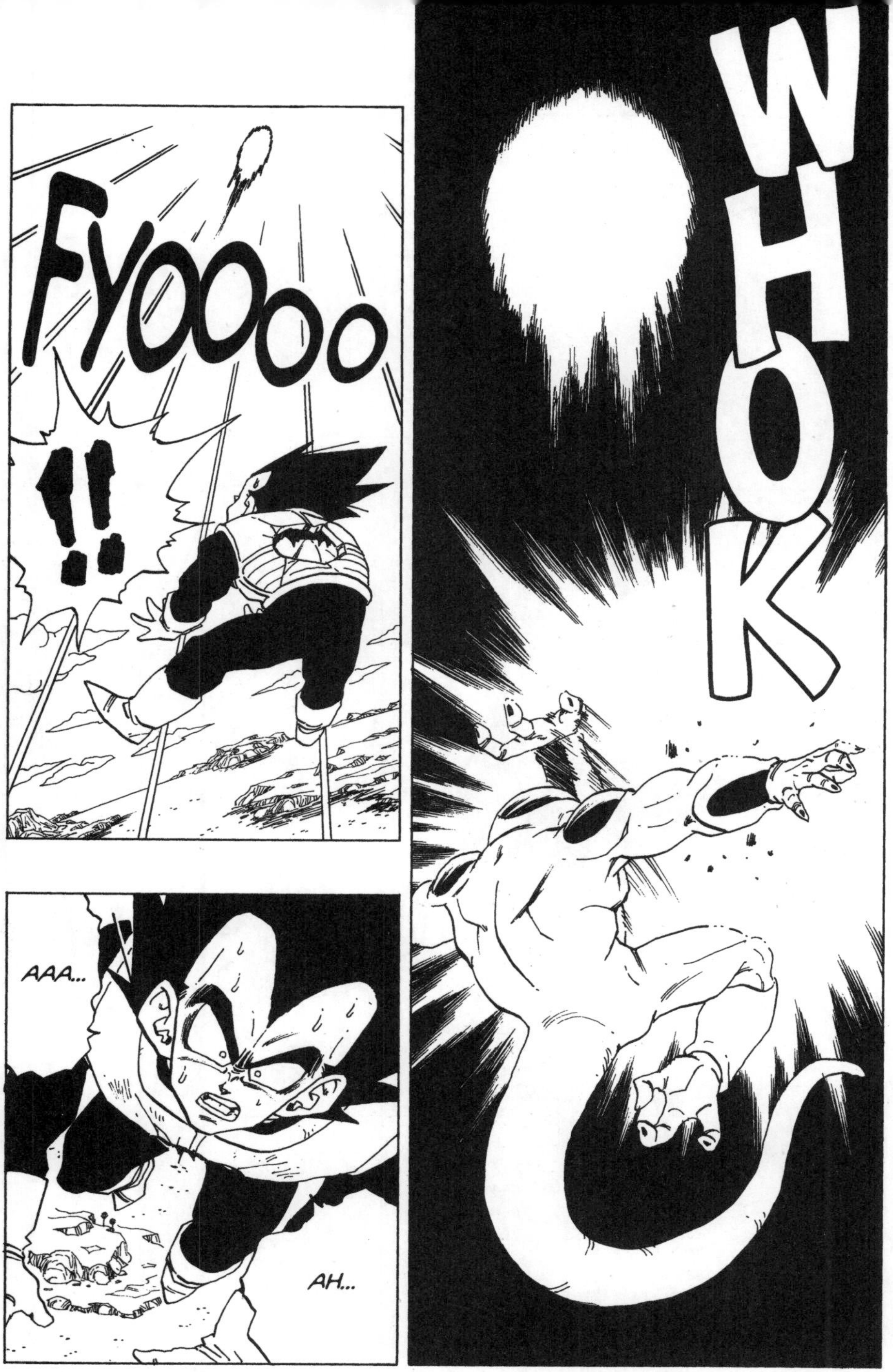
WHOK
FYOOOO
!!
AAA...
AH...

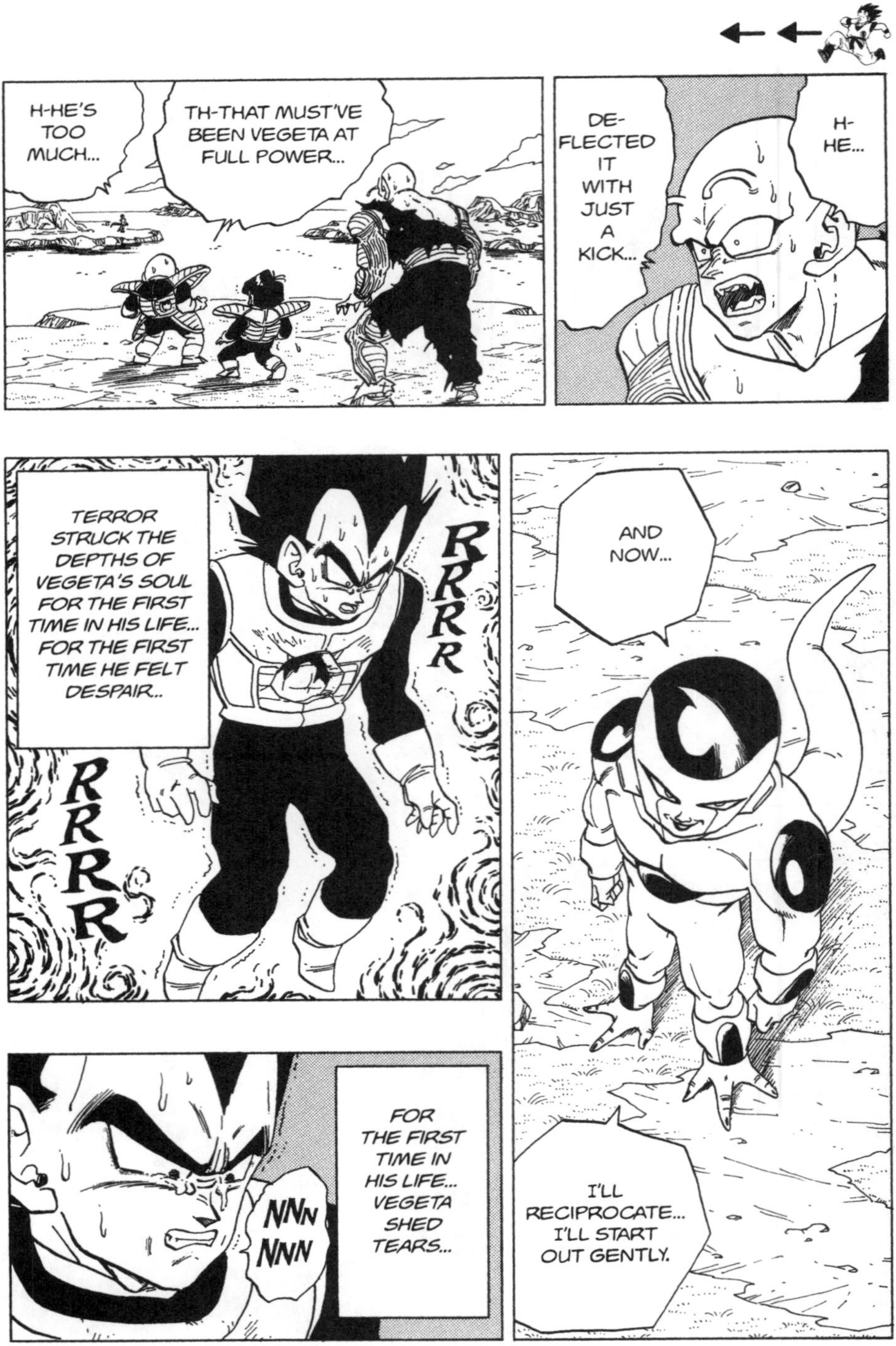
H- HE...
DE- FLECTED IT WITH JUST A KICK...
TH-THAT MUST'VE BEEN VEGETA AT FULL POWER...
H-HE'S TOO MUCH...
AND NOW...
I'LL RECIPROCATE... I'LL START OUT GENTLY.
TERROR STRUCK THE DEPTHS OF VEGETA'S SOUL FOR THE FIRST TIME IN HIS LIFE... FOR THE FIRST TIME HE FELT DESPAIR...
RRRR
RRRR
FOR THE FIRST TIME IN HIS LIFE... VEGETA SHED TEARS...
NNN NNN

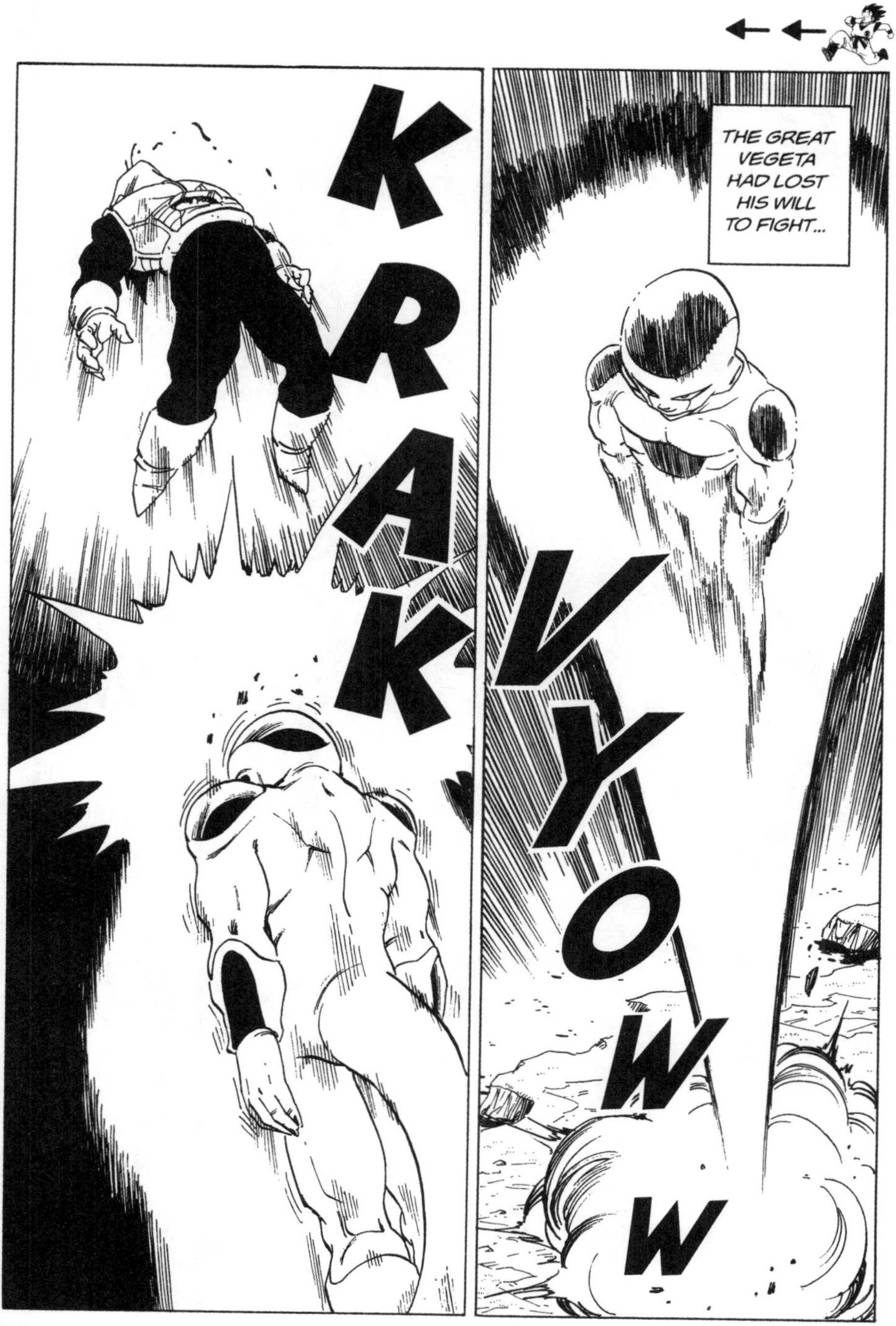
THE GREAT VEGETA HAD LOST HIS WILL TO FIGHT...
VYOWW
KRAKK

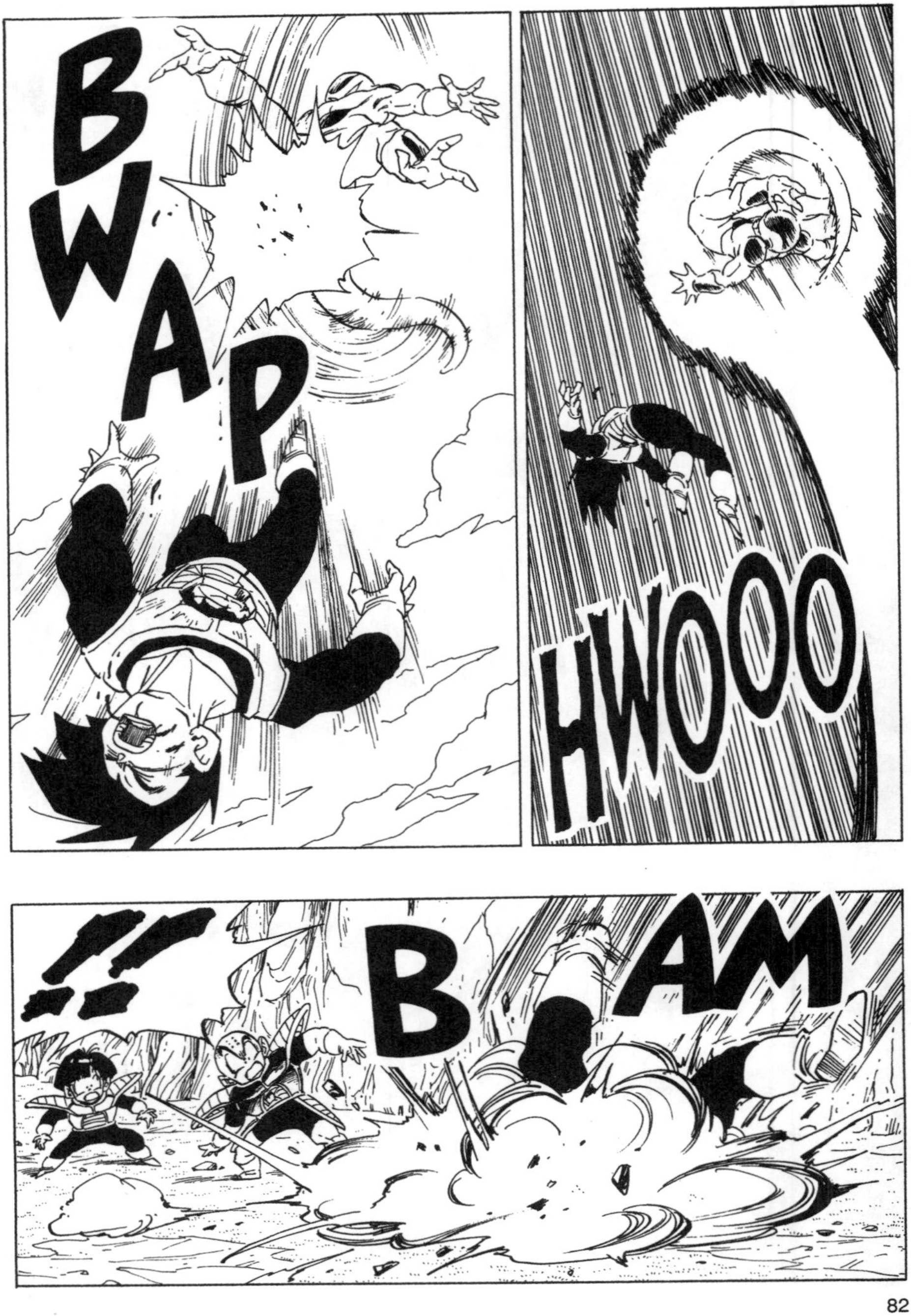
HWOOO
BWAP
BAM
!!

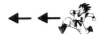

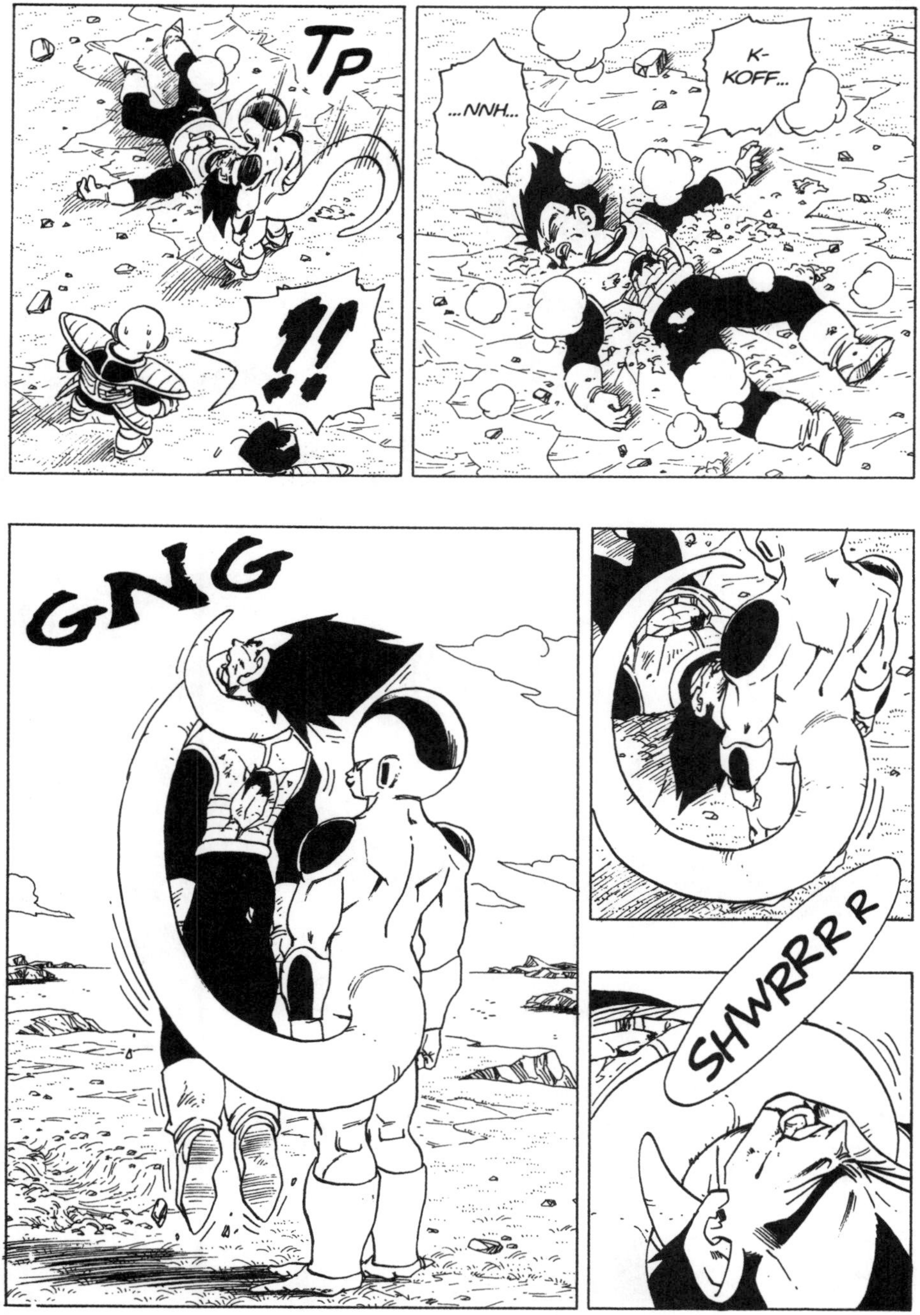
K-KOFF...
...NNH...
TP
!!
SHWRRRR
GNG

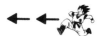

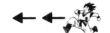

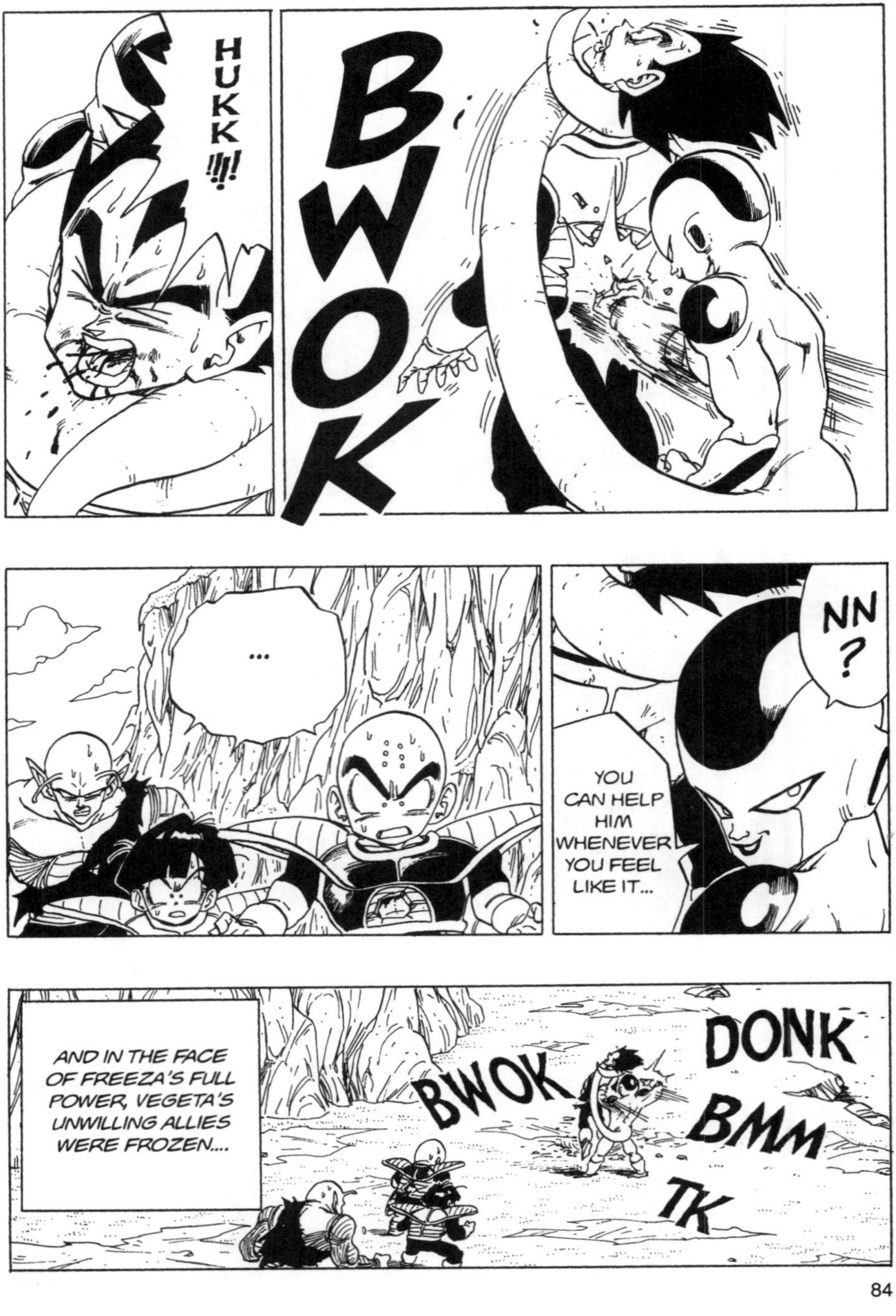
BWOK
HUKK!!!
NN?
YOU CAN HELP HIM WHENEVER YOU FEEL LIKE IT...
...
DONK
AND IN THE FACE OF FREEZA'S FULL POWER, VEGETA'S UNWILLING ALLIES WERE FROZEN....
BWOK
BMM
TK

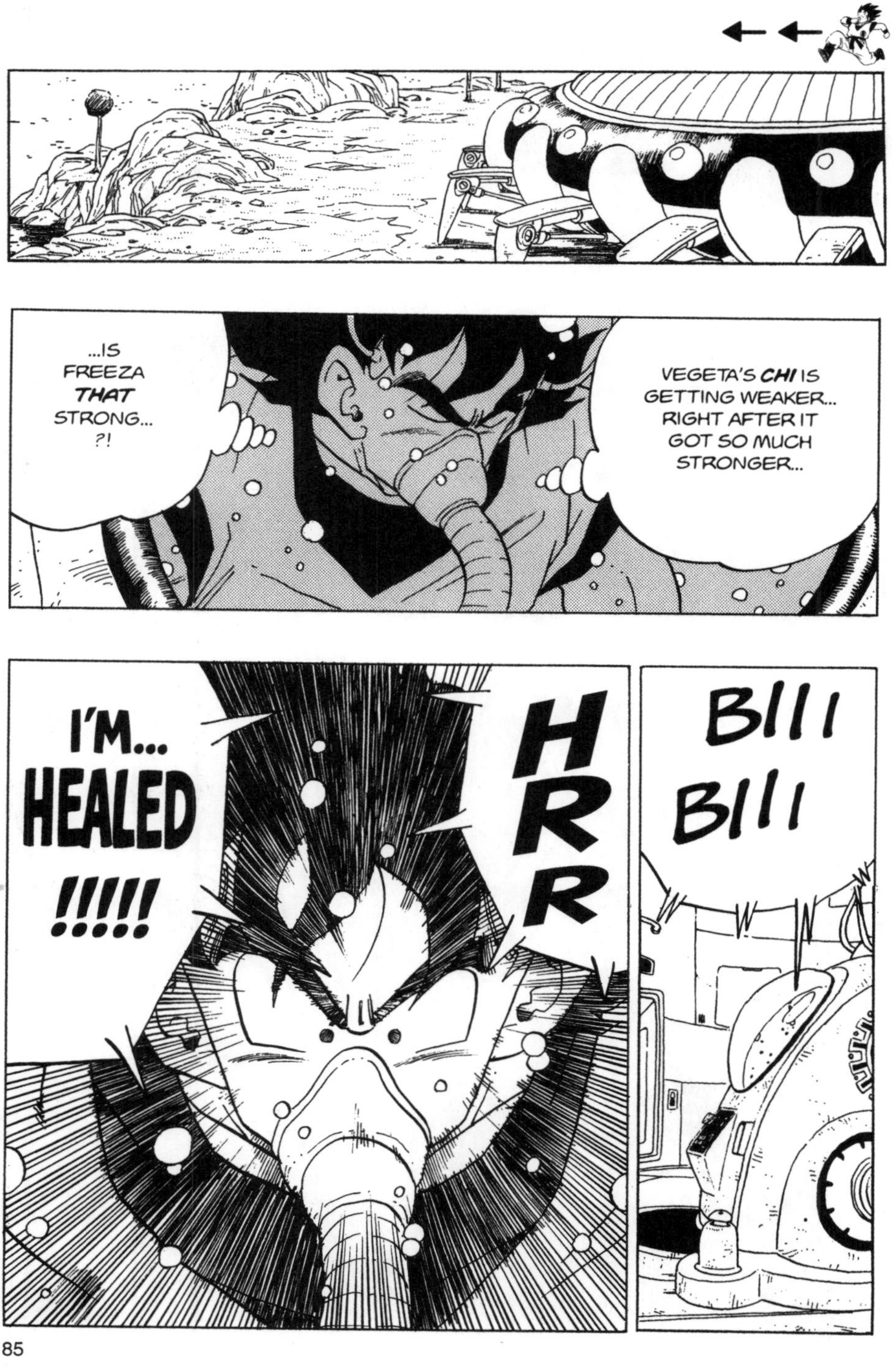
VEGETA'S CHI IS GETTING WEAKER... RIGHT AFTER IT GOT SO MUCH STRONGER...
...IS FREEZA THAT STRONG...?!
BIII BIII
HRR
I'M... HEALED!!!!!

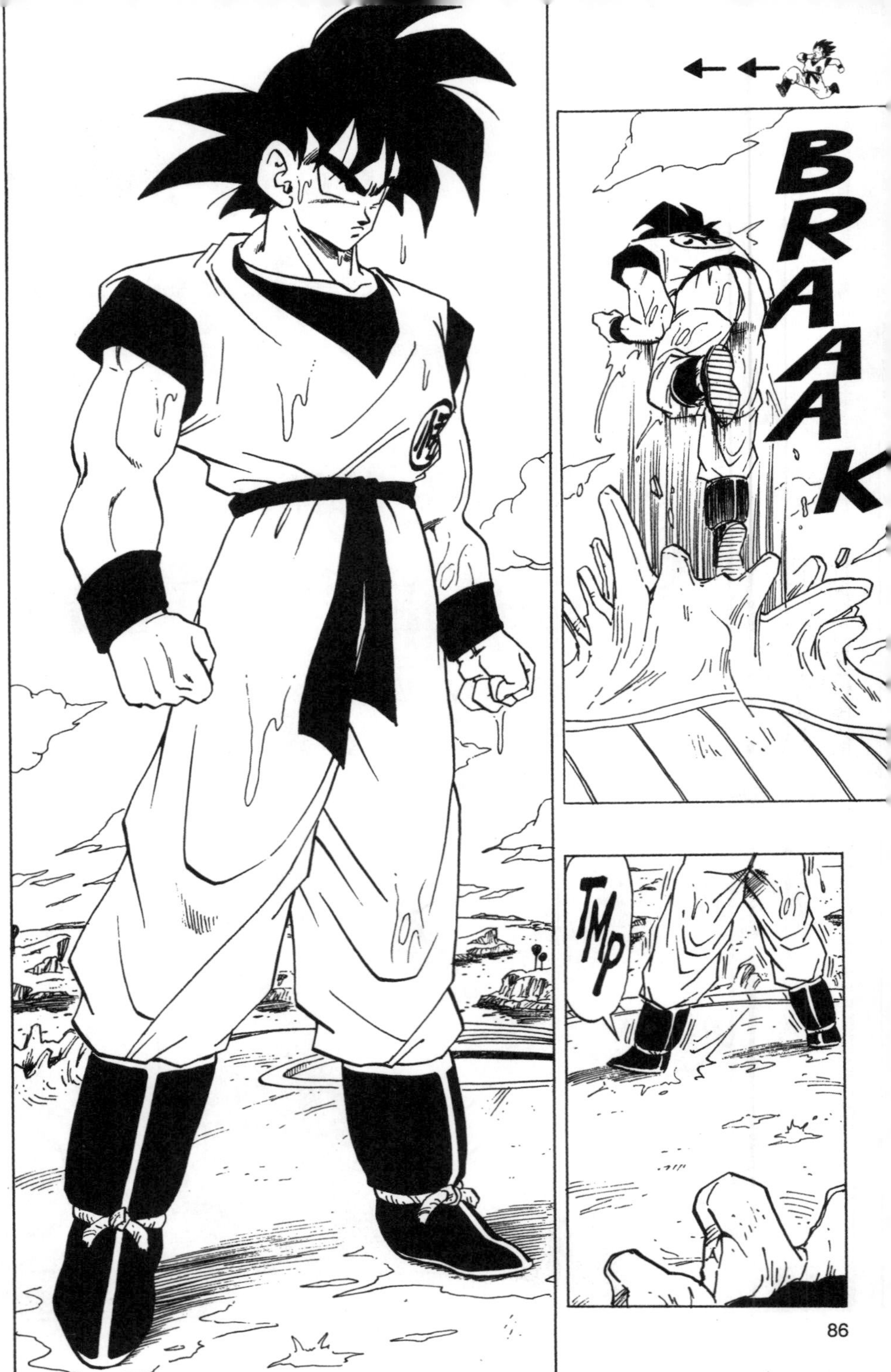
BRAAAK
TMP

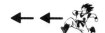

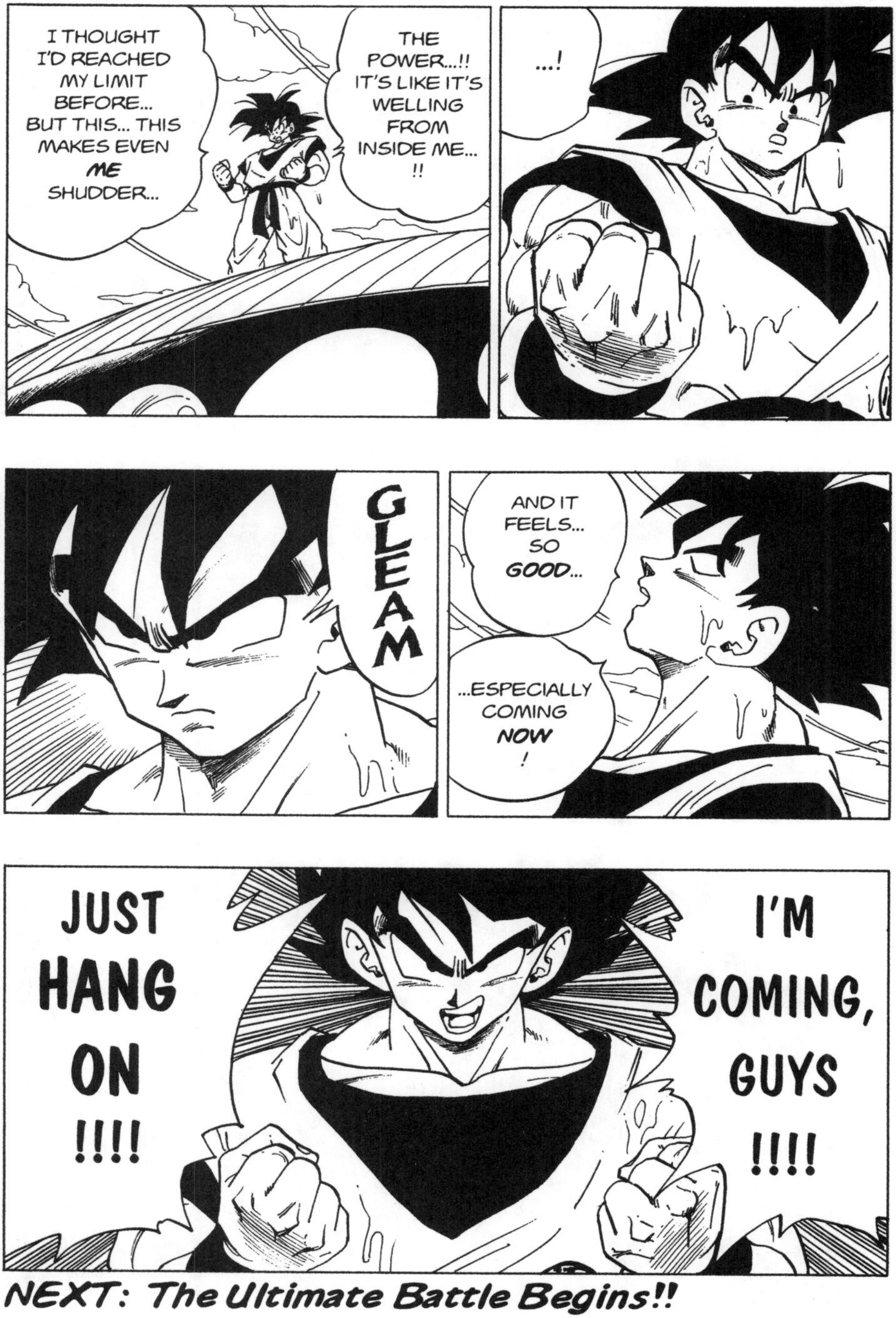
...!
THE POWER...!! IT'S LIKE IT'S WELLING FROM INSIDE ME...!!
I THOUGHT I'D REACHED MY LIMIT BEFORE... BUT THIS... THIS MAKES EVEN ME SHUDDER...
AND IT FEELS... SO GOOD...
...ESPECIALLY COMING NOW!
GLEAM
I'M COMING, GUYS!!!!
JUST HANG ON!!!!

NEXT: The Ultimate Battle Begins!!

## DBZ:113 • The Ultimate Battle Begins!

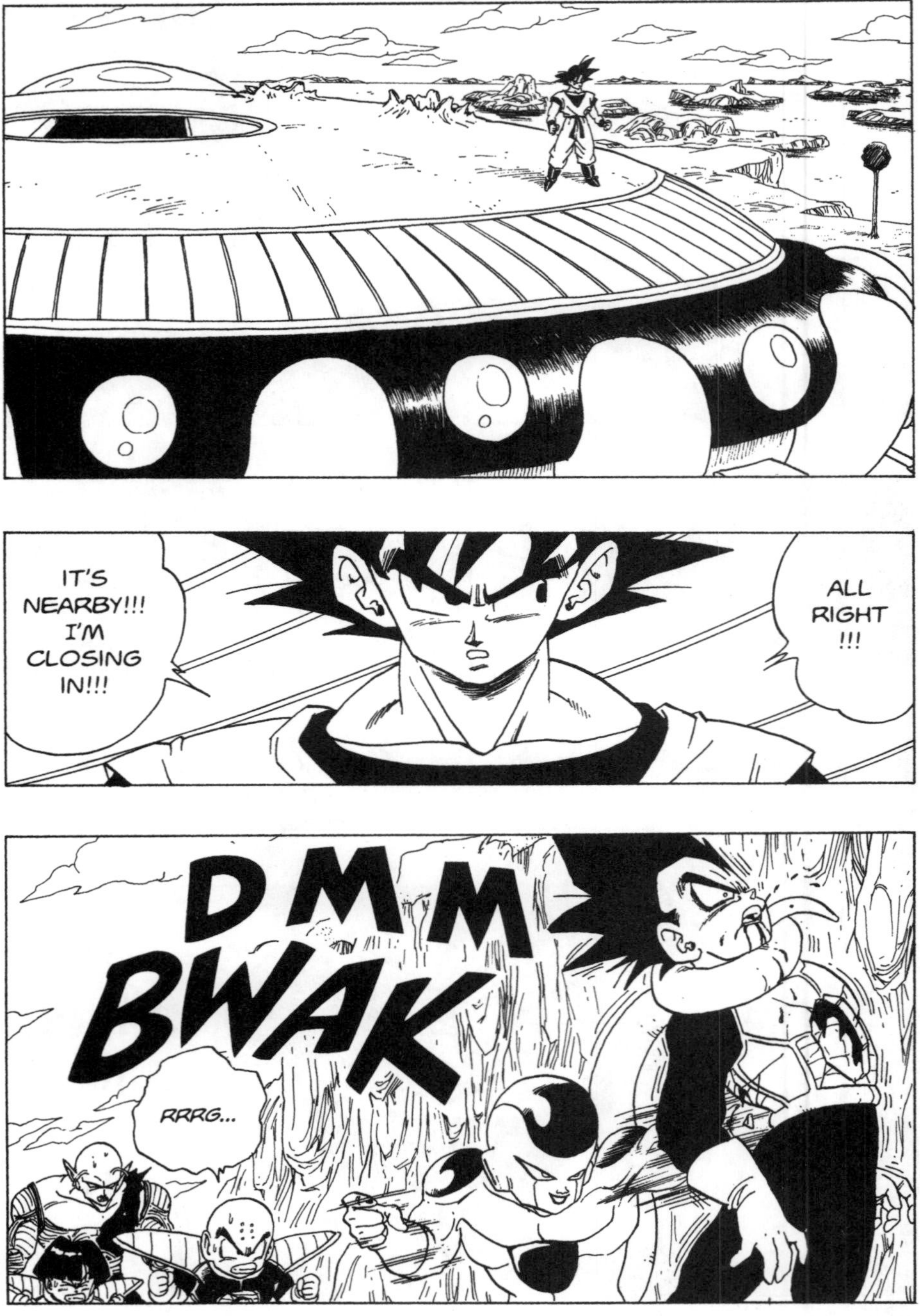

ALL RIGHT !!!
IT'S NEARBY!!! I'M CLOSING IN!!!
DMM
BWAK
RRRG...

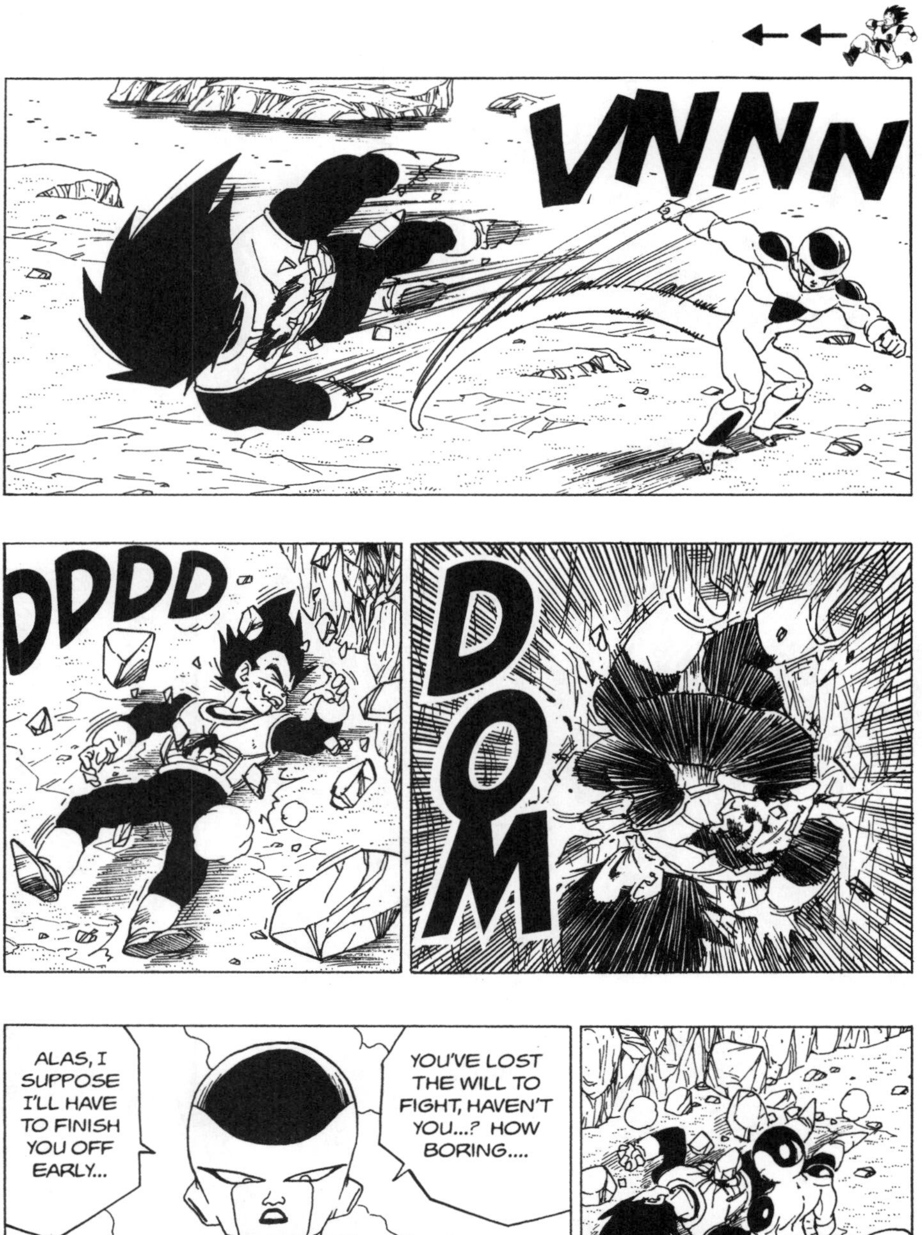
VNNN
DOM
DDDD
YOU'VE LOST THE WILL TO FIGHT, HAVEN'T YOU...? HOW BORING....
ALAS, I SUPPOSE I'LL HAVE TO FINISH YOU OFF EARLY...

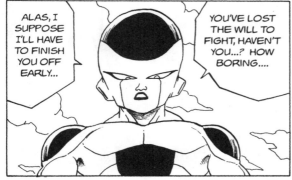

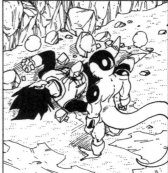

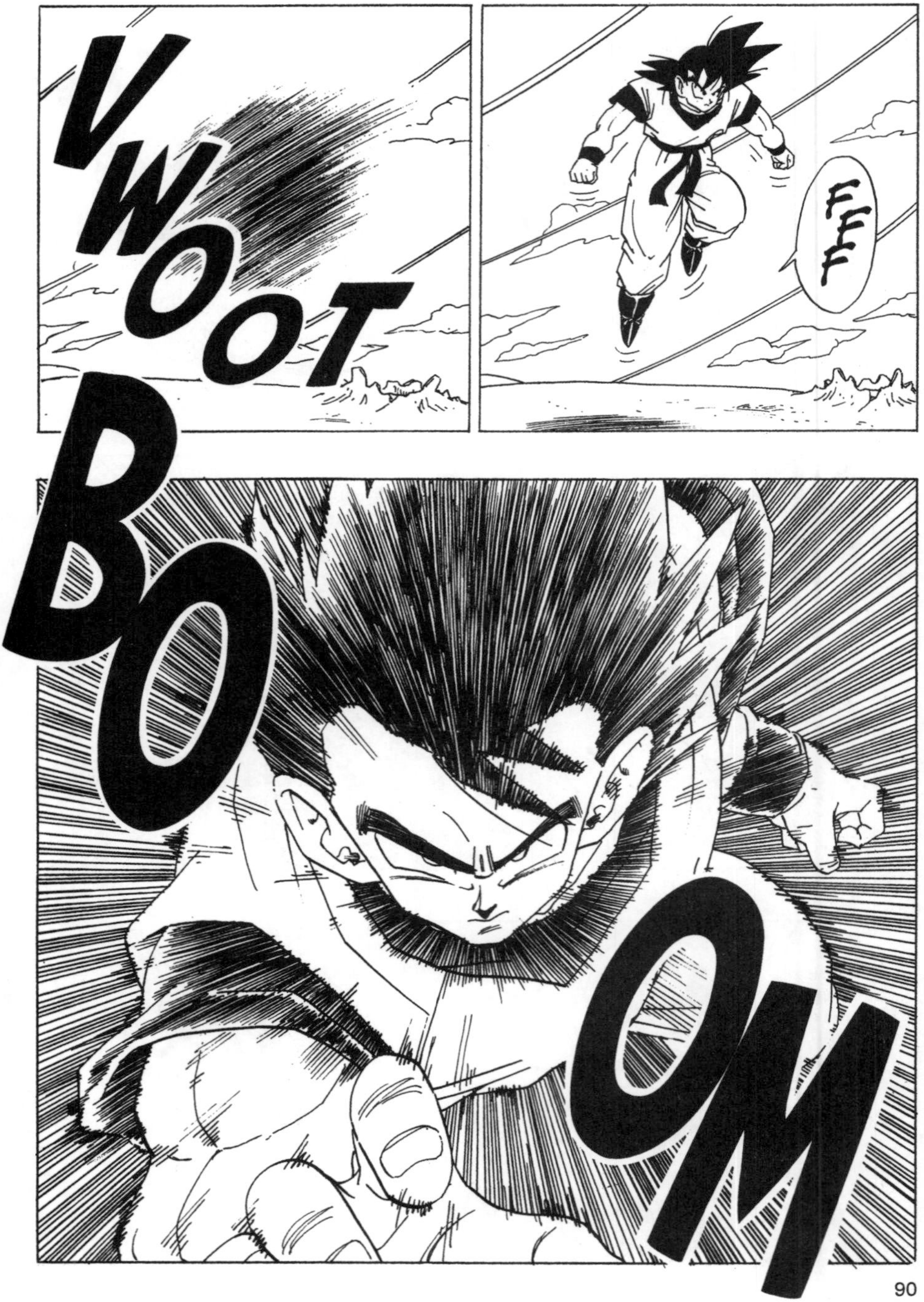
FFF
VWOOT
BOOM

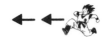

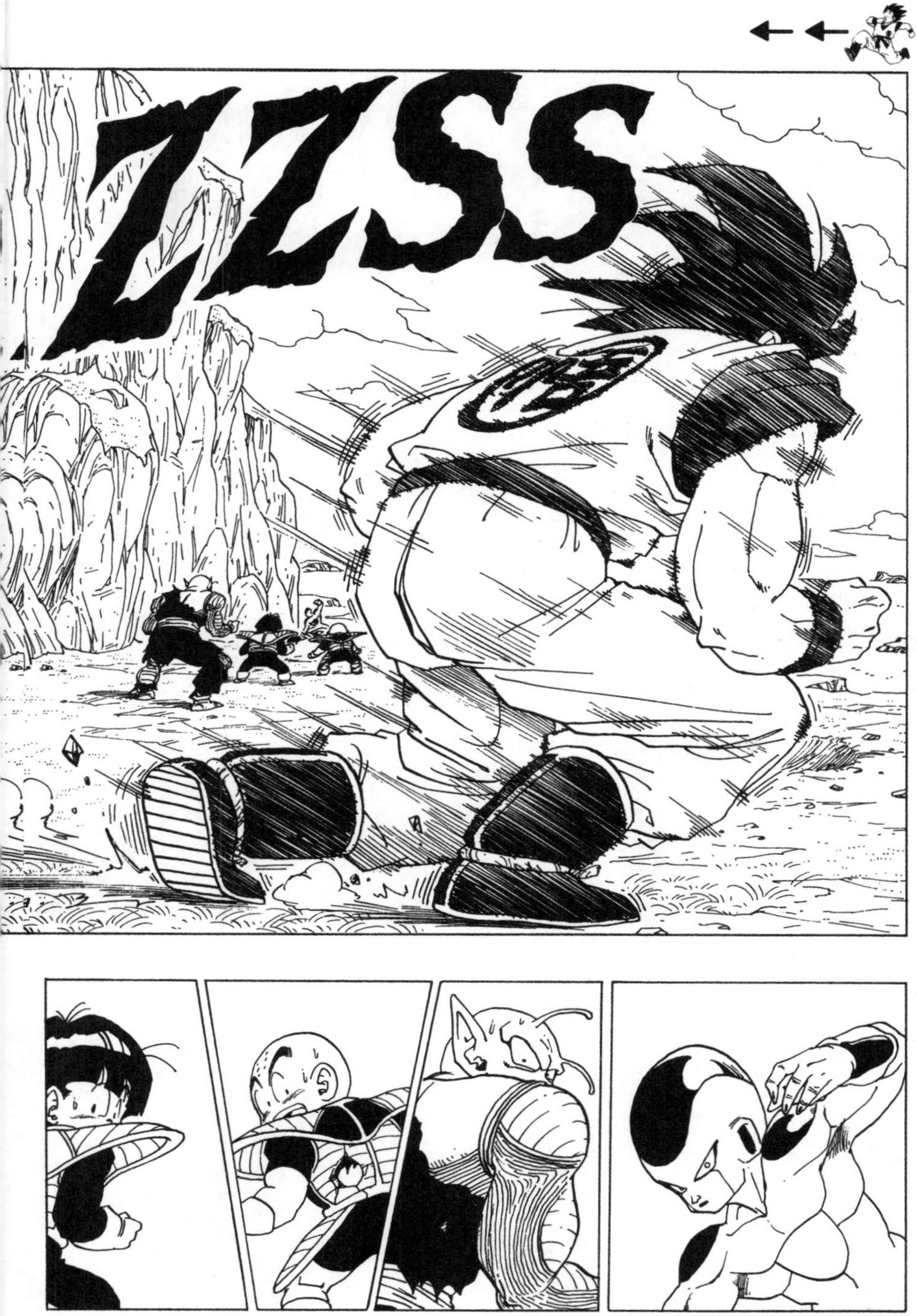
ZZSS

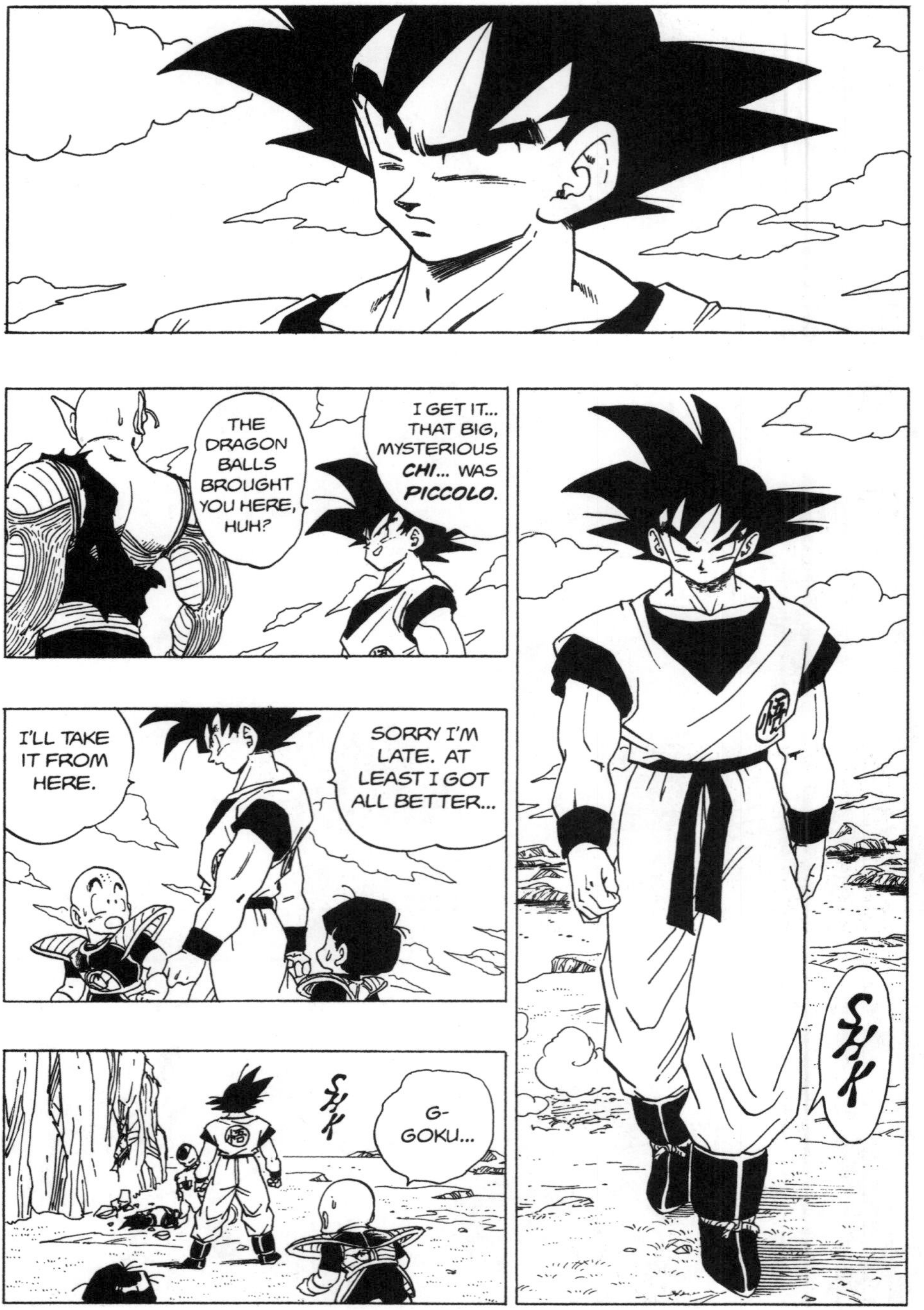
SHK
I GET IT... THAT BIG, MYSTERIOUS CHI... WAS PICCOLO.
THE DRAGON BALLS BROUGHT YOU HERE, HUH?
SORRY I'M LATE. AT LEAST I GOT ALL BETTER...
I'LL TAKE IT FROM HERE.
G-GOKU...
SHK

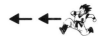

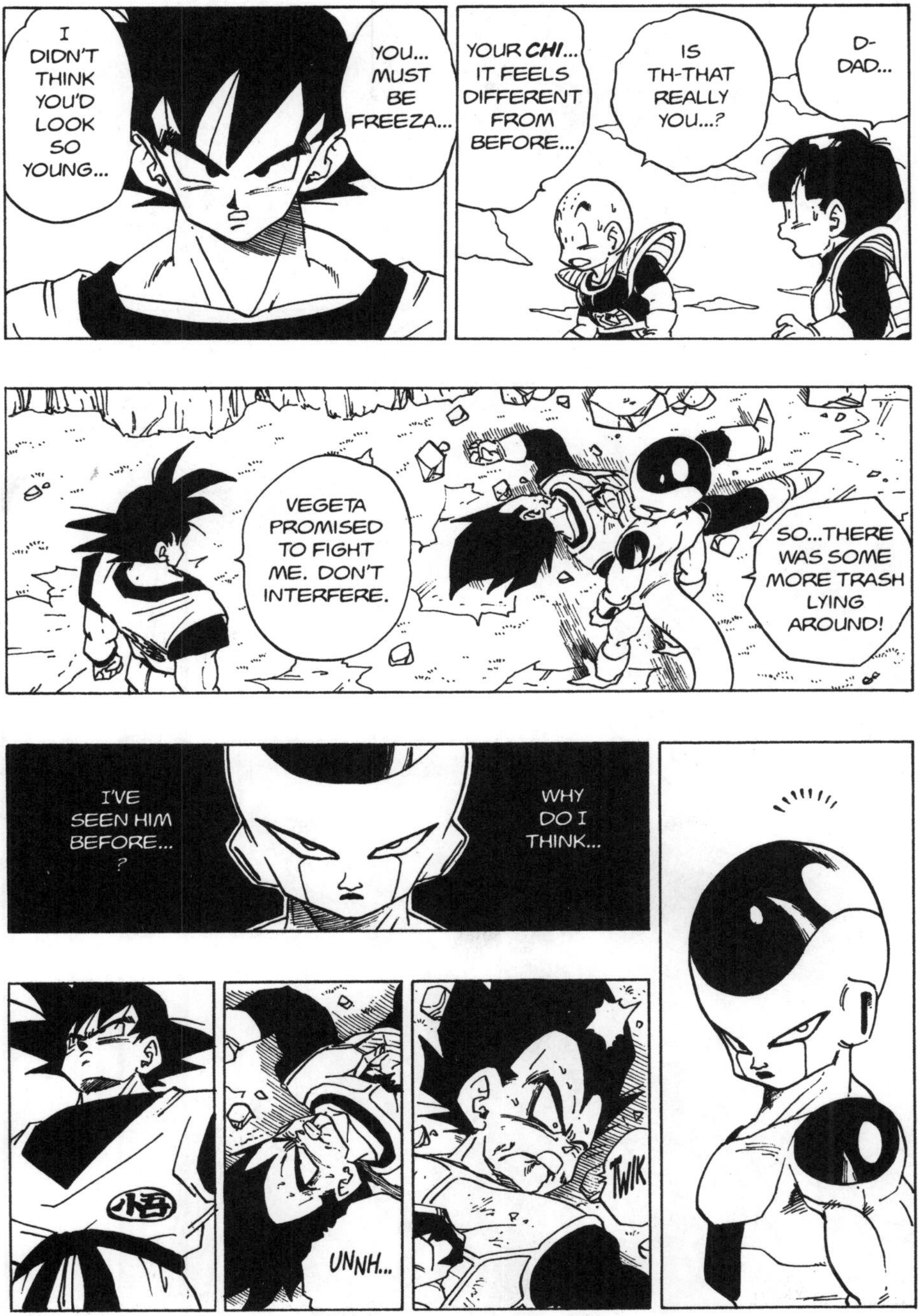
D-DAD...
IS TH-THAT REALLY YOU...?
YOUR **CHI**... IT FEELS DIFFERENT FROM BEFORE...
YOU... MUST BE FREEZA...
I DIDN'T THINK YOU'D LOOK SO YOUNG...
SO...THERE WAS SOME MORE TRASH LYING AROUND!
VEGETA PROMISED TO FIGHT ME. DON'T INTERFERE.
WHY DO I THINK...
I'VE SEEN HIM BEFORE...?
TWIK
UNNH...

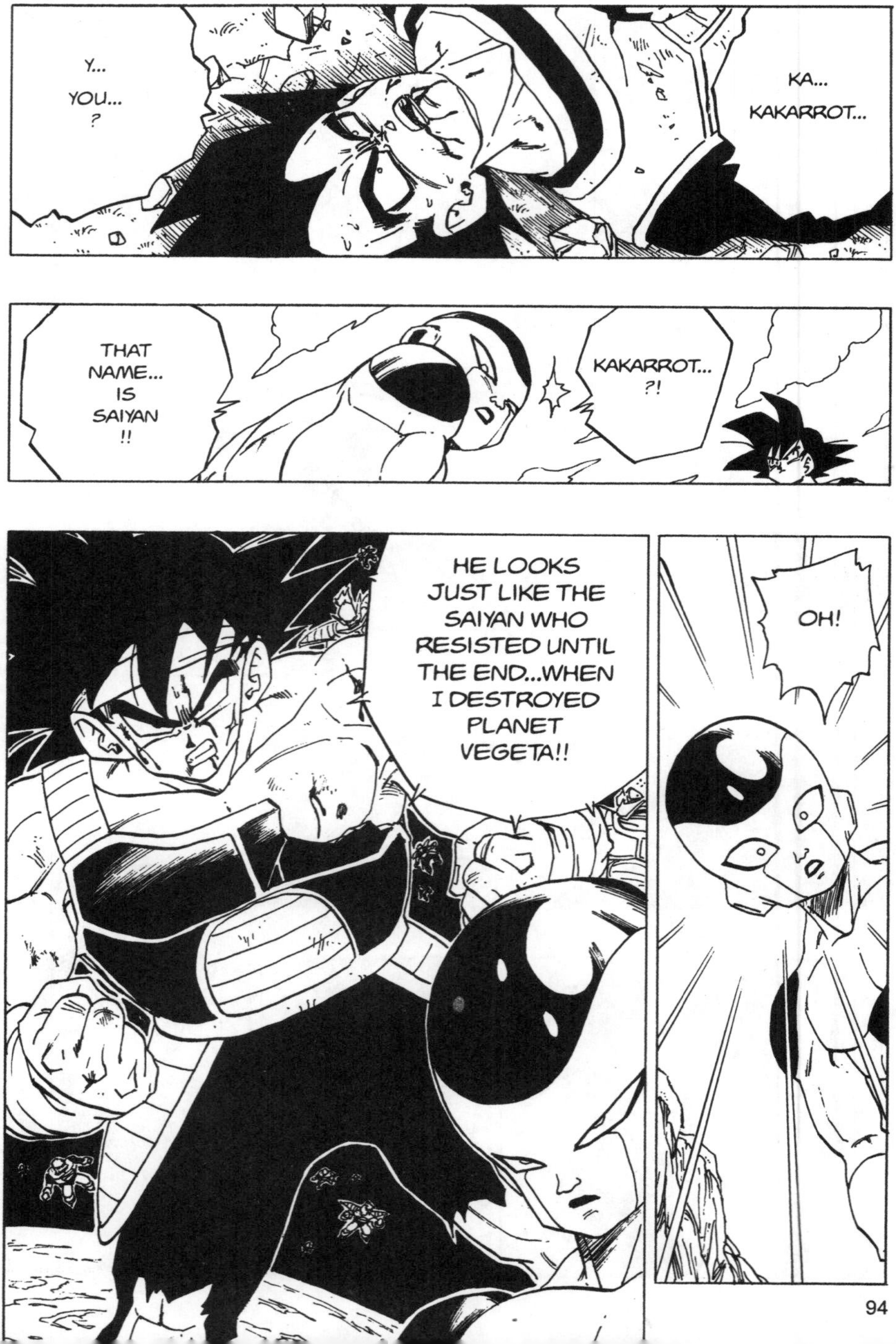
KA... KAKARROT...
Y... YOU... ?
KAKARROT... ?!
THAT NAME... IS SAIYAN !!
OH!
HE LOOKS JUST LIKE THE SAIYAN WHO RESISTED UNTIL THE END...WHEN I DESTROYED PLANET VEGETA!!

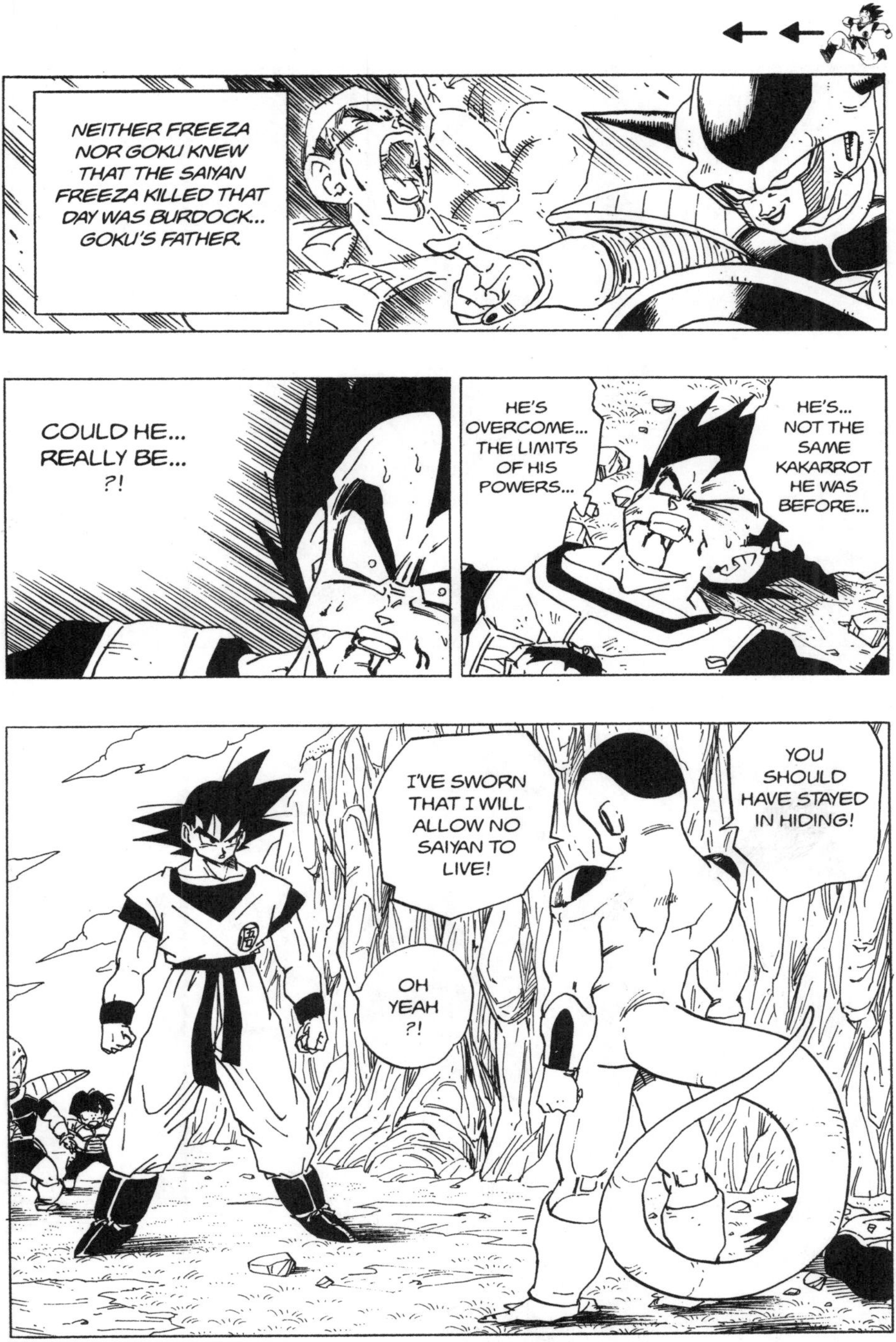
NEITHER FREEZA NOR GOKU KNEW THAT THE SAIYAN FREEZA KILLED THAT DAY WAS BURDOCK... GOKU'S FATHER.
HE'S... NOT THE SAME KAKARROT HE WAS BEFORE...
HE'S OVERCOME... THE LIMITS OF HIS POWERS...
COULD HE... REALLY BE... ?!
YOU SHOULD HAVE STAYED IN HIDING!
I'VE SWORN THAT I WILL ALLOW NO SAIYAN TO LIVE!
OH YEAH ?!

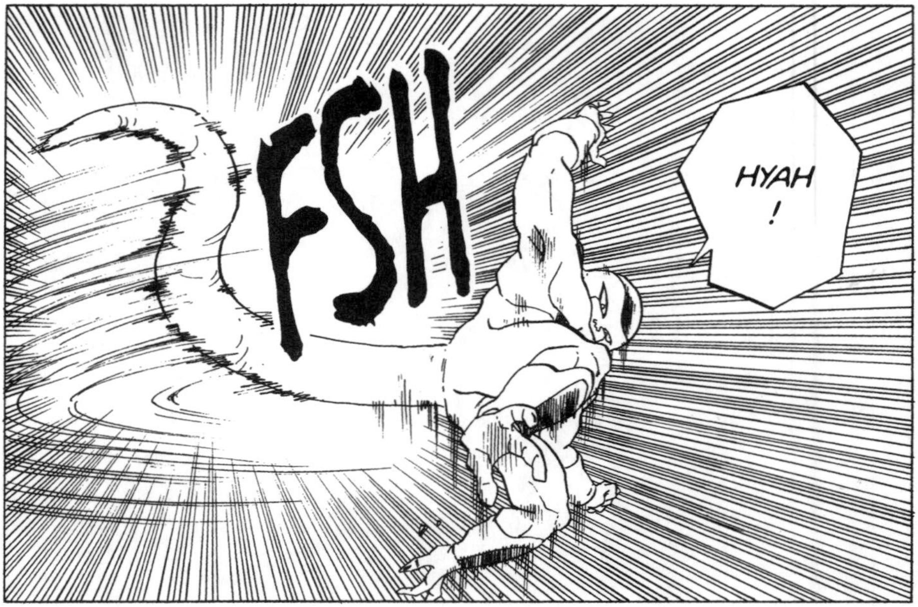
HYAH
!
FSH

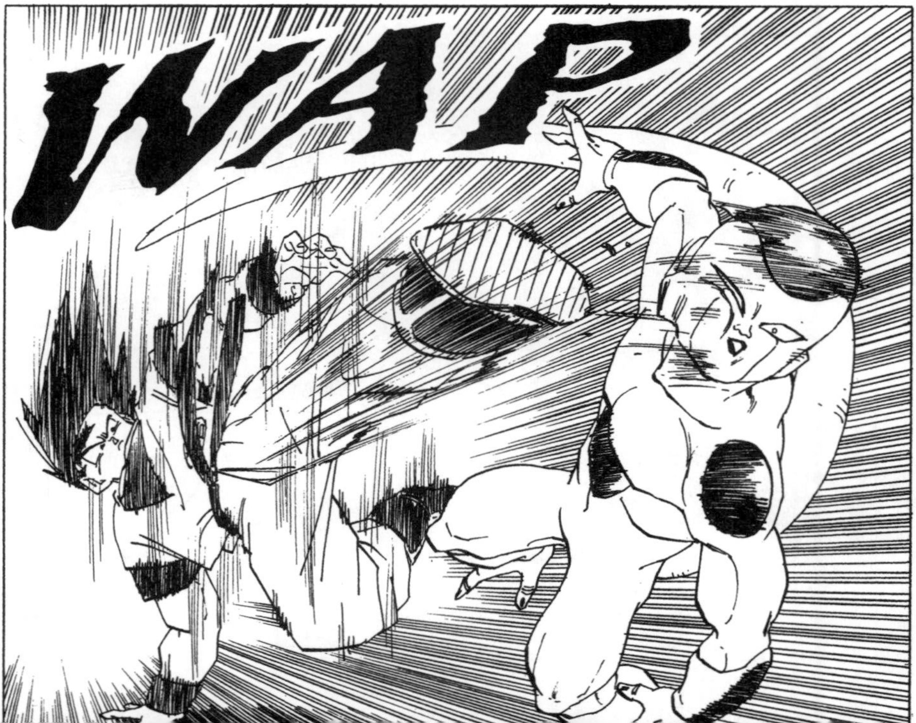
WAP

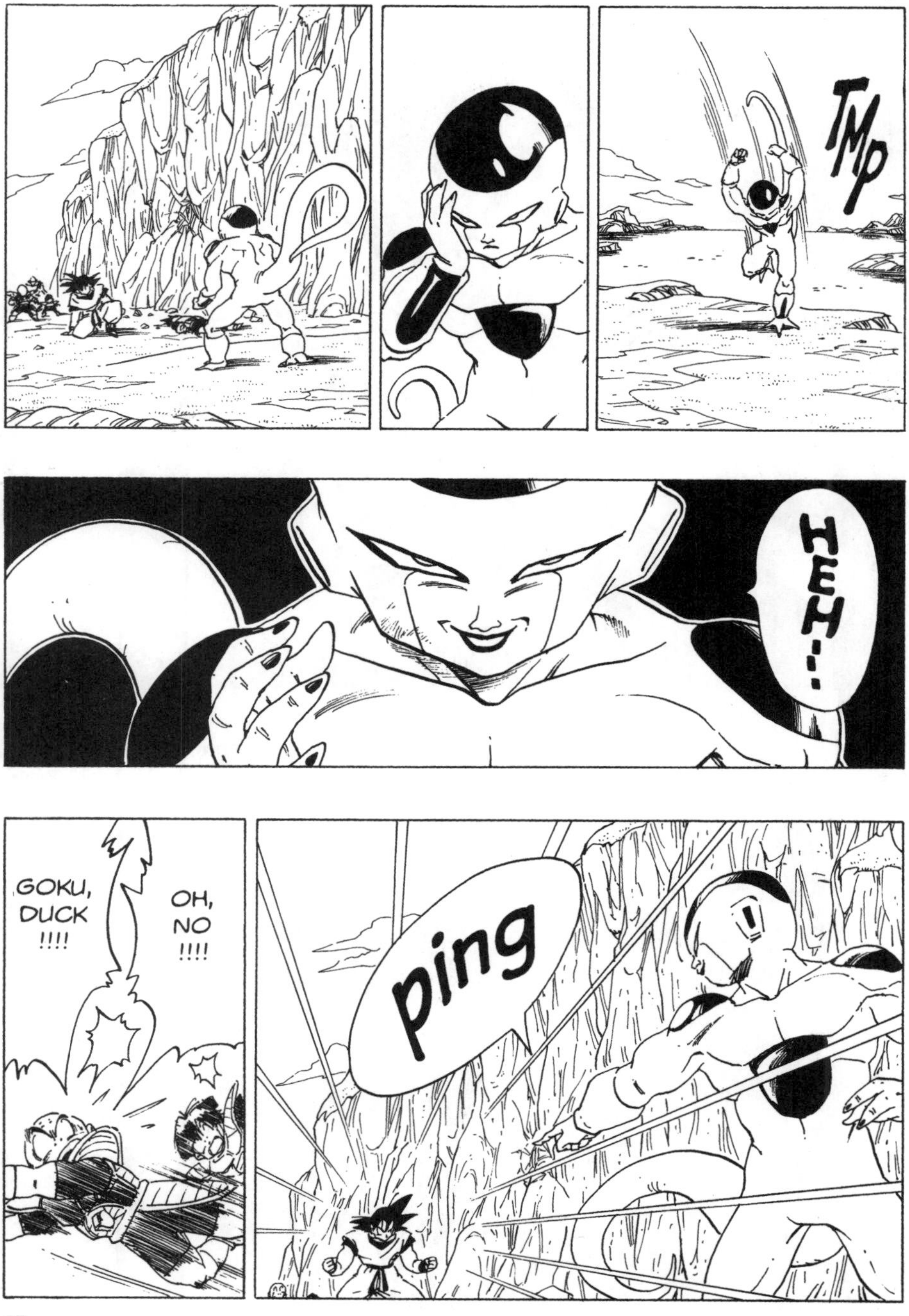
TMP
HEH!!
ping
!
OH, NO !!!!
GOKU, DUCK !!!!

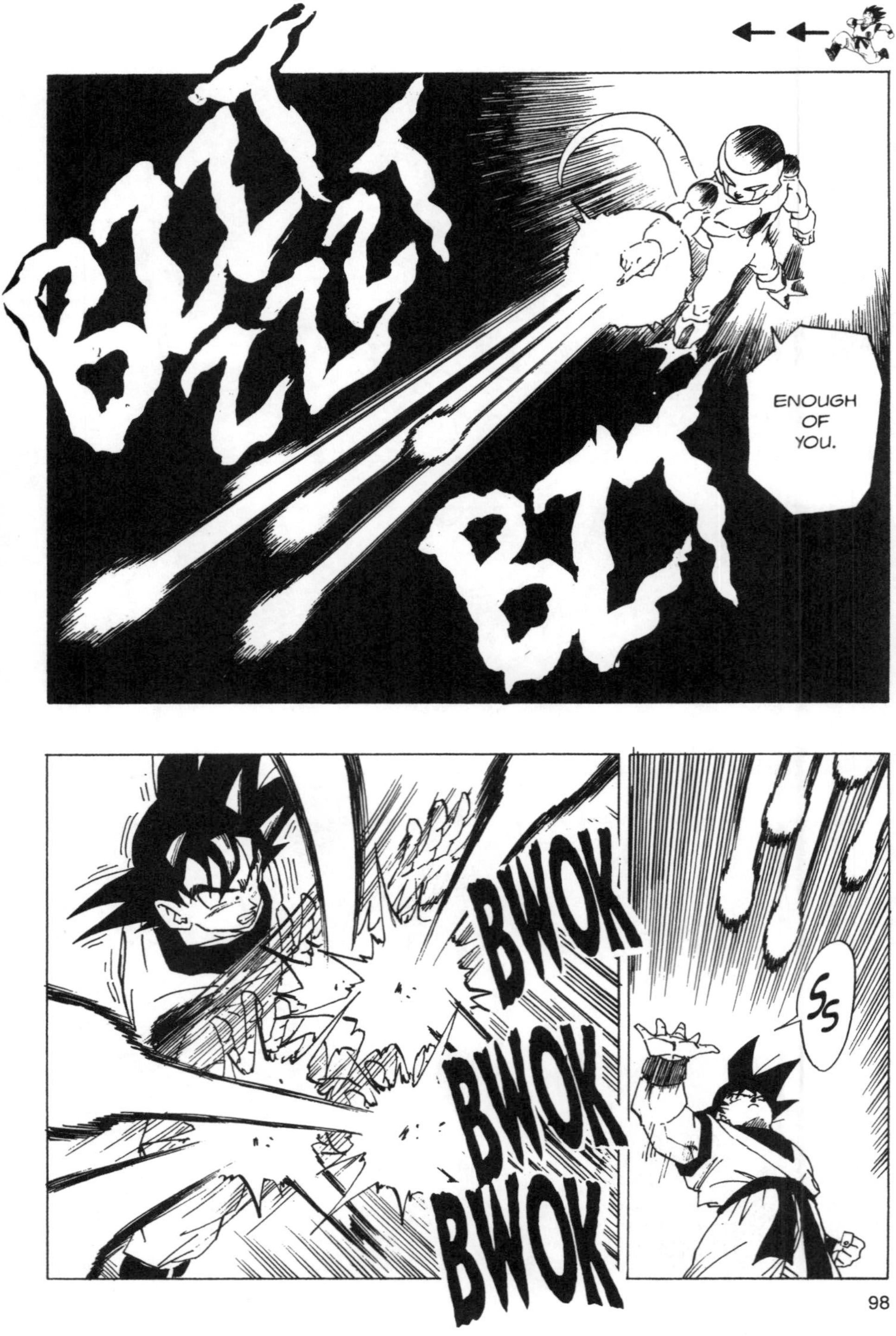
ENOUGH OF YOU.
BZZT
BZZZT
BZT
SS
BWOK
BWOK
BWOK

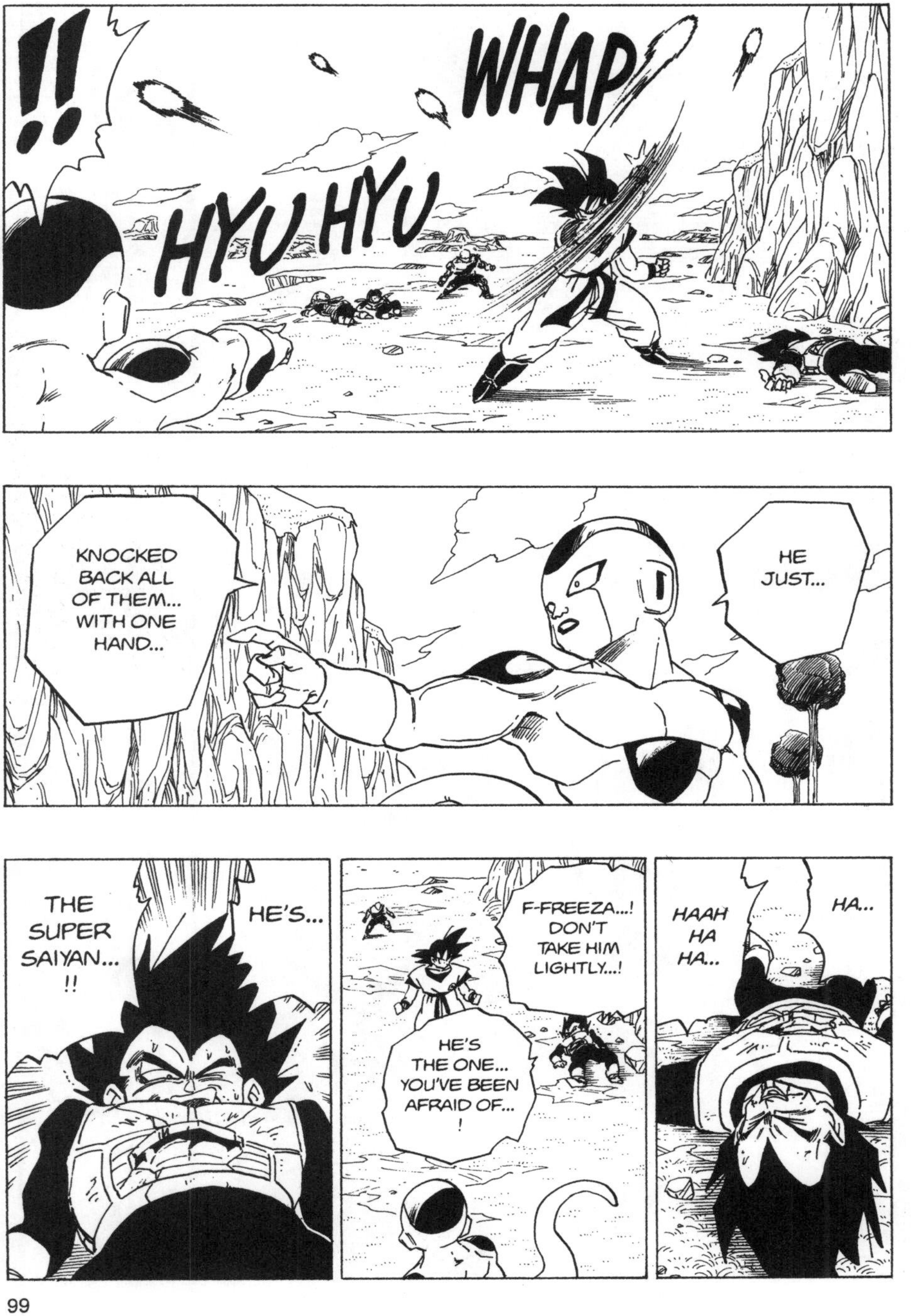

WHAP
!!
HYU HYU
HE JUST...
KNOCKED BACK ALL OF THEM... WITH ONE HAND...
HA...
HAAH HA HA...
F-FREEZA...! DON'T TAKE HIM LIGHTLY...!
HE'S THE ONE... YOU'VE BEEN AFRAID OF... !
HE'S...
THE SUPER SAIYAN... !!

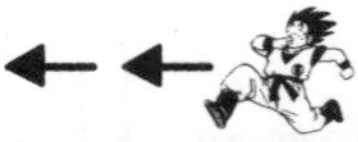

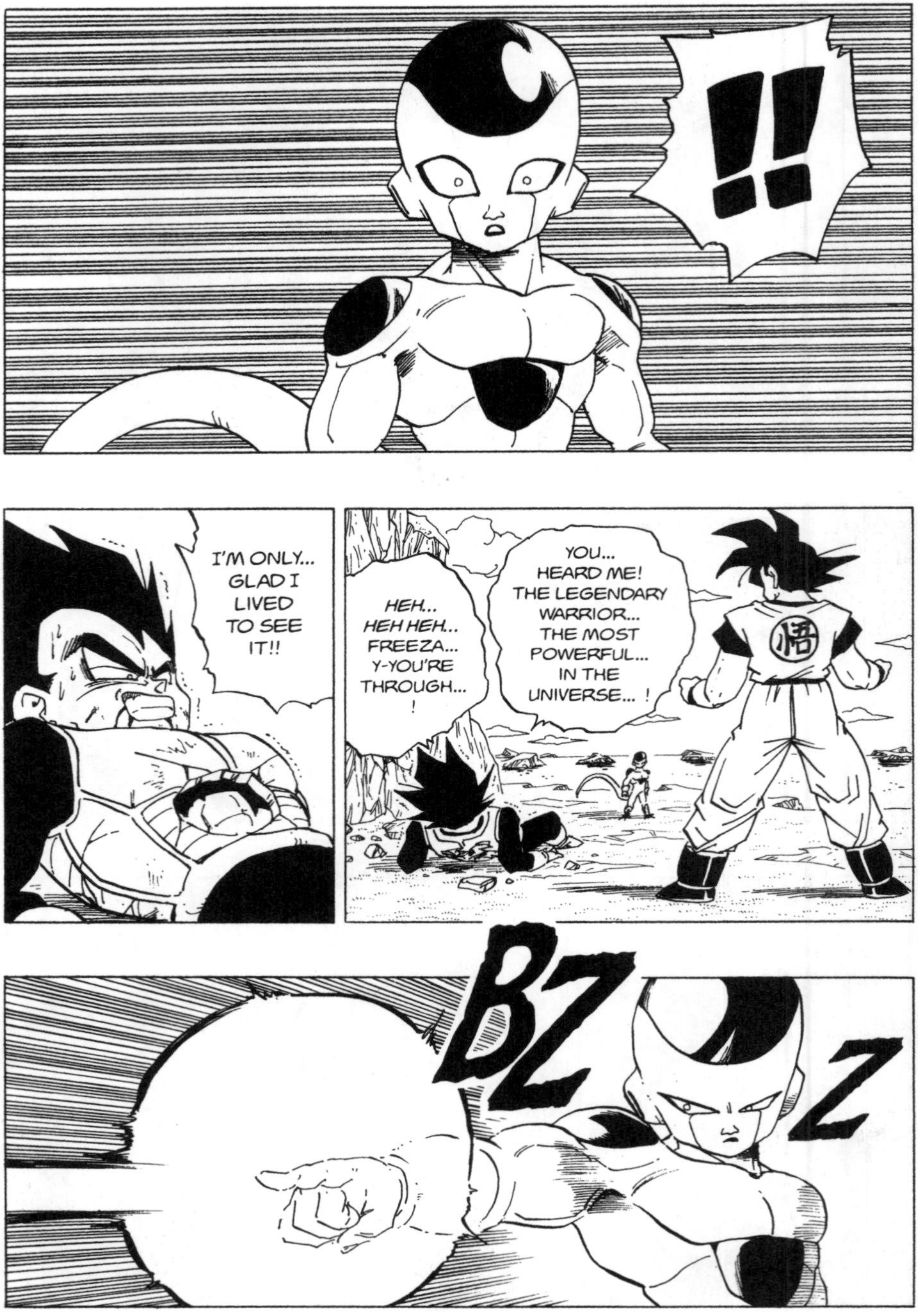
!!
YOU... HEARD ME! THE LEGENDARY WARRIOR... THE MOST POWERFUL... IN THE UNIVERSE... !
HEH... HEH HEH... FREEZA... Y-YOU'RE THROUGH... !
I'M ONLY... GLAD I LIVED TO SEE IT!!
BZZZ

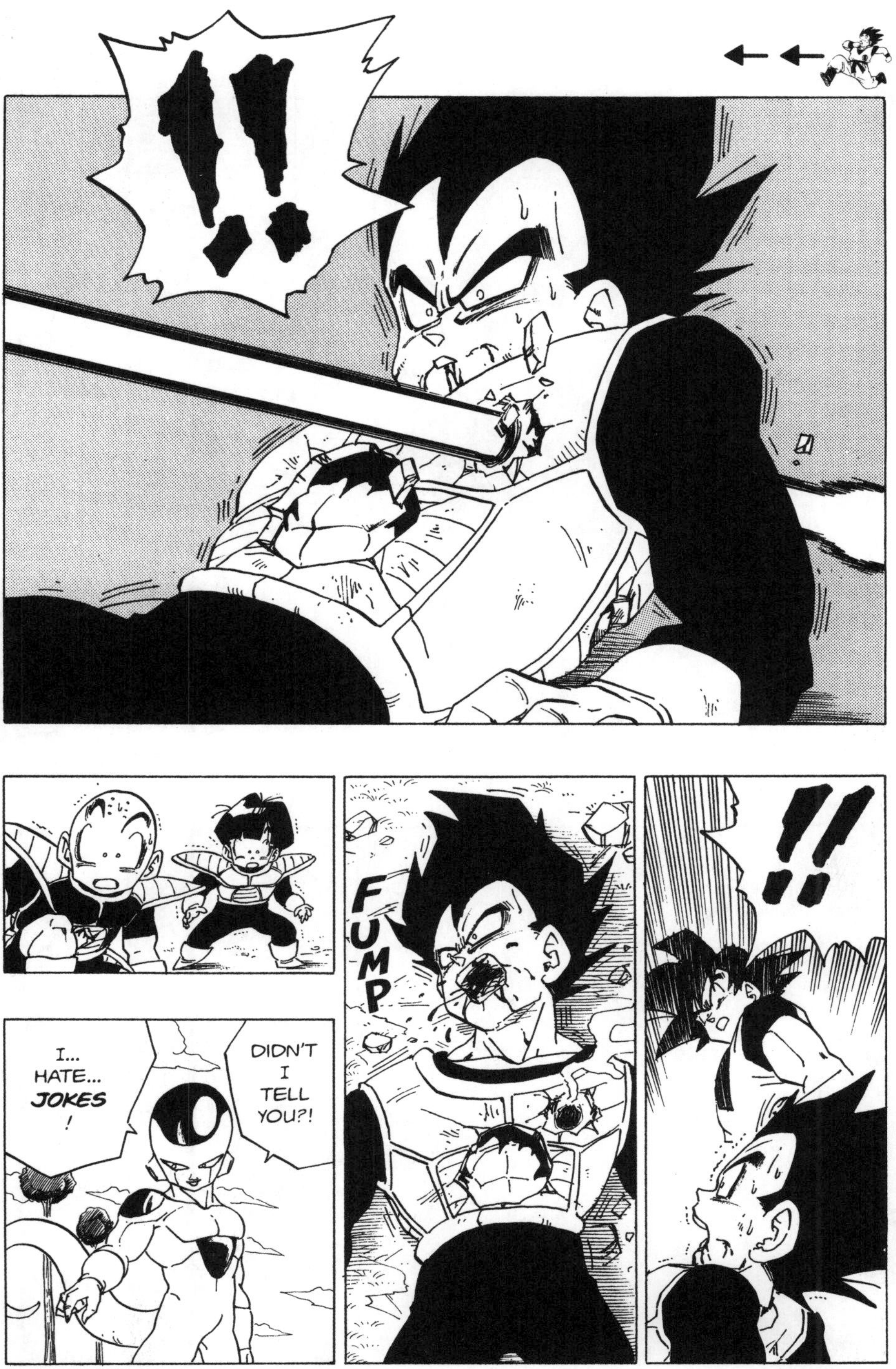
!!
!!
FUMP
DIDN'T I TELL YOU?!
I... HATE... JOKES!

NEXT: Vegeta Dies!!

# DBZ:114 • The Death of Vegeta

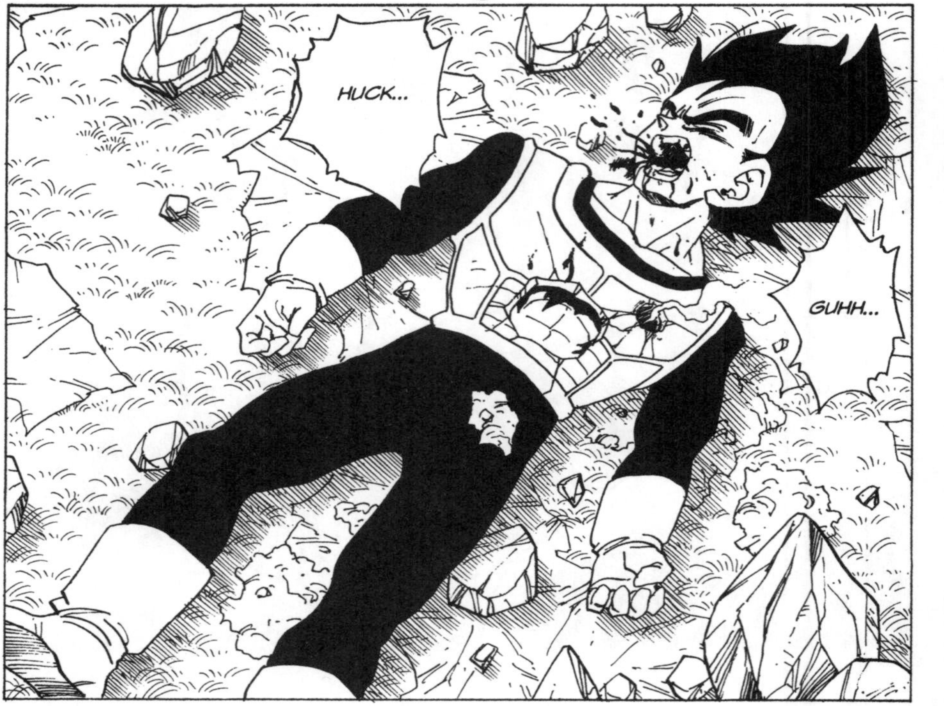
HUCK...
GUHH...

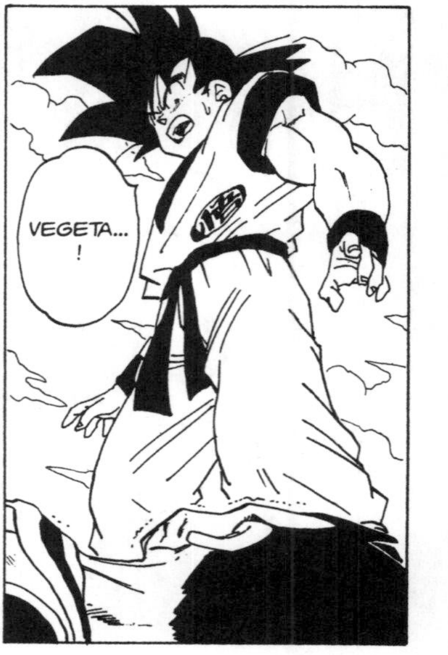
VEGETA... !

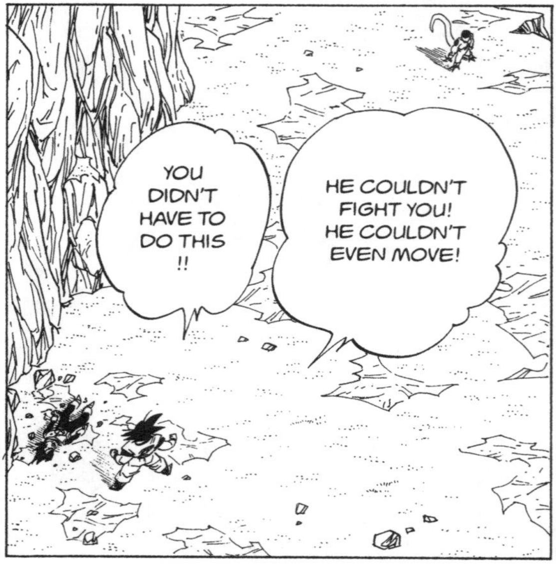
HE COULDN'T FIGHT YOU! HE COULDN'T EVEN MOVE!
YOU DIDN'T HAVE TO DO THIS !!

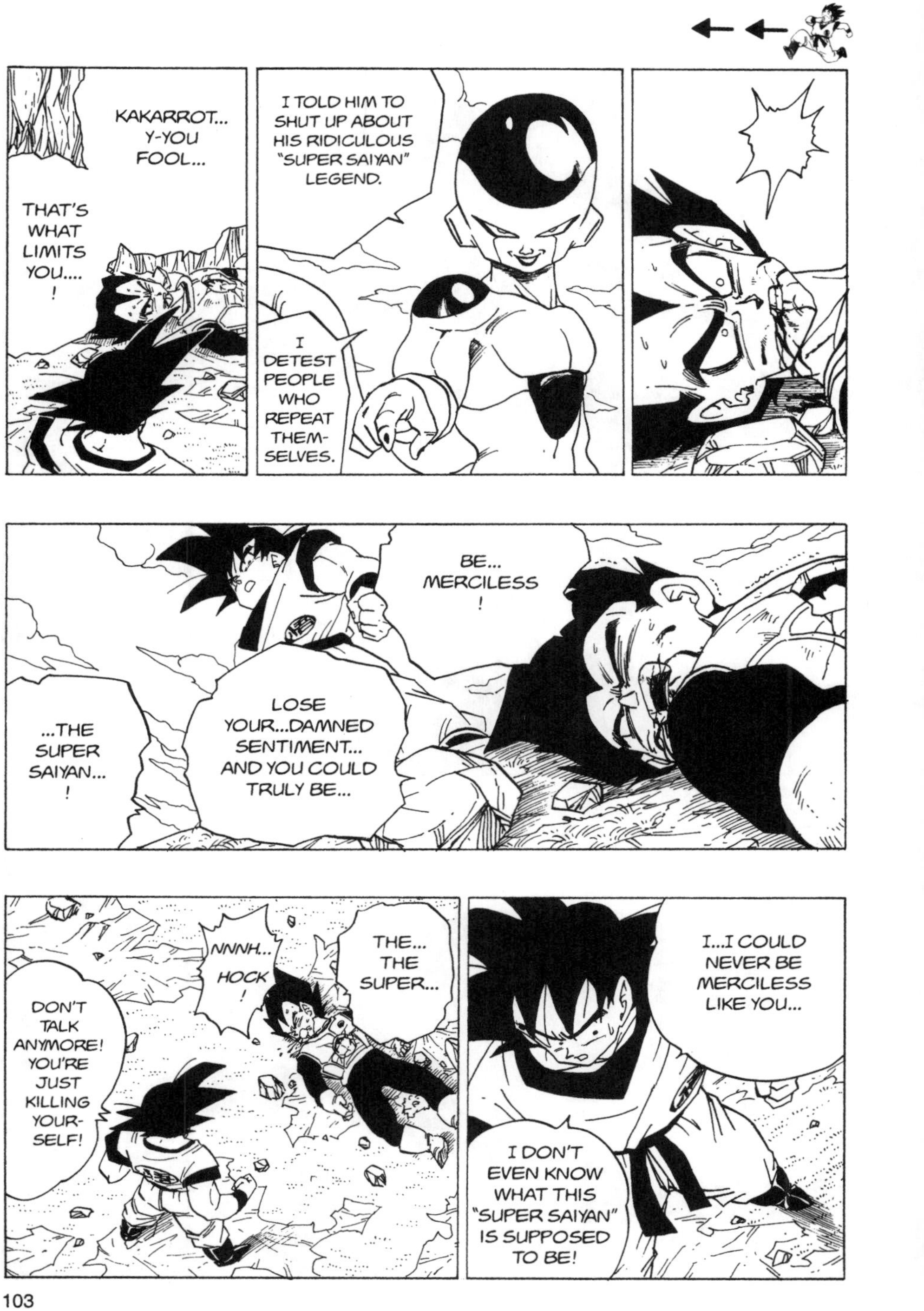
I TOLD HIM TO SHUT UP ABOUT HIS RIDICULOUS "SUPER SAIYAN" LEGEND.
I DETEST PEOPLE WHO REPEAT THEM-SELVES.
KAKARROT... Y-YOU FOOL...
THAT'S WHAT LIMITS YOU....!
BE... MERCILESS!
LOSE YOUR...DAMNED SENTIMENT... AND YOU COULD TRULY BE...
...THE SUPER SAIYAN...!
I...I COULD NEVER BE MERCILESS LIKE YOU...
I DON'T EVEN KNOW WHAT THIS "SUPER SAIYAN" IS SUPPOSED TO BE!
THE... THE SUPER...
NNNH... HOCK!
DON'T TALK ANYMORE! YOU'RE JUST KILLING YOUR-SELF!

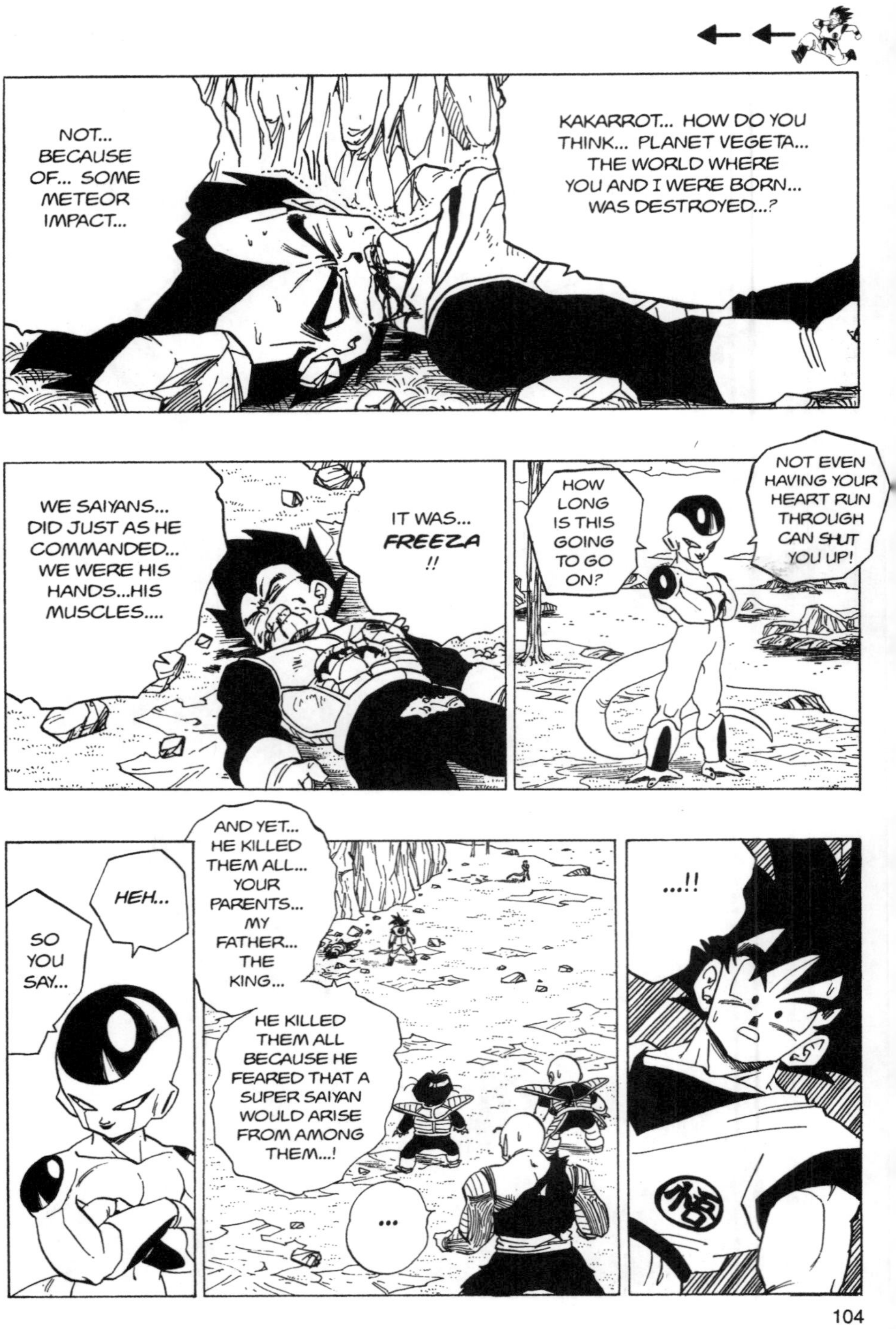
KAKARROT... HOW DO YOU THINK... PLANET VEGETA... THE WORLD WHERE YOU AND I WERE BORN... WAS DESTROYED...?
NOT... BECAUSE OF... SOME METEOR IMPACT...
NOT EVEN HAVING YOUR HEART RUN THROUGH CAN SHUT YOU UP!
HOW LONG IS THIS GOING TO GO ON?
IT WAS... *FREEZA* !!
WE SAIYANS... DID JUST AS HE COMMANDED... WE WERE HIS HANDS...HIS MUSCLES....
...!!
AND YET... HE KILLED THEM ALL... YOUR PARENTS... MY FATHER... THE KING...
HE KILLED THEM ALL BECAUSE HE FEARED THAT A SUPER SAIYAN WOULD ARISE FROM AMONG THEM...!
...
*HEH...*
SO YOU SAY...

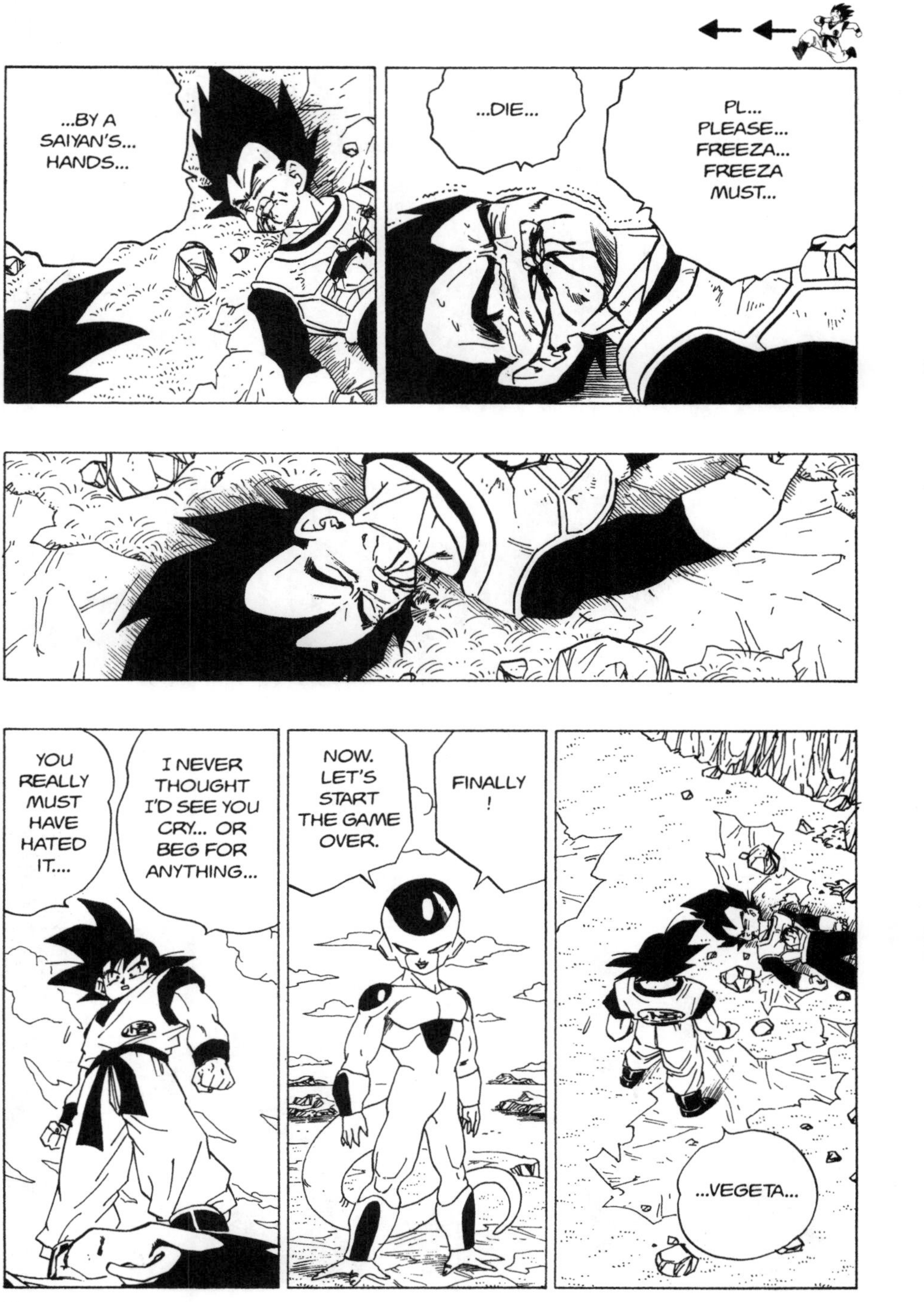
PL... PLEASE... FREEZA... FREEZA MUST...
...DIE...
...BY A SAIYAN'S... HANDS...
...VEGETA...
FINALLY!
NOW. LET'S START THE GAME OVER.
I NEVER THOUGHT I'D SEE YOU CRY... OR BEG FOR ANYTHING...
YOU REALLY MUST HAVE HATED IT....

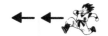

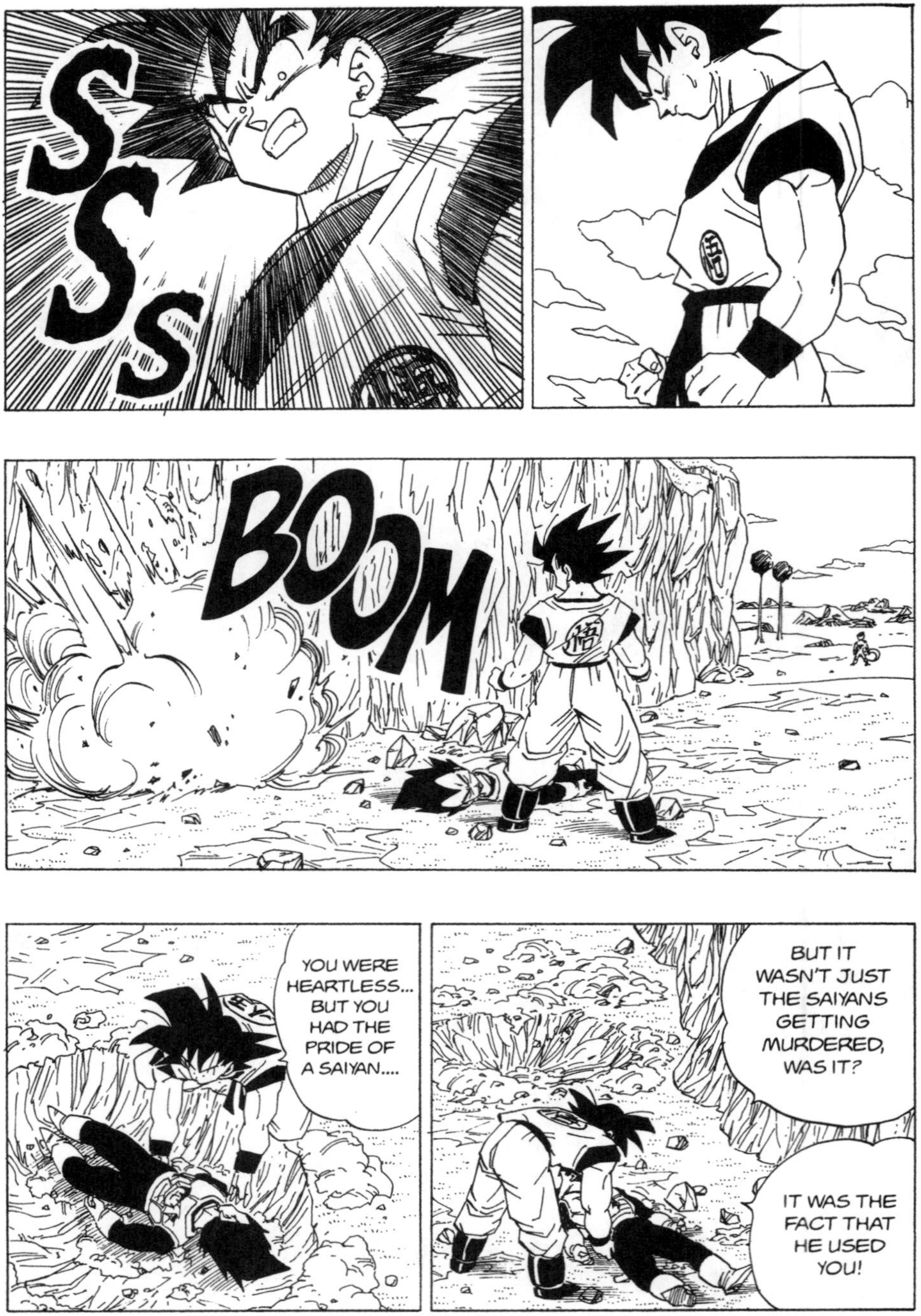
SSS
BOOM
BUT IT WASN'T JUST THE SAIYANS GETTING MURDERED, WAS IT?
IT WAS THE FACT THAT HE USED YOU!
YOU WERE HEARTLESS... BUT YOU HAD THE PRIDE OF A SAIYAN....

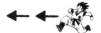

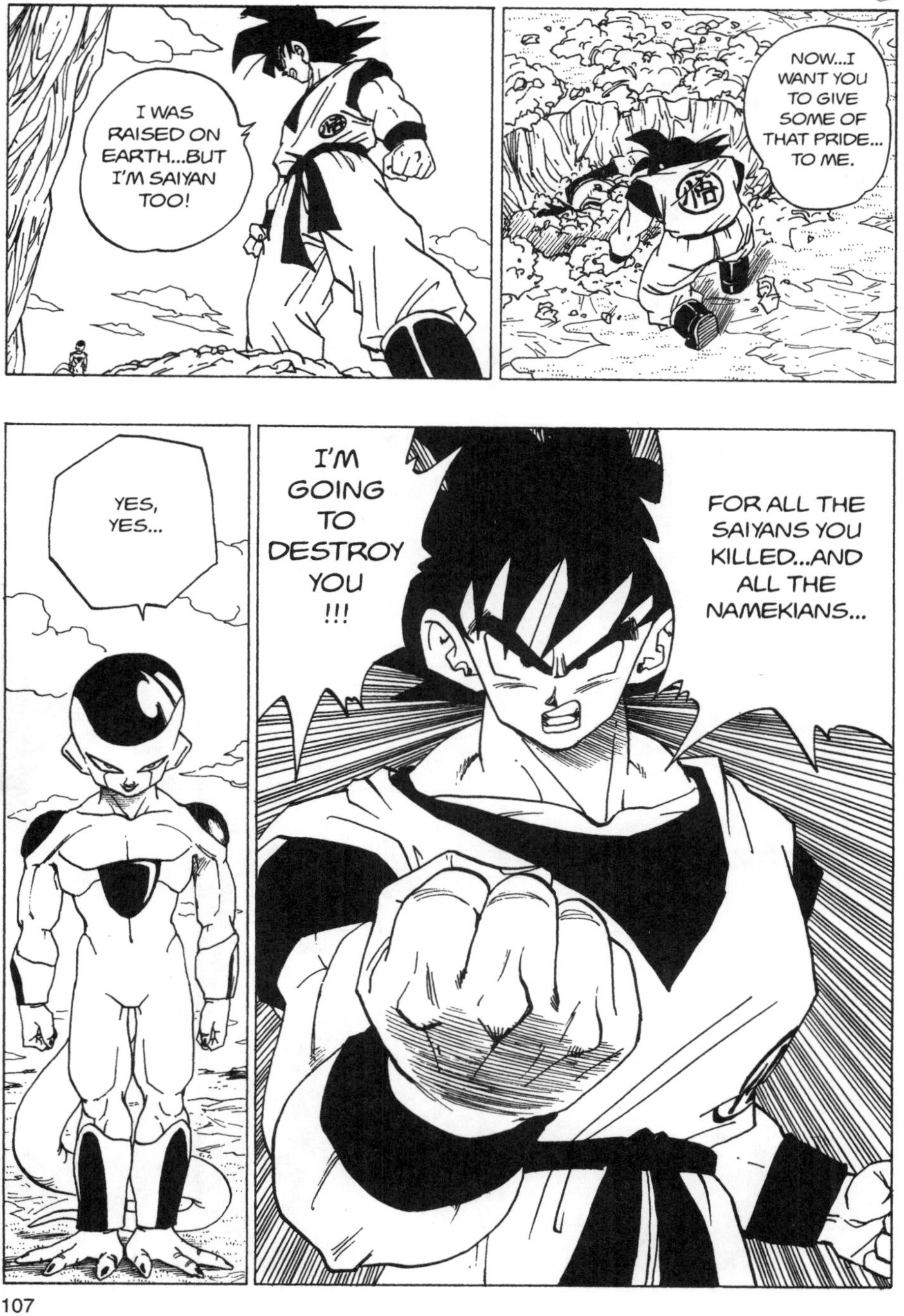
NOW...I WANT YOU TO GIVE SOME OF THAT PRIDE... TO ME.
I WAS RAISED ON EARTH...BUT I'M SAIYAN TOO!
FOR ALL THE SAIYANS YOU KILLED...AND ALL THE NAMEKIANS...
I'M GOING TO DESTROY YOU !!!
YES, YES...

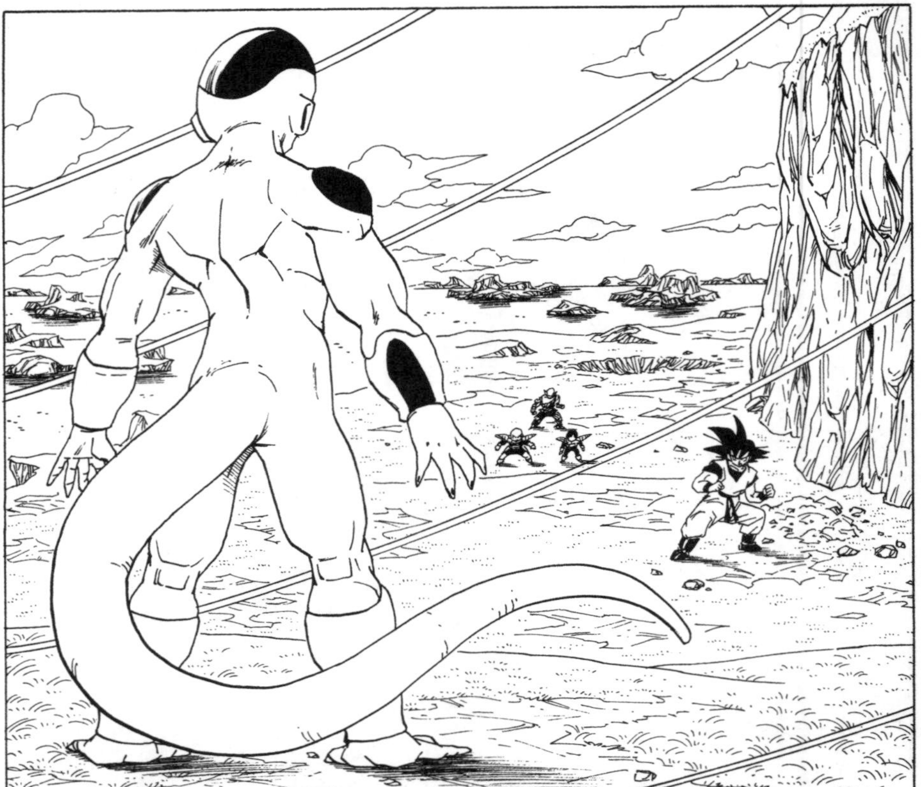

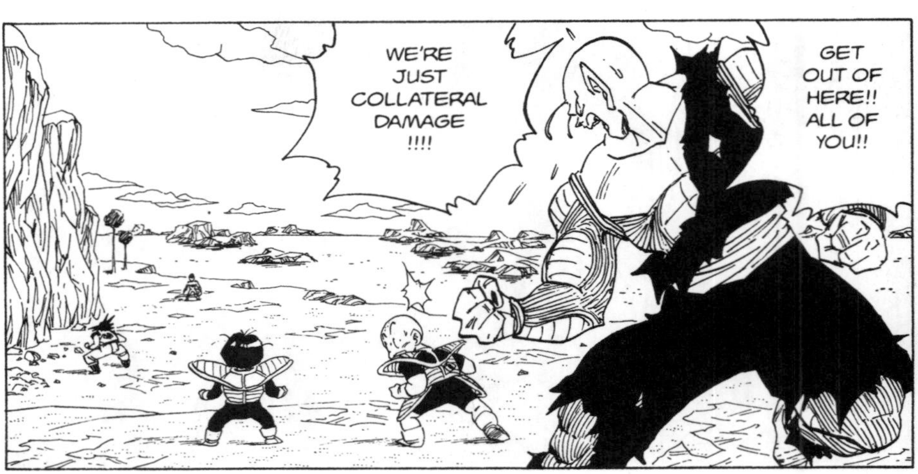
GET OUT OF HERE!! ALL OF YOU!!
WE'RE JUST COLLATERAL DAMAGE !!!!

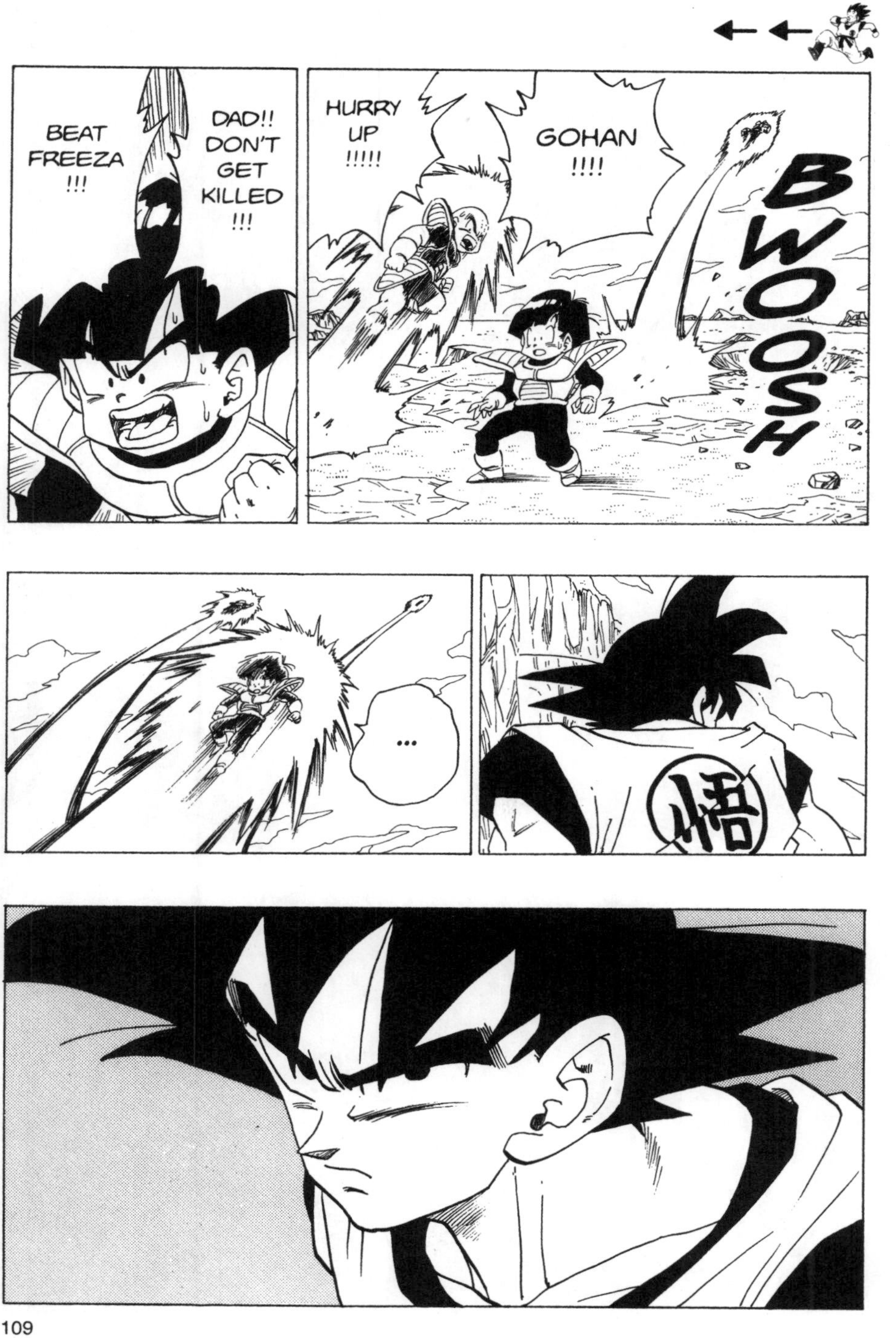
BWOOSH
GOHAN !!!!
HURRY UP !!!!!
DAD!! DON'T GET KILLED !!!
BEAT FREEZA !!!
...

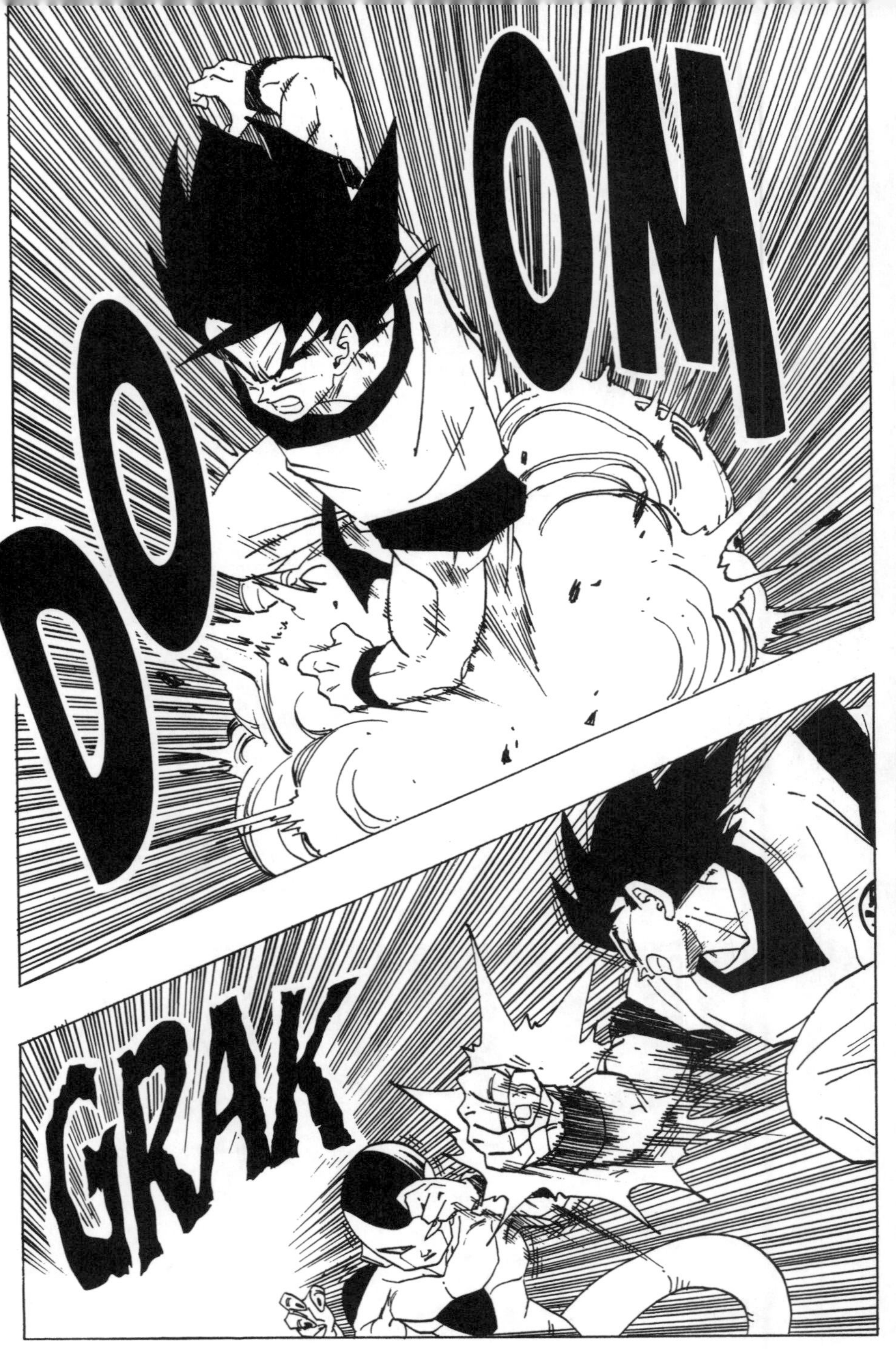
DOOOM
GRAK

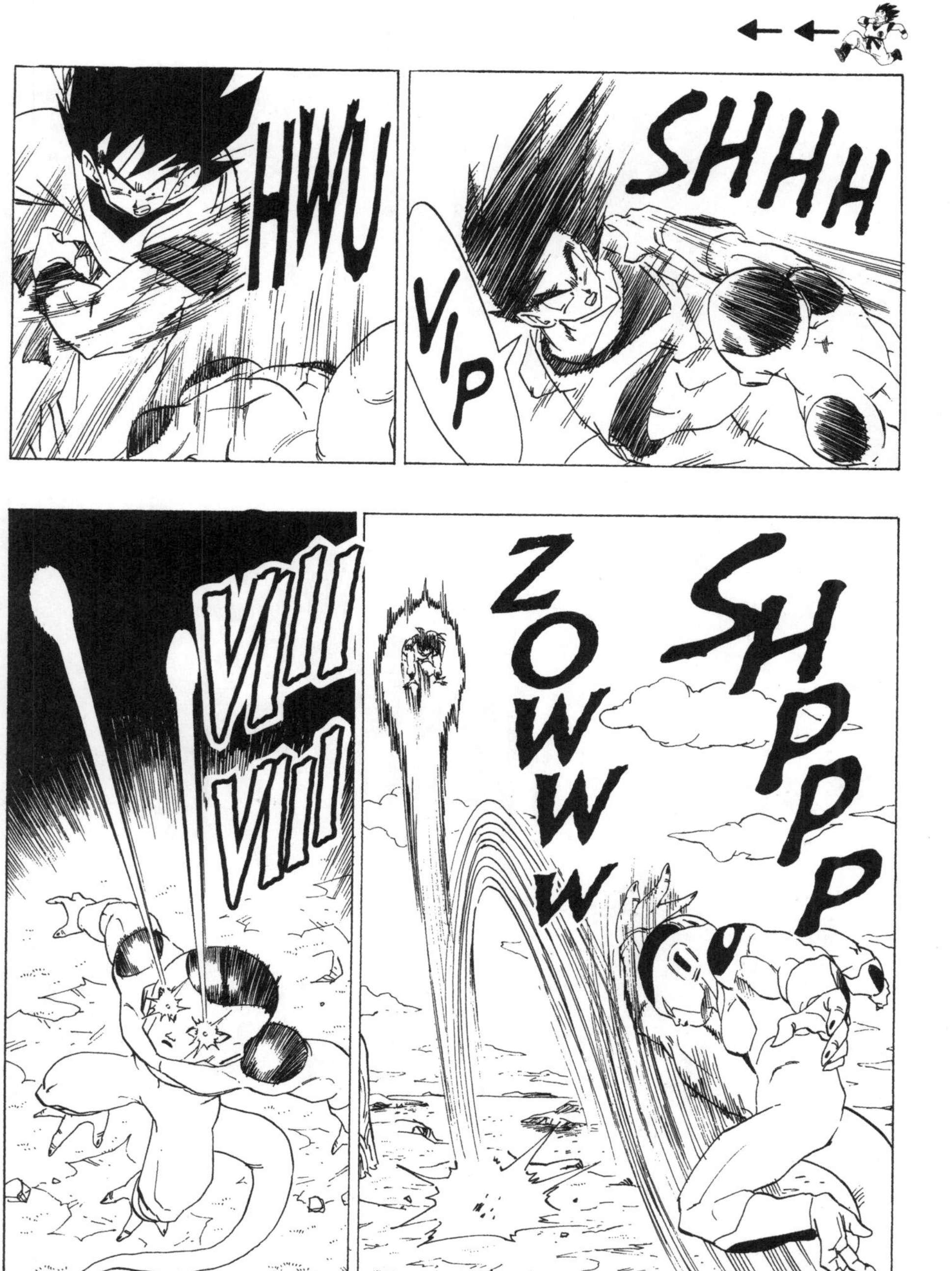
SHHH
VIP
HWU
SHPPP
ZOWWW
VIII
VIII

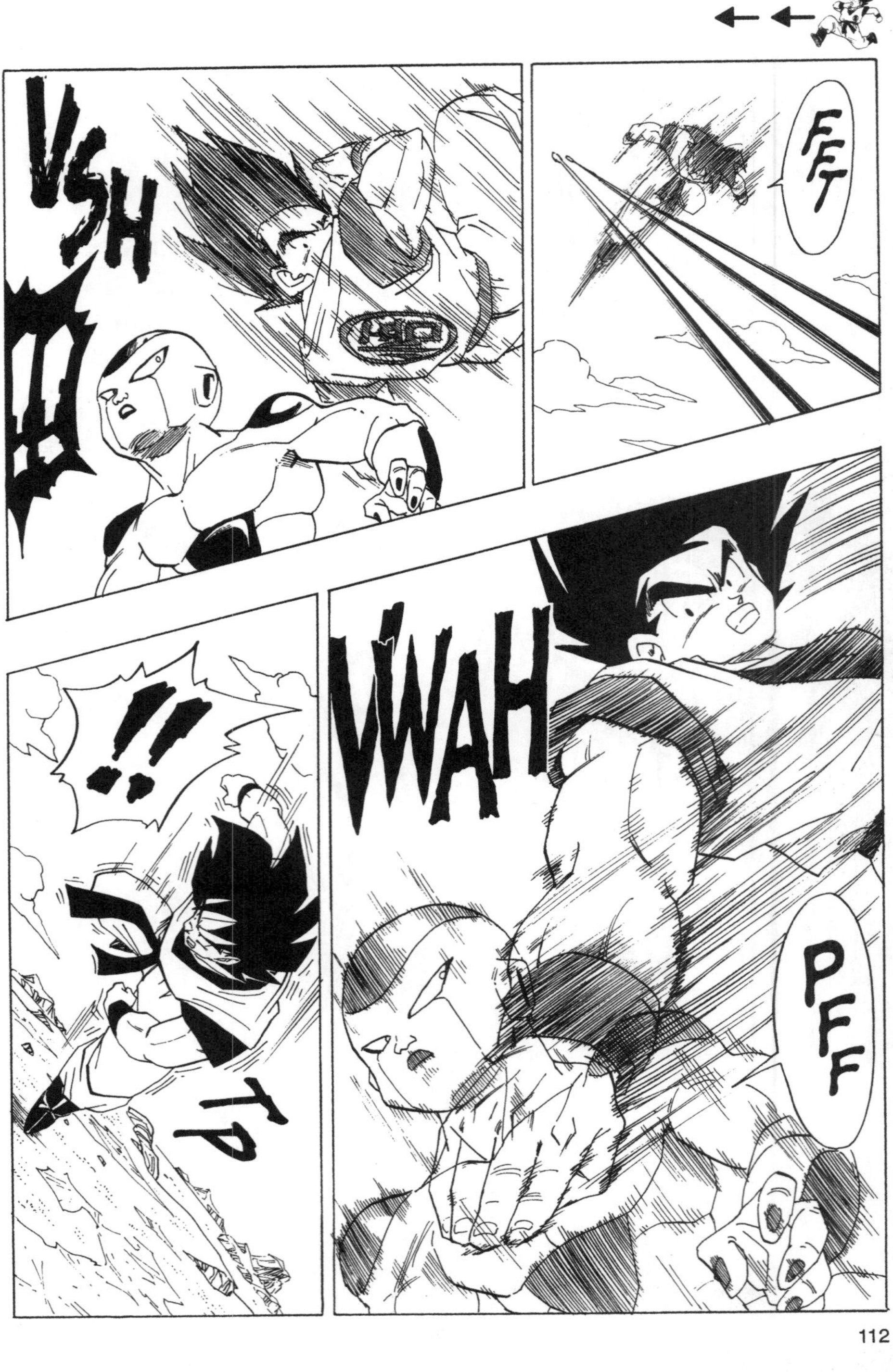
FFT
VSH!!
VWAH
PFF
!!
TP

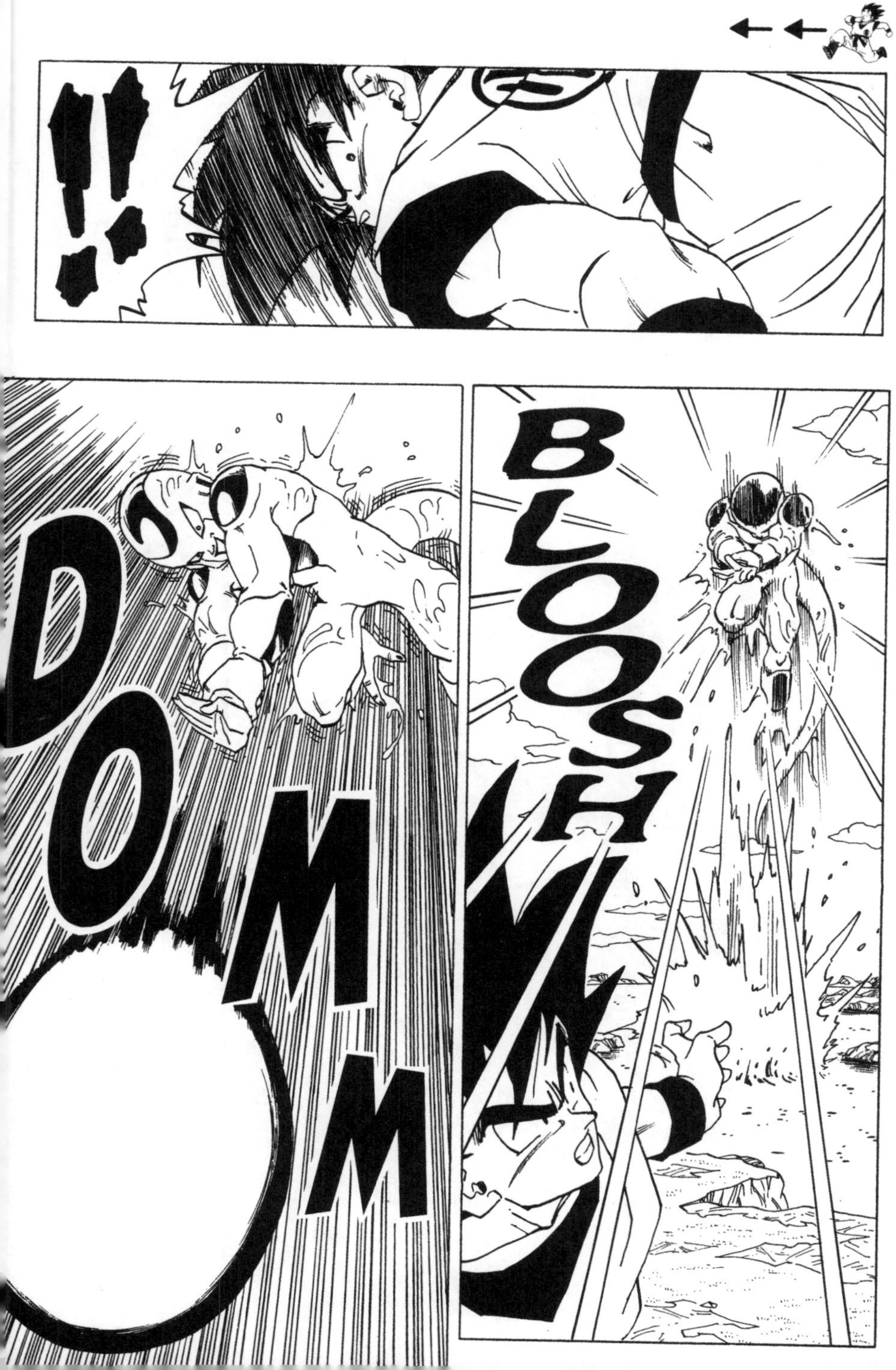
!!
BLOOSH
DOMMM

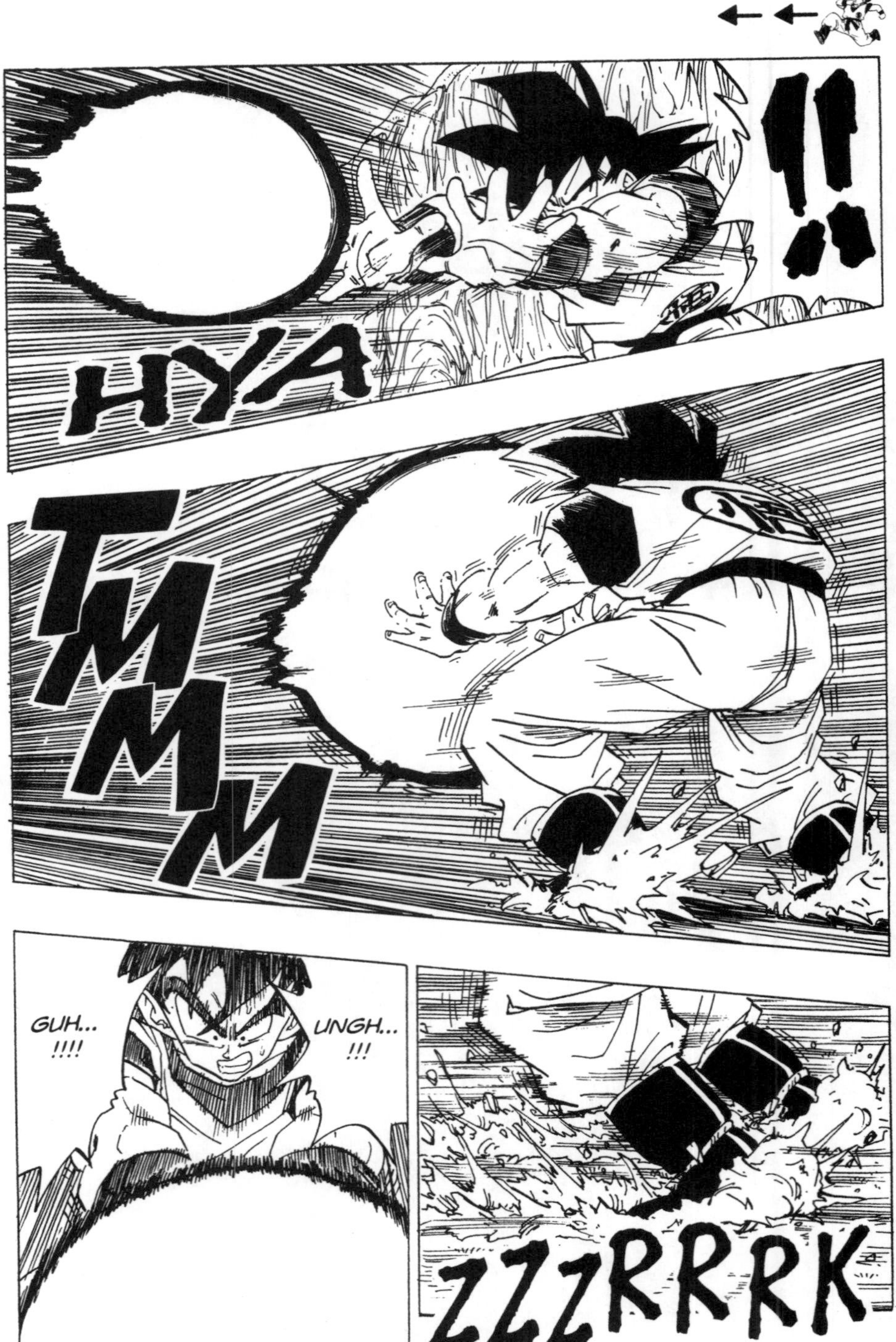
!!
HYA
TMMM
ZZZRRRK
UNGH... !!!
GUH... !!!!

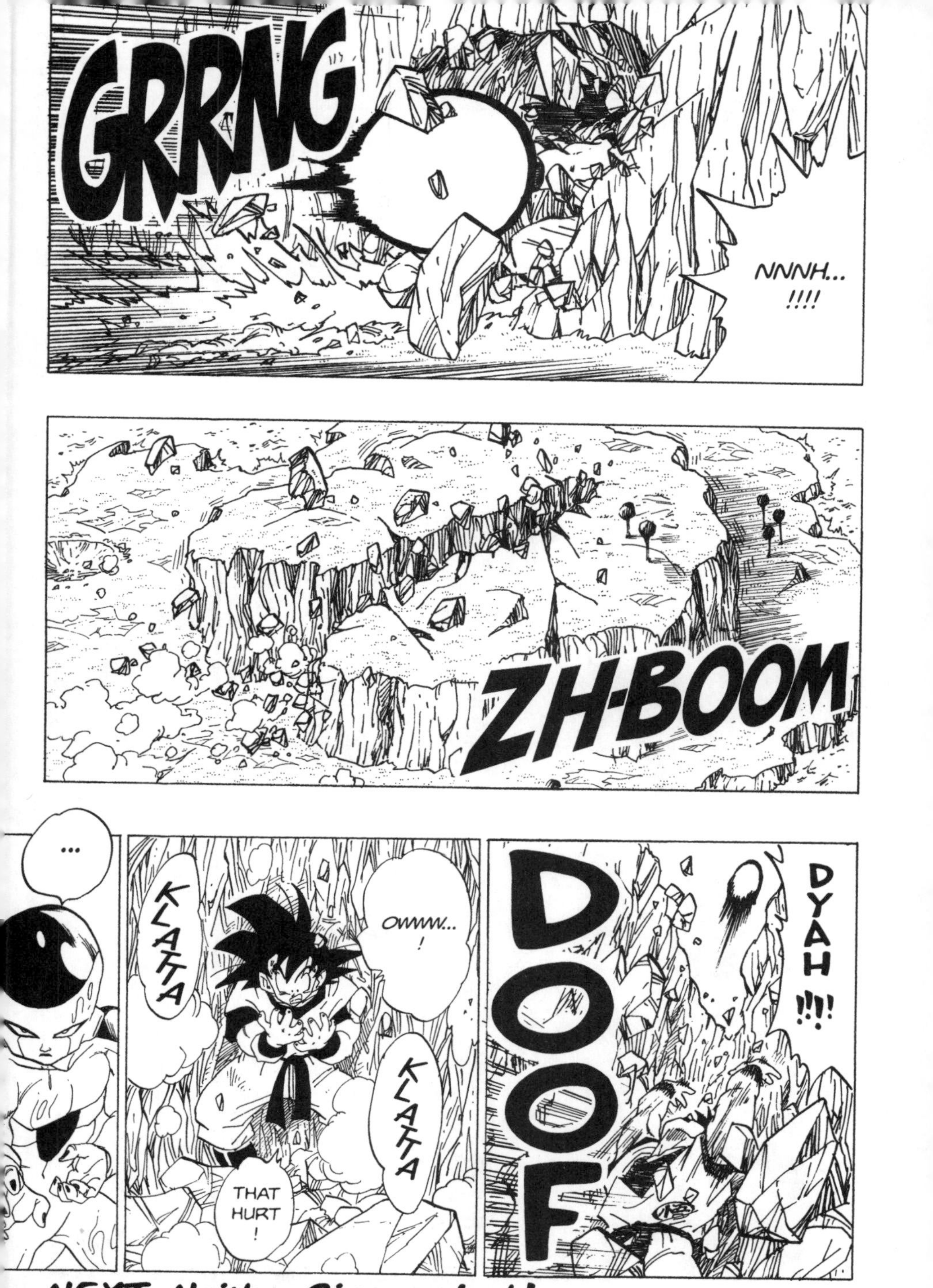
NNNH... !!!!
GRRNG
ZH-BOOM
DYAH !!!!
DOOF
OWWW... !
KLATTA
KLATTA
THAT HURT !
...

NEXT: Neither Gives an Inch!

# DBZ:115 • Underwater Battle

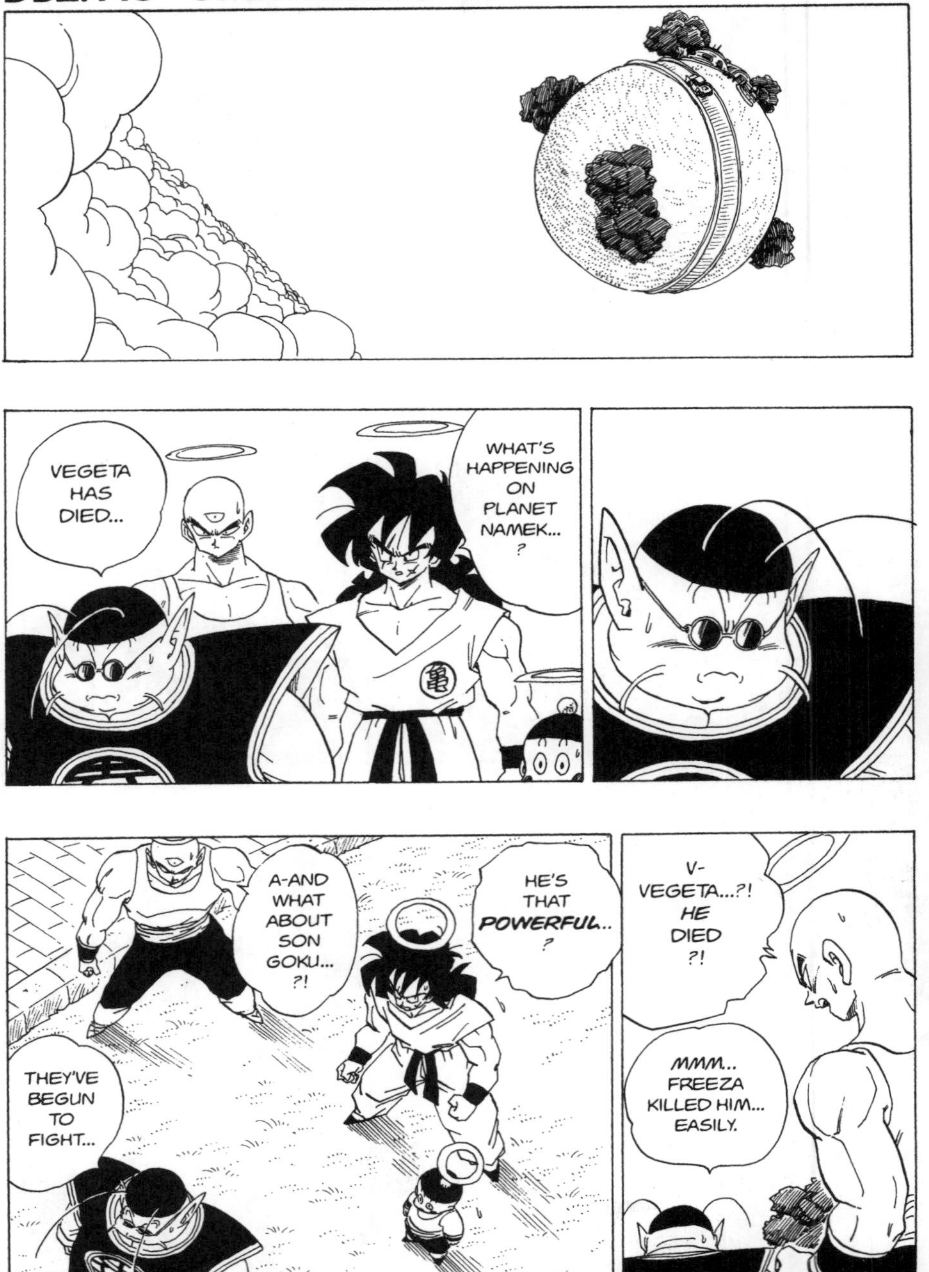
WHAT'S HAPPENING ON PLANET NAMEK...?
VEGETA HAS DIED...
V-VEGETA...?! HE DIED?!
MMM... FREEZA KILLED HIM... EASILY.
HE'S THAT **POWERFUL**...?
A-AND WHAT ABOUT SON GOKU...?!
THEY'VE BEGUN TO FIGHT...

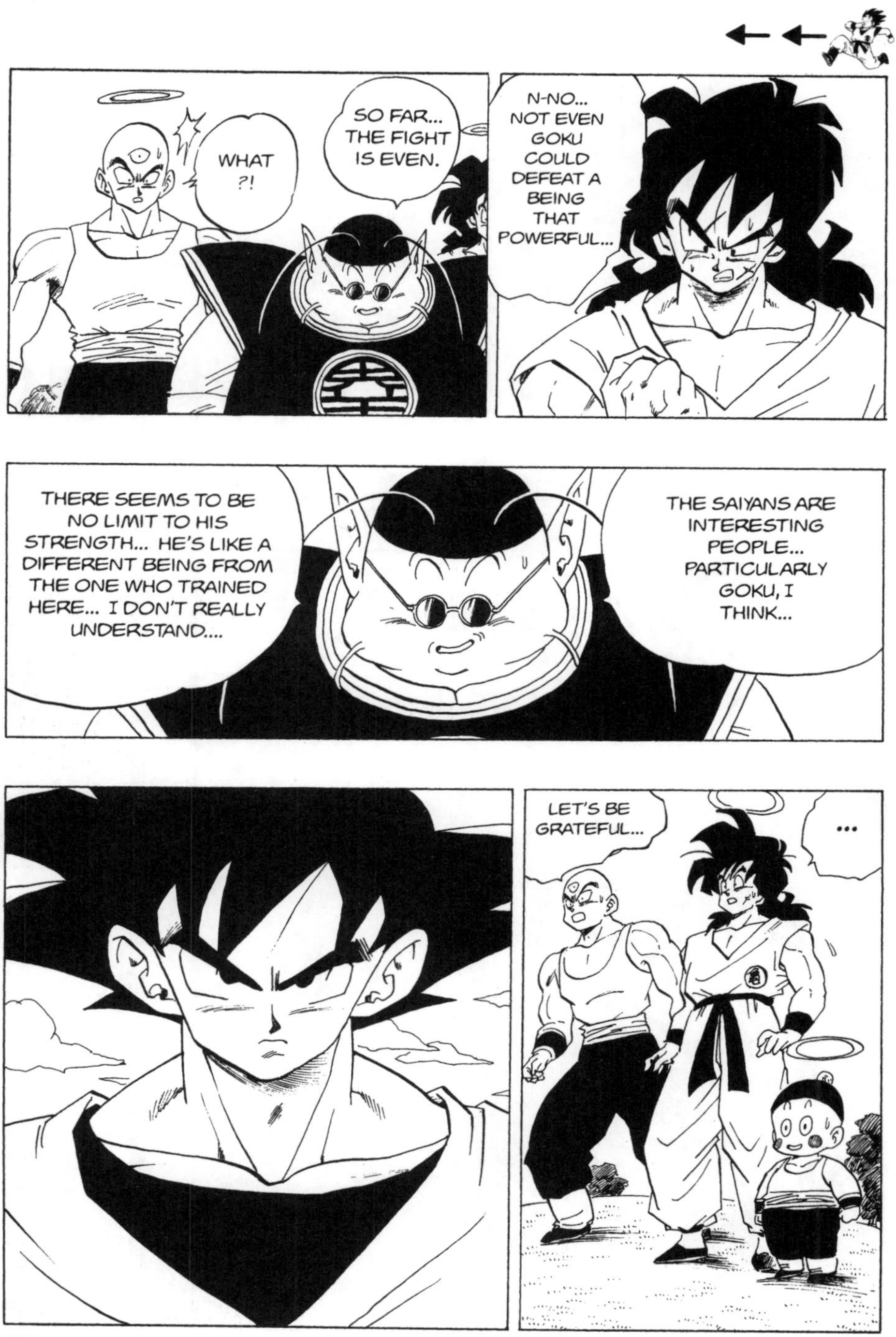
N-NO... NOT EVEN GOKU COULD DEFEAT A BEING THAT POWERFUL...
SO FAR... THE FIGHT IS EVEN.
WHAT ?!
THE SAIYANS ARE INTERESTING PEOPLE... PARTICULARLY GOKU, I THINK...
THERE SEEMS TO BE NO LIMIT TO HIS STRENGTH... HE'S LIKE A DIFFERENT BEING FROM THE ONE WHO TRAINED HERE... I DON'T REALLY UNDERSTAND....
...
LET'S BE GRATEFUL...

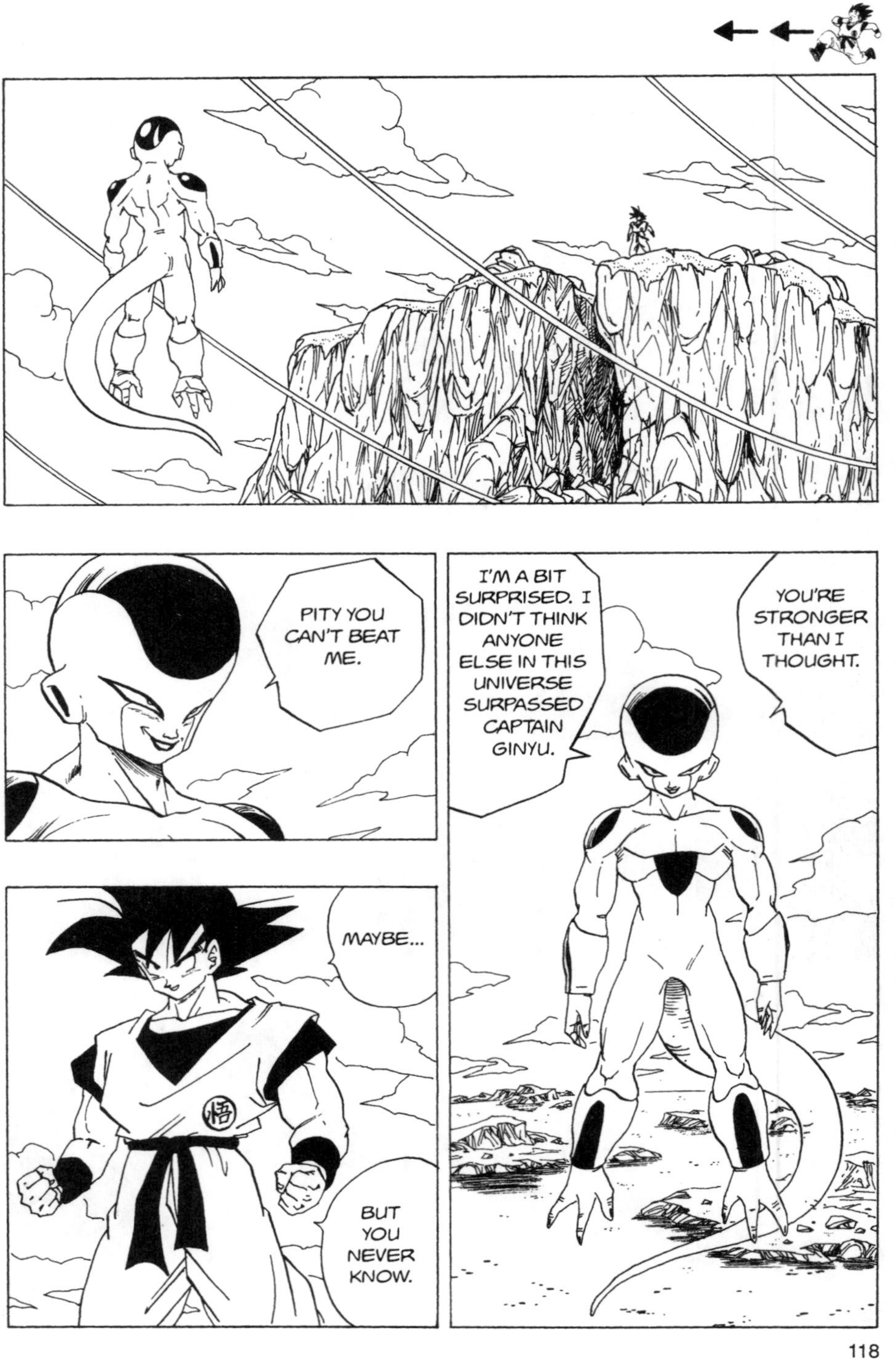
YOU'RE STRONGER THAN I THOUGHT.
I'M A BIT SURPRISED. I DIDN'T THINK ANYONE ELSE IN THIS UNIVERSE SURPASSED CAPTAIN GINYU.
PITY YOU CAN'T BEAT ME.
MAYBE...
BUT YOU NEVER KNOW.

YOU'LL KNOW.

OH, HO HO...

SSS

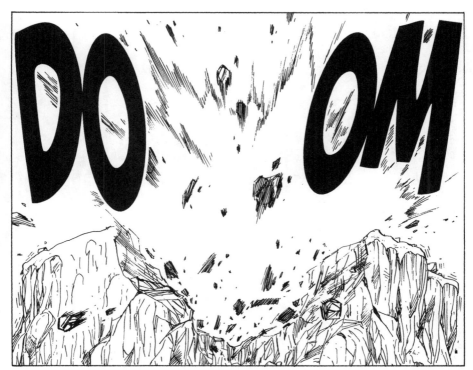

DOOM

RIGHT BACK AT YOU!!

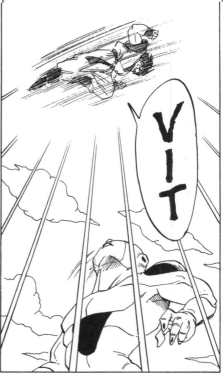

VIT

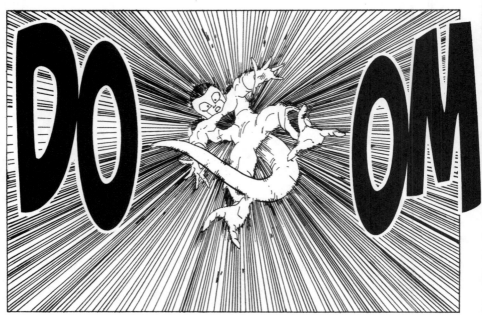

DOOM

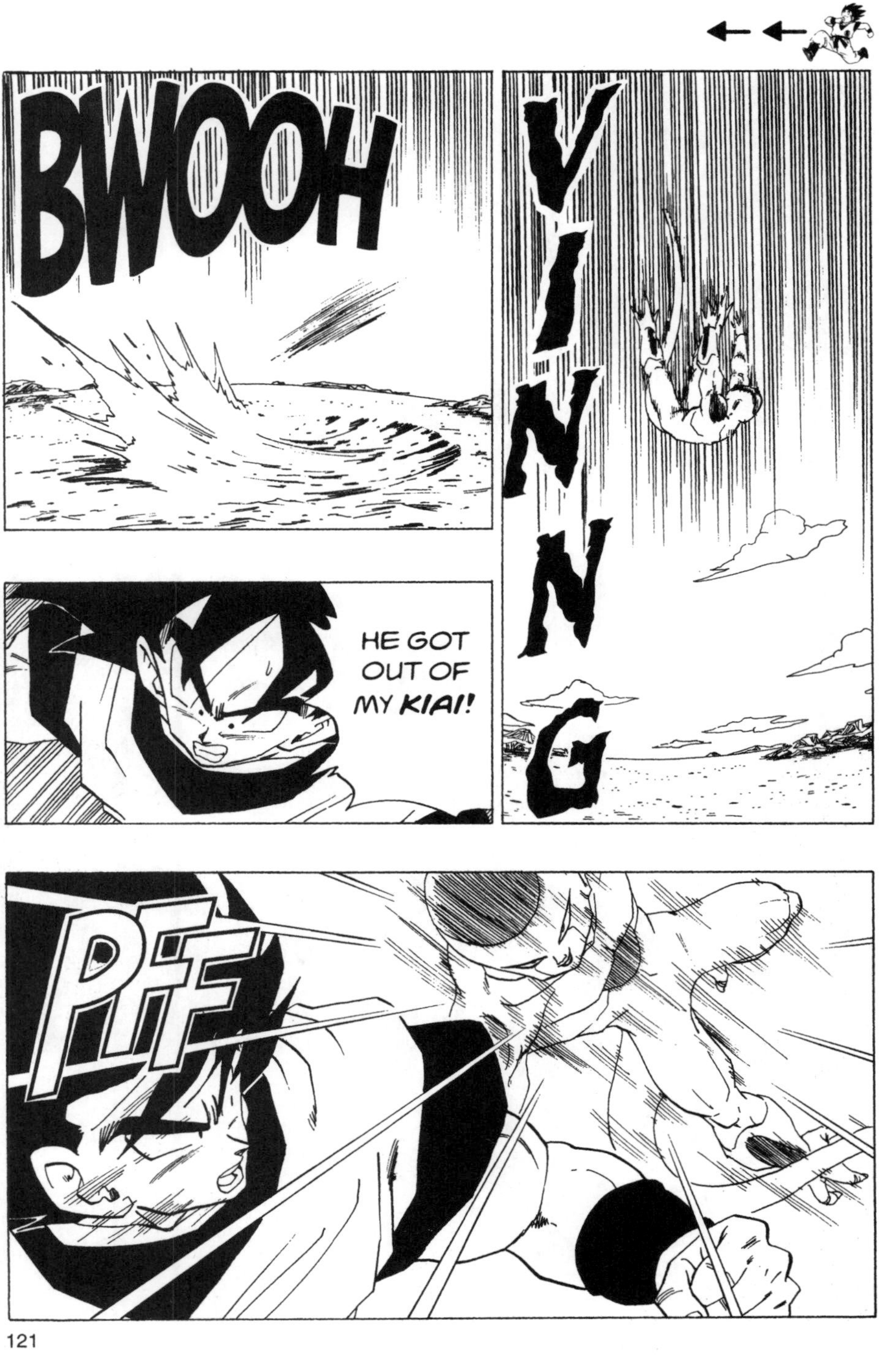
VINNG
BWOOH
HE GOT OUT OF MY KIAI!
PFF

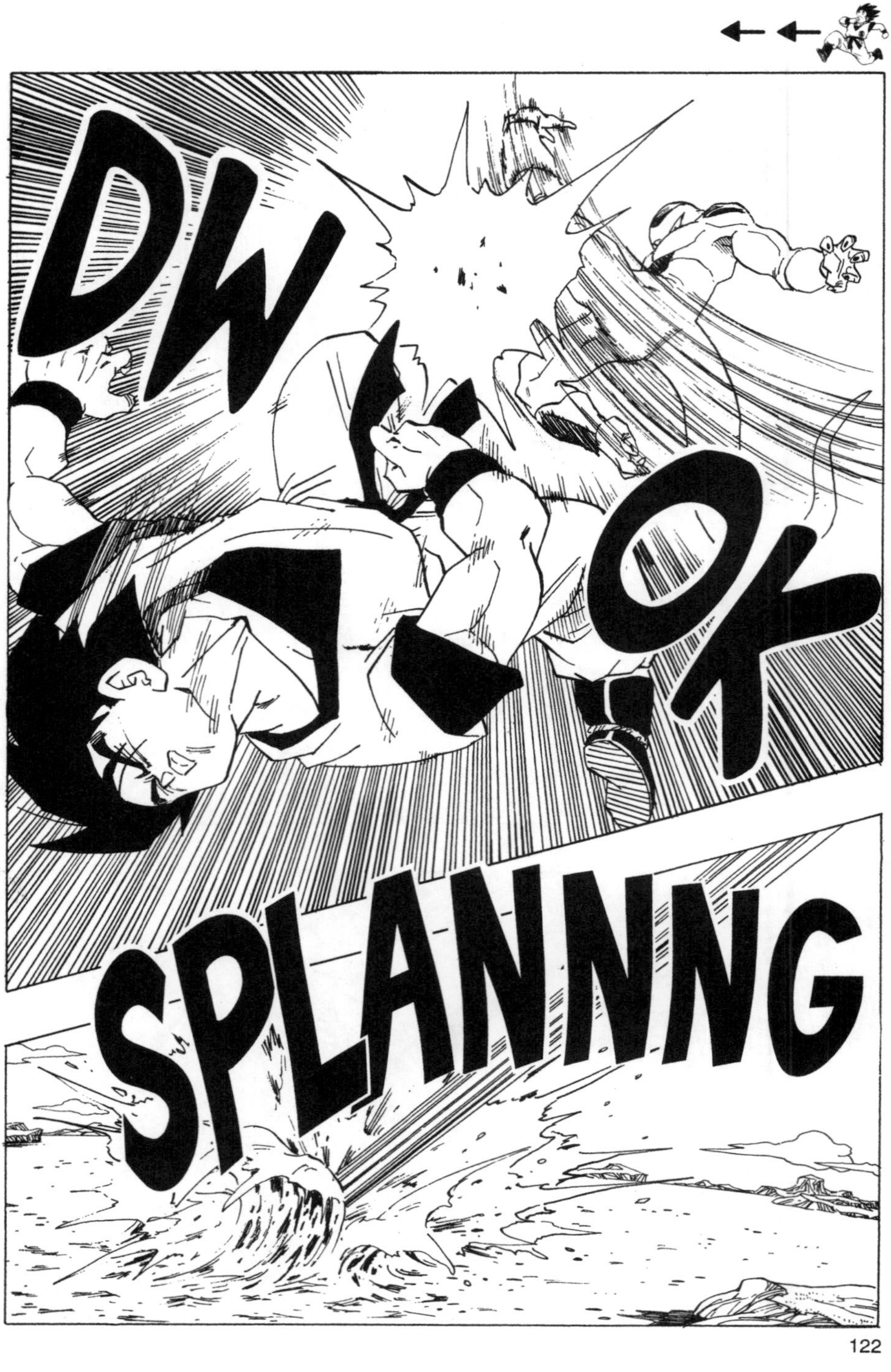
DWOK
SPLANNG

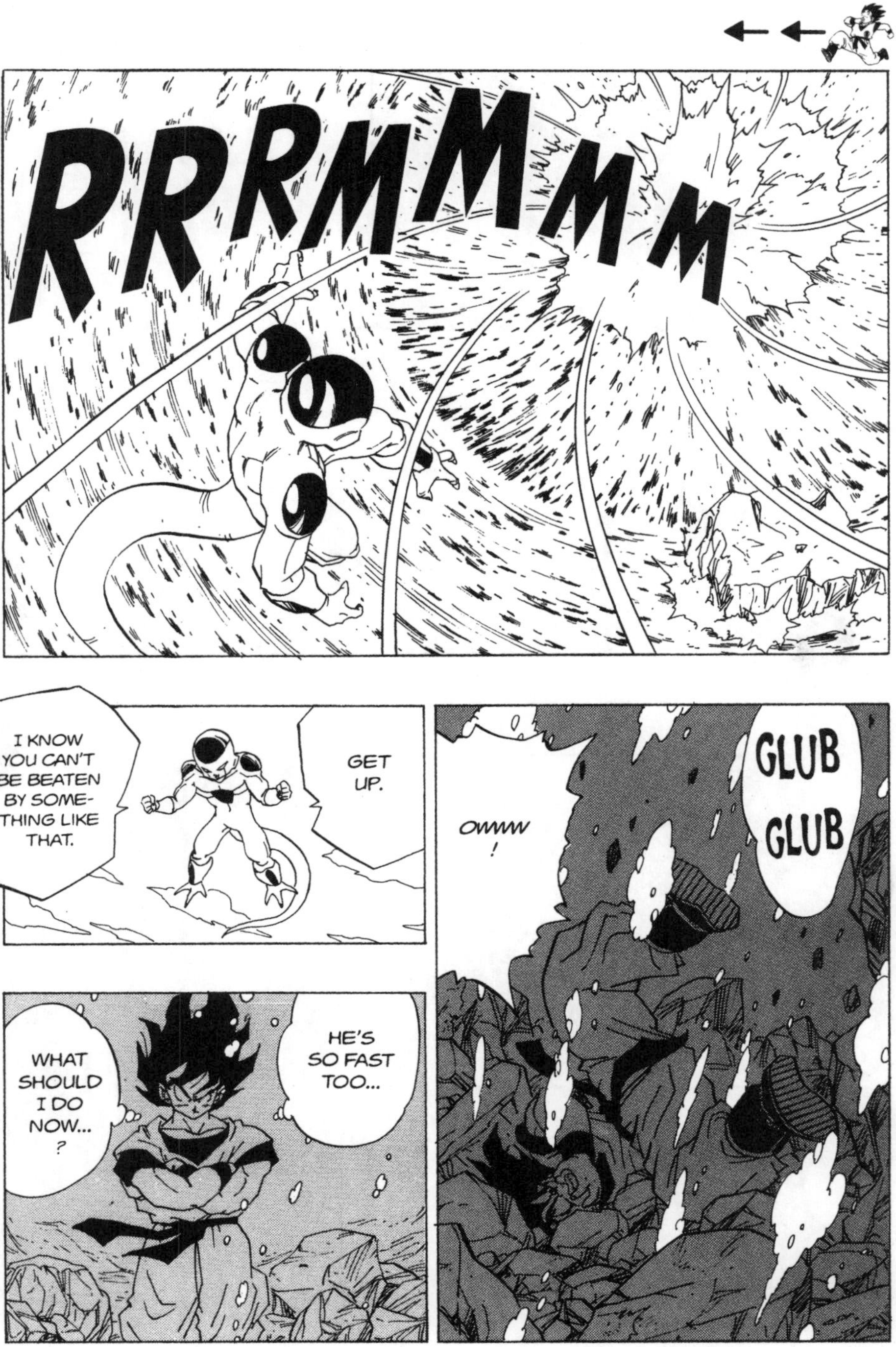
RRRMMMM
GLUB GLUB
OWWW !
GET UP.
I KNOW YOU CAN'T BE BEATEN BY SOME-THING LIKE THAT.
HE'S SO FAST TOO...
WHAT SHOULD I DO NOW... ?

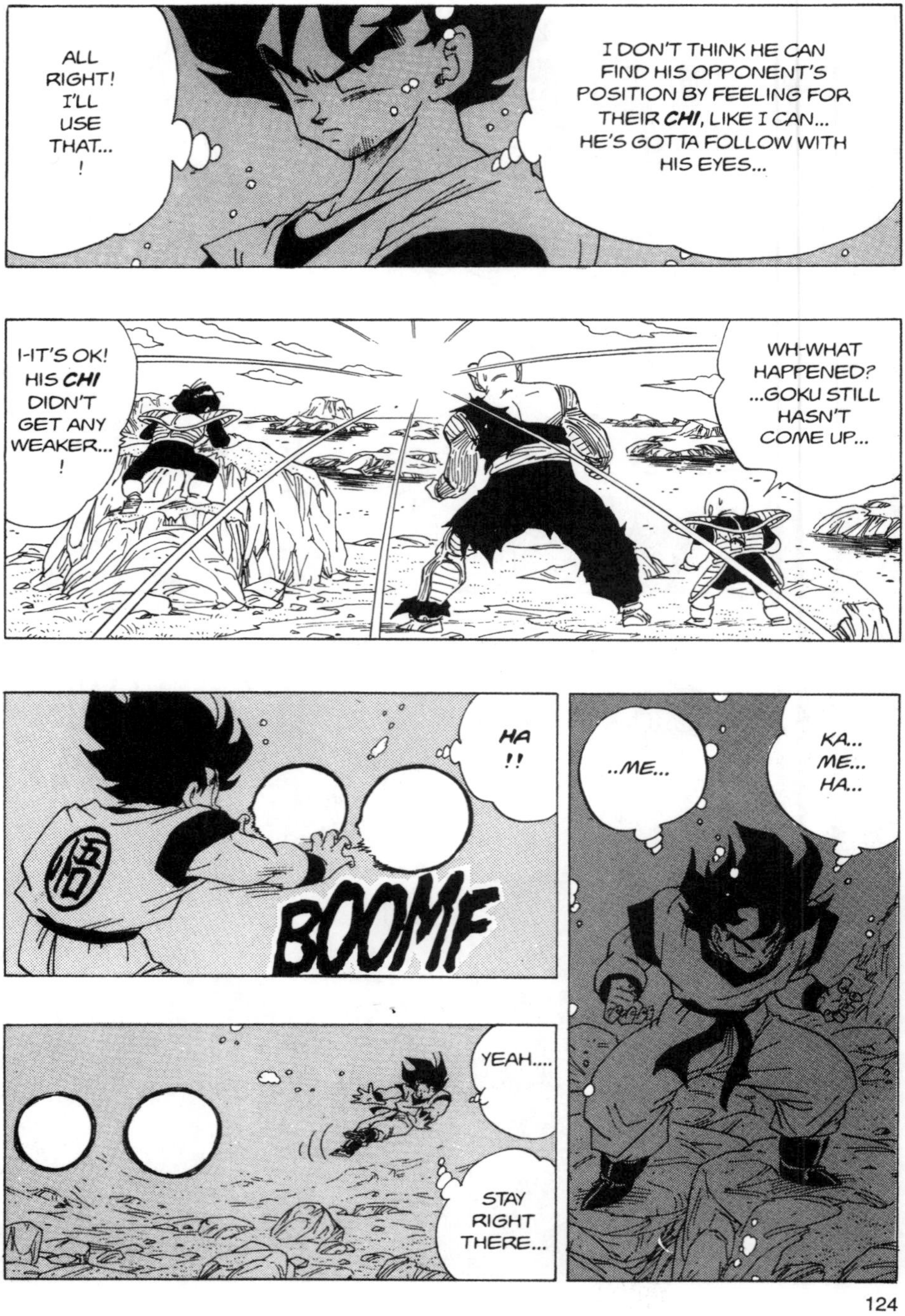

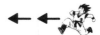

I DON'T THINK HE CAN FIND HIS OPPONENT'S POSITION BY FEELING FOR THEIR **CHI**, LIKE I CAN... HE'S GOTTA FOLLOW WITH HIS EYES...
ALL RIGHT! I'LL USE THAT... !
WH-WHAT HAPPENED? ...GOKU STILL HASN'T COME UP...
I-IT'S OK! HIS **CHI** DIDN'T GET ANY WEAKER... !
KA... ME... HA...
..ME...
HA !!
BOOMF
YEAH....
STAY RIGHT THERE...

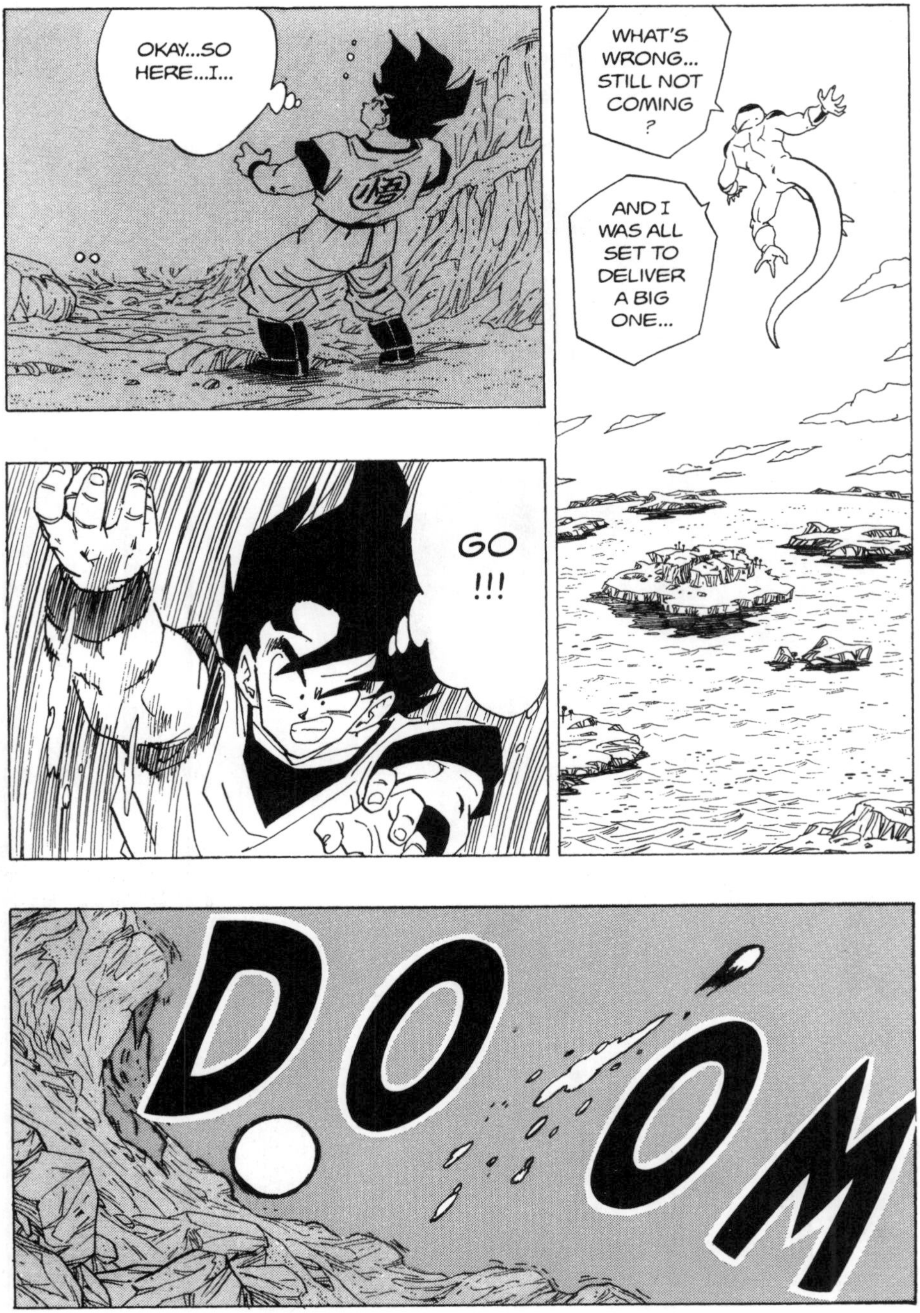
WHAT'S WRONG... STILL NOT COMING ?
AND I WAS ALL SET TO DELIVER A BIG ONE...
OKAY...SO HERE...I...
GO !!!
DOOM

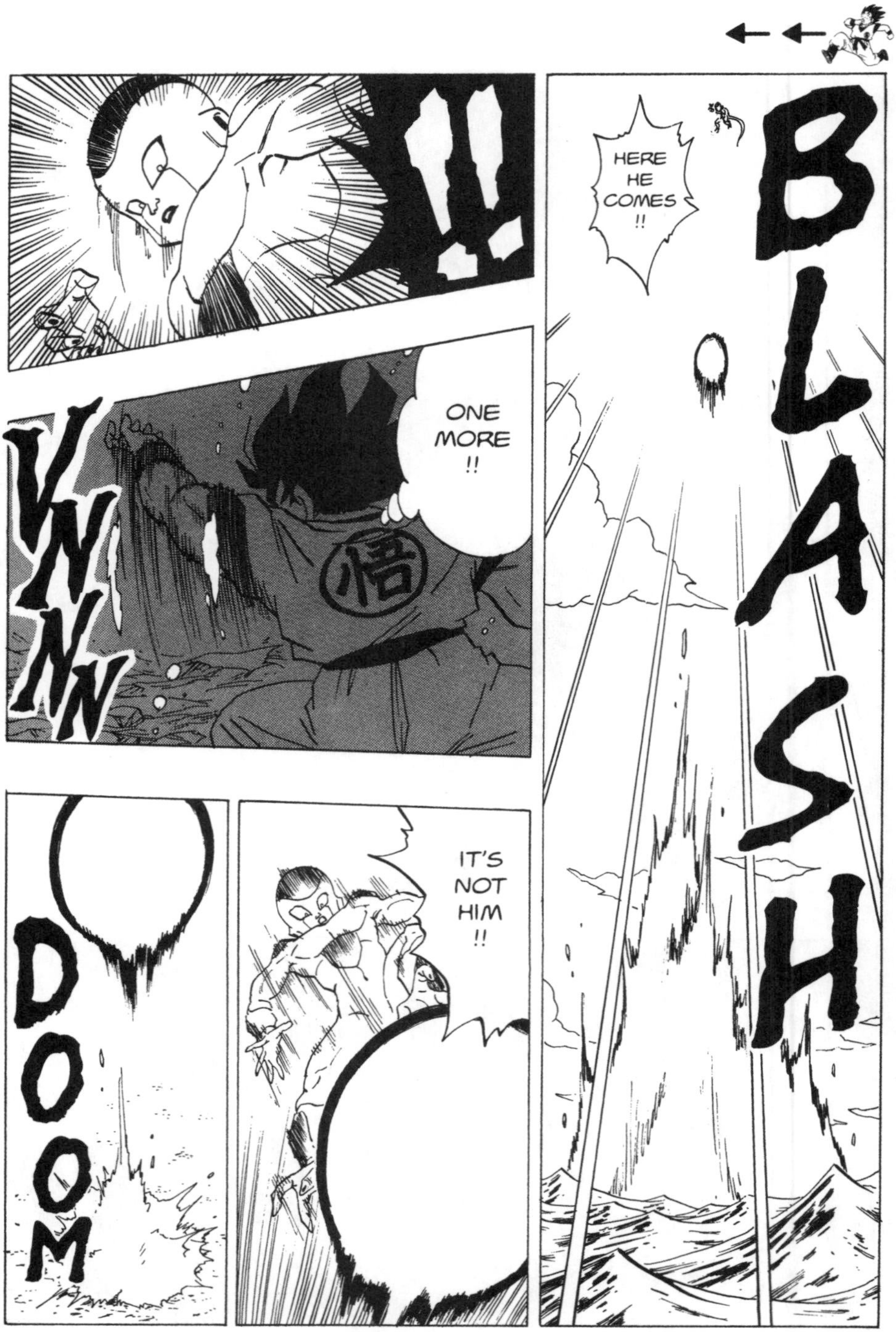
HERE HE COMES !!
BLASH
!!
VNNNN
ONE MORE !!
IT'S NOT HIM !!
DOOM

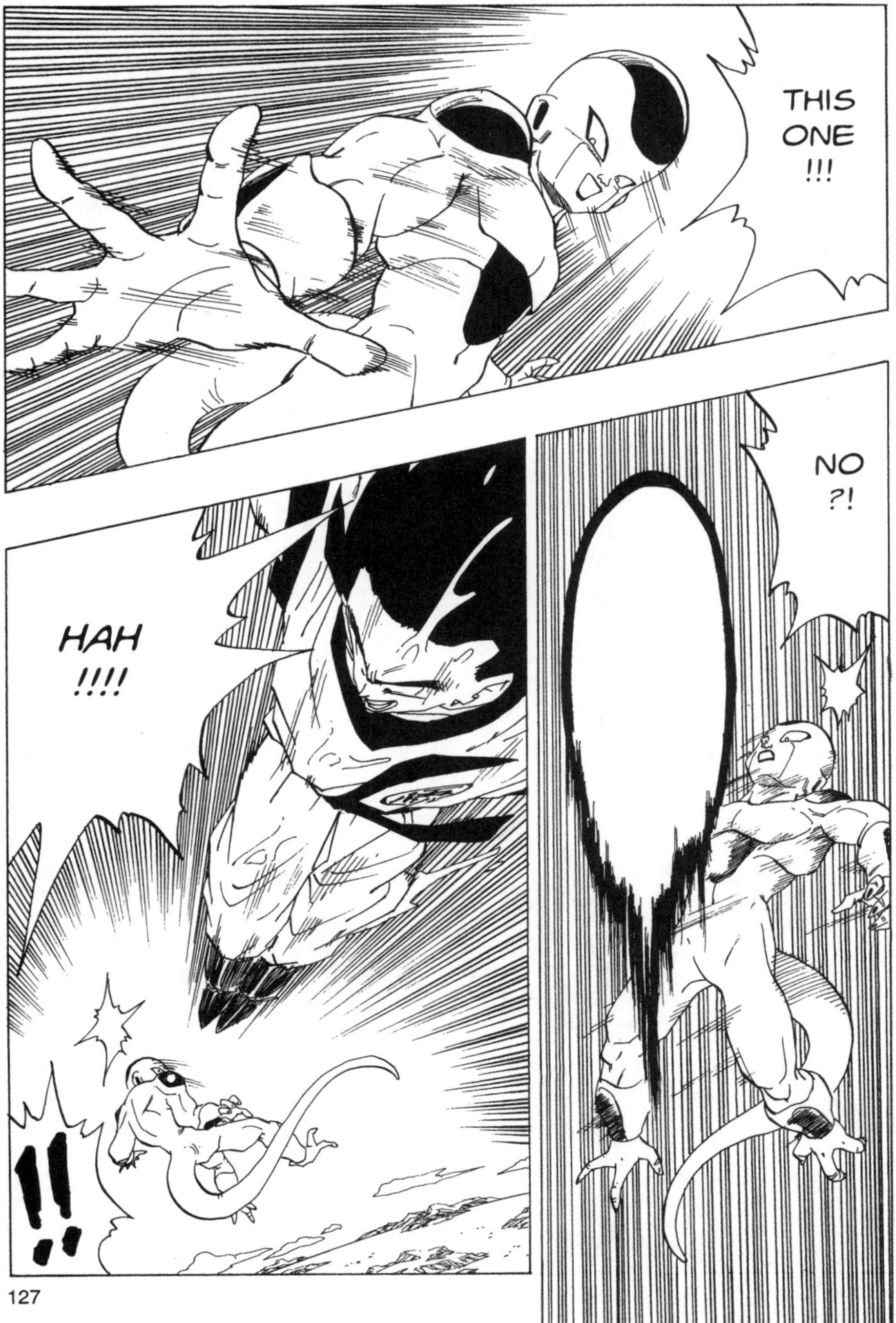
THIS ONE !!!
NO ?!
HAH !!!!
!!

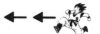

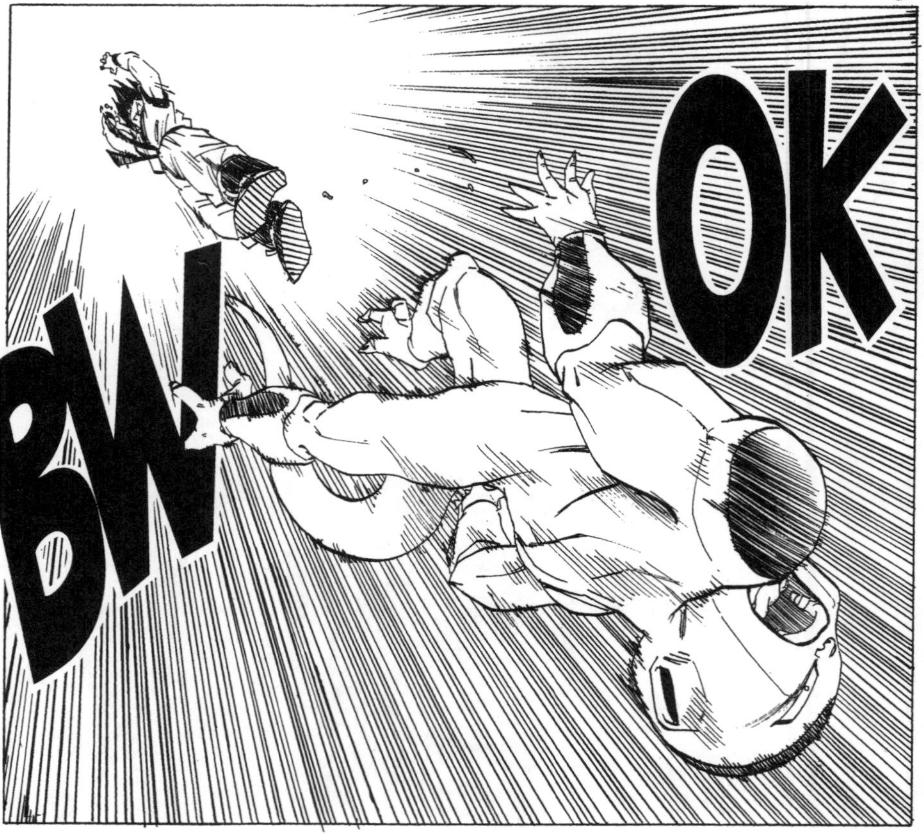
BWOK

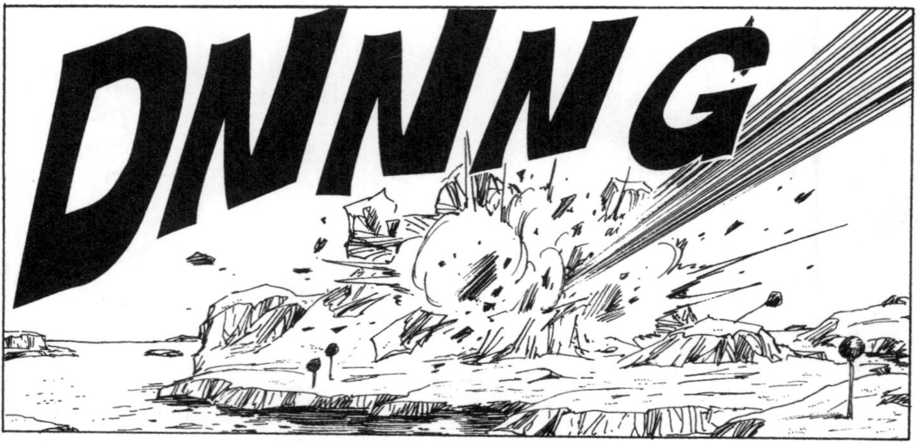
DNNNG

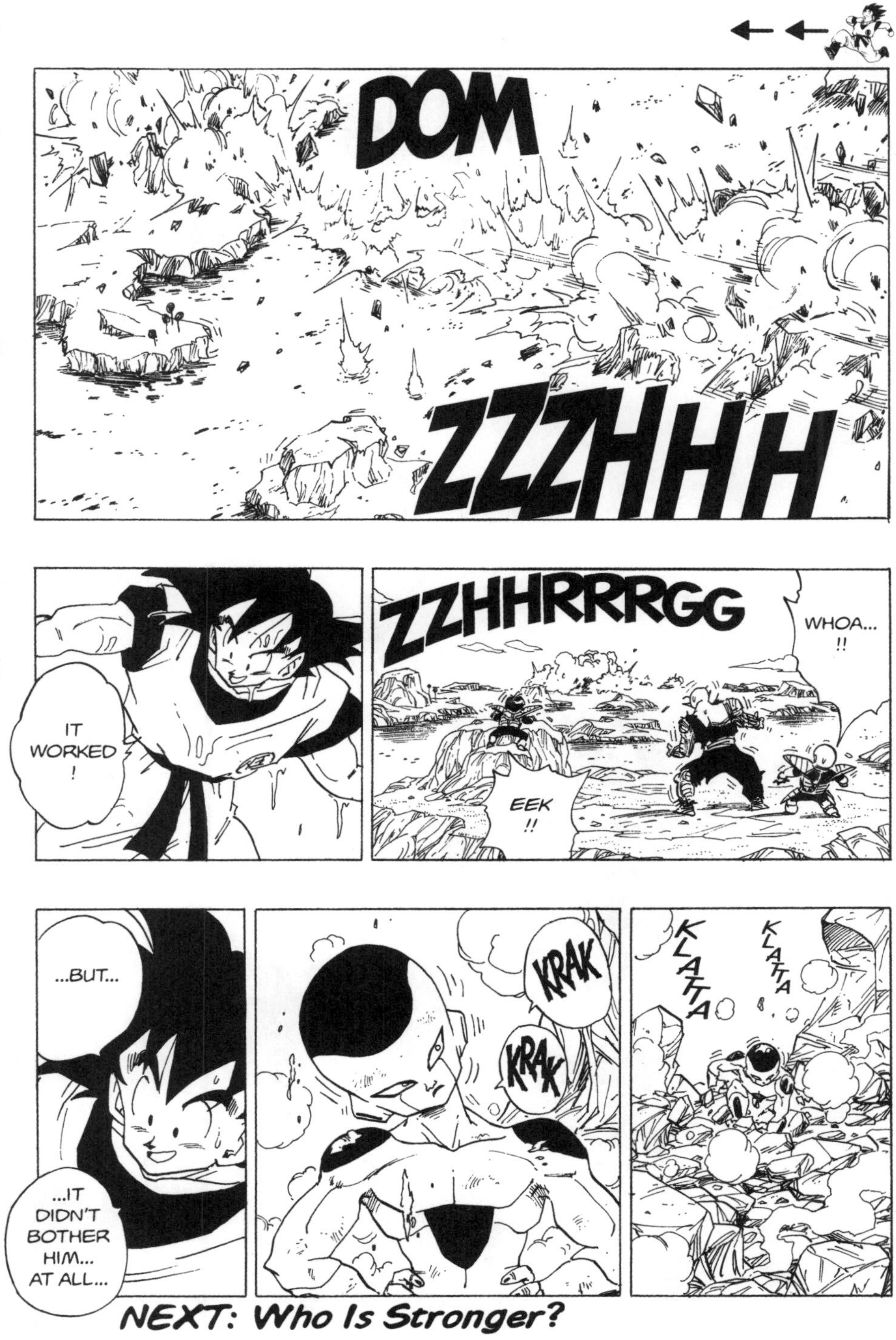
DOM
ZZZHHH
ZZHHRRRGG
WHOA... !!
EEK !!
IT WORKED !
KLATTA
KLATTA
KRAK
KRAK
...BUT...
...IT DIDN'T BOTHER HIM... AT ALL...

**NEXT: Who Is Stronger?**

# DBZ:116 • Aerial Battle

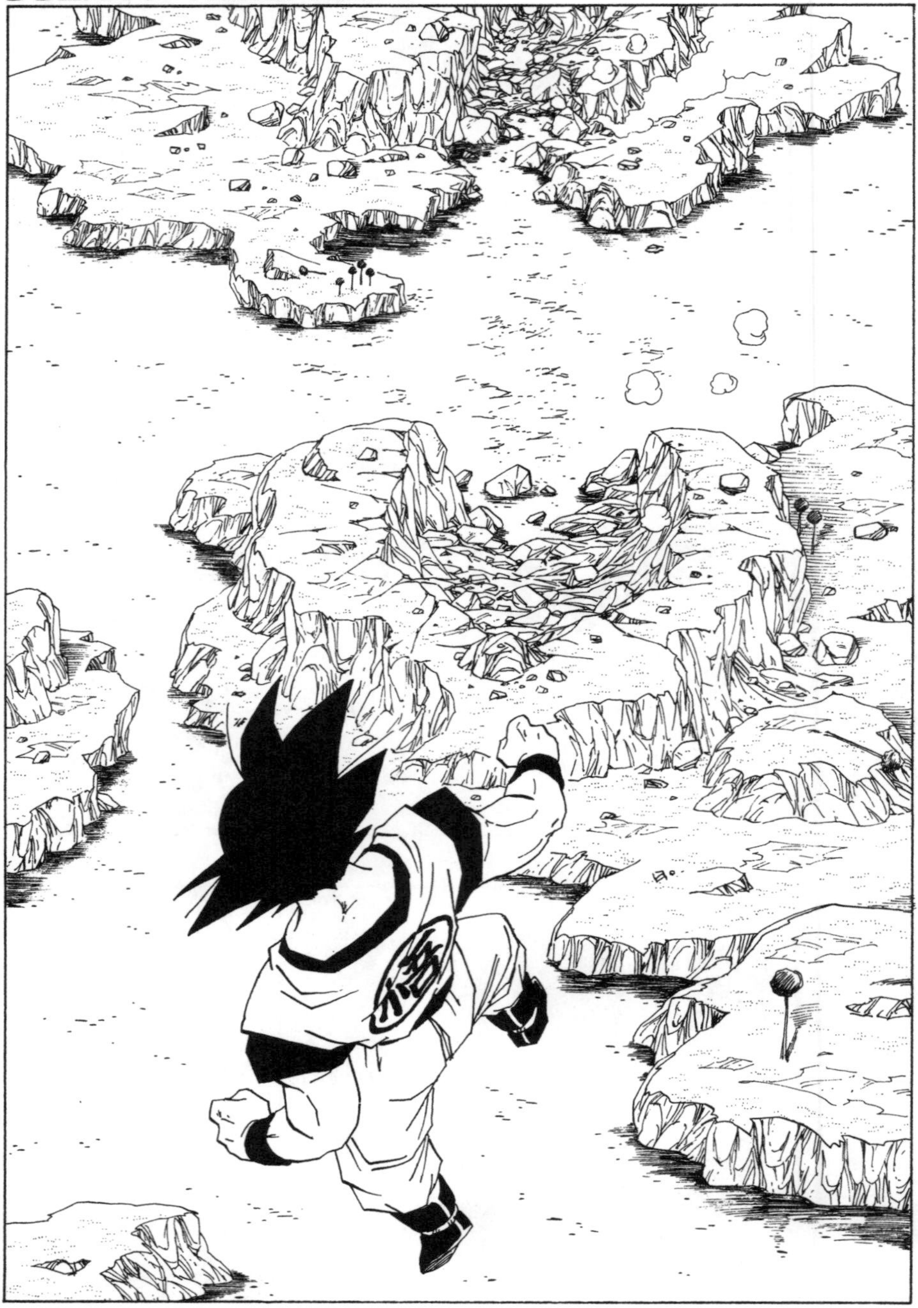

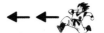

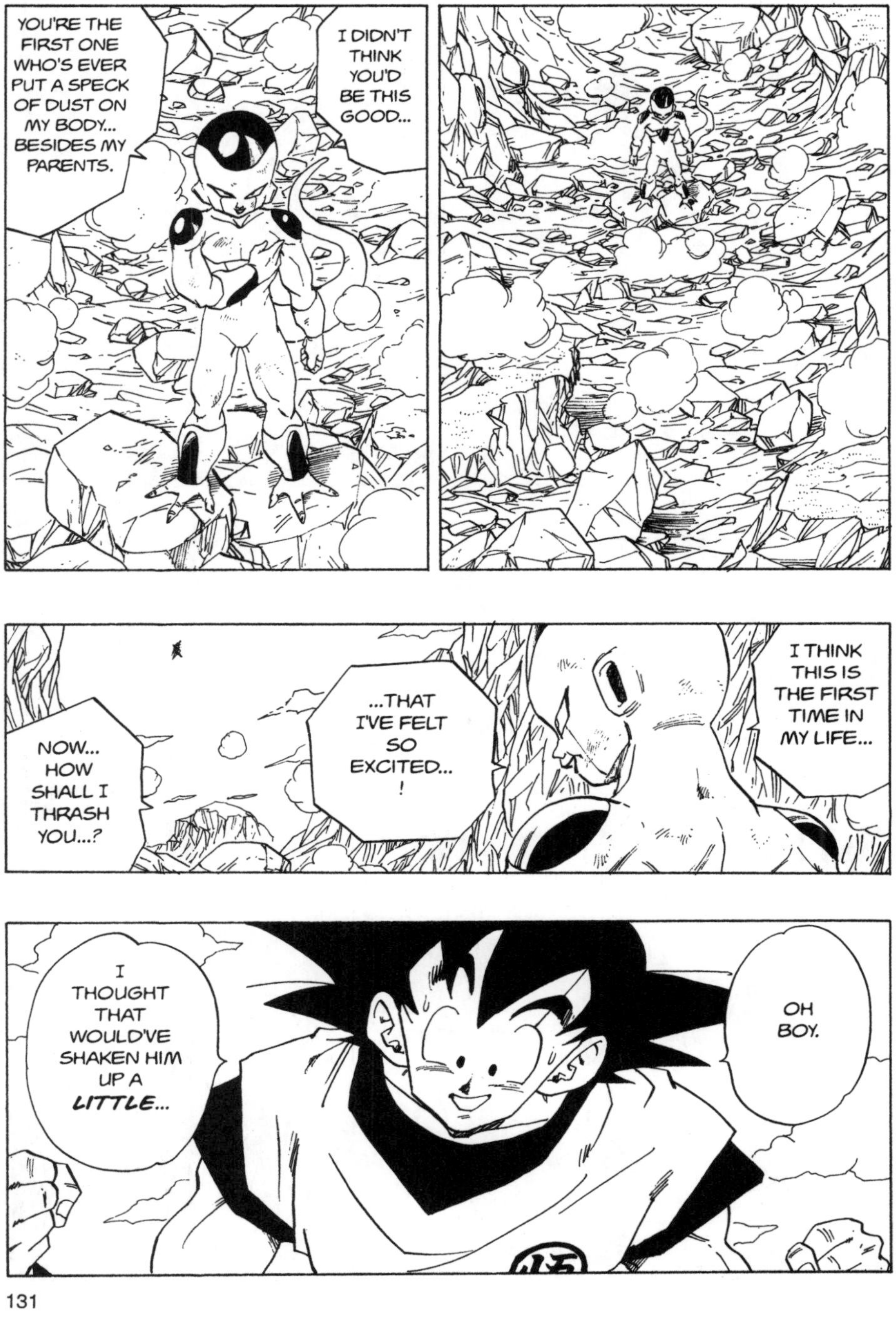
I DIDN'T THINK YOU'D BE THIS GOOD...
YOU'RE THE FIRST ONE WHO'S EVER PUT A SPECK OF DUST ON MY BODY... BESIDES MY PARENTS.
I THINK THIS IS THE FIRST TIME IN MY LIFE...
...THAT I'VE FELT SO EXCITED...!
NOW... HOW SHALL I THRASH YOU...?
OH BOY.
I THOUGHT THAT WOULD'VE SHAKEN HIM UP A *LITTLE*...

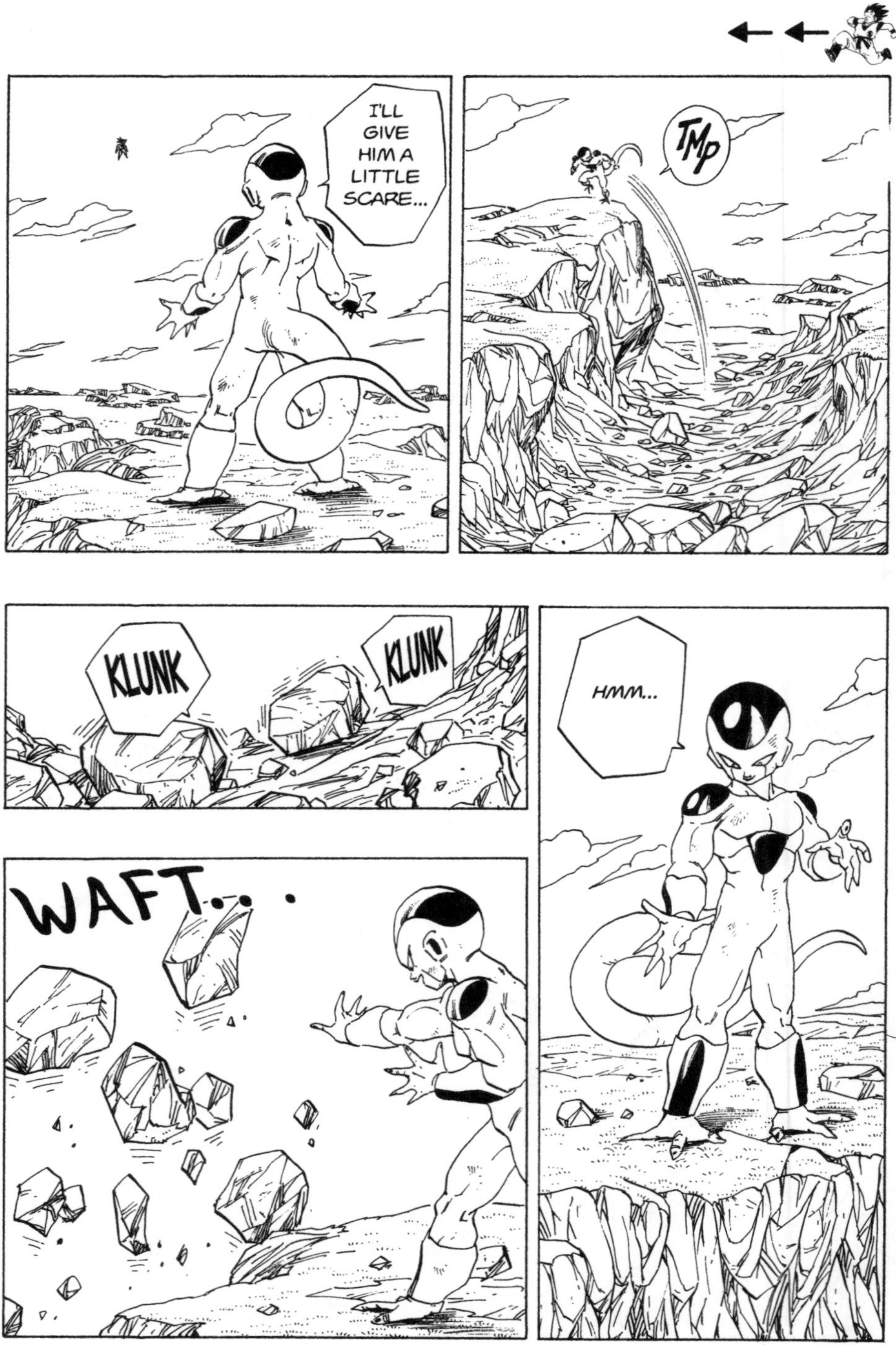
TMP
I'LL GIVE HIM A LITTLE SCARE...
HMM...
KLUNK
KLUNK
WAFT...

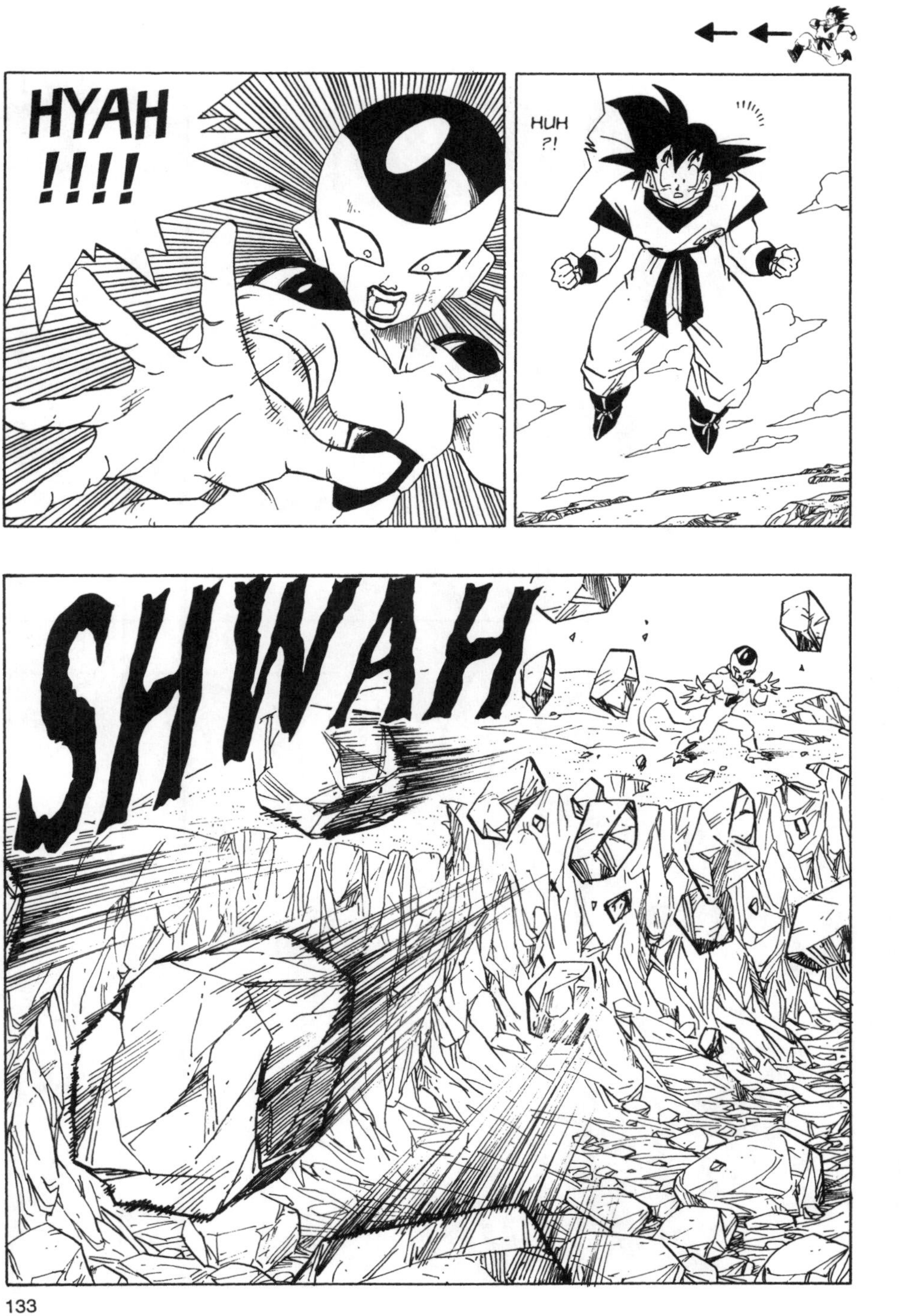
HUH ?!
HYAH !!!!
SHWAH

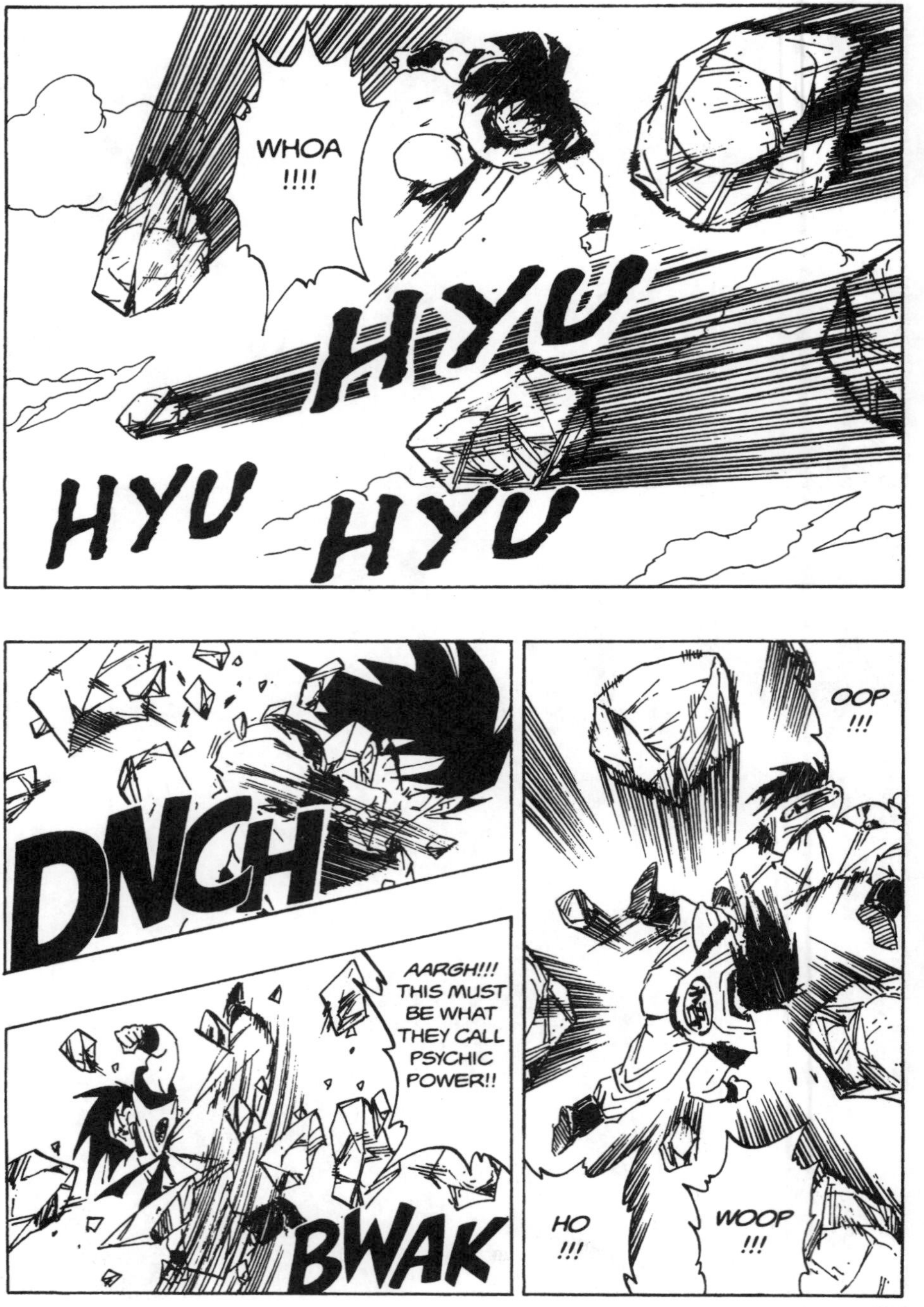
WHOA !!!!
HYU
HYU
HYU
OOP !!!
WOOP !!!
HO !!!
DNCH
AARGH!!! THIS MUST BE WHAT THEY CALL PSYCHIC POWER!!
BWAK

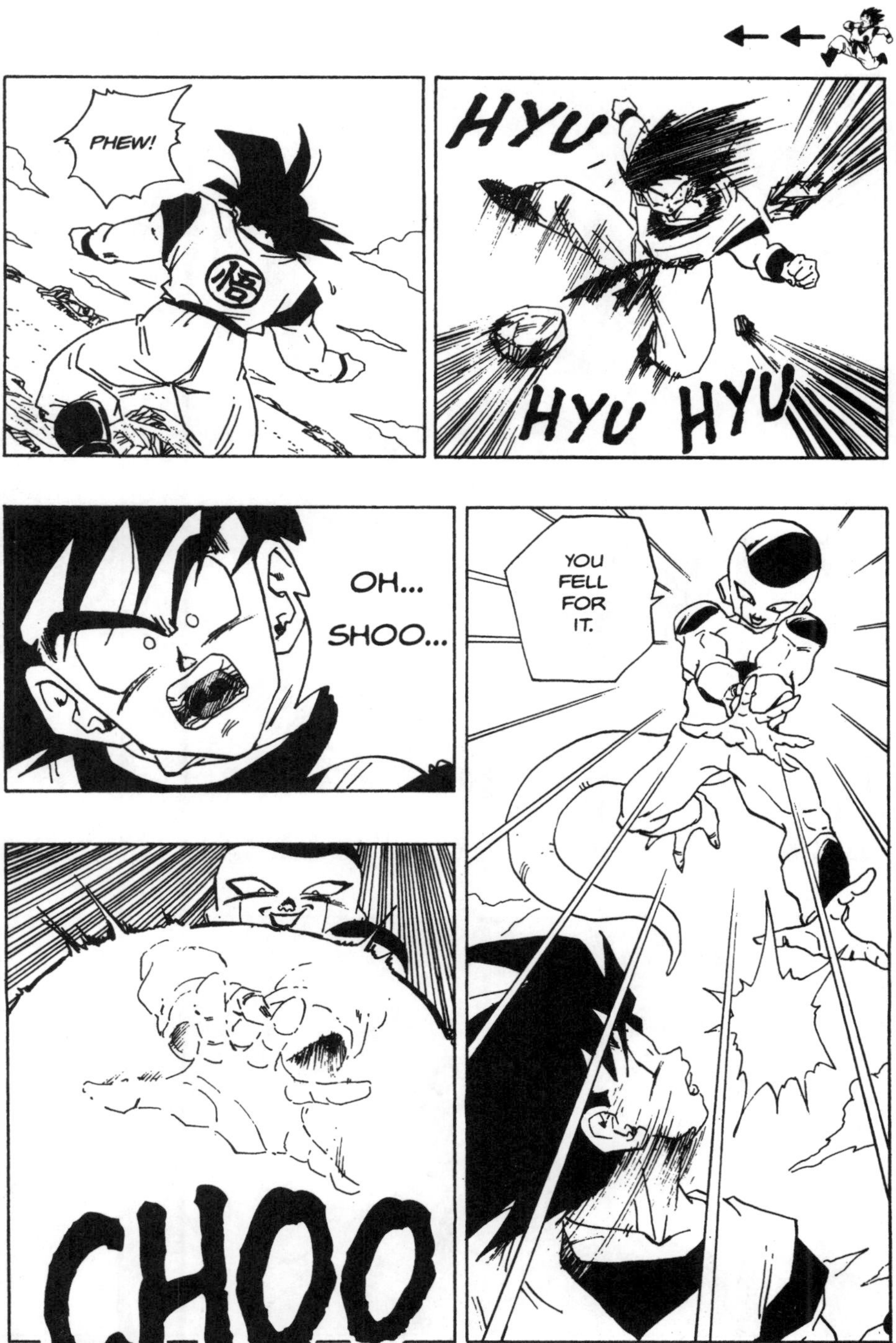
HYU
HYU HYU
PHEW!
YOU FELL FOR IT.
OH... SHOO...
CHOO

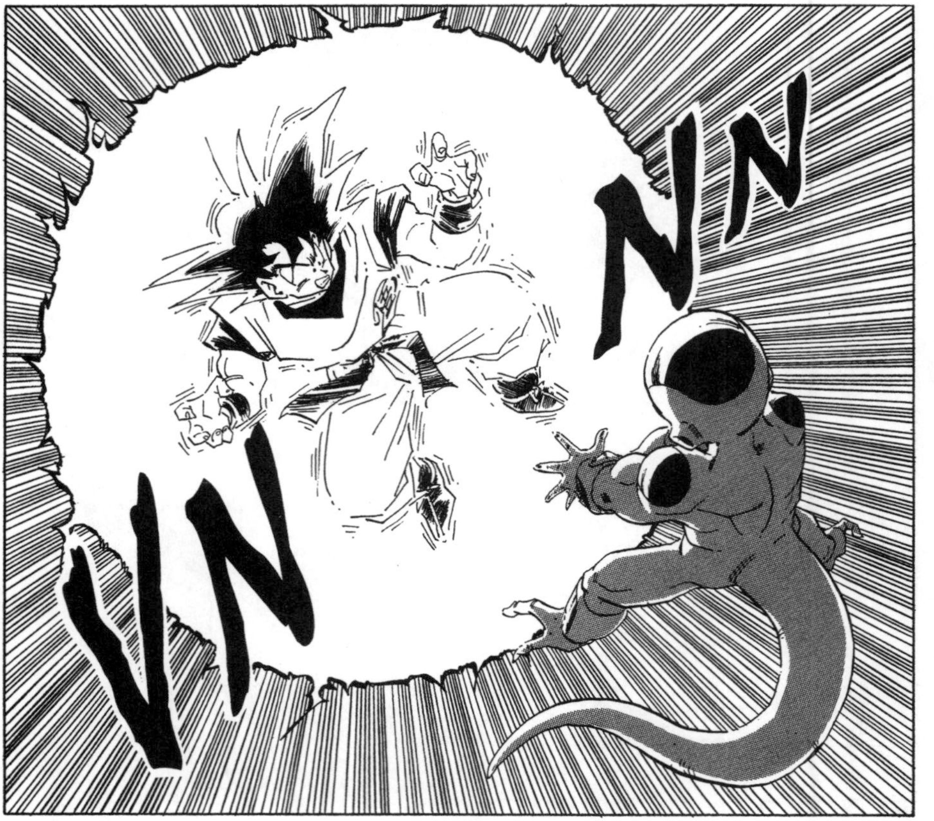
VN NN
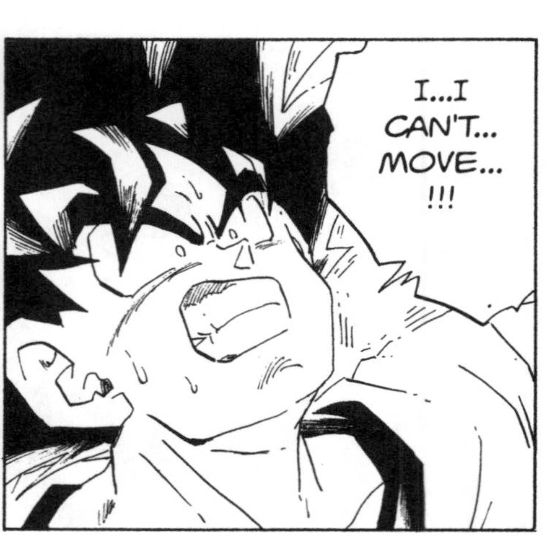
I...I CAN'T... MOVE... !!!
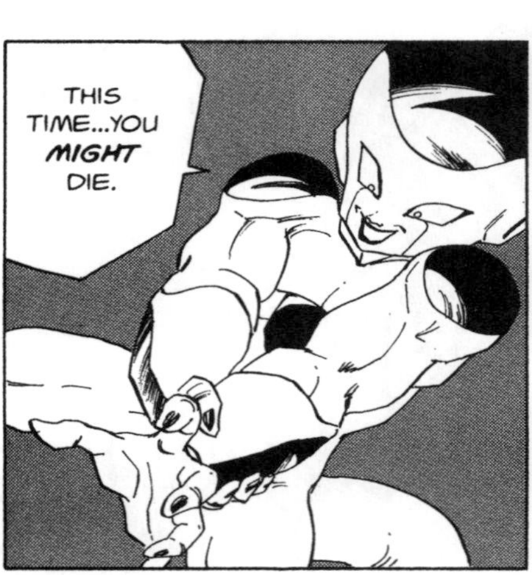
THIS TIME...YOU ***MIGHT*** DIE.

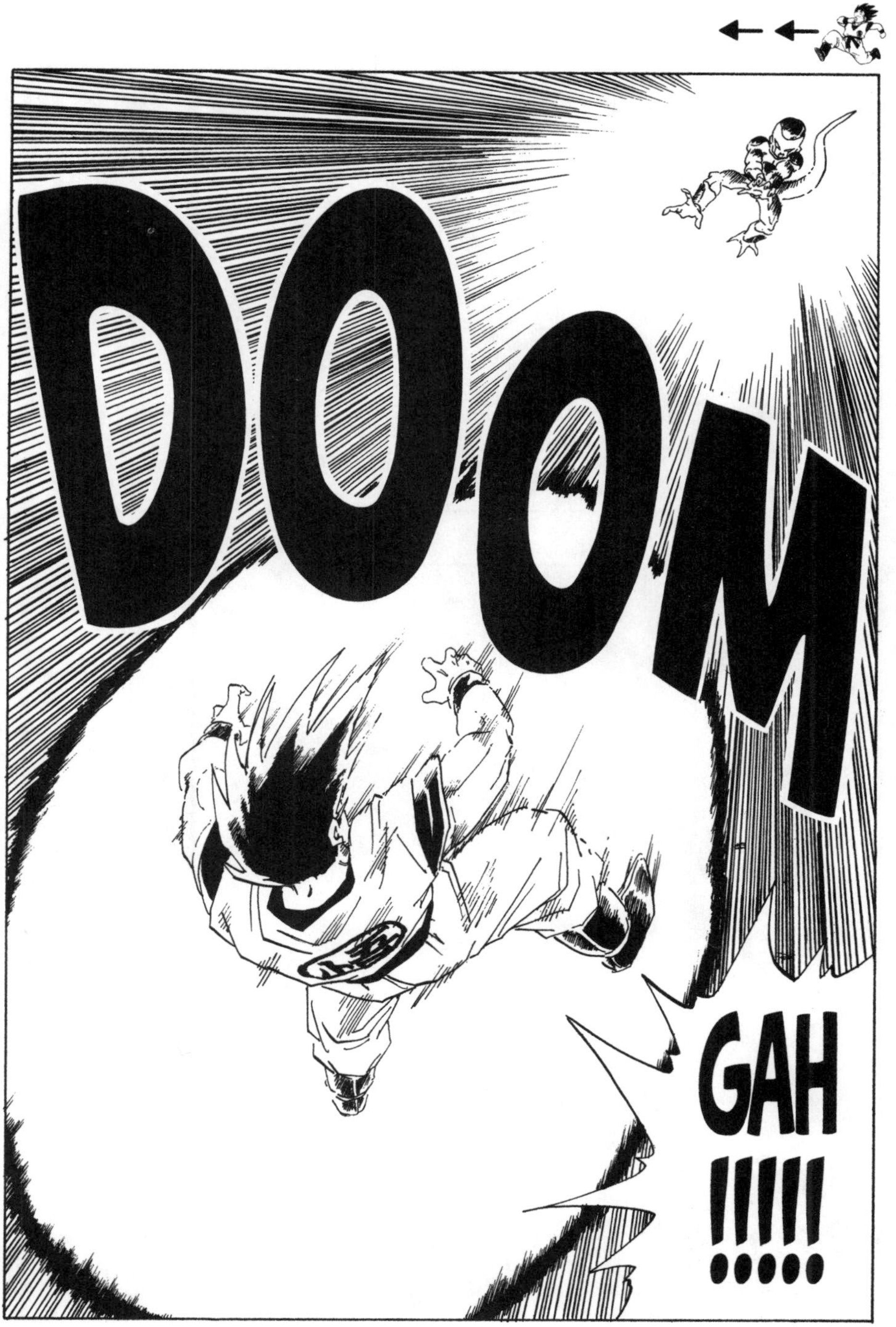
DOOM
GAH!!!!!

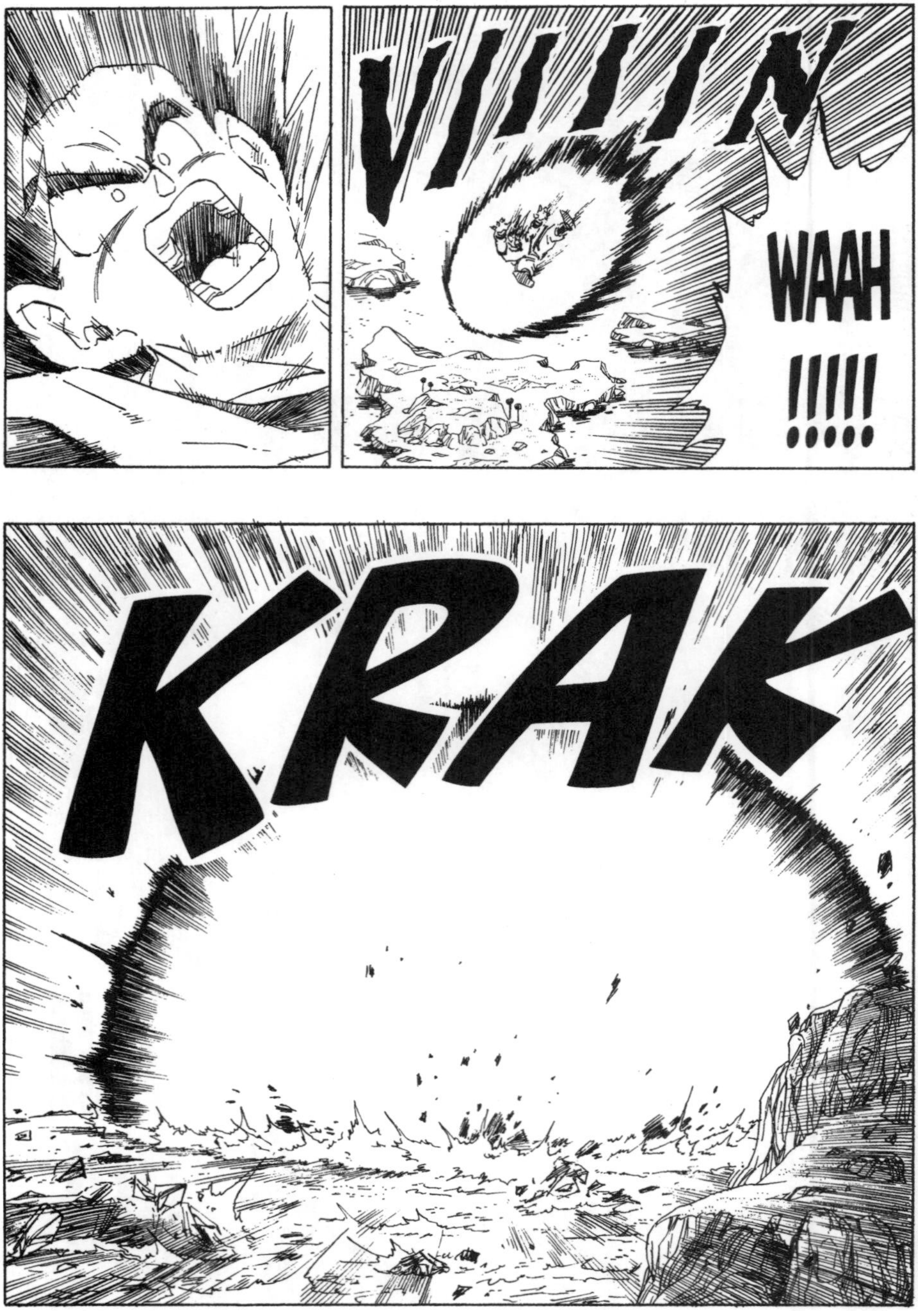
VIIIIN
WAAH!!!!!!
KRAK

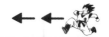

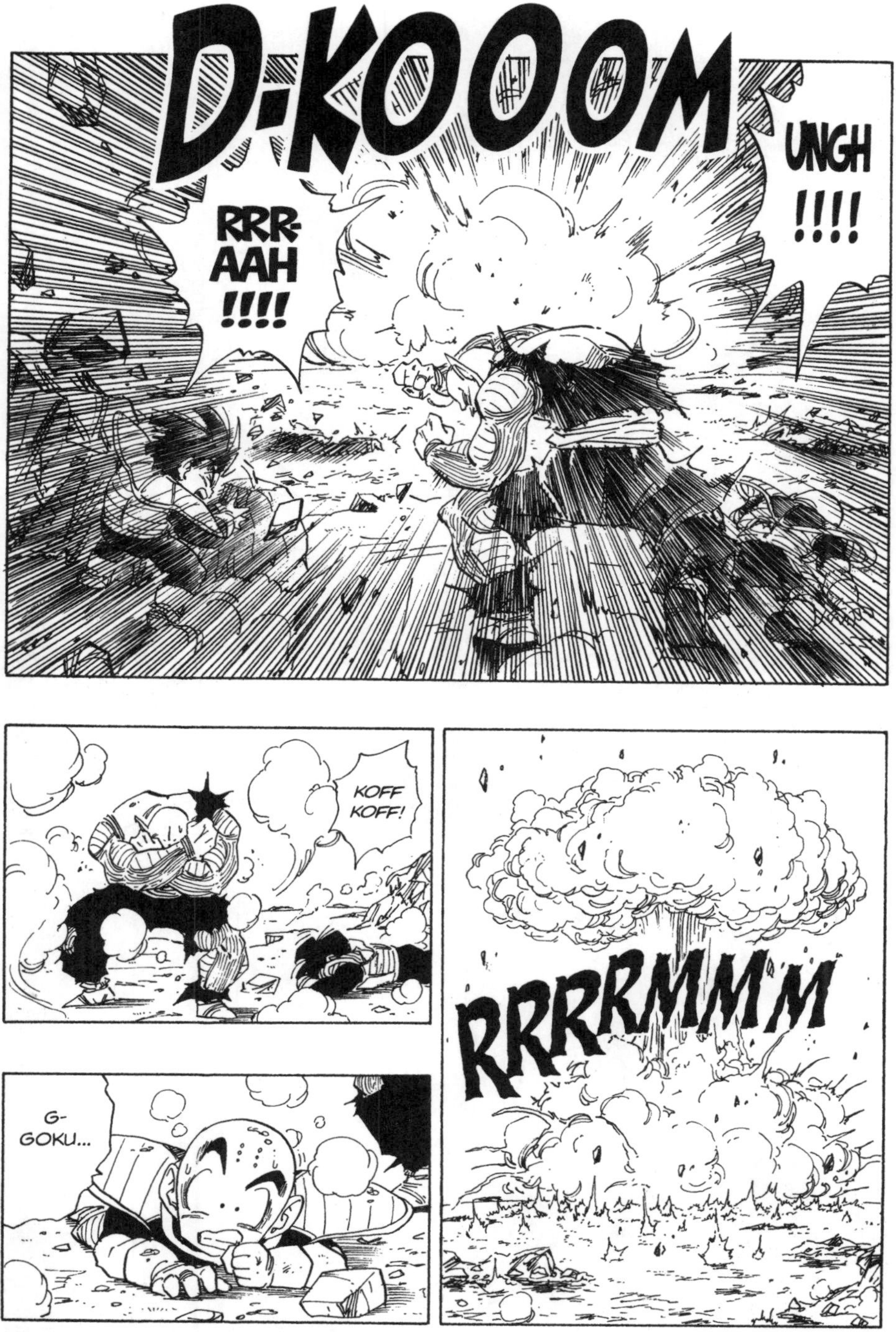
D-KOOOM
UNGH !!!!
RRR-AAH !!!!
RRRRMMMM
KOFF KOFF!
G-GOKU...

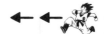

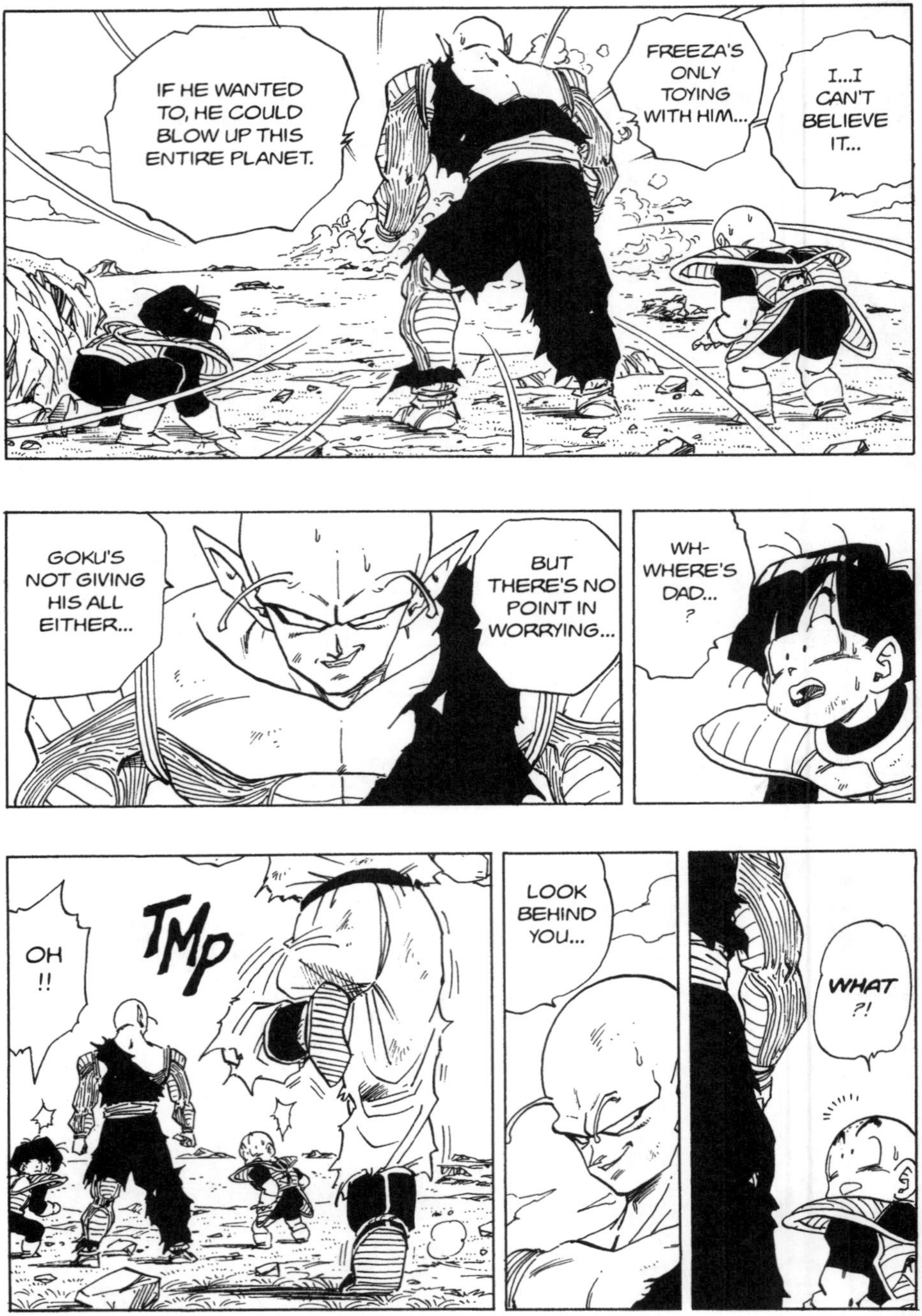
I...I CAN'T BELIEVE IT...
FREEZA'S ONLY TOYING WITH HIM...
IF HE WANTED TO, HE COULD BLOW UP THIS ENTIRE PLANET.
WH- WHERE'S DAD...?
BUT THERE'S NO POINT IN WORRYING...
GOKU'S NOT GIVING HIS ALL EITHER...
WHAT ?!
LOOK BEHIND YOU...
TMP
OH !!

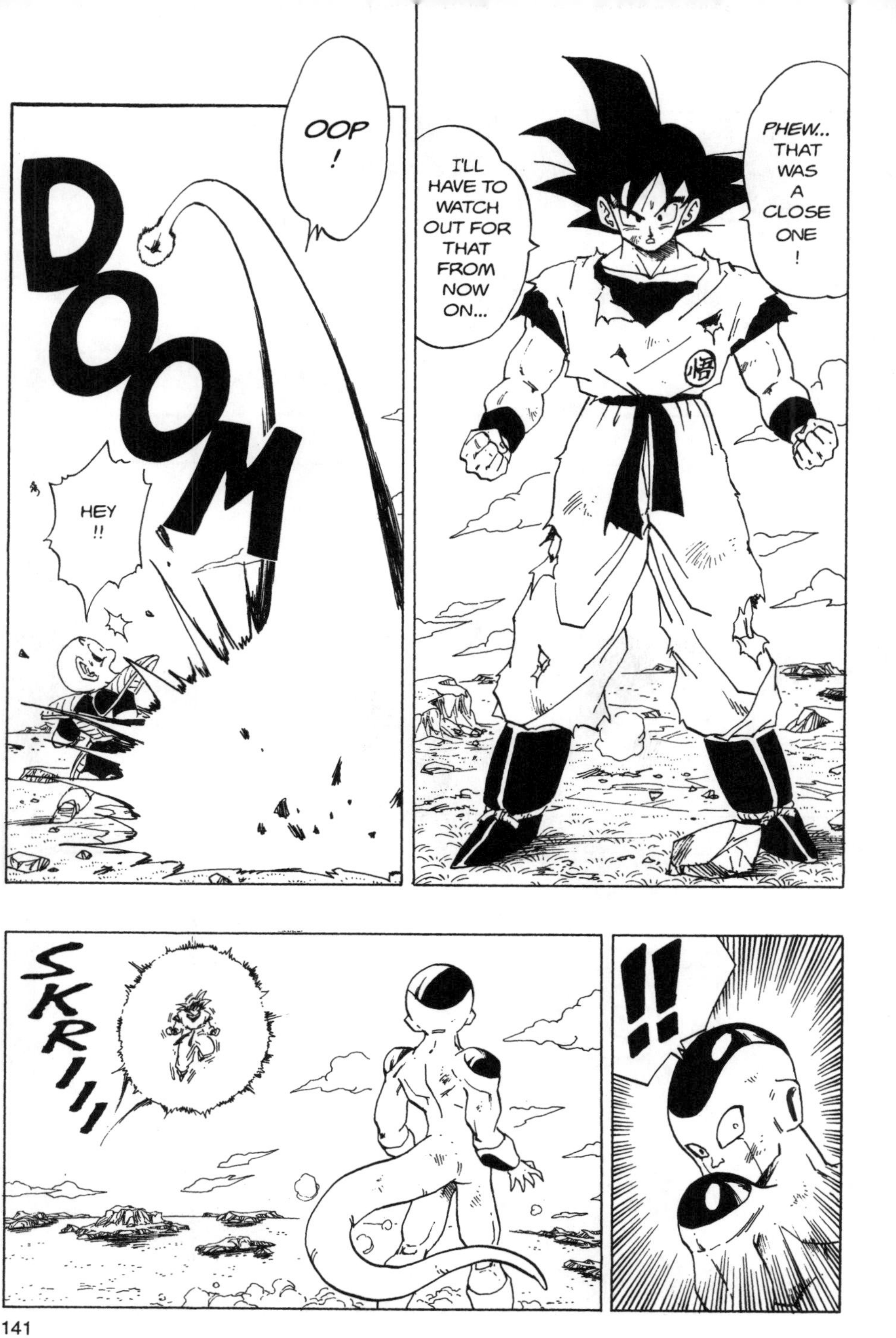
PHEW... THAT WAS A CLOSE ONE !
I'LL HAVE TO WATCH OUT FOR THAT FROM NOW ON...
OOP !
DOOM
HEY !!
!!
SKRIIII

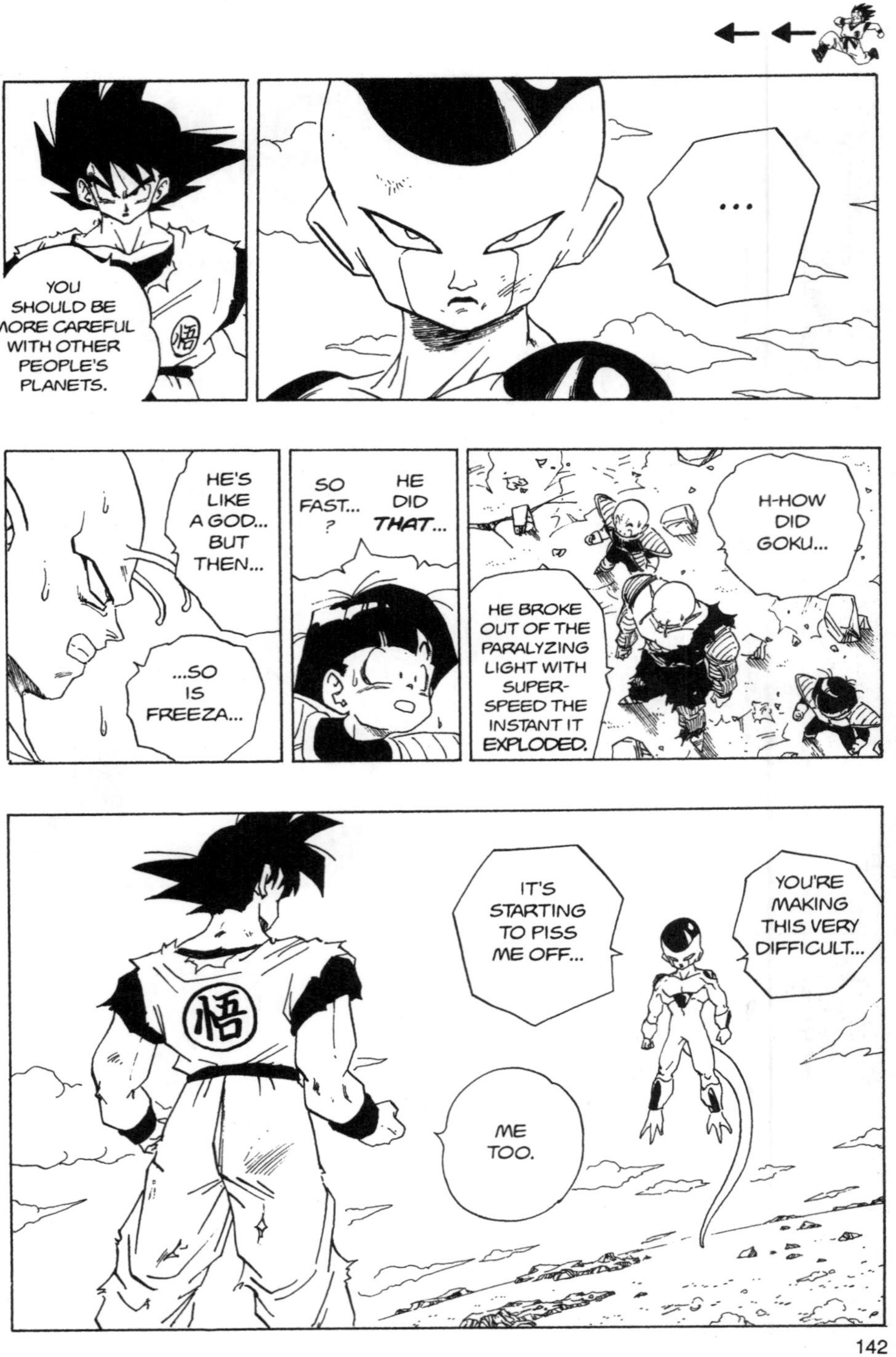
...
YOU SHOULD BE MORE CAREFUL WITH OTHER PEOPLE'S PLANETS.
H-HOW DID GOKU...
HE BROKE OUT OF THE PARALYZING LIGHT WITH SUPER-SPEED THE INSTANT IT EXPLODED.
HE DID *THAT*...
SO FAST... ?
HE'S LIKE A GOD... BUT THEN...
...SO IS FREEZA...
YOU'RE MAKING THIS VERY DIFFICULT...
IT'S STARTING TO PISS ME OFF...
ME TOO.

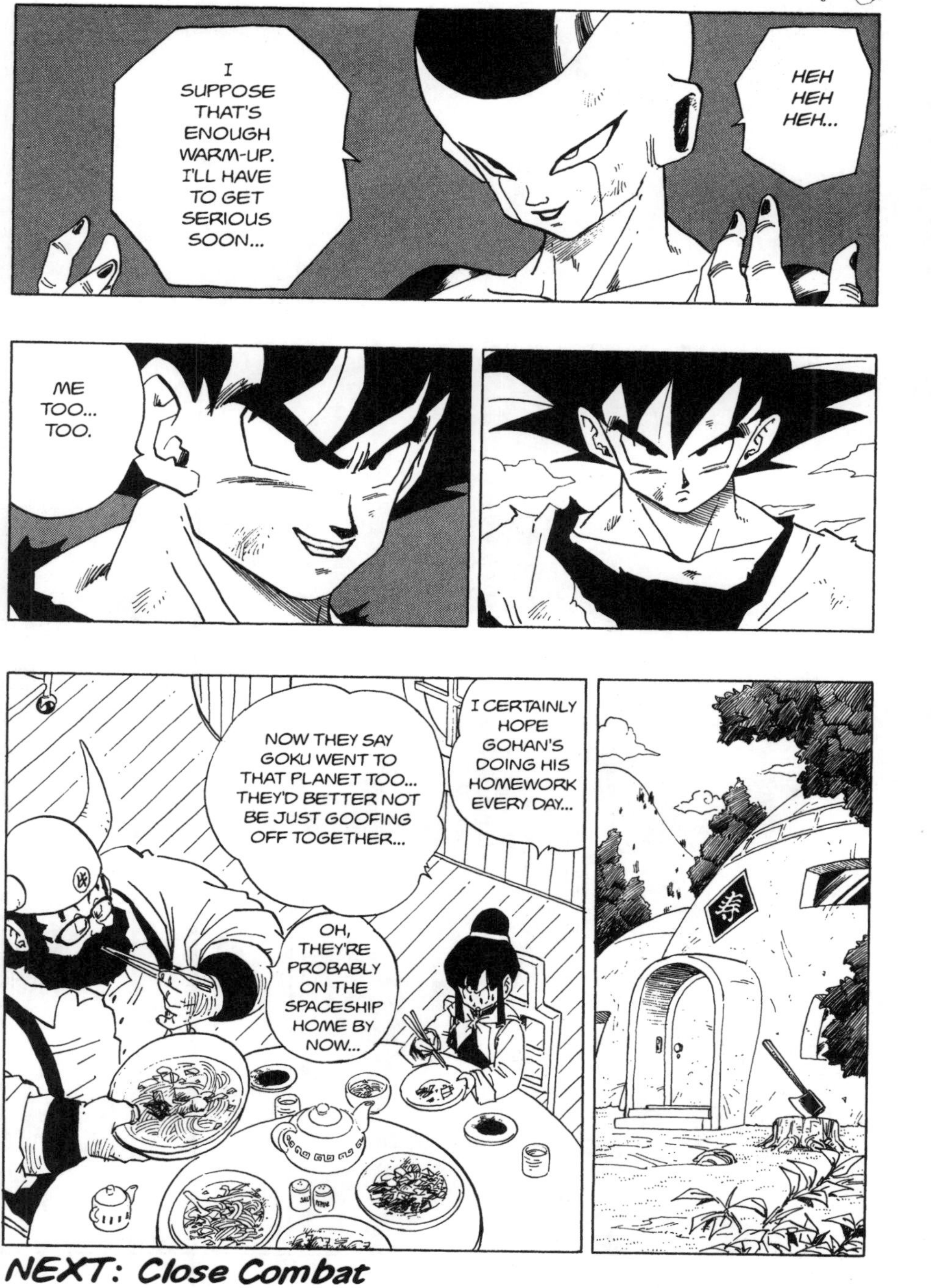
HEH HEH HEH...
I SUPPOSE THAT'S ENOUGH WARM-UP. I'LL HAVE TO GET SERIOUS SOON...
ME TOO... TOO.
I CERTAINLY HOPE GOHAN'S DOING HIS HOMEWORK EVERY DAY...
NOW THEY SAY GOKU WENT TO THAT PLANET TOO... THEY'D BETTER NOT BE JUST GOOFING OFF TOGETHER...
OH, THEY'RE PROBABLY ON THE SPACESHIP HOME BY NOW...

**NEXT: Close Combat**

# DBZ:117 • Hand to Foot

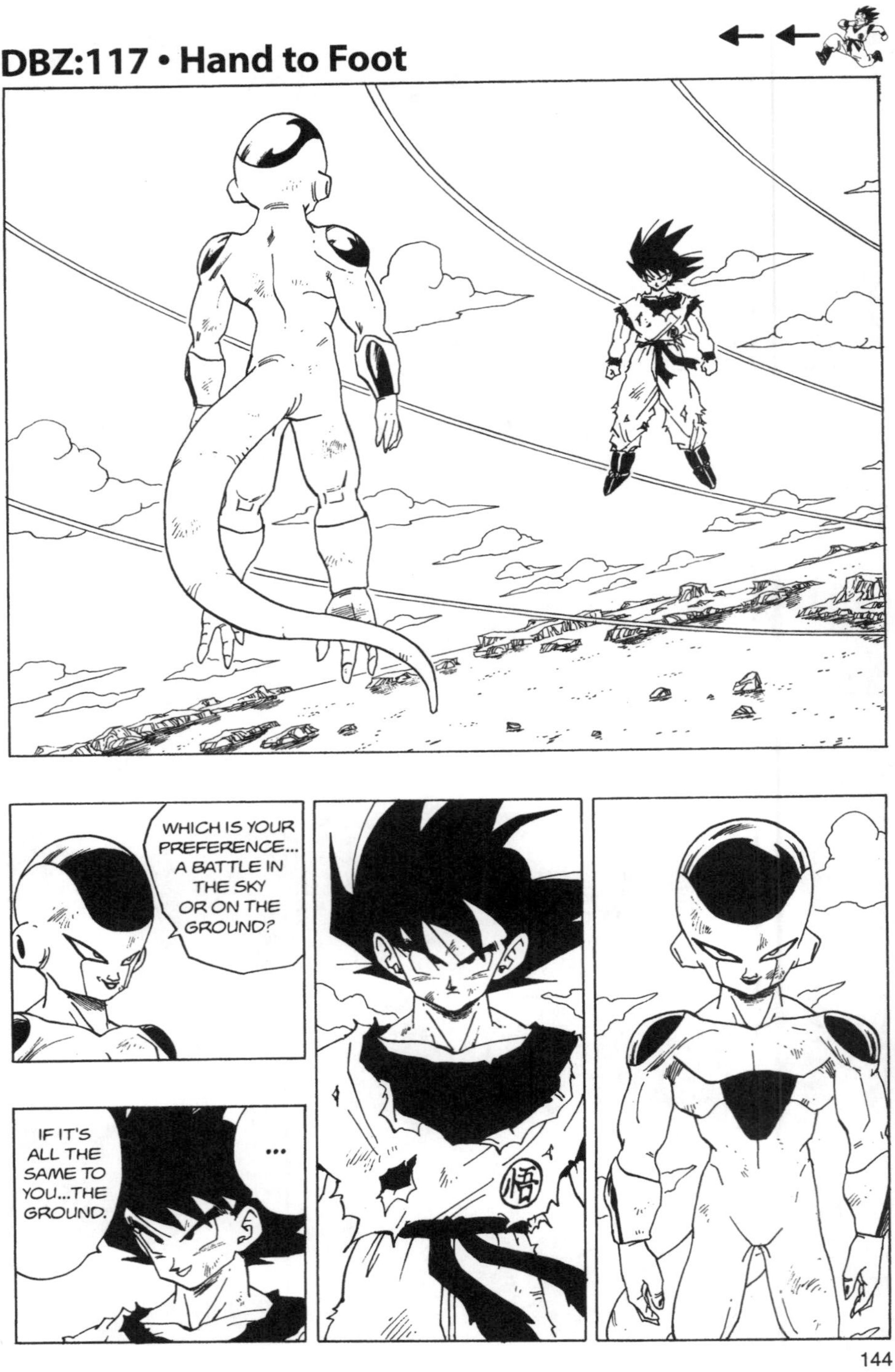
WHICH IS YOUR PREFERENCE... A BATTLE IN THE SKY OR ON THE GROUND?
...
IF IT'S ALL THE SAME TO YOU...THE GROUND.

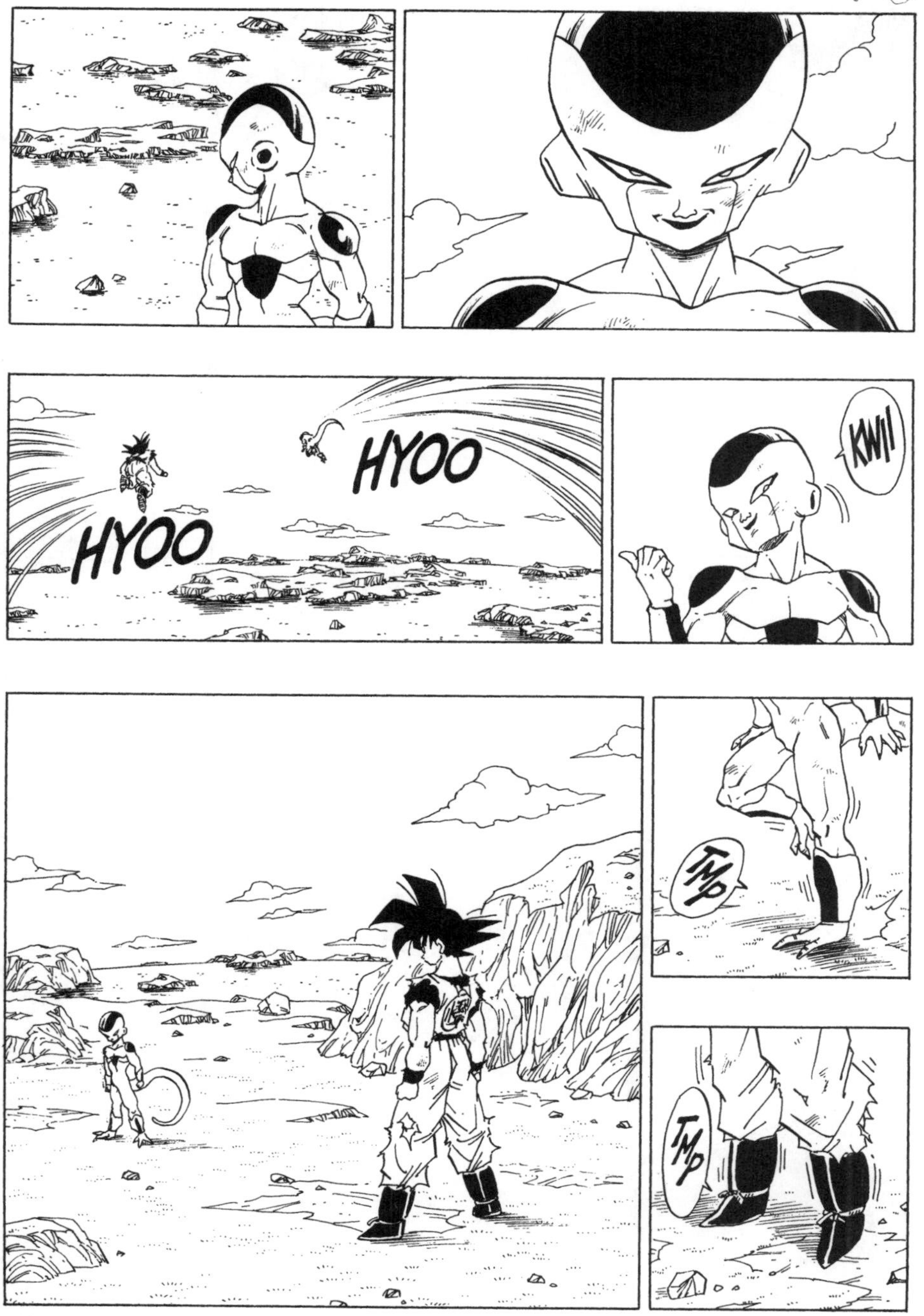
KWII
HYOO
HYOO
TMP
TMP

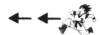

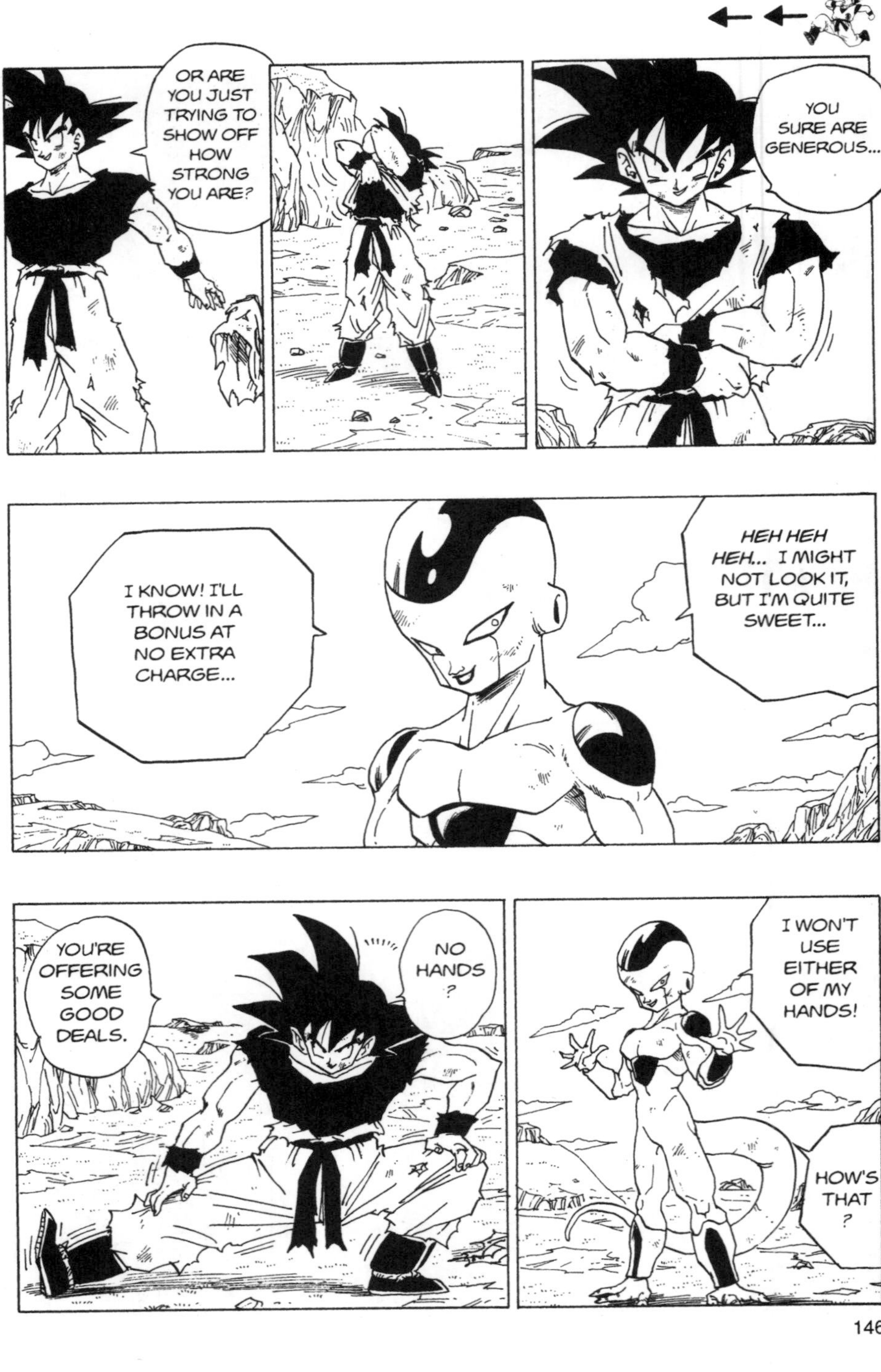
YOU SURE ARE GENEROUS...
OR ARE YOU JUST TRYING TO SHOW OFF HOW STRONG YOU ARE?
HEH HEH HEH... I MIGHT NOT LOOK IT, BUT I'M QUITE SWEET...
I KNOW! I'LL THROW IN A BONUS AT NO EXTRA CHARGE...
I WON'T USE EITHER OF MY HANDS!
HOW'S THAT?
NO HANDS?
YOU'RE OFFERING SOME GOOD DEALS.

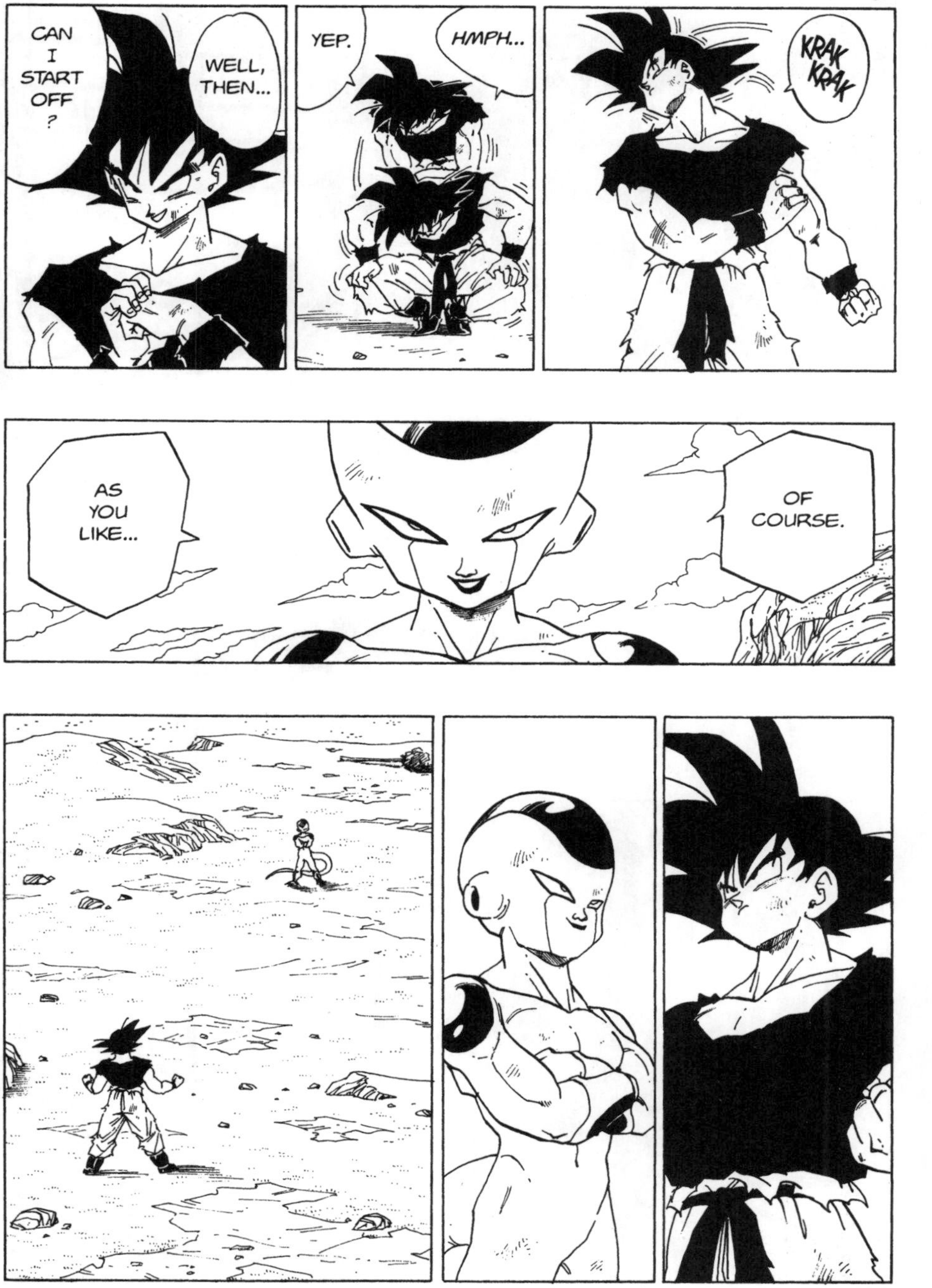
KRAK KRAK
HMPH...
YEP.
WELL, THEN...
CAN I START OFF ?
OF COURSE.
AS YOU LIKE...

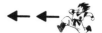

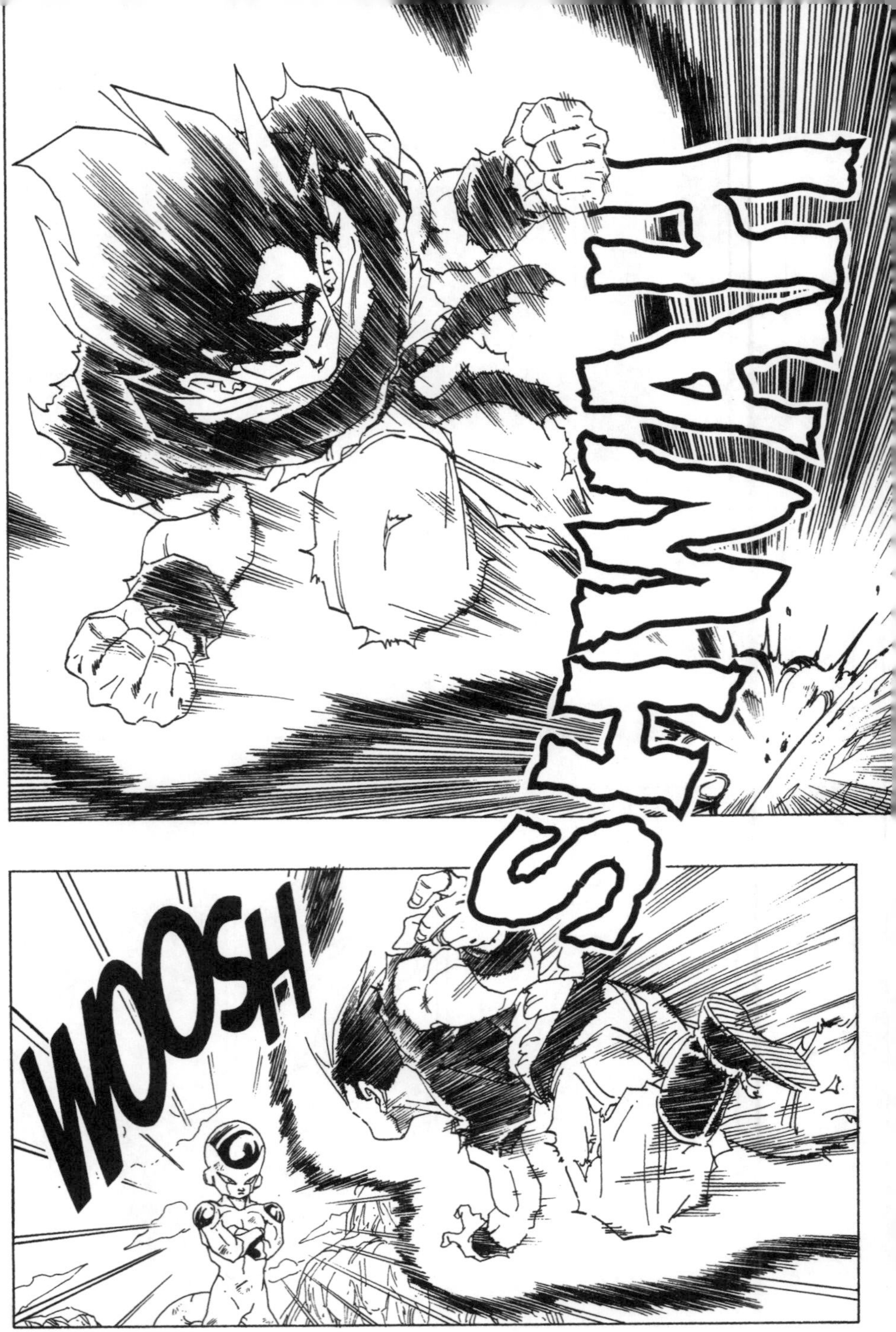
SHWAH
WOOSH

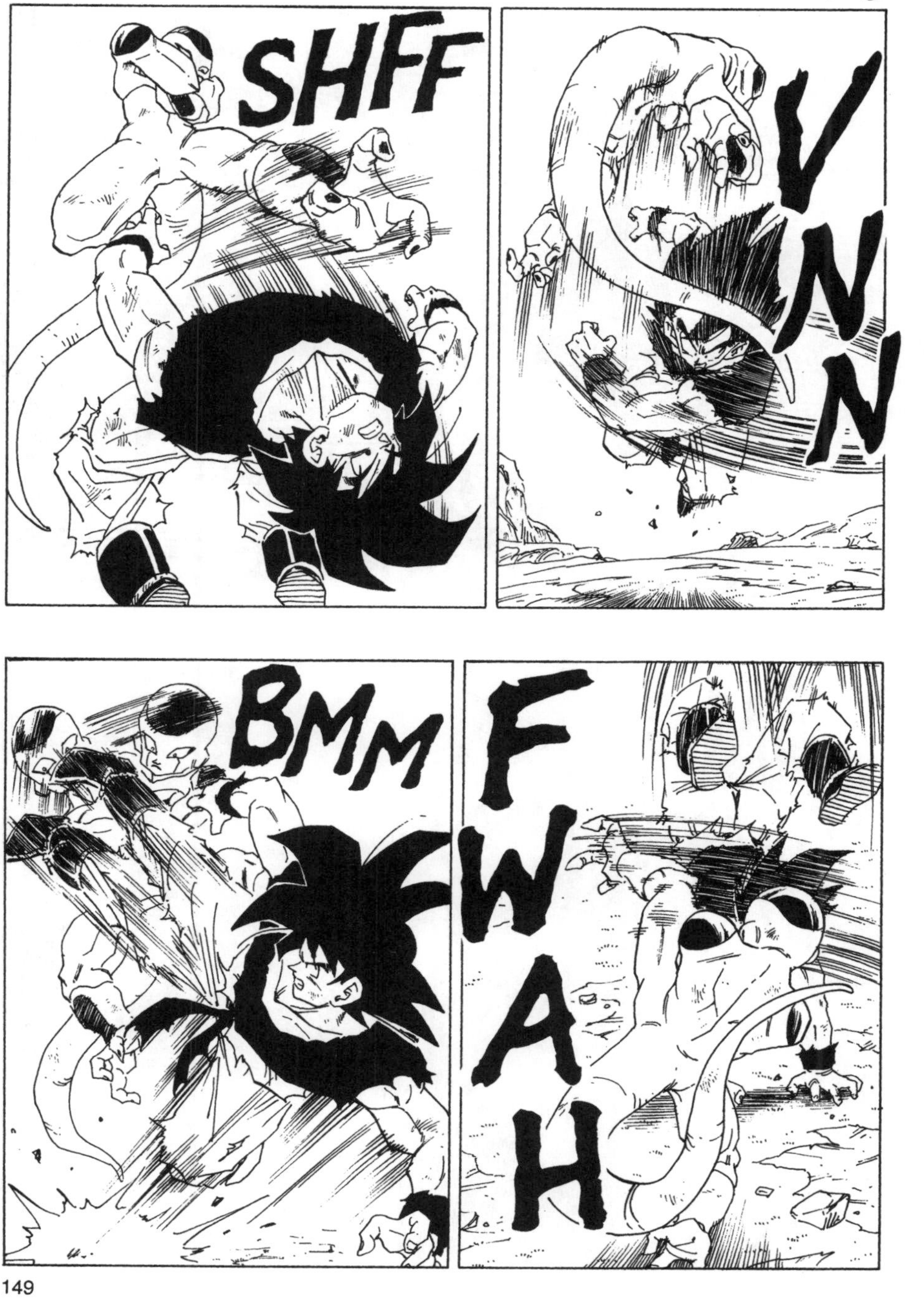
VNNN
SHFF
FWAH
BMM

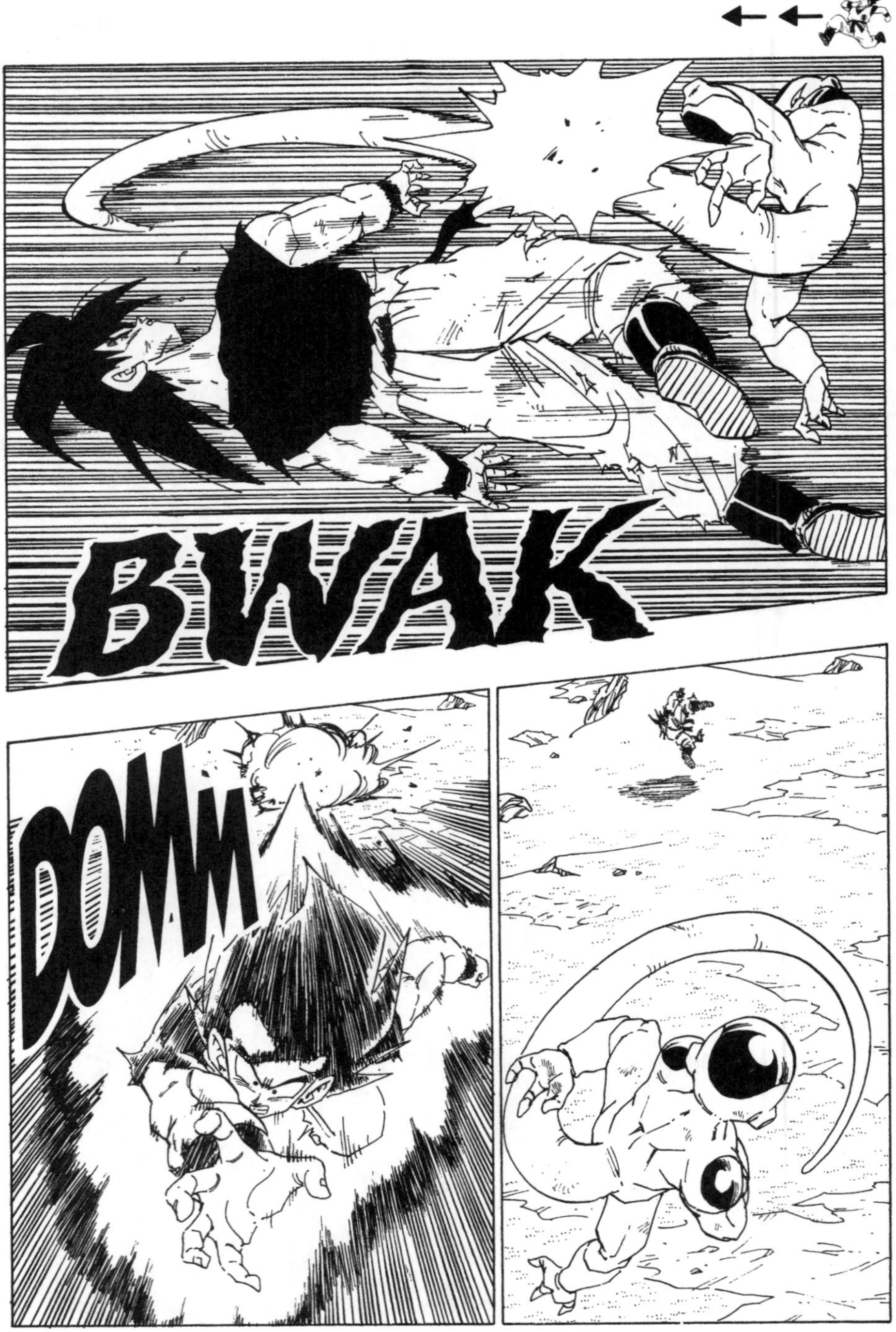
BWAK
DOMM

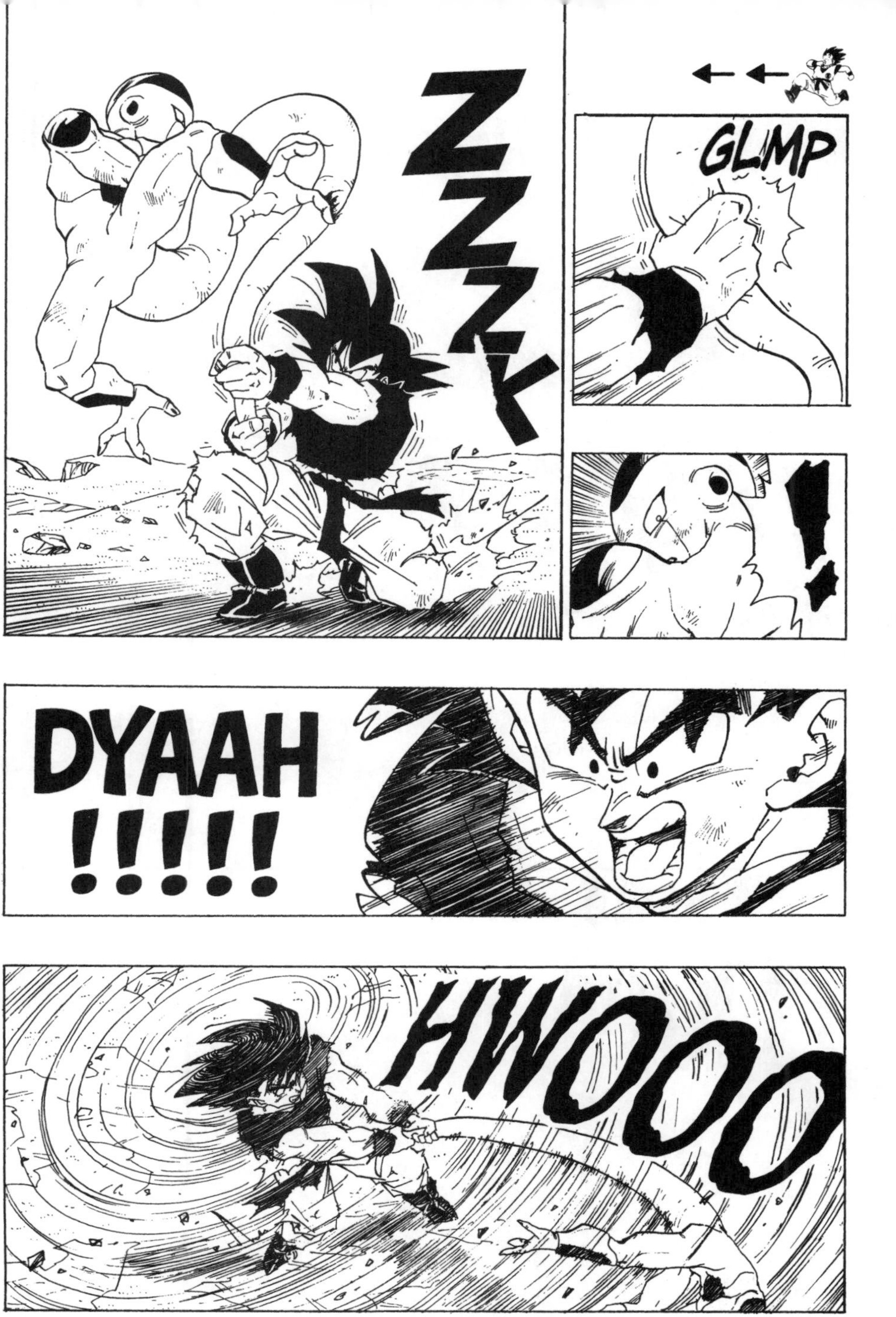
GLMP
!
ZZZK
DYAAH!!!!!
HWOOO

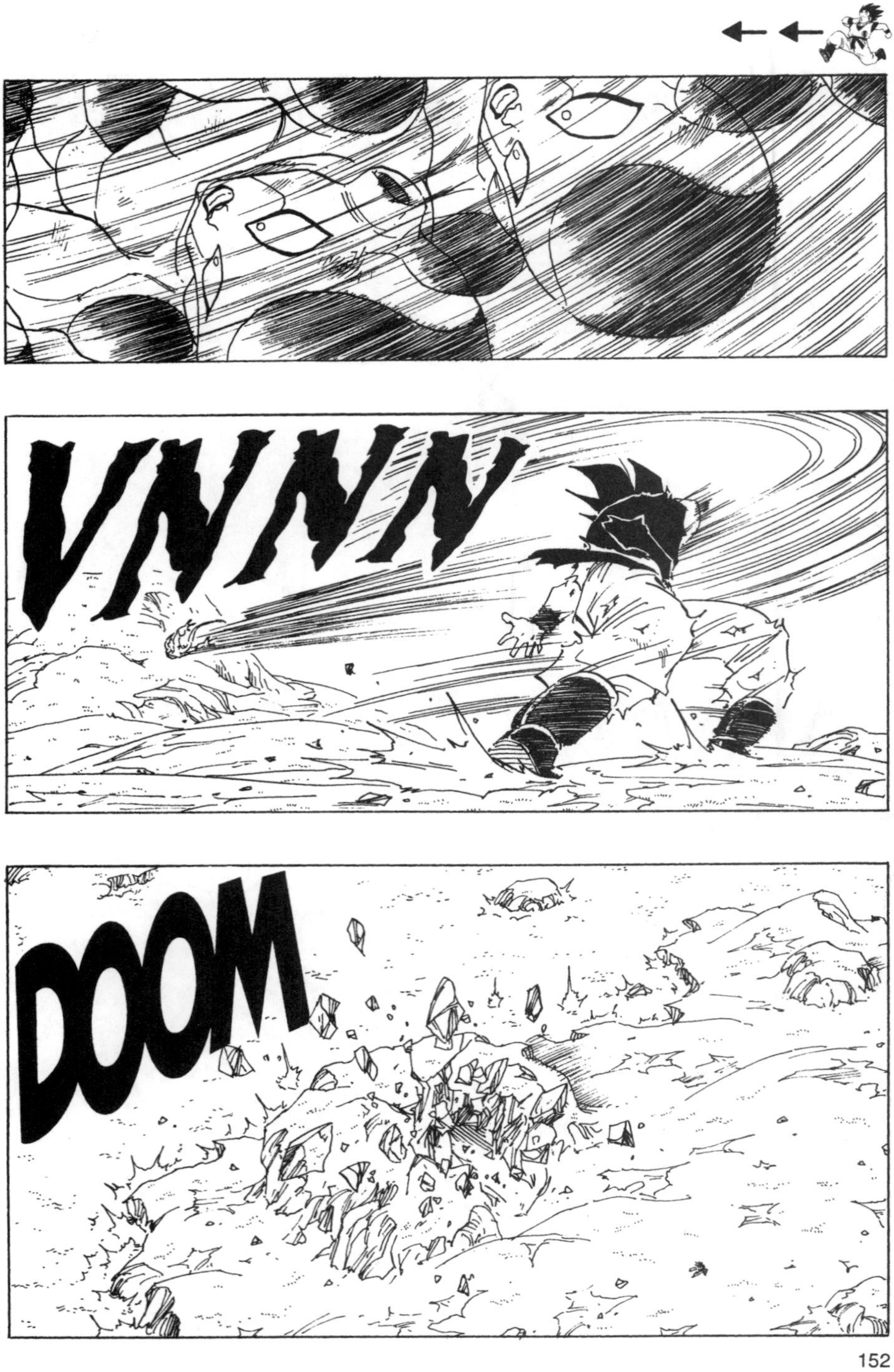
VNNN
DOOM

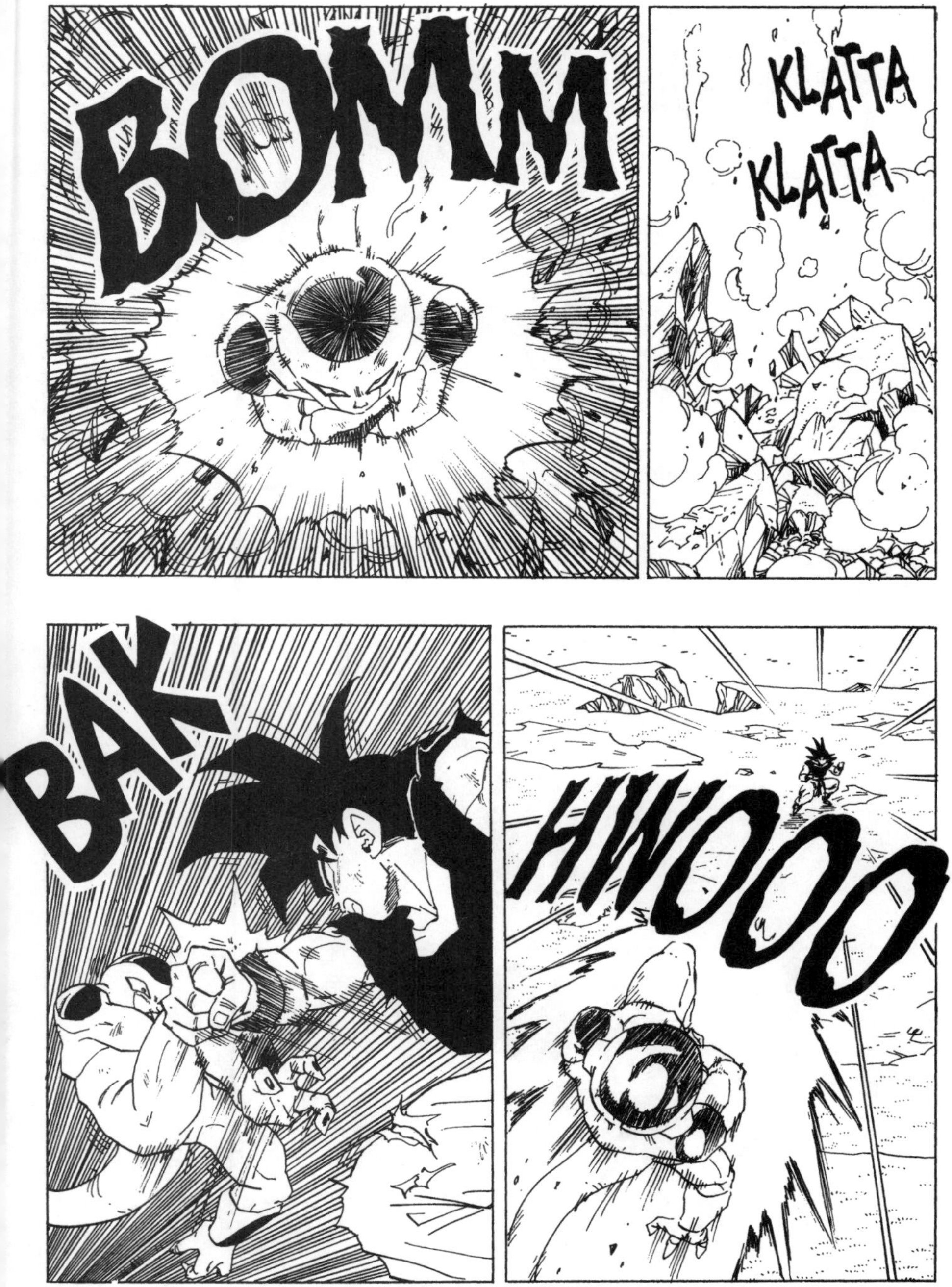
KLATTA
KLATTA
BOMM
HWOOO
BAK

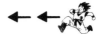

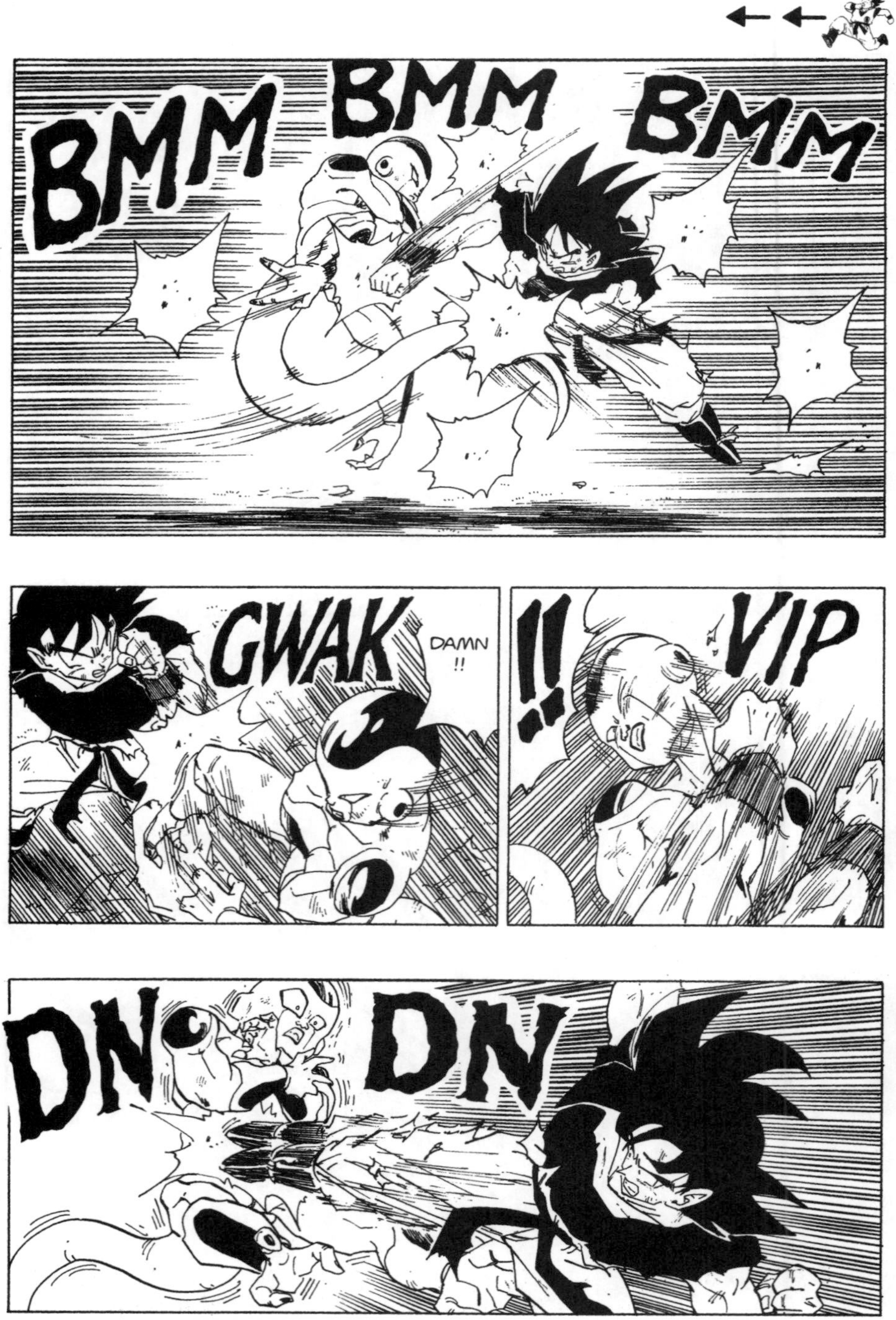
BMM
BMM
BMM
VIP
!!
GWAK
DAMN !!
DN
DN

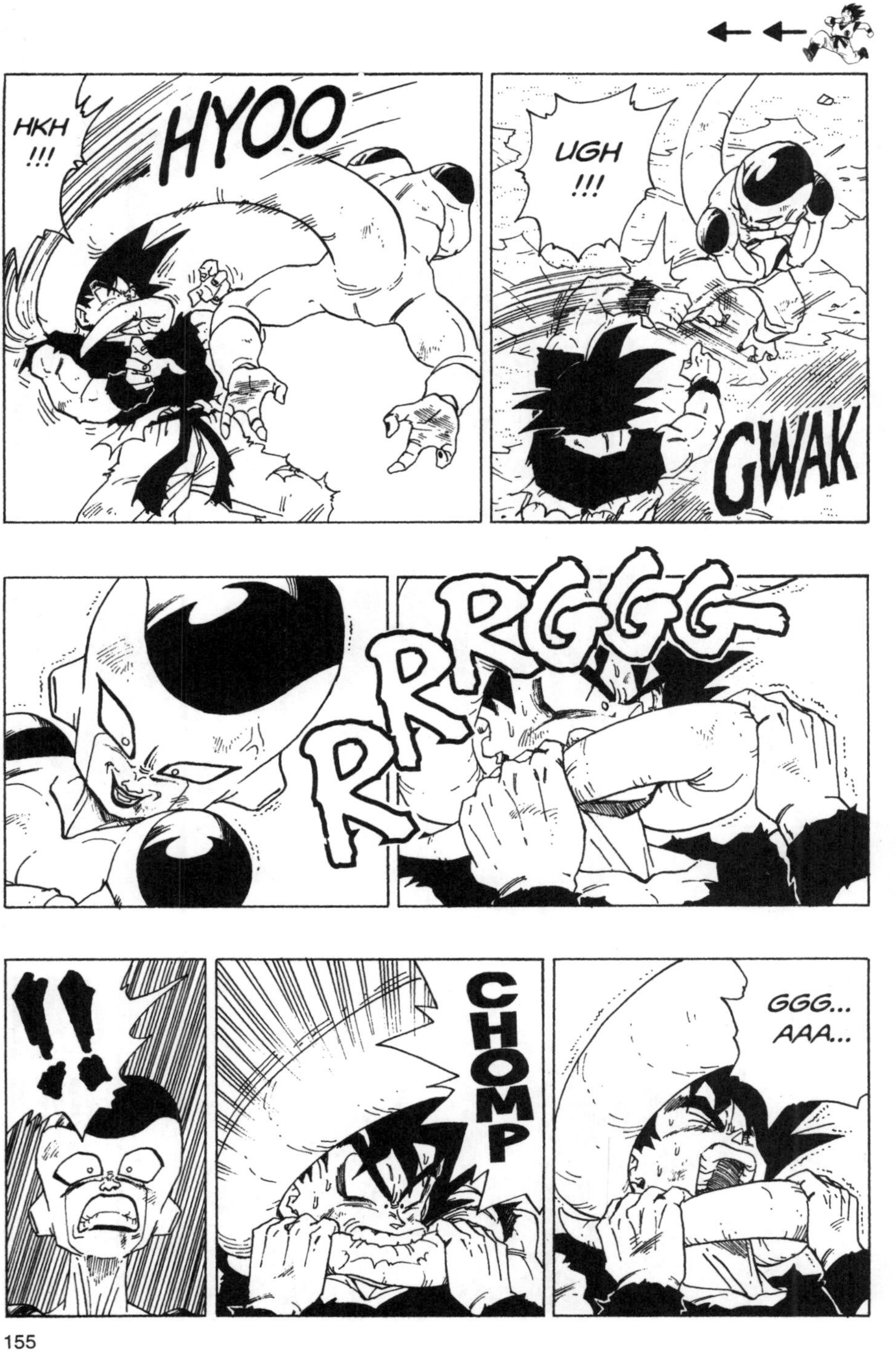
UGH !!!
GWAK
HKH !!!
HYOO
RRRGGG-
GGG... AAA...
CHOMP
!!

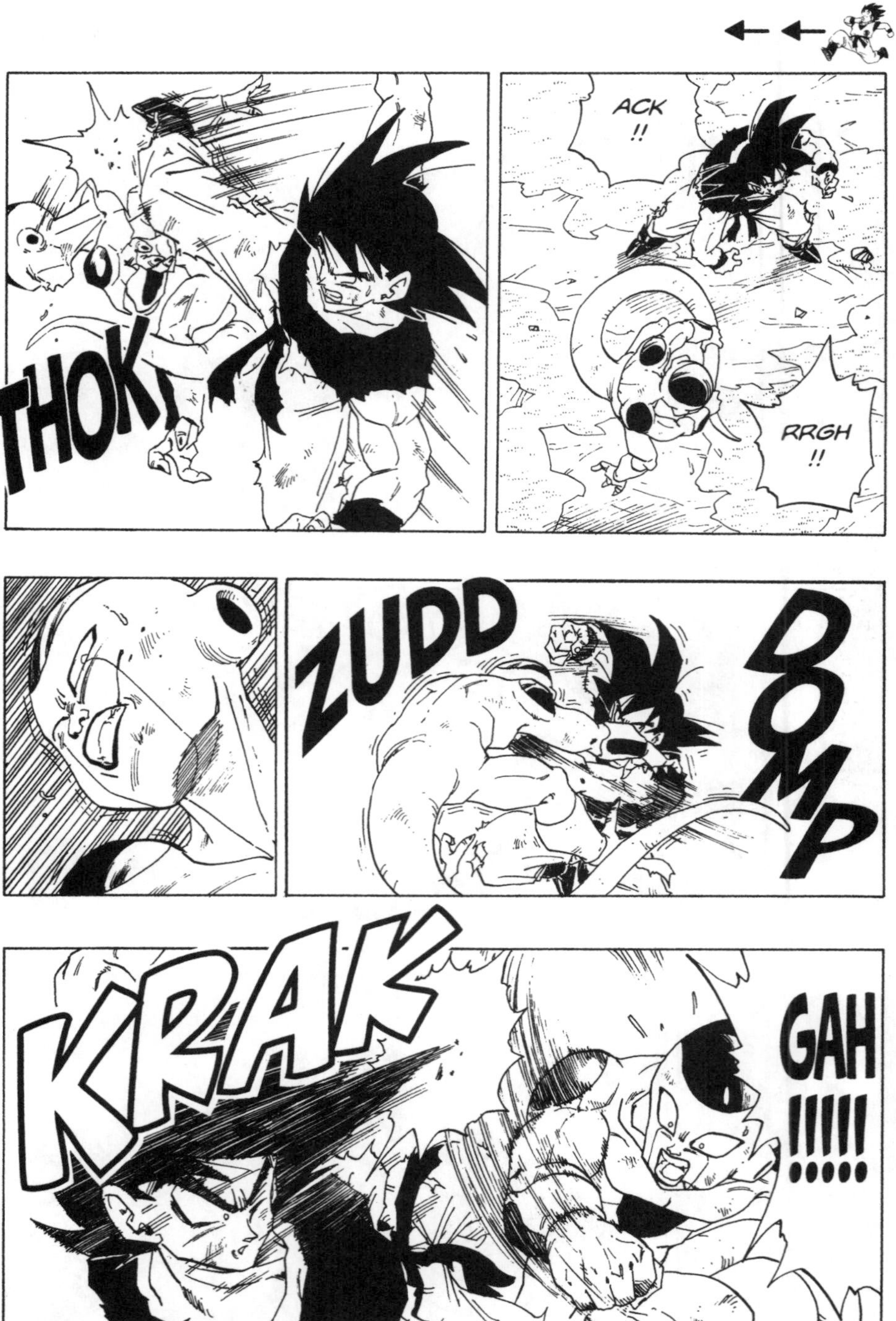
ACK !!
RRGH !!
THOK
DOMP
ZUDD
KRAK
GAH !!!!!

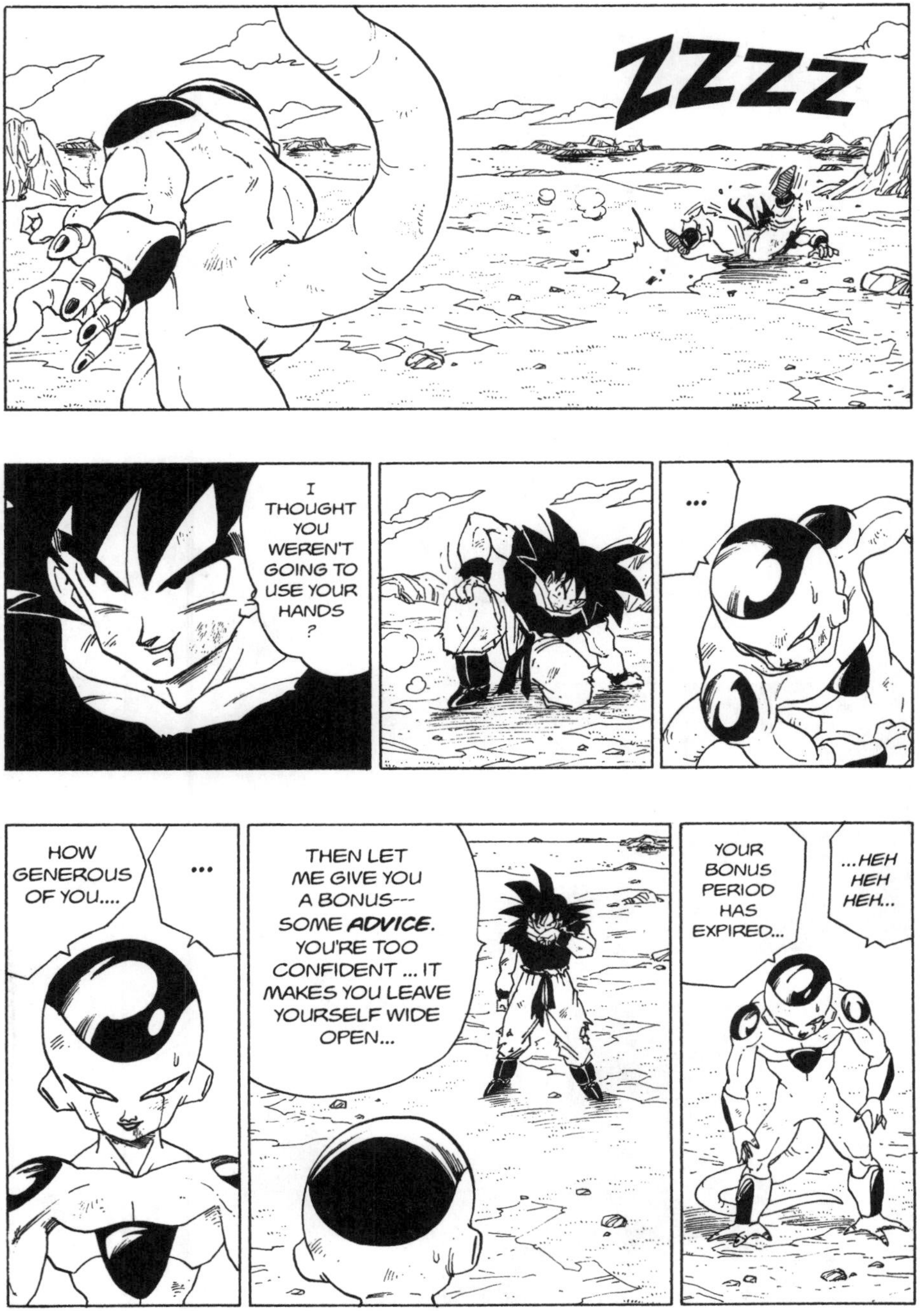
ZZZZ
...
I THOUGHT YOU WEREN'T GOING TO USE YOUR HANDS ?
...HEH HEH HEH...
YOUR BONUS PERIOD HAS EXPIRED...
THEN LET ME GIVE YOU A BONUS--- SOME ***ADVICE***. YOU'RE TOO CONFIDENT ... IT MAKES YOU LEAVE YOURSELF WIDE OPEN...
...
HOW GENEROUS OF YOU....

***NEXT*: Freeza Gets Serious**

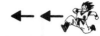

# DBZ:118 • 50% Maximum Power

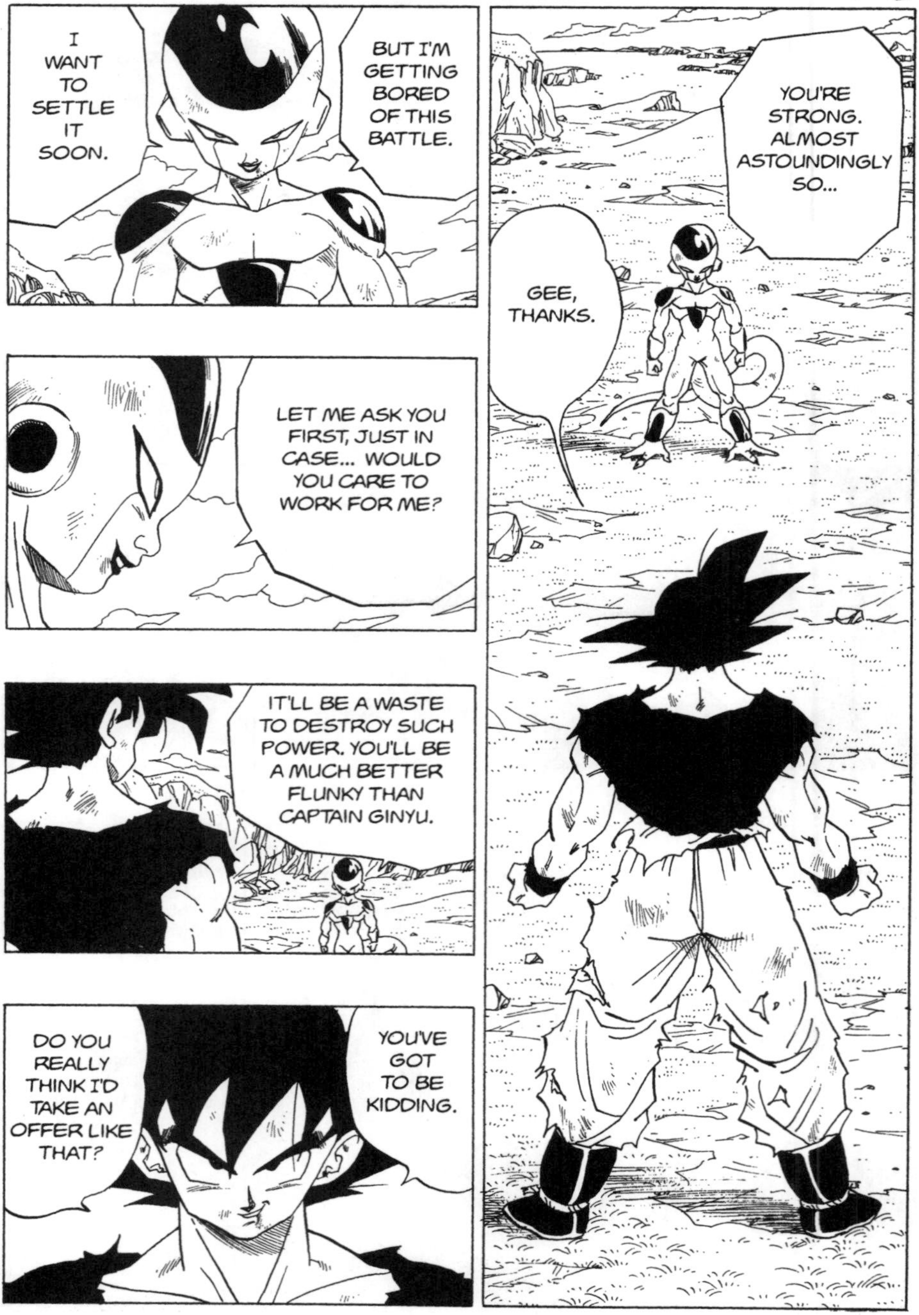
YOU'RE STRONG. ALMOST ASTOUNDINGLY SO...
GEE, THANKS.
BUT I'M GETTING BORED OF THIS BATTLE.
I WANT TO SETTLE IT SOON.
LET ME ASK YOU FIRST, JUST IN CASE... WOULD YOU CARE TO WORK FOR ME?
IT'LL BE A WASTE TO DESTROY SUCH POWER. YOU'LL BE A MUCH BETTER FLUNKY THAN CAPTAIN GINYU.
YOU'VE GOT TO BE KIDDING.
DO YOU REALLY THINK I'D TAKE AN OFFER LIKE THAT?

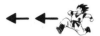

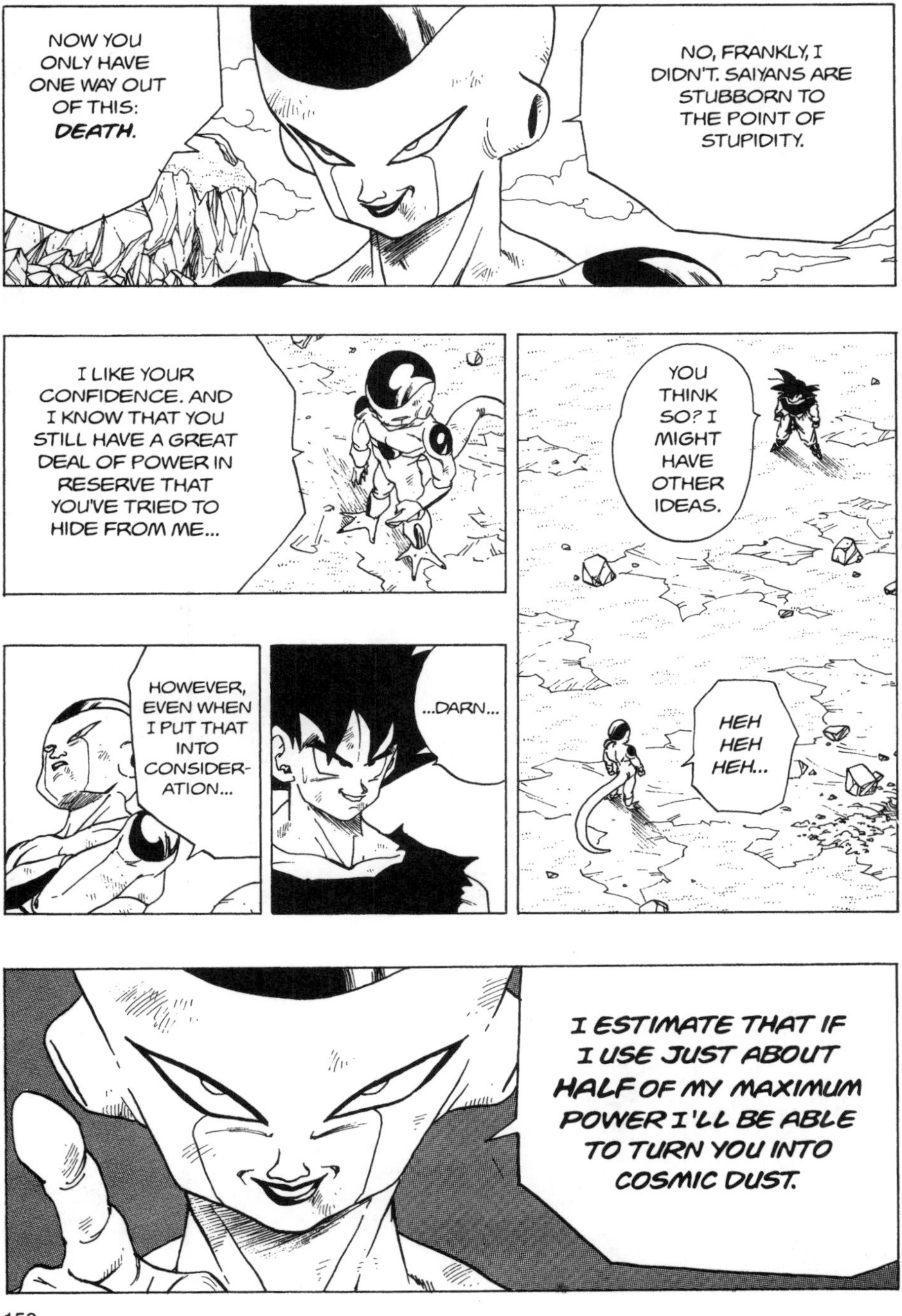
NO, FRANKLY, I DIDN'T. SAIYANS ARE STUBBORN TO THE POINT OF STUPIDITY.
NOW YOU ONLY HAVE ONE WAY OUT OF THIS: *DEATH*.
YOU THINK SO? I MIGHT HAVE OTHER IDEAS.
HEH HEH HEH...
I LIKE YOUR CONFIDENCE. AND I KNOW THAT YOU STILL HAVE A GREAT DEAL OF POWER IN RESERVE THAT YOU'VE TRIED TO HIDE FROM ME...
...DARN...
HOWEVER, EVEN WHEN I PUT THAT INTO CONSIDER-ATION...
I ESTIMATE THAT IF I USE JUST ABOUT HALF OF MY MAXIMUM POWER I'LL BE ABLE TO TURN YOU INTO COSMIC DUST.

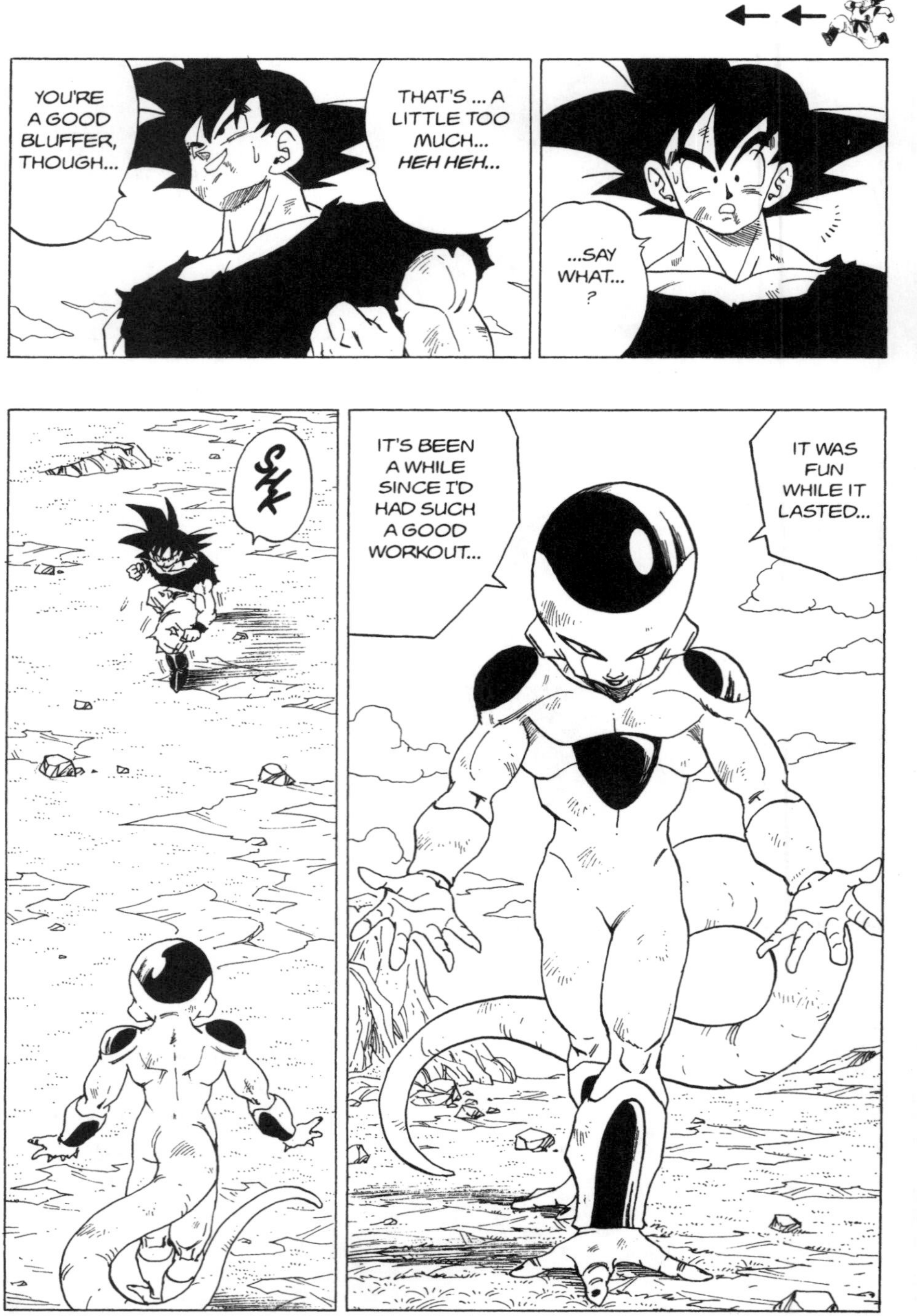
...SAY WHAT... ?
THAT'S ... A LITTLE TOO MUCH... *HEH HEH...*
YOU'RE A GOOD BLUFFER, THOUGH...
IT WAS FUN WHILE IT LASTED...
IT'S BEEN A WHILE SINCE I'D HAD SUCH A GOOD WORKOUT...
SNK

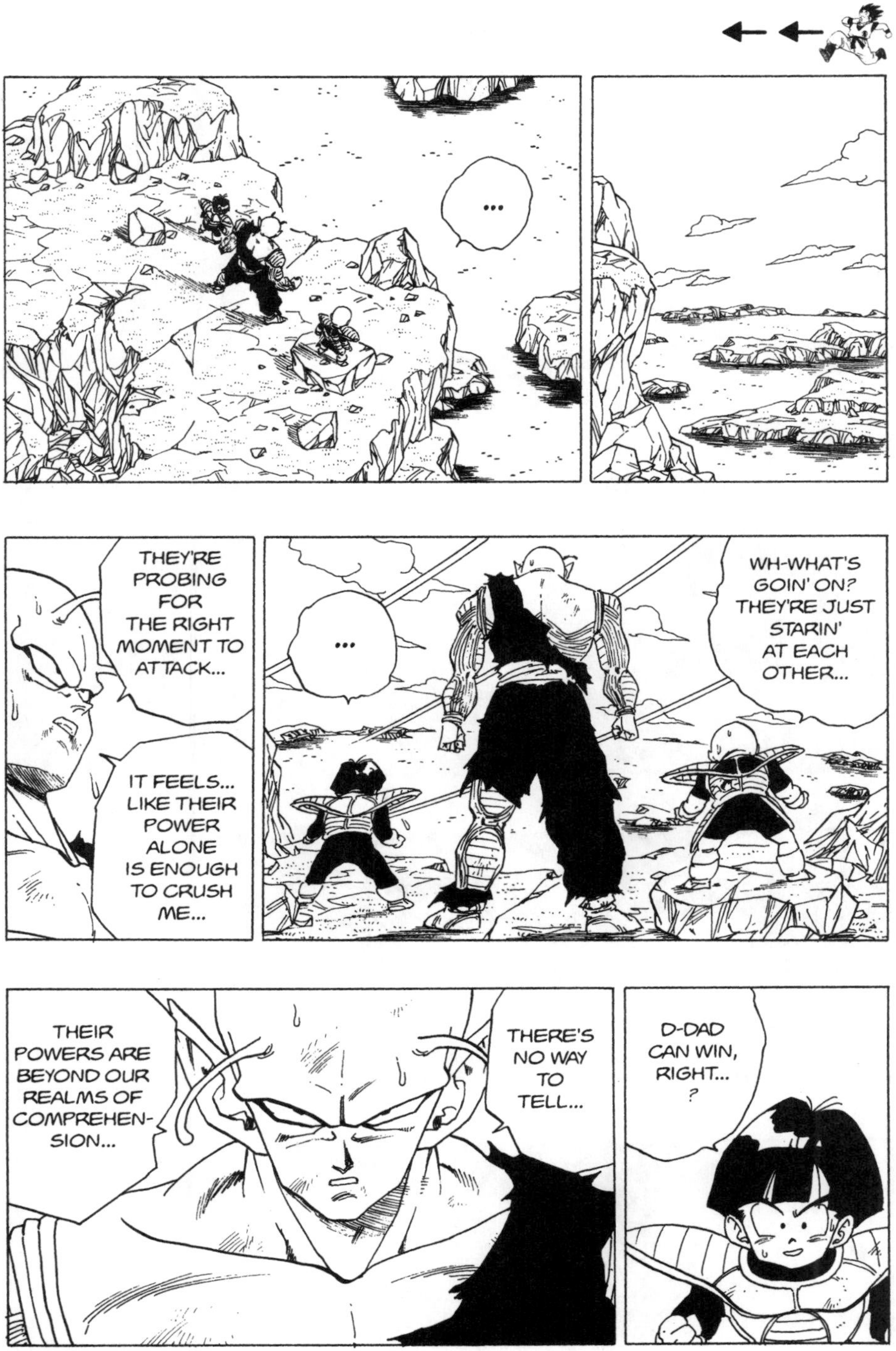
...
WH-WHAT'S GOIN' ON? THEY'RE JUST STARIN' AT EACH OTHER...
...
THEY'RE PROBING FOR THE RIGHT MOMENT TO ATTACK...
IT FEELS... LIKE THEIR POWER ALONE IS ENOUGH TO CRUSH ME...
D-DAD CAN WIN, RIGHT...?
THERE'S NO WAY TO TELL...
THEIR POWERS ARE BEYOND OUR REALMS OF COMPREHENSION...

...HOO BOY...

...

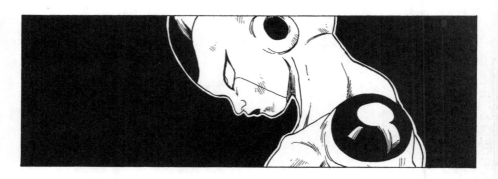

...NOT BLUFFING... !!!

H- HE'S...

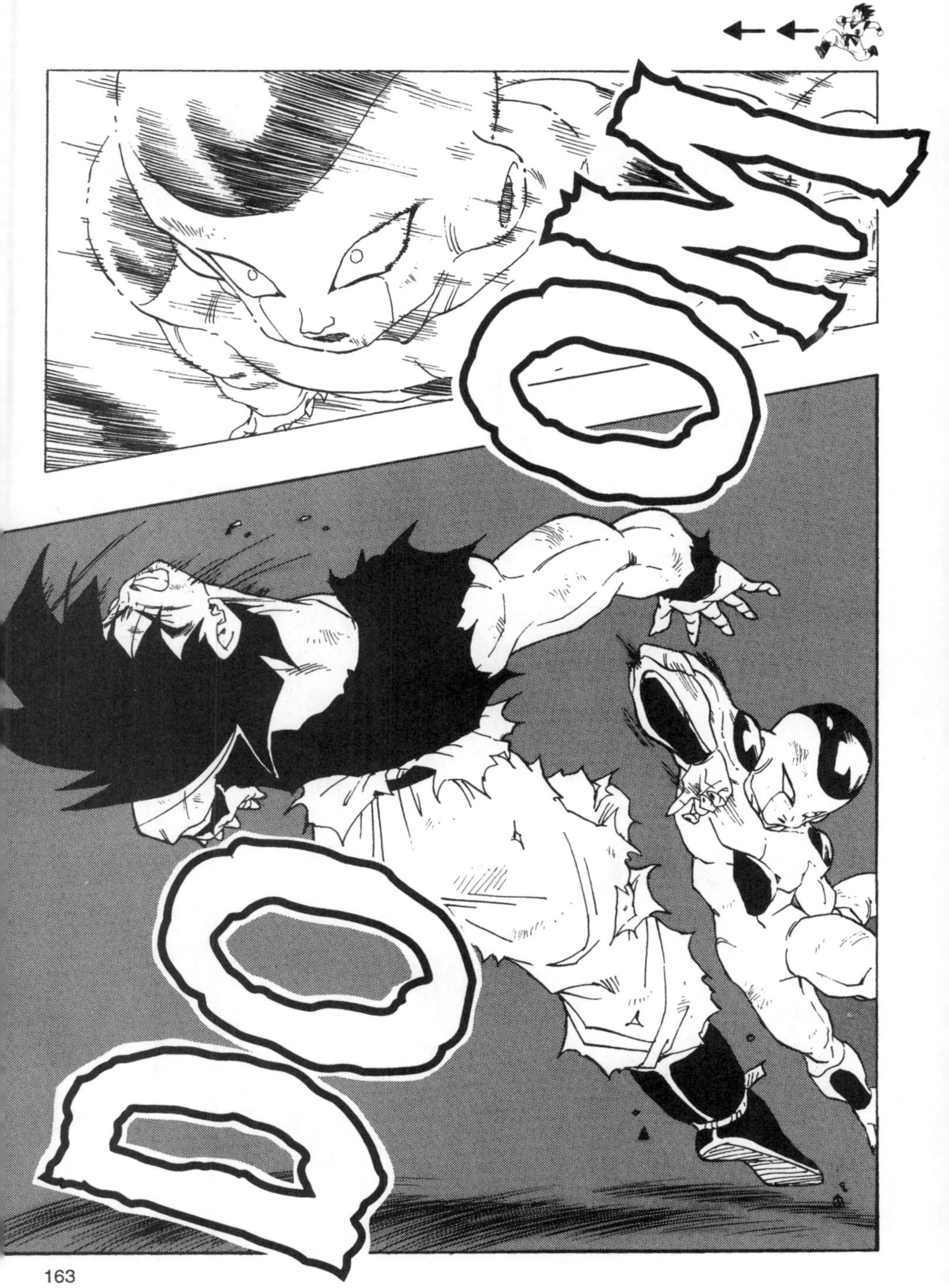
DOOM

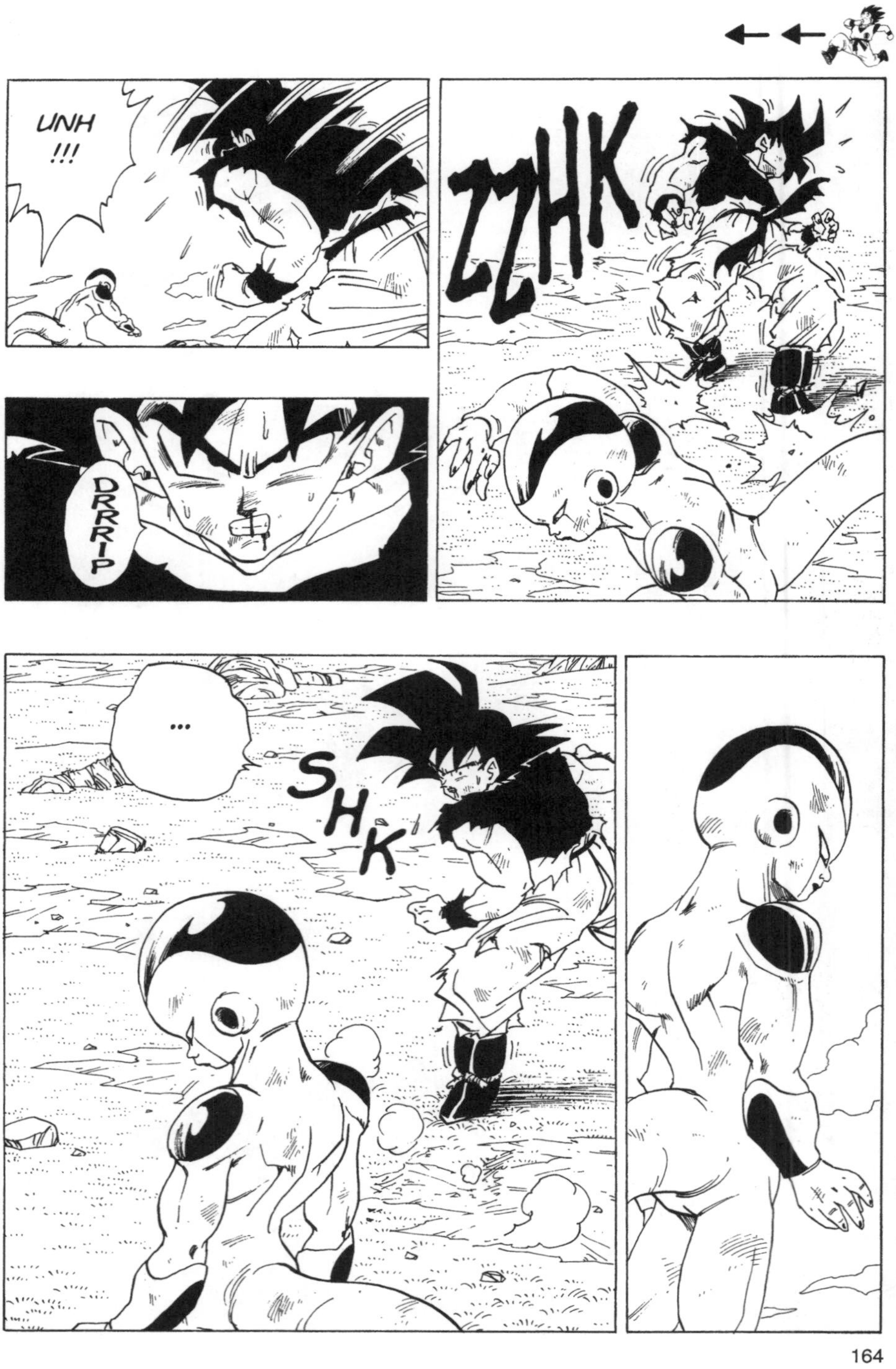
ZZHK
UNH !!!
DRRRIP
...
SHK

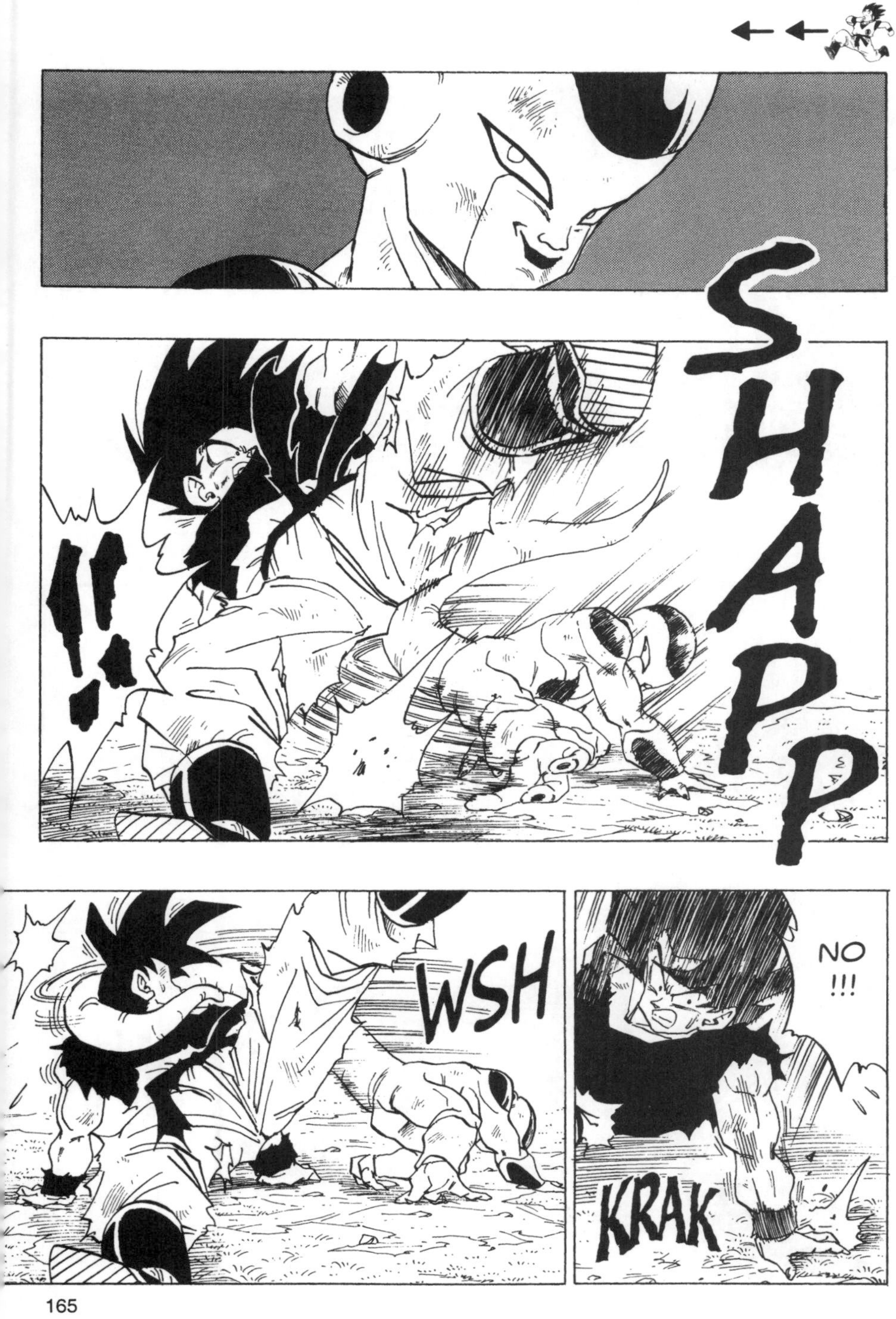
SHAPP
!!
NO !!!
KRAK
WSH

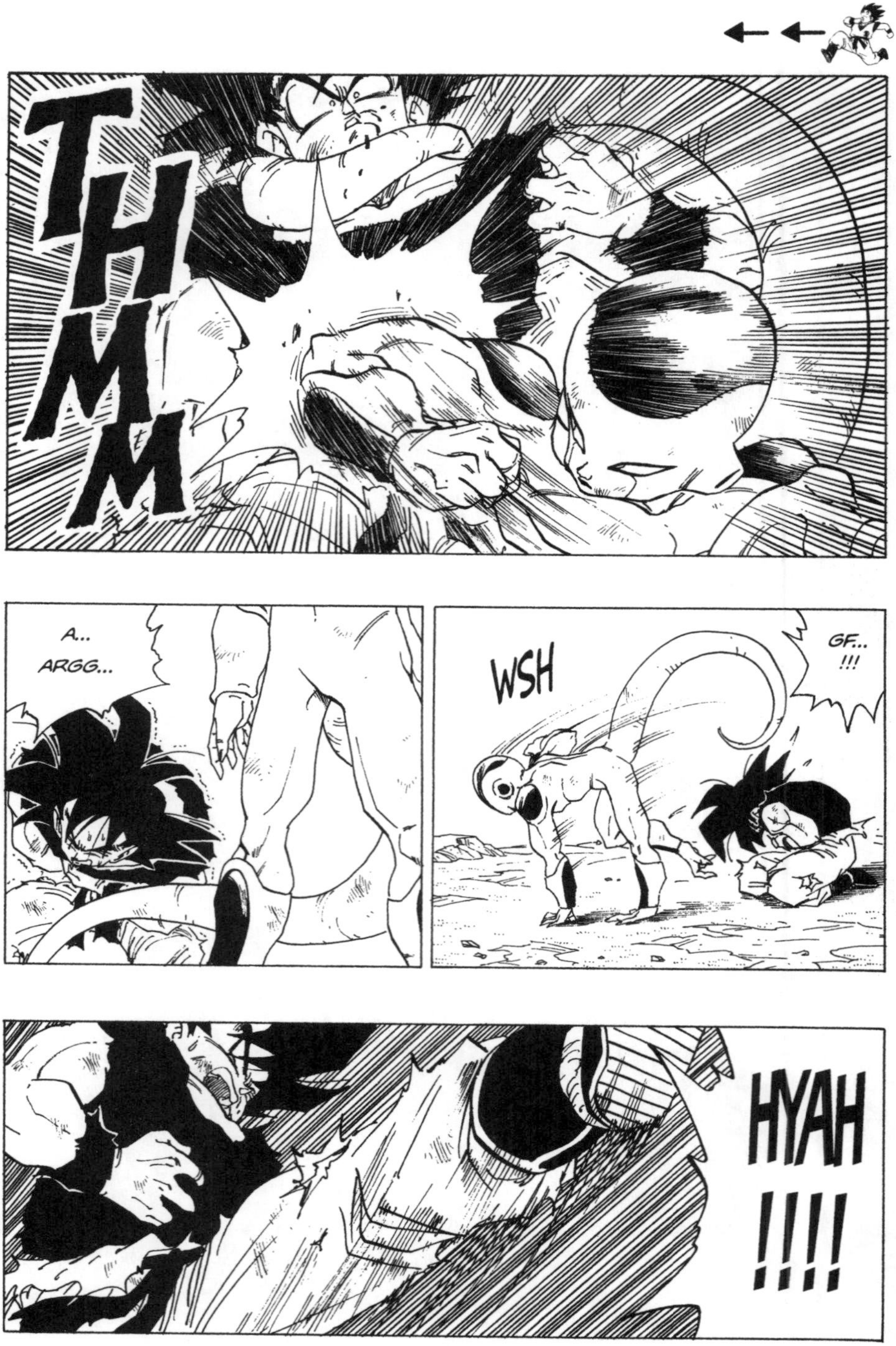
THMM
WSH
GF... !!!
A... ARGG...
HYAH !!!!!

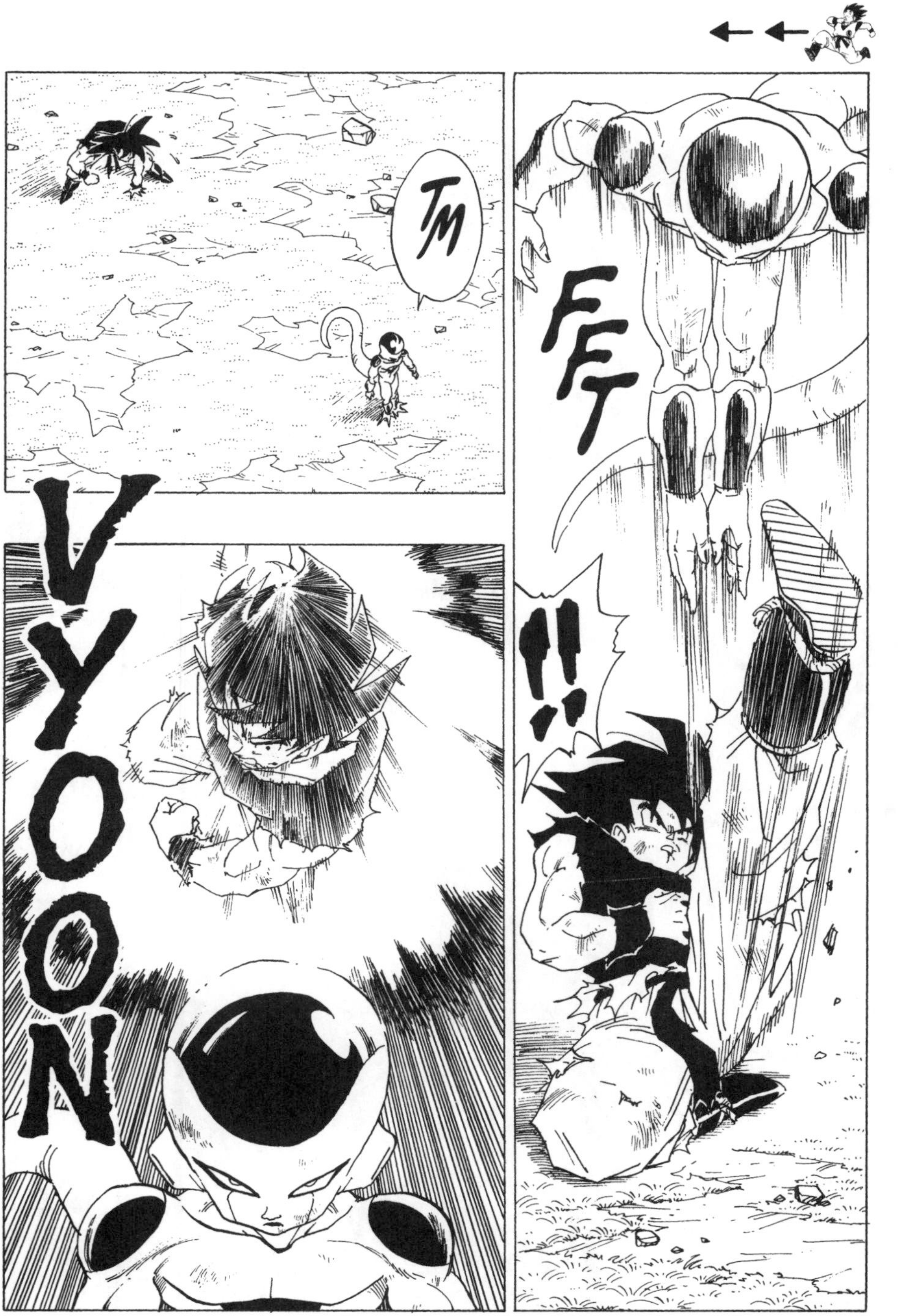
FFT
!!
TM
VYOON

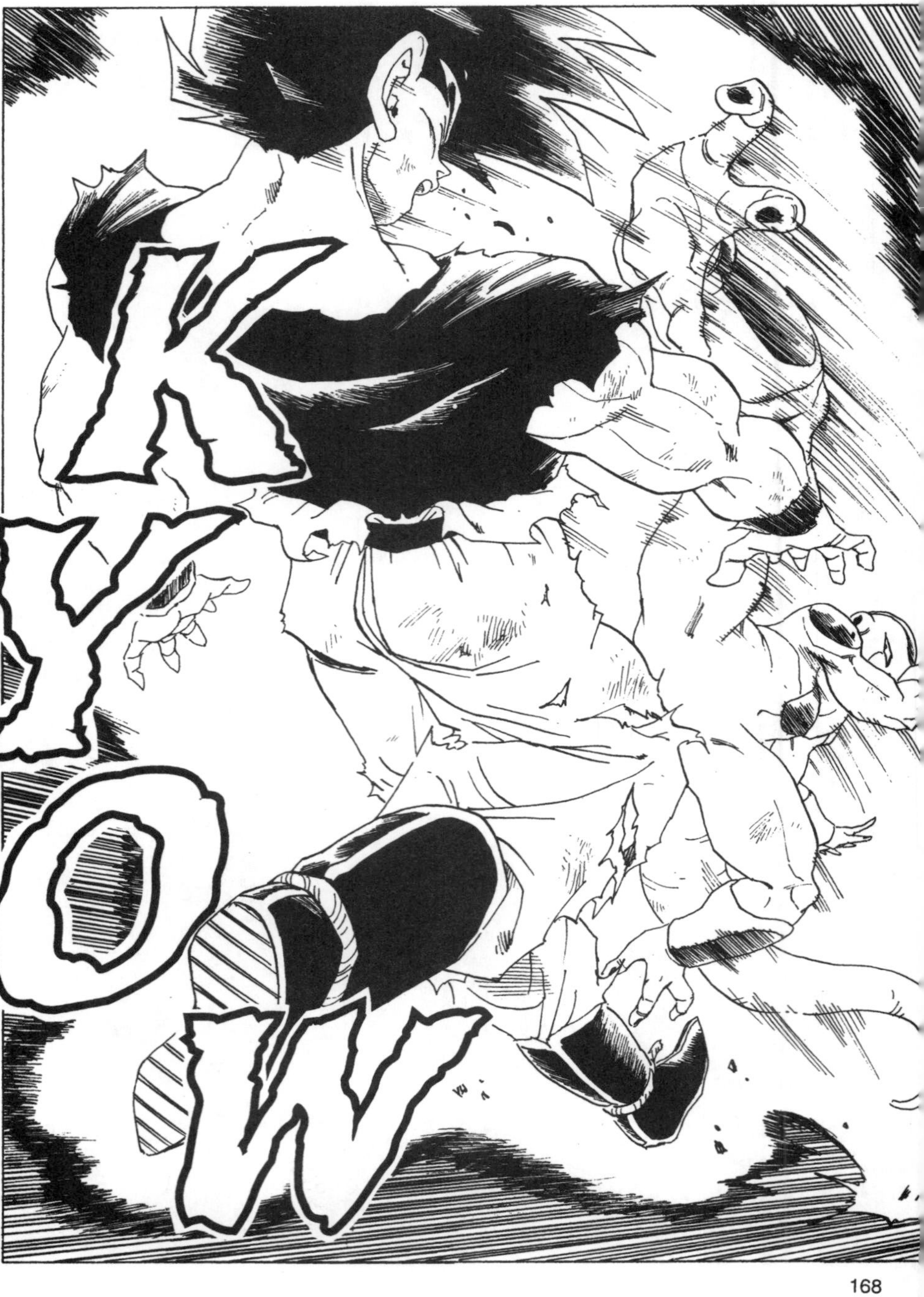
KYOW

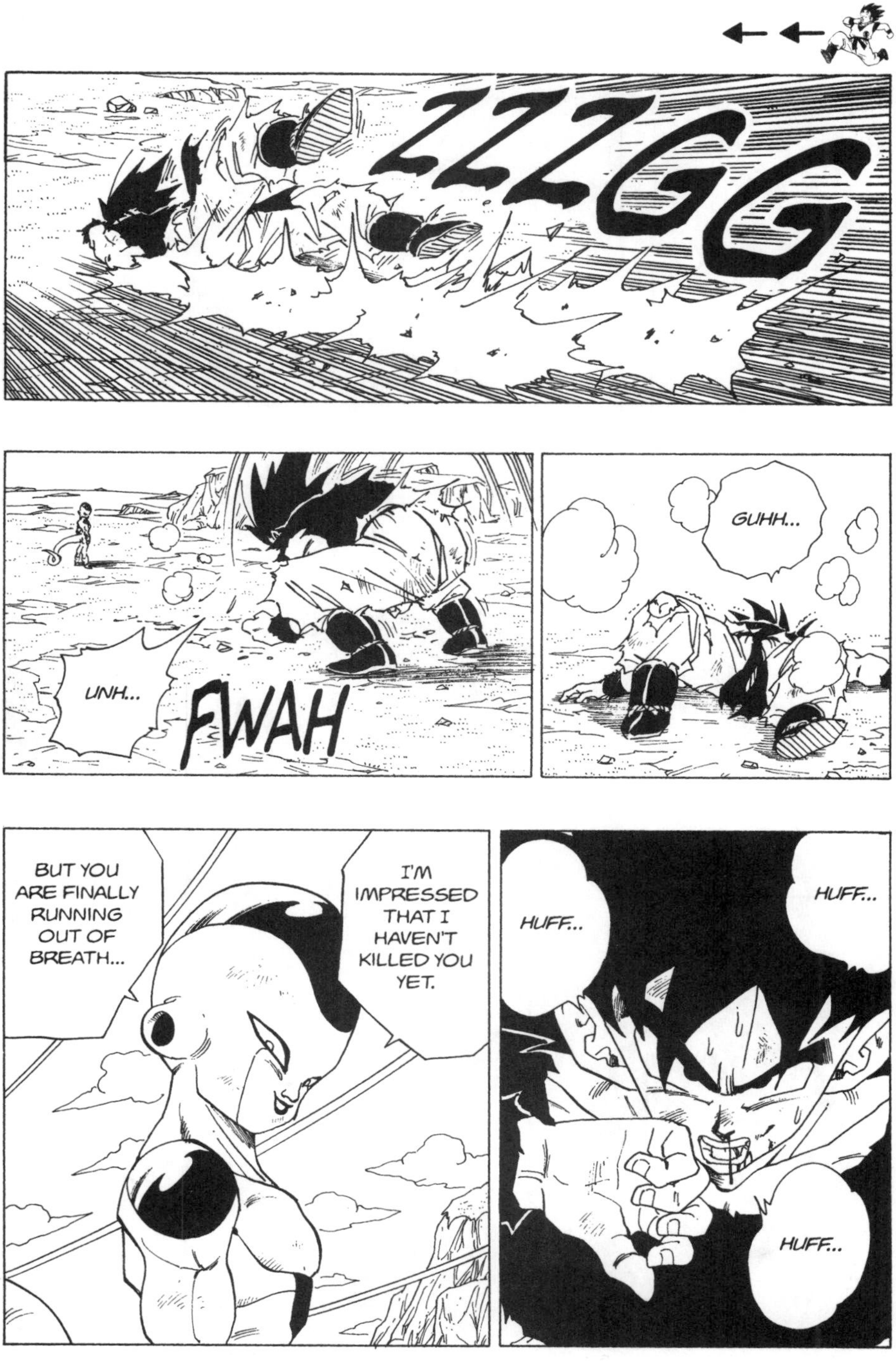
ZZZGG
GUHH...
UNH...
FWAH
HUFF...
HUFF...
HUFF...
I'M IMPRESSED THAT I HAVEN'T KILLED YOU YET.
BUT YOU ARE FINALLY RUNNING OUT OF BREATH...

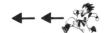

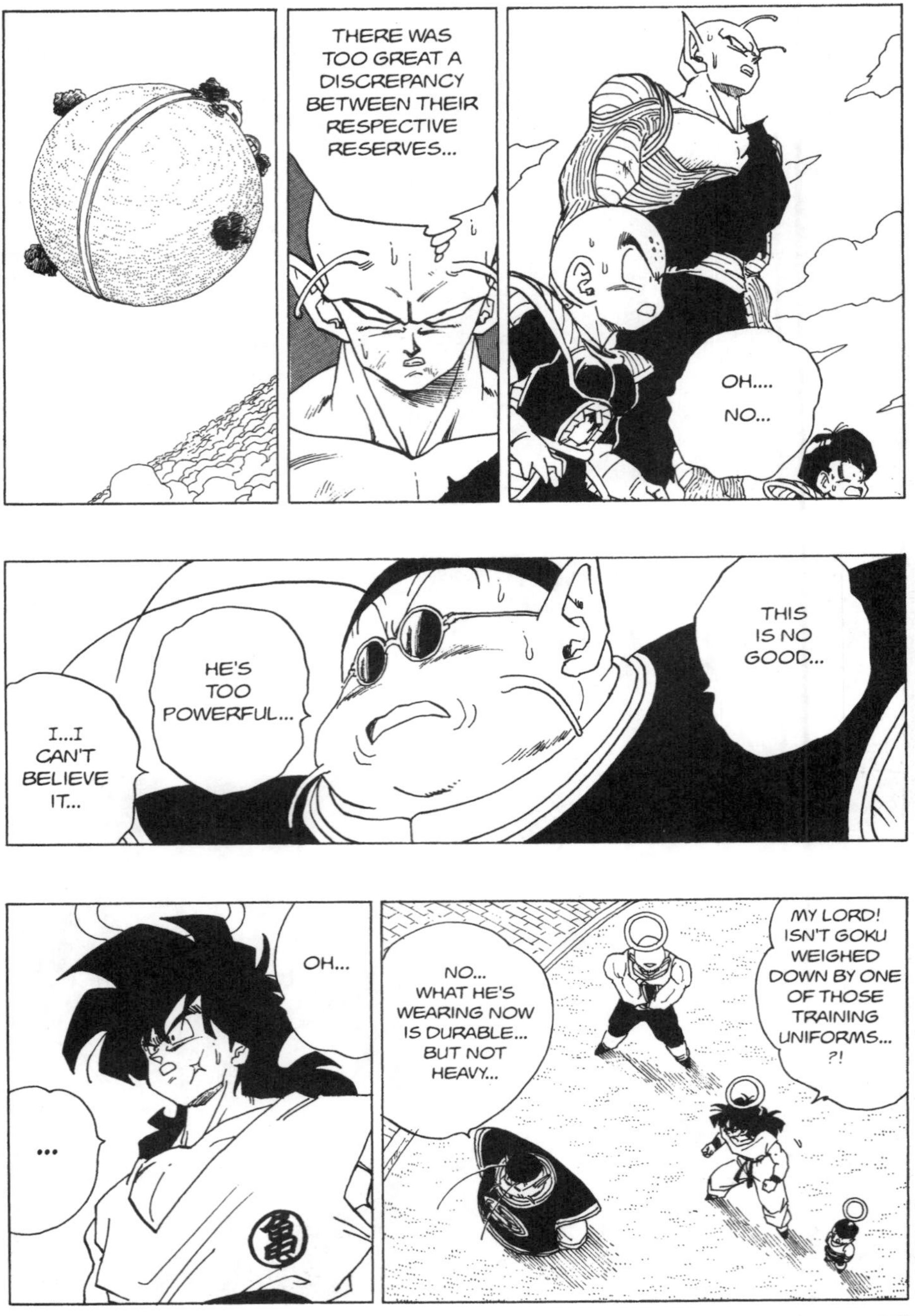
OH....
NO...
THERE WAS TOO GREAT A DISCREPANCY BETWEEN THEIR RESPECTIVE RESERVES...
THIS IS NO GOOD...
HE'S TOO POWERFUL...
I...I CAN'T BELIEVE IT...
MY LORD! ISN'T GOKU WEIGHED DOWN BY ONE OF THOSE TRAINING UNIFORMS...?!
NO... WHAT HE'S WEARING NOW IS DURABLE... BUT NOT HEAVY...
OH...
...

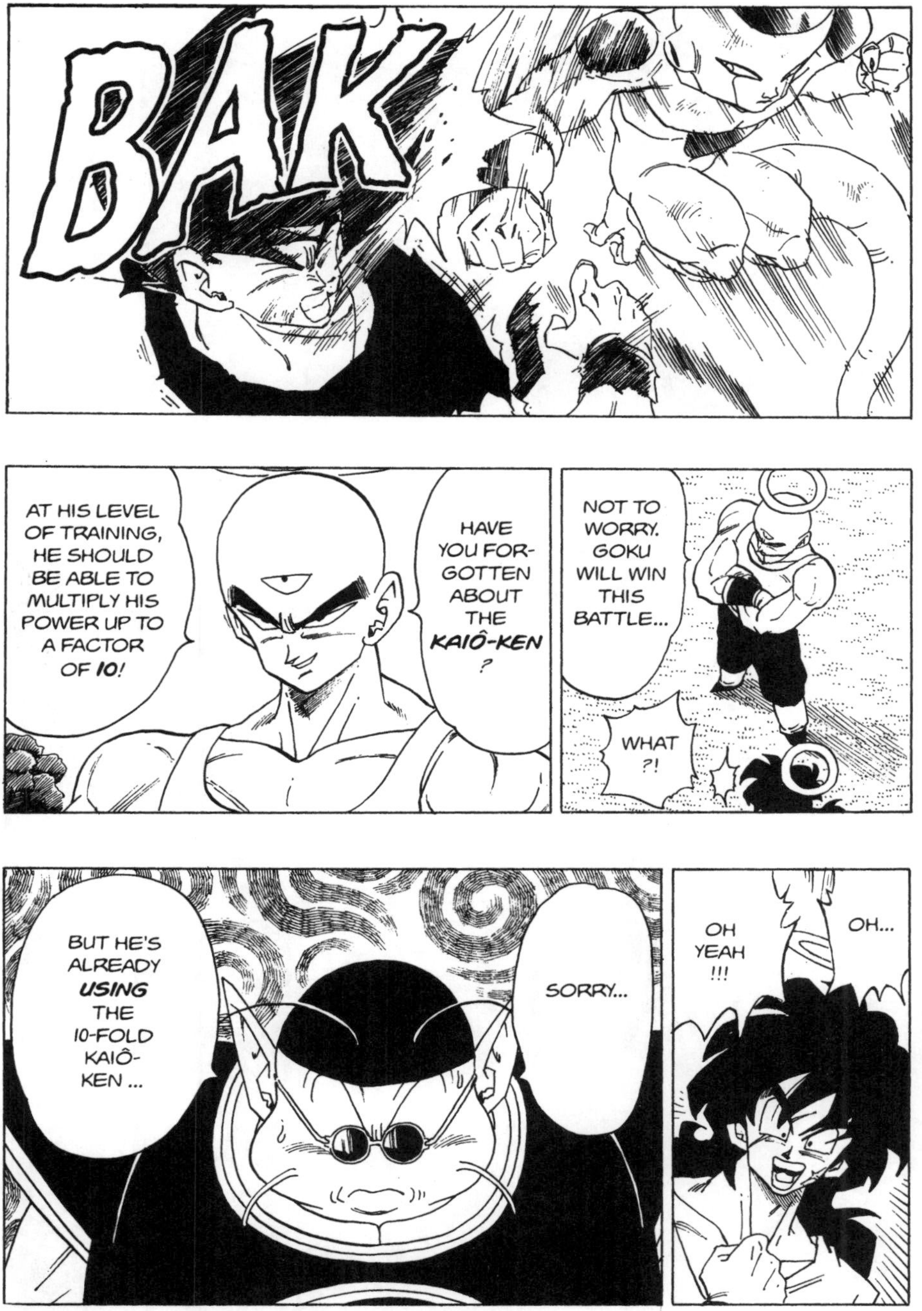
BAK
NOT TO WORRY. GOKU WILL WIN THIS BATTLE...
WHAT?!
HAVE YOU FORGOTTEN ABOUT THE KAIÔ-KEN?
AT HIS LEVEL OF TRAINING, HE SHOULD BE ABLE TO MULTIPLY HIS POWER UP TO A FACTOR OF 10!
OH...
OH YEAH!!!
SORRY...
BUT HE'S ALREADY USING THE 10-FOLD KAIÔ-KEN ...

*NEXT: Kaiô-ken times 20!!!*

# DBZ:119 • Kaiô-ken times 20!!!

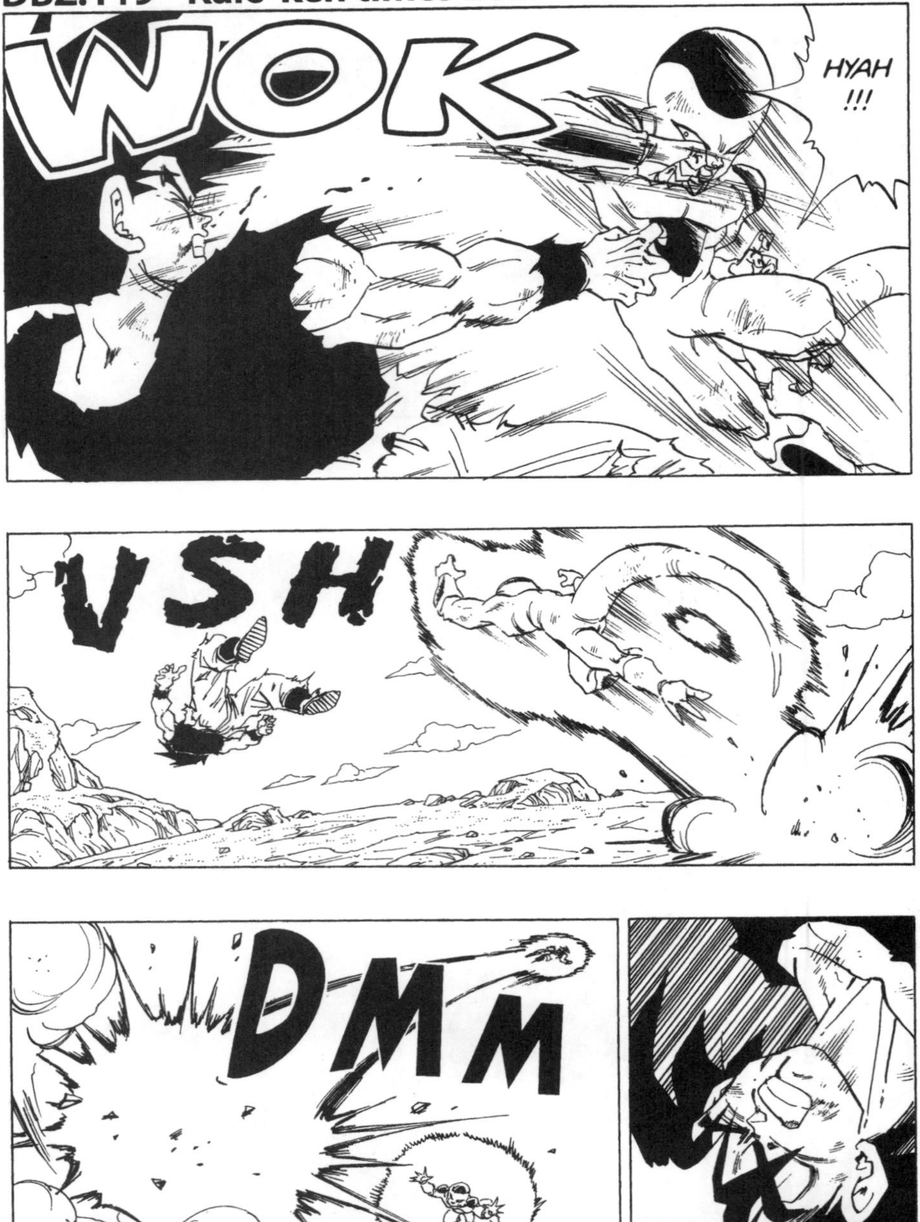
HYAH !!!
WOK
VSH
UGH... !!!!
DMM

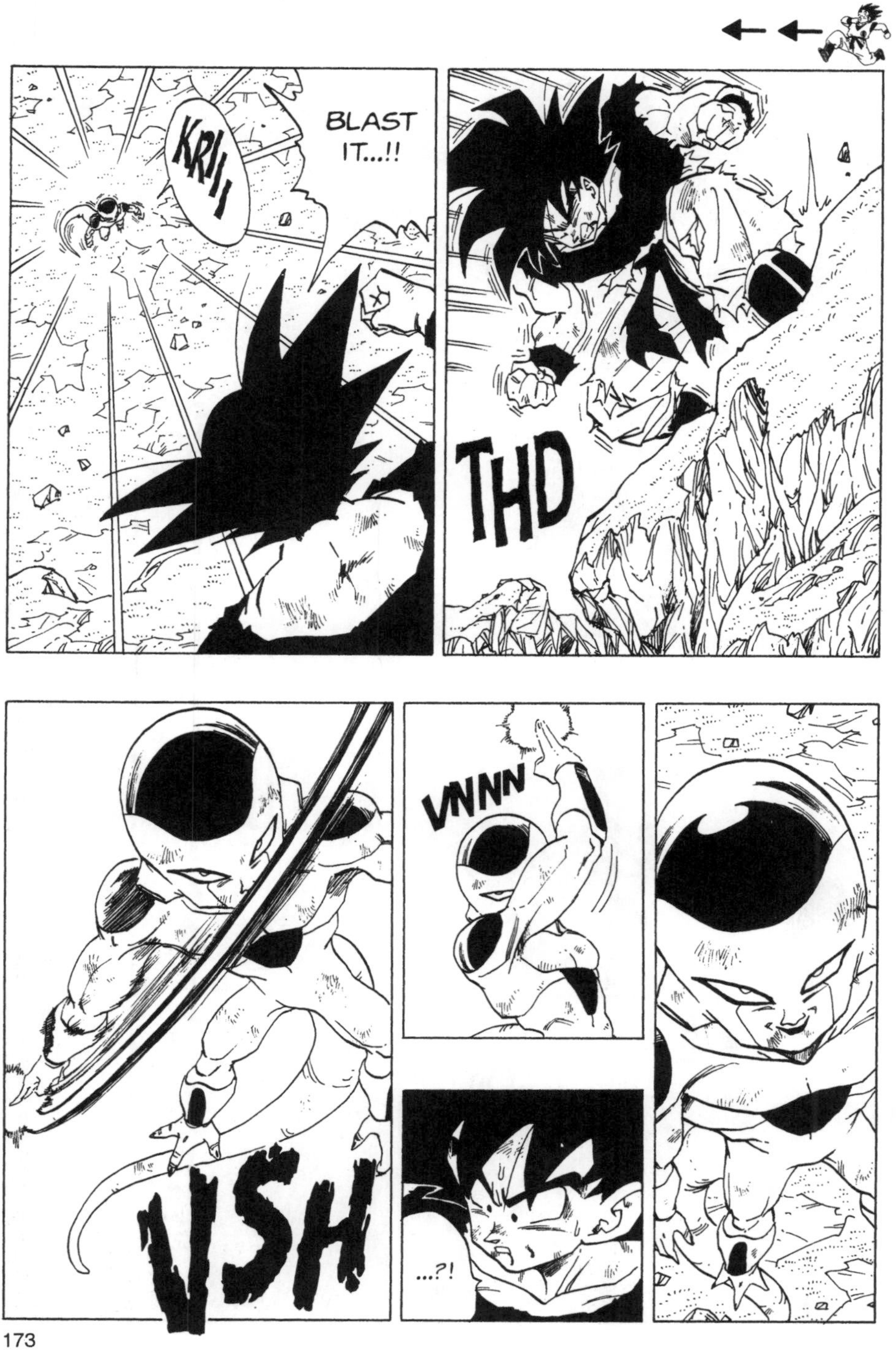
THD
BLAST IT...!!
KRIII
VNNN
...?!
VSH

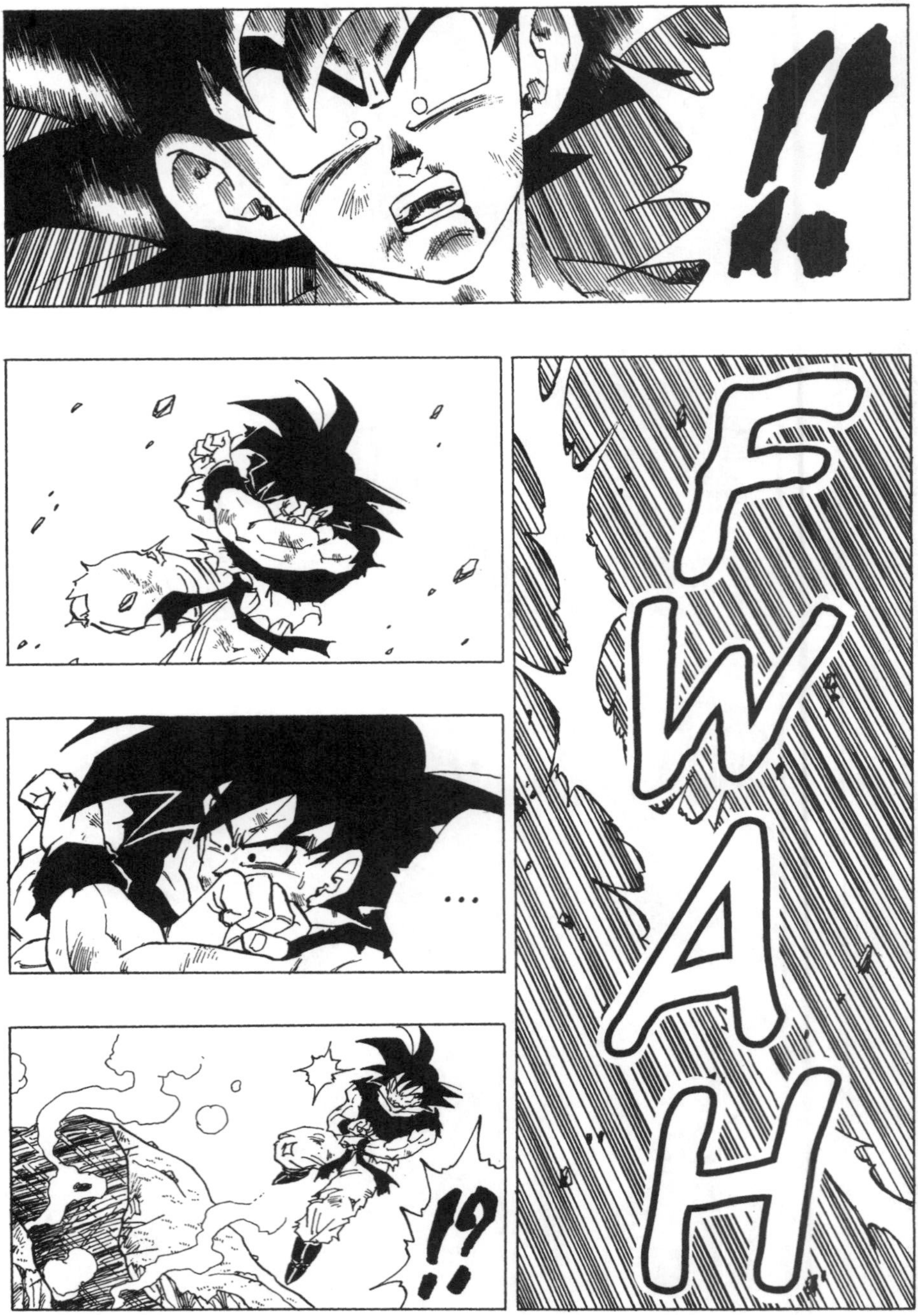
!!
FWAH
...
!?!!

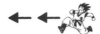

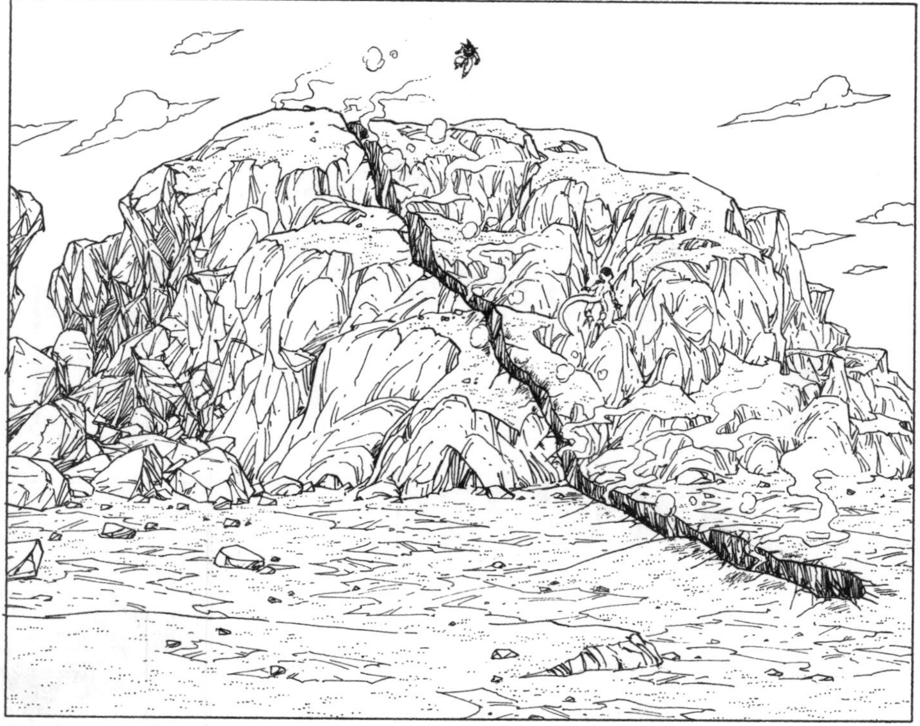

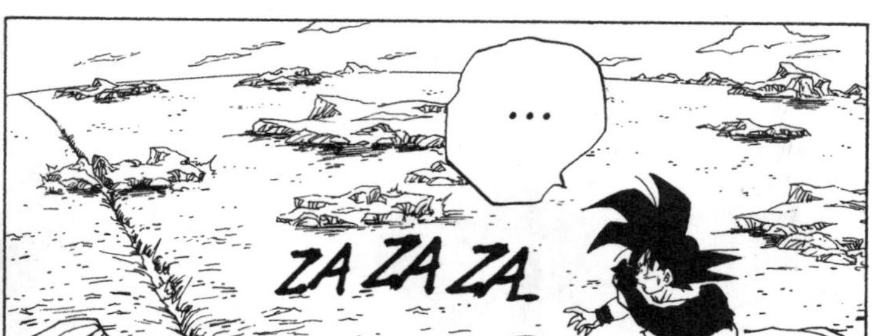
...
ZA ZA ZA

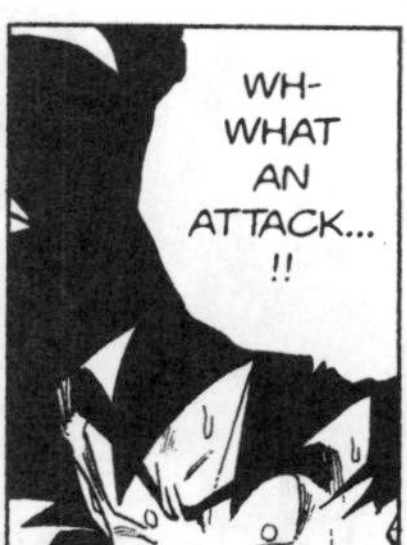
WH-WHAT AN ATTACK... !!

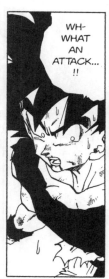

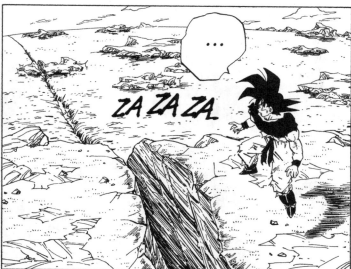

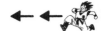

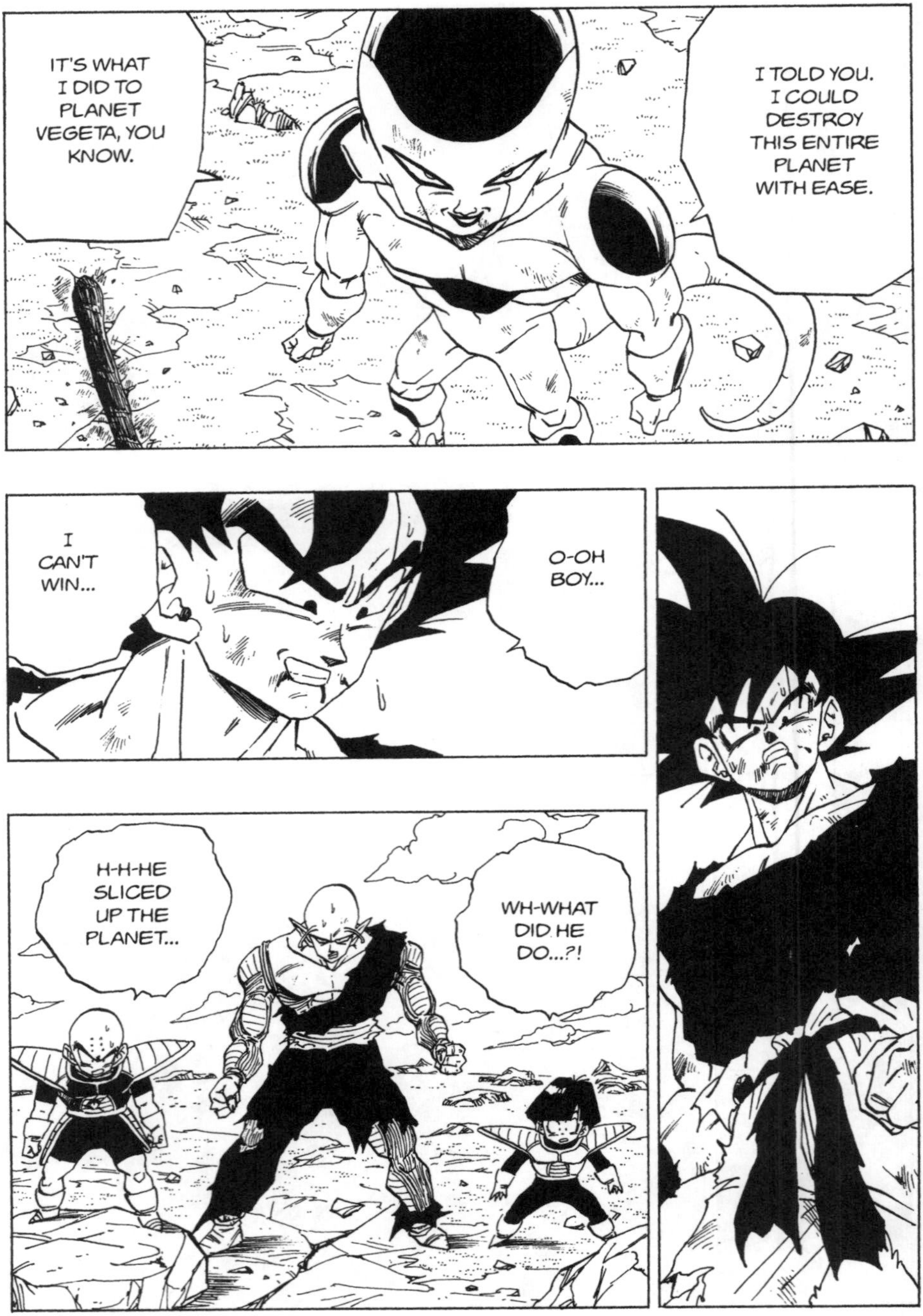
I TOLD YOU. I COULD DESTROY THIS ENTIRE PLANET WITH EASE.
IT'S WHAT I DID TO PLANET VEGETA, YOU KNOW.
O-OH BOY...
I CAN'T WIN...
WH-WHAT DID HE DO...?!
H-H-HE SLICED UP THE PLANET...

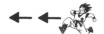

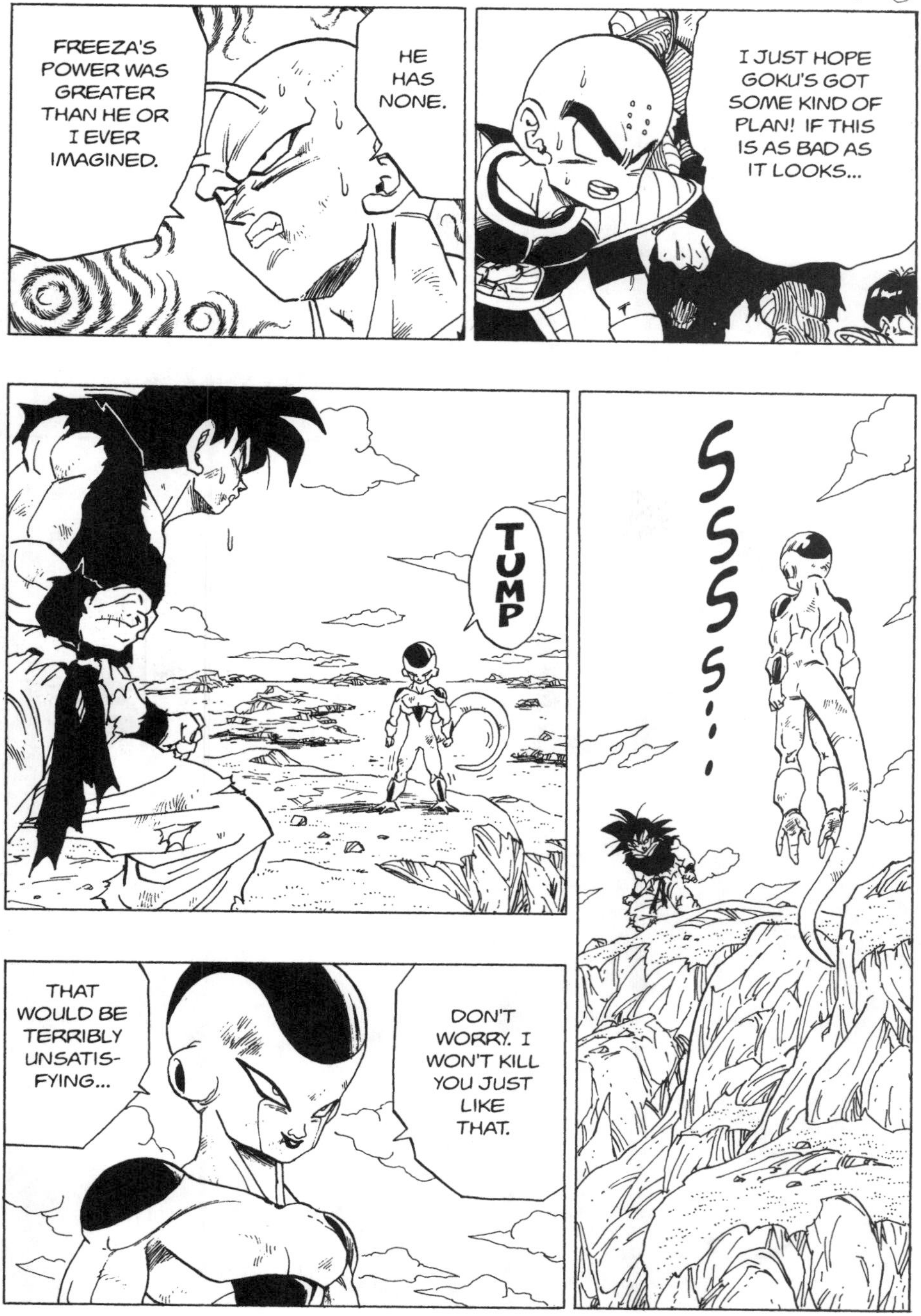
I JUST HOPE GOKU'S GOT SOME KIND OF PLAN! IF THIS IS AS BAD AS IT LOOKS...
HE HAS NONE.
FREEZA'S POWER WAS GREATER THAN HE OR I EVER IMAGINED.
SSSS...
TUMP
DON'T WORRY. I WON'T KILL YOU JUST LIKE THAT.
THAT WOULD BE TERRIBLY UNSATIS-FYING...

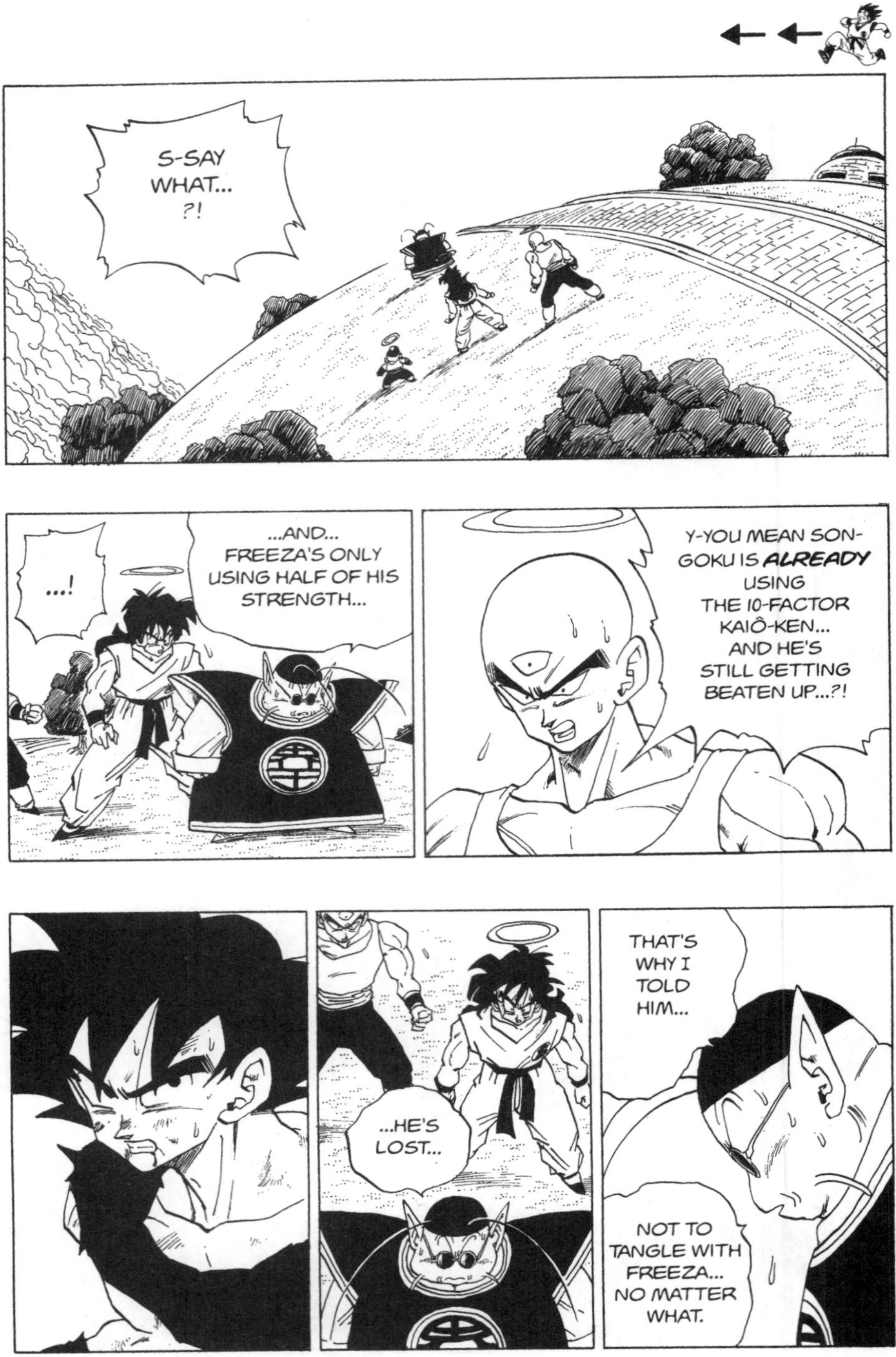
S-SAY WHAT... ?!
Y-YOU MEAN SON-GOKU IS ***ALREADY*** USING THE 10-FACTOR KAIÔ-KEN... AND HE'S STILL GETTING BEATEN UP...?!
...AND... FREEZA'S ONLY USING HALF OF HIS STRENGTH...
...!
THAT'S WHY I TOLD HIM...
NOT TO TANGLE WITH FREEZA... NO MATTER WHAT.
...HE'S LOST...

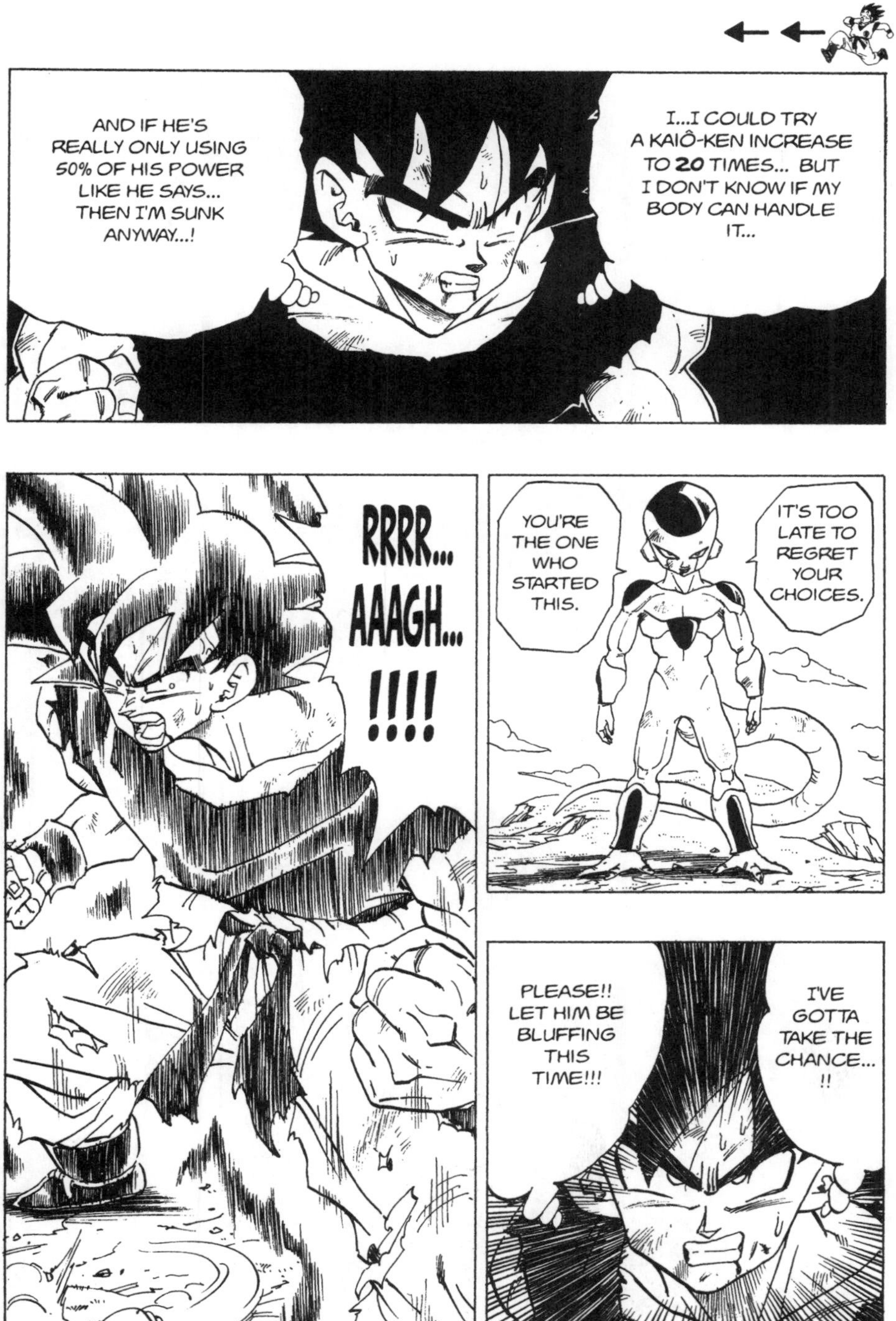
I...I COULD TRY A KAIÔ-KEN INCREASE TO 20 TIMES... BUT I DON'T KNOW IF MY BODY CAN HANDLE IT...
AND IF HE'S REALLY ONLY USING 50% OF HIS POWER LIKE HE SAYS... THEN I'M SUNK ANYWAY...!
IT'S TOO LATE TO REGRET YOUR CHOICES.
YOU'RE THE ONE WHO STARTED THIS.
I'VE GOTTA TAKE THE CHANCE... !!
PLEASE!! LET HIM BE BLUFFING THIS TIME!!!
RRRR... AAAGH... !!!!

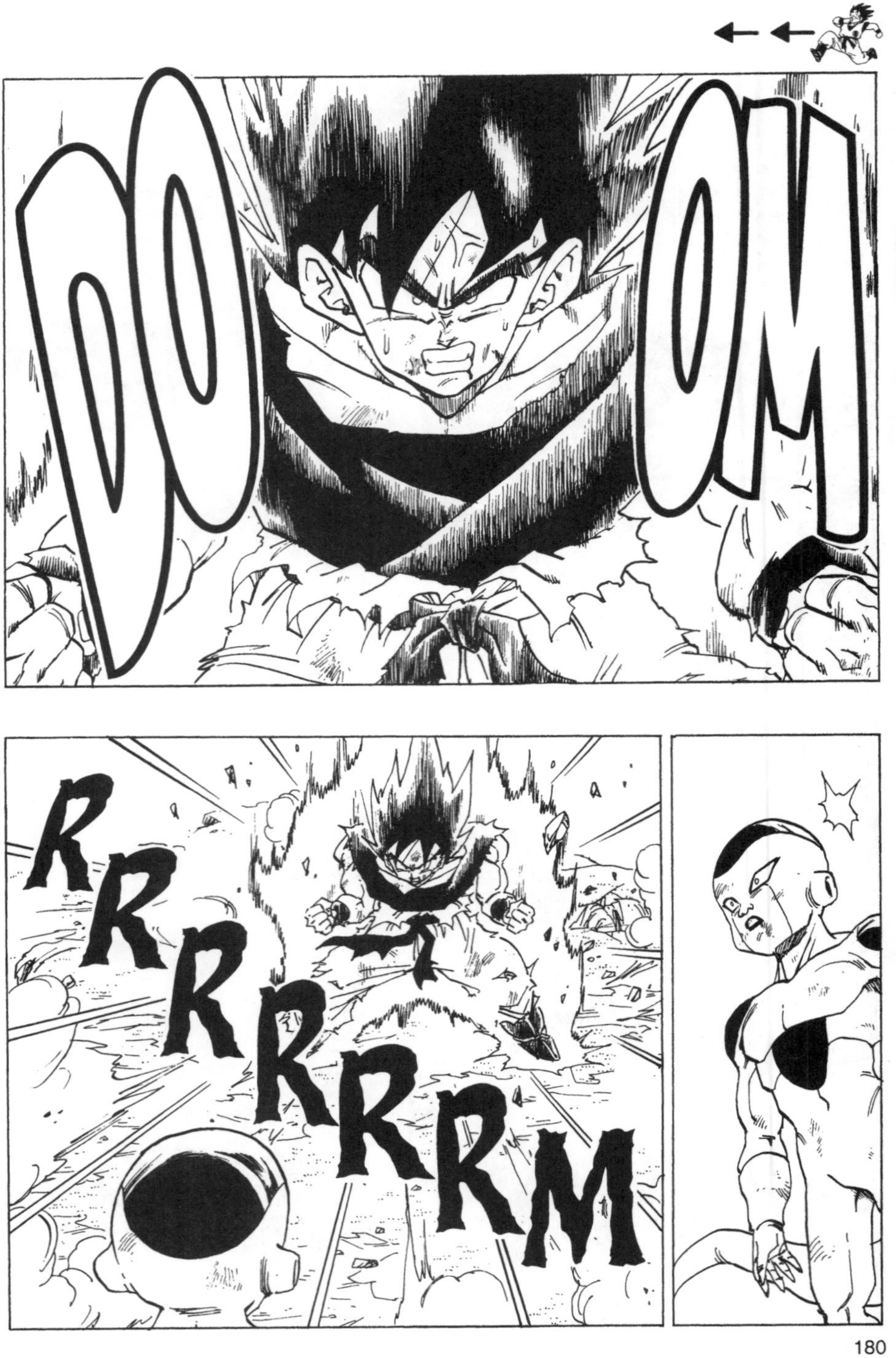
DOOOM
RRRRRRRM

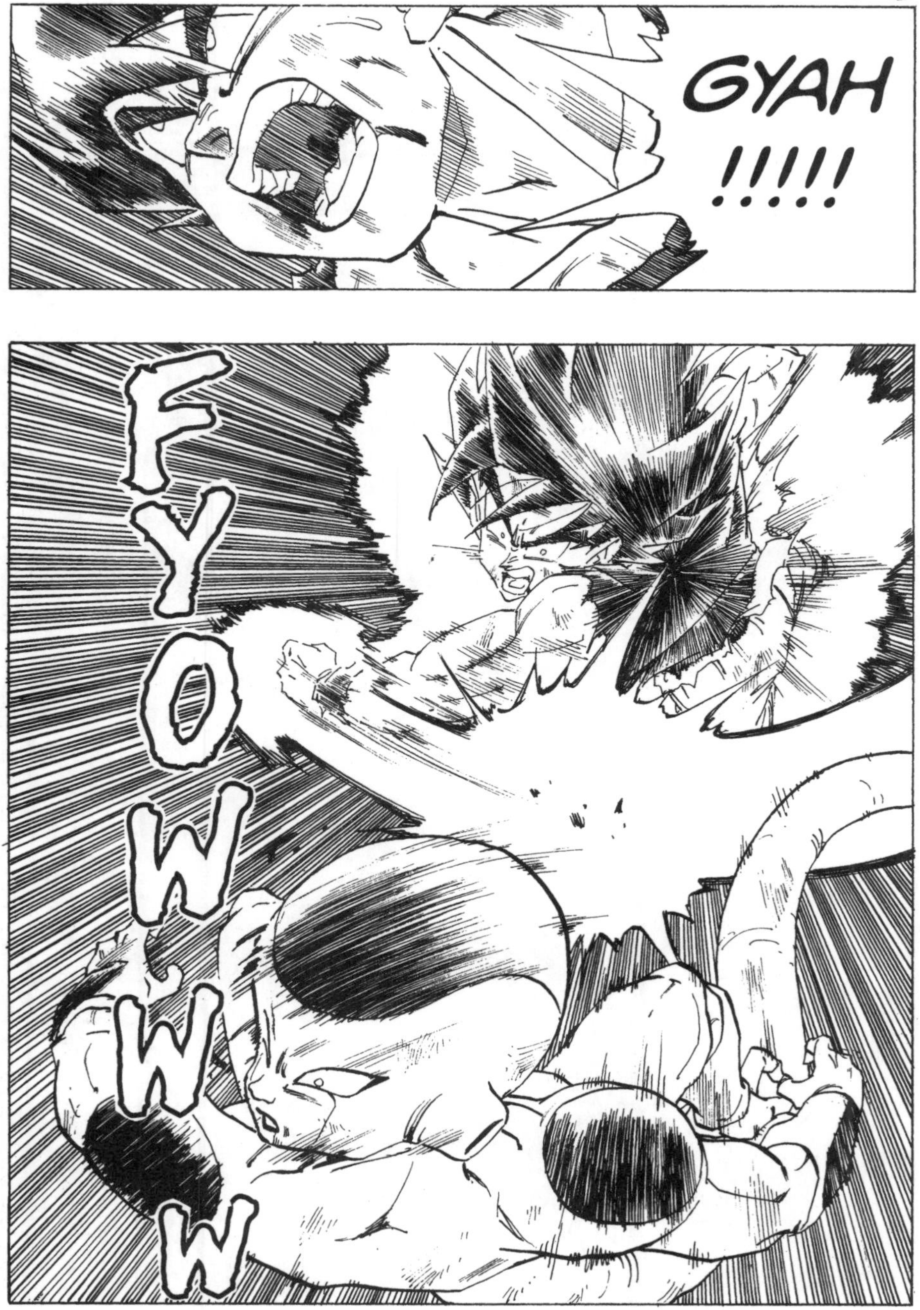
GYAH
!!!!!
FYOWWW

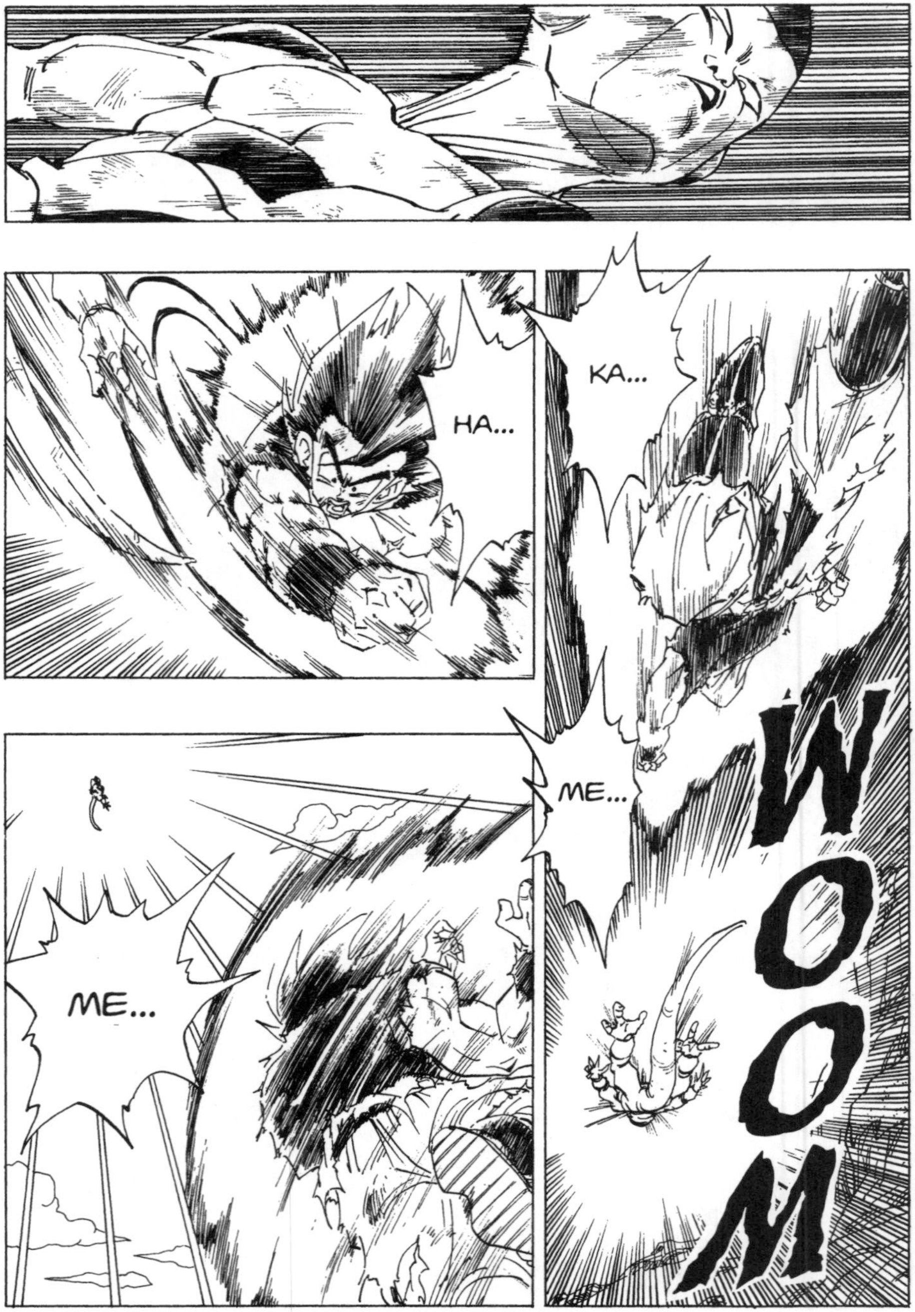
KA...
ME...
WOOM
HA...
ME...

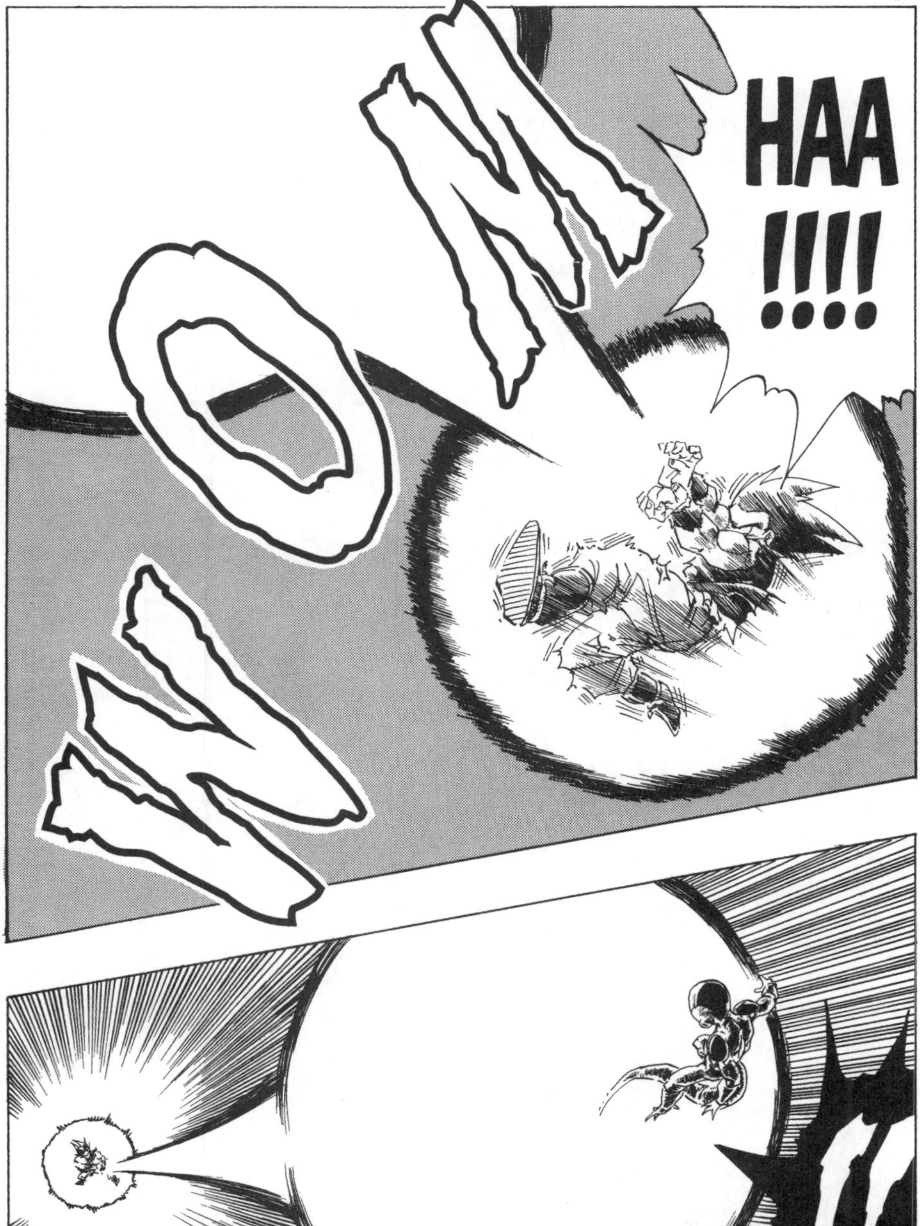
HAA!!!!!
!!

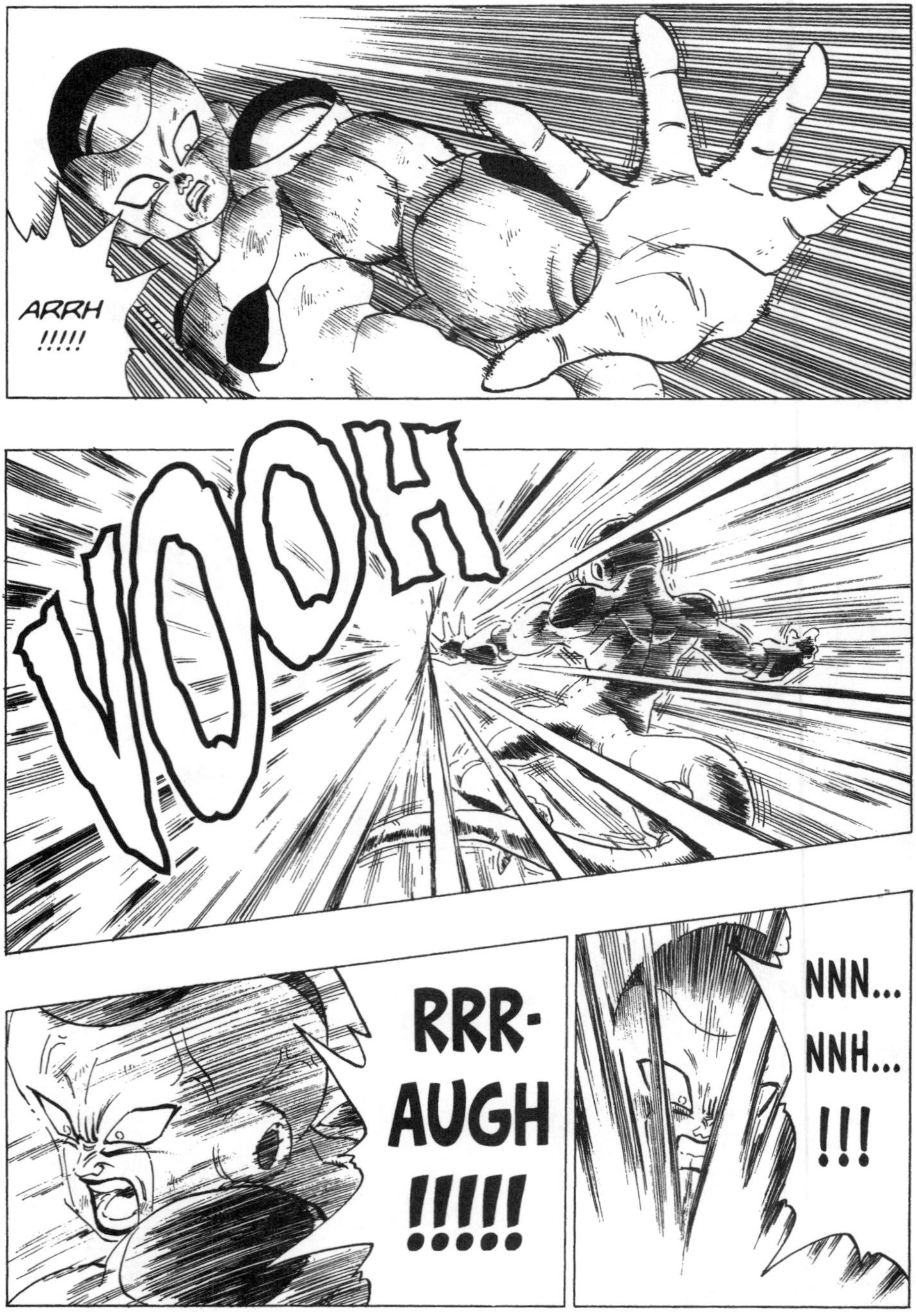
ARRH
!!!!!
VOOH
NNN...
NNH...
!!!
RRR-
AUGH
!!!!!

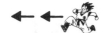

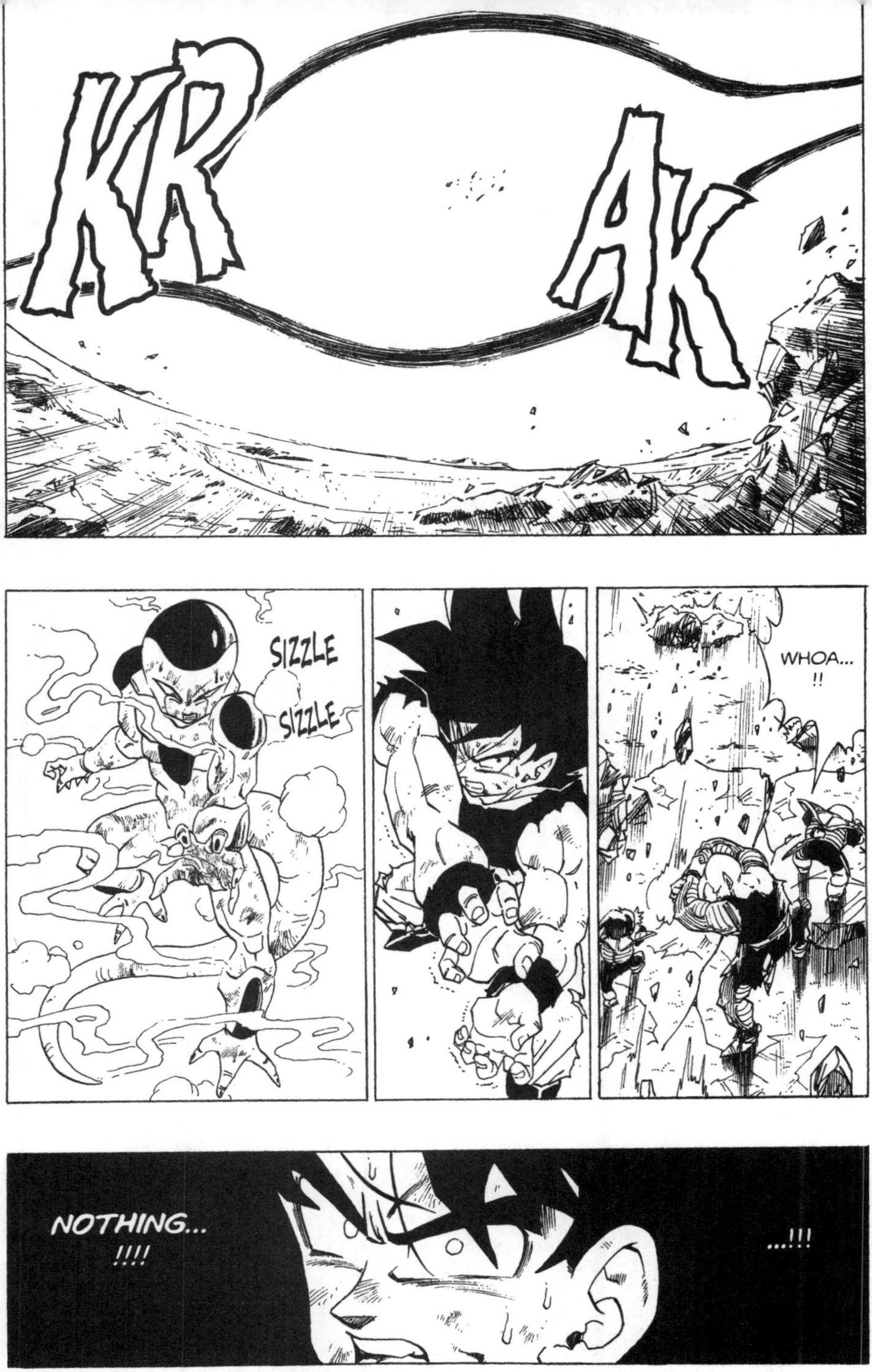
KRAK
WHOA... !!
SIZZLE
SIZZLE
...!!!
NOTHING... !!!!

**NEXT: Goku Folds Up!**

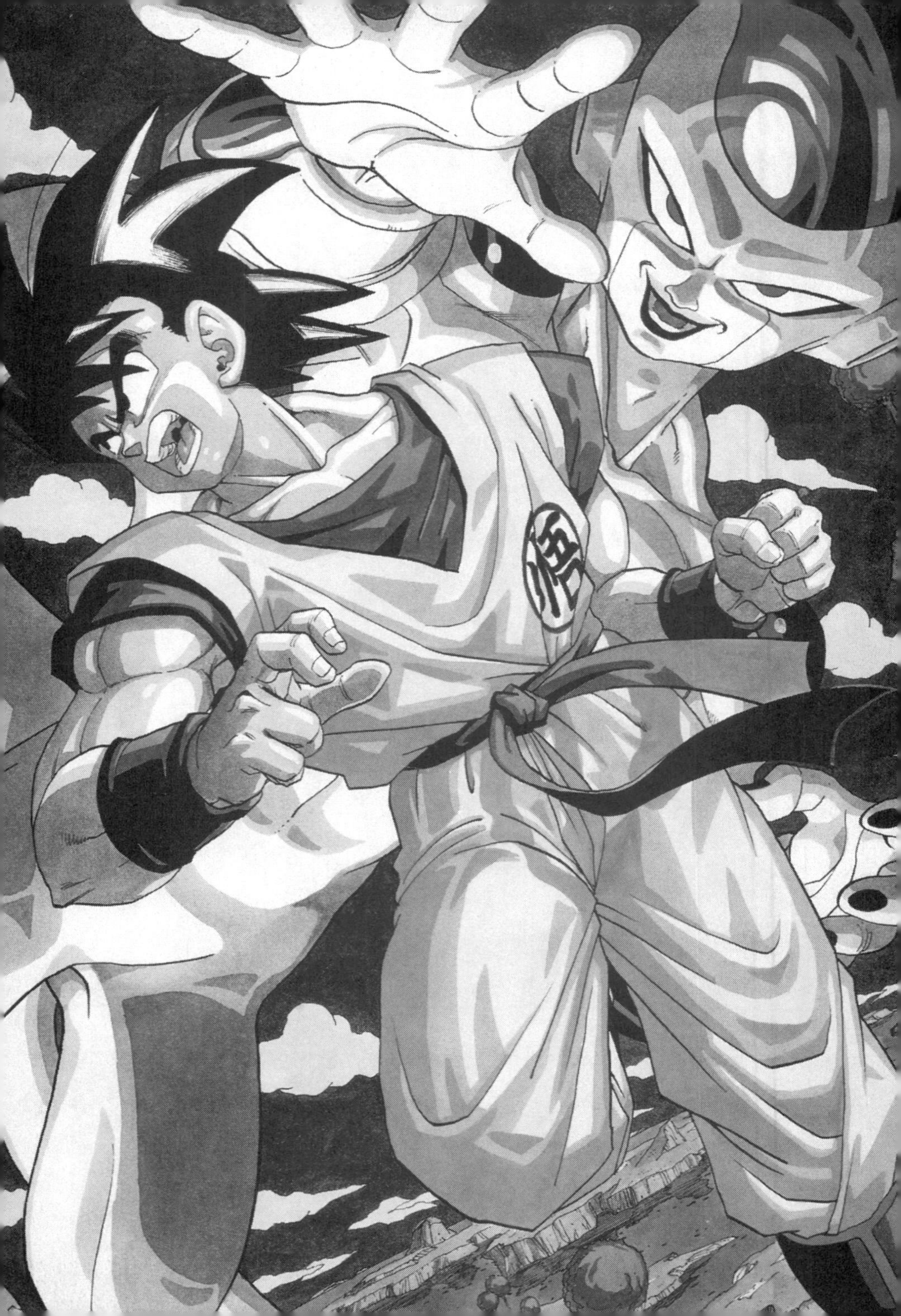

# TITLE PAGE GALLERY

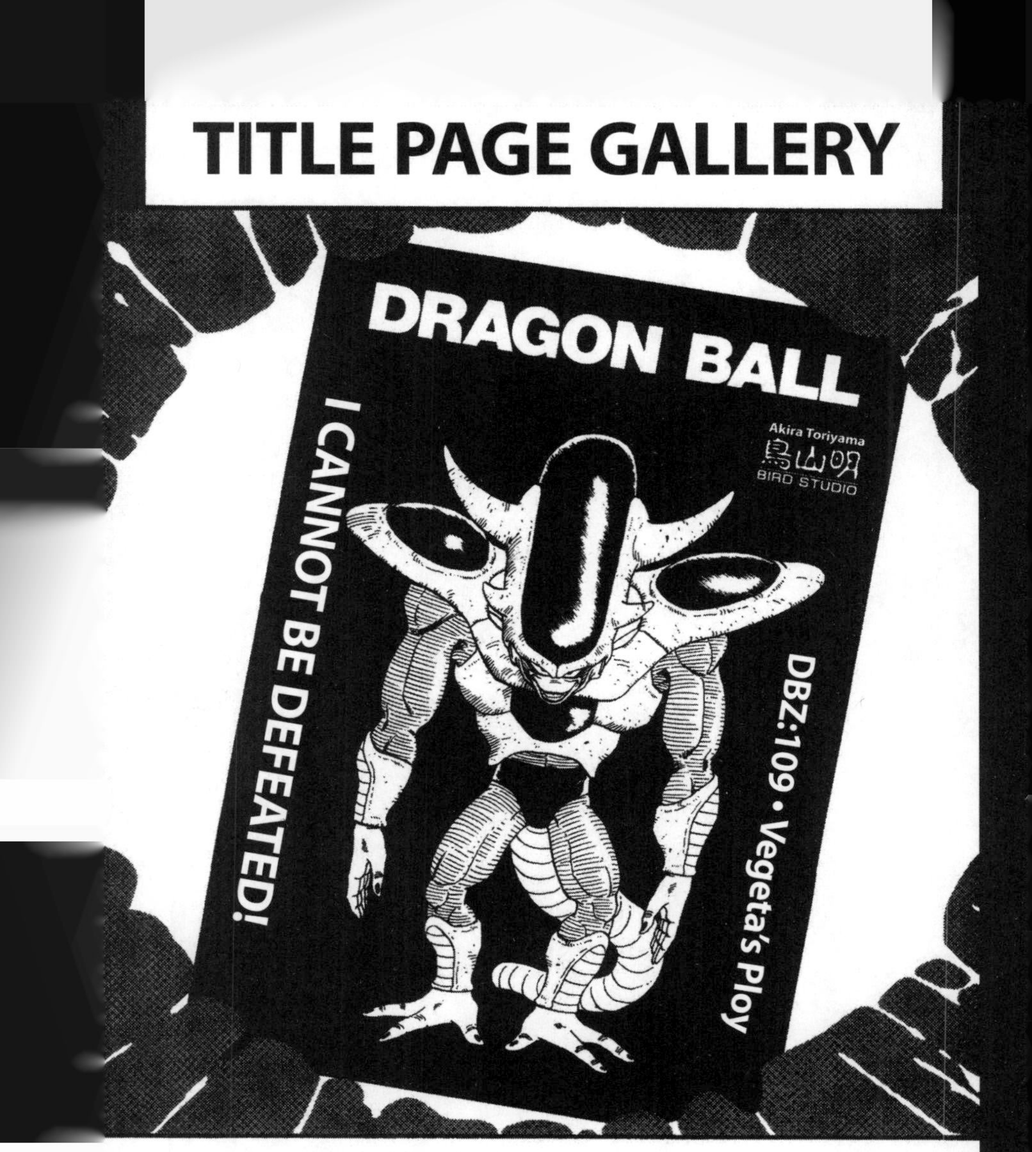
DRAGON BALL
Akira Toriyama
鳥山明
BIRD STUDIO
I CANNOT BE DEFEATED!
DBZ:109 • Vegeta's Ploy

**These chapter title pages were used when these episodes of *Dragon Ball* were originally published in 1991 in Japan in *Shonen Jump* magazine.**

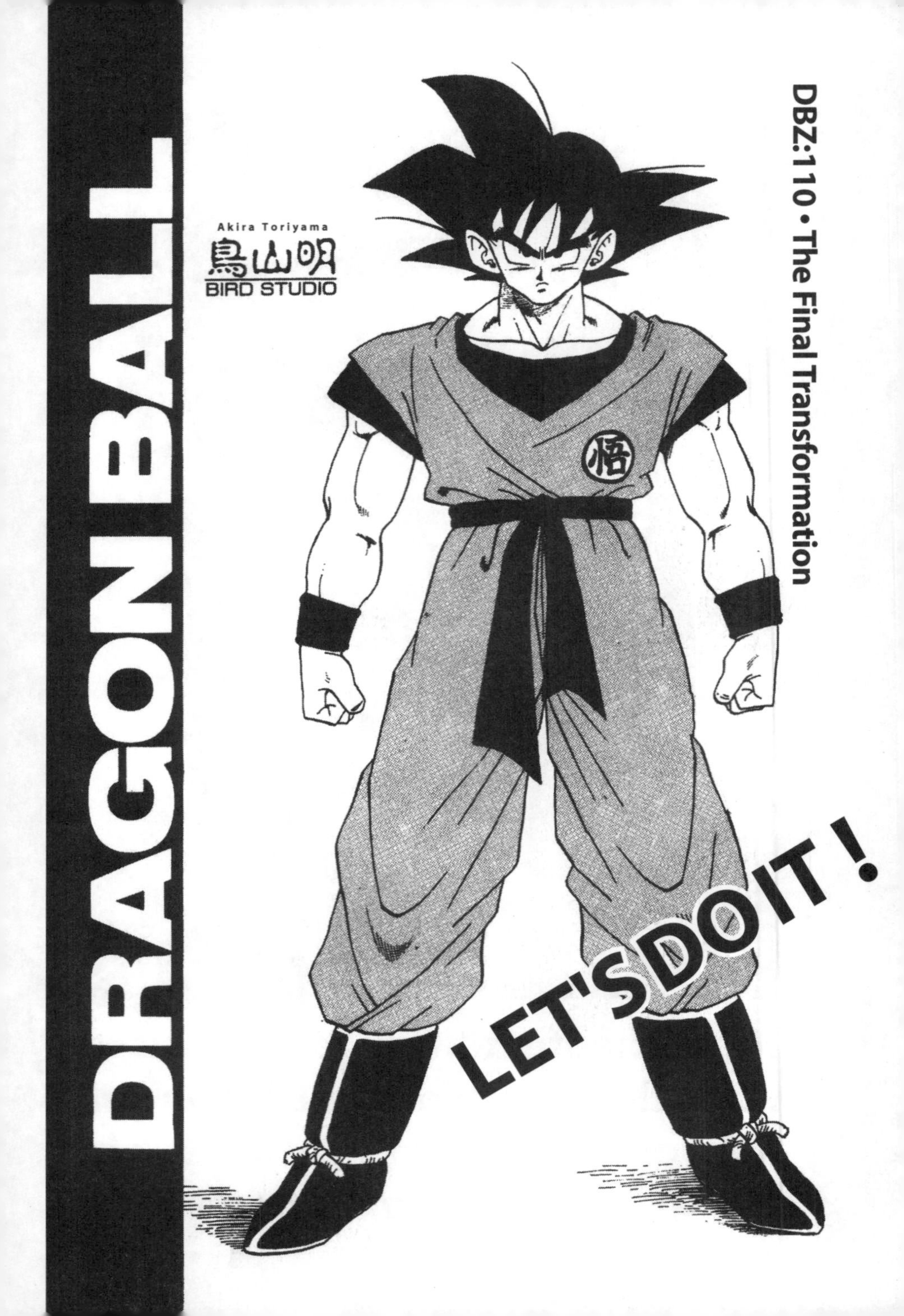
DBZ:110 • The Final Transformation
DRAGON BALL
Akira Toriyama
鳥山明
BIRD STUDIO
LET'S DO IT!

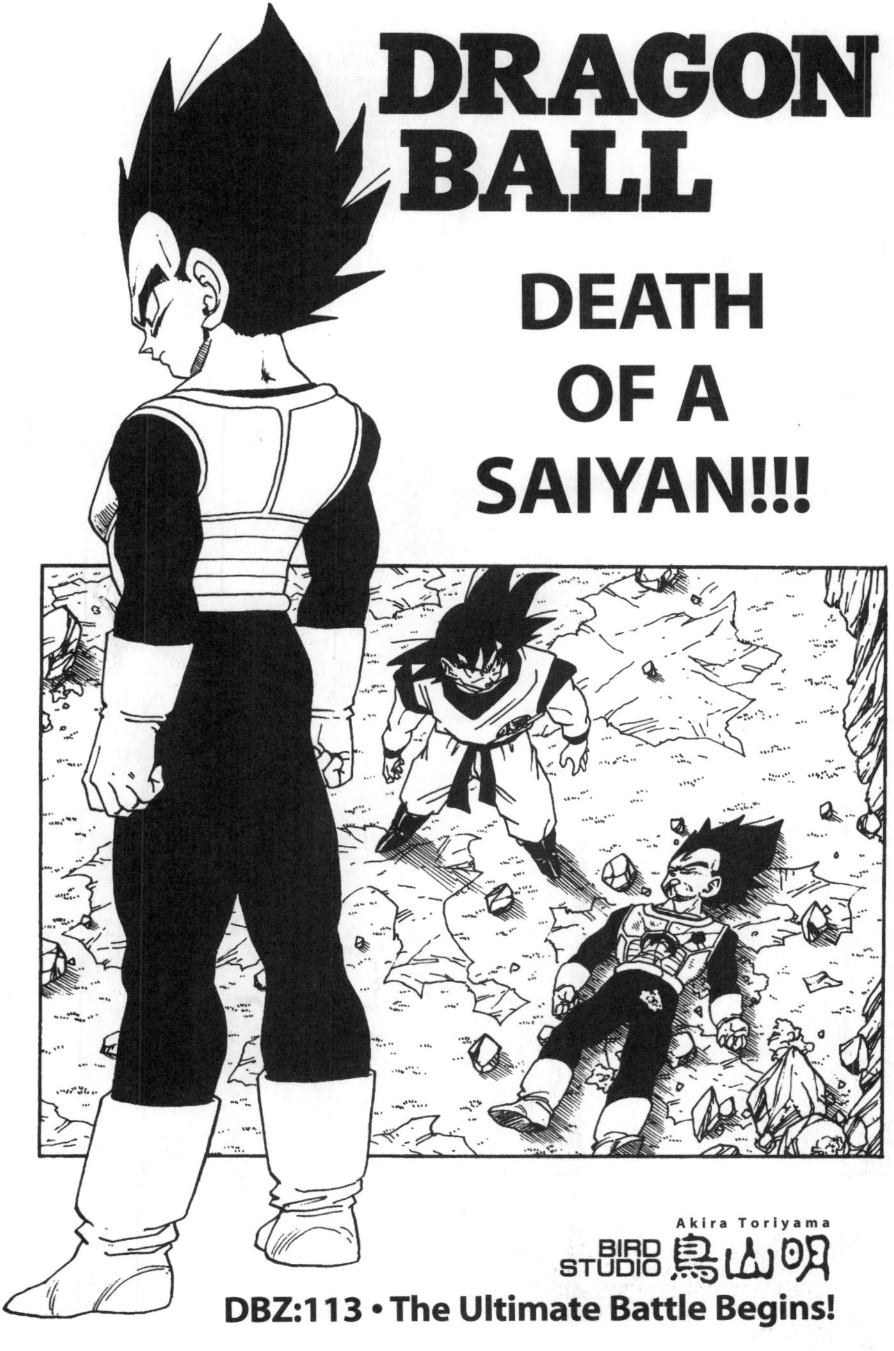
DRAGON BALL
DEATH OF A SAIYAN!!!
Akira Toriyama
BIRD STUDIO 鳥山明
DBZ:113 • The Ultimate Battle Begins!

# DRAGON BALL

## DBZ:116 • Aerial Battle

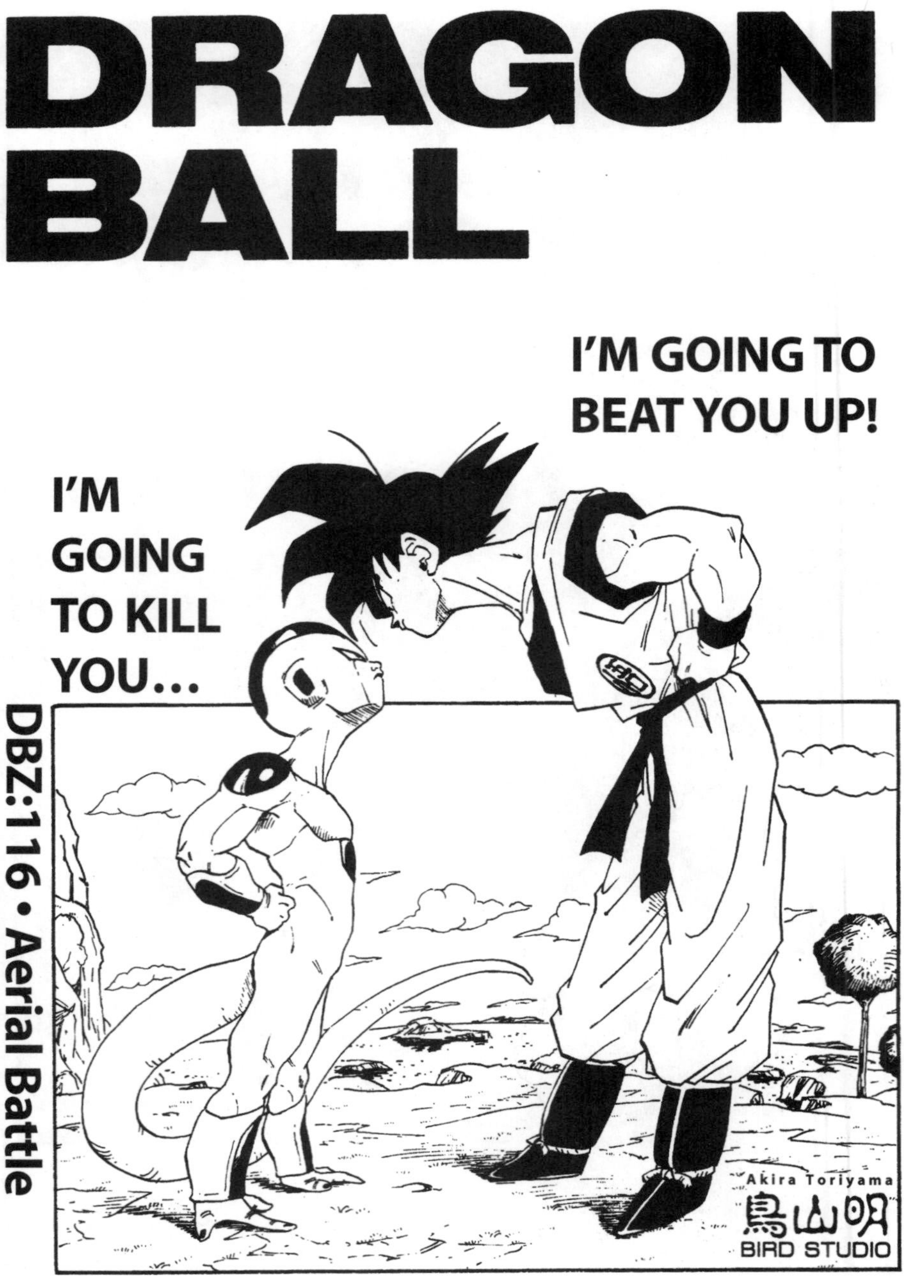
I'M GOING TO BEAT YOU UP!
I'M GOING TO KILL YOU...
Akira Toriyama
鳥山明
BIRD STUDIO

# DRAGON BALL

BIRD STUDIO 鳥山明
Akira Toriyama

## CLASH OF THE SUPER POWERS!

DBZ:119 • Kaiô-ken times 20!!!

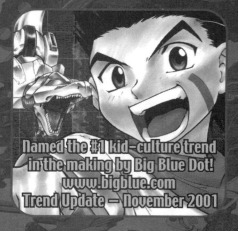